**Algorithms and Networking for
Computer Games**

Algorithms and Networking for Computer Games

Second Edition

Jouni Smed
University of Turku
Turku, FI

Harri Hakonen
Turku, FI

Registered Offices
John Wiley & Sons, Inc., 111 River Street, Hoboken, NJ 07030, USA
John Wiley & Sons, Ltd. The Atrium, Southern Gate, Chichester, West Sussex, PO19 8SQ, UK

Editorial Office
The Atrium, Southern Gate, Chichester, West Sussex, PO19 8SQ, UK

For details of our global editorial offices, customer services, and more information about Wiley products visit us at www.wiley.com.

Wiley also publishes its books in a variety of electronic formats and by print-on-demand. Some content that appears in standard print versions of this book may not be available in other formats.

Library of Congress Cataloging-in-Publication Data

Names: Smed, Jouni, author. | Hakonen, Harri, author.
Title: Algorithms and networking for computer games / Jouni Smed, Harri Hakonen.
Description: Second edition. | Hoboken, NJ, USA : John Wiley & Sons Inc., 2017. |
    Includes bibliographical references and index.
Identifiers: LCCN 2017005948 (print) | LCCN 2017006972 (ebook) | ISBN 9781119259763 (cloth) |
    ISBN 9781119259824 (Adobe PDF) | ISBN 9781119259831 (ePub)
Subjects: LCSH: Computer games–Programming. | Computer algorithms.
Classification: LCC QA76.76.C672 S62 2017 (print) | LCC QA76.76.C672 (ebook) |
    DDC 794.8/1526–dc23
LC record available at https://lccn.loc.gov/2017005948

Cover Design: Wiley
Cover Image: © Pobytov / Getty Images

Set in 10/12pt WarnockPro by Aptara Inc., New Delhi, India
Printed and bound in Malaysia by Vivar Printing Sdn Bhd

10 9 8 7 6 5 4 3 2 1

Contents

List of Figures

List of Tables

List of Algorithms

Preface

When students at MIT competed against each other in the first real-time graphical computer game *Spacewar* in 1962 (Graetz 1981), probably none of them could have dreamt how realistic and complex computer games would develop in five decades and how large a business would grow around them. Commercial arcade games such as *Pong* and *Space Invaders* arrived in the 1970s, and home computers brought computer games within the reach of all enthusiasts in the 1980s. Since then game development has grown from small amateur enterprises into an industry, which is now – in spite of popular claims – the second largest branch of the entertainment industry, steadily narrowing the lead of the film industry (Newzoo 2014; Statista 2016).

Games are also becoming ever more pervasive in our lives. Smartphones and mobile gaming are a handy pastime in almost any situation, and technological advances in augmented and virtual reality along with internet of things are pushing forward the frontiers of gaming. This has coincided with a change in the ecosystem for game distribution from bricks-and-mortar stores into digital online stores and new monetization methods. Single-player mode – which is an anomaly in the known 5000-year history of games starting from the Egyptian Senet and the Sumerian Royal Game of Ur – is no longer the standard playmode, and networking can now bring massive numbers of players together to participate in the same game. We have witnessed the rise of gamification and application areas outside of pure entertainment to assist, guide, rehabilitate and teach children, youngsters, adults and elders alike. Game development has also become more democratized, because the development platforms make it easy and quick for everyone to create digital games. Finally, there is more knowledge and research on various aspects of games from design to productization, and modern game developers are more educated and aware of the possibilities of their medium. Behind the seven established forms of art (Canudo, 1988a,b; Hegel 1975), games are truly emerging as the eighth art form.

The first edition of this book was published ten years ago in 2006. It was a time before smartphones, tablets, digital distribution and social networks. Massive multiplayer games such as *World of Warcraft* and *Eve Online* had just been released and were gathering momentum, the social media of today were still in their infancy, and the verb 'to google' had just been added to the *Oxford English Dictionary*. The single-player PC games delivered in DVDs were the top of the line, and mobile games resembled simple games from the early 1980s. If we were back then careful in asserting that computer games are a valid topic for academic research, there is today no argument as to their importance.

Despite the changes, something still remains the same: the algorithms and networking making it all possible. Game programming is not an isolated field of study but intersects many essential research areas of 'traditional' computer science. Solving an algorithmic or networking problem is always more than just getting it done as quickly as possible; it is about analysing what is behind the problem and what possibilities there are to solve it. This is the the motivation for this book, and our intention – right from the beginning – has been to provide the reader with a glance into the world of computer games as seen from the perspective of a computer scientist.

We assume that the reader is familiar with the fundamentals of algorithms and data structures (e.g. complexity analysis and graph theory). In a case of uncertainty, the reader can consult basic textbooks such as *Introduction to Algorithms* (Cormen et al. 2001) and, of course, the ever inspirational *The Art of Computer Programming* (Knuth 1998a,b,c, 2011). We describe classical game algorithms and review problems encountered in commercial computer games. Thus, in selecting material for this book we have walked a tight-rope between these two worlds. The current selection may seem a bit of a ragbag, but the common factor in the choice of the topics has been a combination of algorithmic and practical interest.

Going through the original LaTeX files of the first edition, we were pleasantly surprised how fresh many of the ideas have remained. Hardly anything was outdated; rather the problems the developers are facing today are still the same. It also inspired us to continue and expand the work with a similar mindset. We have tried again to pick relevant topics from both academic literature and trade journals, forum posts and blogs to squeeze out their essence. We have still refrained from tying our hands with a particular platform (of which there have been many throughout the past decade) and programming language (of which there have been equally many). We are aware that that has been a common critique over the years, but we have strived to unlock the timeless beauty that many of the ideas conceal. Granted, there are many things that escape our grasp or which we could only briefly introduce, which is why we provide references to the works of the wiser and better informed. Also, the exercises at the end of each chapter hide many gold nuggets and possibilities for expanding one's thoughts and even venturing into uncharted waters.

Revising and expanding this book has been a fun process, and a hard process – a task one gladly undertakes once a decade.

Acknowledgements

First of all, we acknowledge our dear friend Dr Timo Kaukoranta's role in gathering and analysing the topics which formed the basis for the first edition of this book. His untimely death was a wake-up call to realize in written form the ideas we had been tossing around for several years. Timo's spirit is still present throughout this book.

Many people have guided us on our journey to view the world as computer scientists. Professor Olli Nevalainen's pivotal role in steering us to the world of algorithms as well as the support from the late Professor Timo Raita have been both inspiring and invaluable to us.

We would like to thank our colleagues and co-authors over the years – of whom we would like to mention here (alphabetically) Andy Best, Sami Hyrynsalmi, Antero

Järvi, Kai Kimppa, Timo Knuutila, Ville Leppänen and Tomi 'bgt' Suovuo – for widening our perspectives and sharpening our thoughts. We are also grateful for the feedback we have received from the students who have taken part in our various game-related projects, courses and seminars in the Department of Information Technology, University of Turku and Turku Centre for Computer Science during 2001–2016.

It has again been a pleasure to work with the people at Wiley. We thank Tiina Wigley for initiating this opportunity to write a second edition, and Sandra Grayson and Preethi Belkese for giving us the freedom to enjoy this treat – it has tasted as sweet as the first one.

Jouni.   First and foremost, I am grateful to Professor Erkki Sutinen for his most positive and encouraging attitude towards this endeavour. I am also in debt to my doctoral students Jussi Laasonen and Tapani Liukkonen as well as my master's students Ilmari Lahti, Eero Itkonen and Juhani Kyrki for their valuable insights. Over the years collaboration with the local game scene has been priceless to me and I would like to thank: Turku Game Lab (Adjunct Professor Mika Luimula, Taisto Suominen, Nataša Bulatović Trygg and the rest of the lab staff), TEPE Research Group on Health Games (Professor Sanna Salanterä, Heidi Parisod and Anni Pakarinen), Game Turku and Turku Science Park (Patrik Uhinki and Marko Puhtila), Up Your Game Network (Aki Koponen and Jukka Vahlo), and IGDA Finland Turku Hub. As always, it was good to team up again with Harri to play a little Lennon–McCartney as this project also marked the twentieth anniversary of co-authoring with him (which is always a pleasure). Finally, Lilia and Julian, thank you for being wonderful, amazing little creatures with your own view of the world – and for inviting Dad to take part in your games. And Iris, my words cannot express my gratitude for all the love, care, wit, warmth and understanding.

Harri.   Thank you to all my friends for your benevolence, encouragement, support, inspiration, and the warm hugs. To my colleagues at Oy LM Ericsson Ab for allowing me to be part of a small and hard-working team of experienced specialists; I am still learning a lot from you all, you gracious *kuomat*! To Jouni, when my writing deep-dived into the tar pit you said 'Do not worry, we'll figure it out, it'll turn out OK as always', and you were right again. To my son Pyry for having the patience to test-read the scribbles and drafts, and then give honest feedback; love has wonderfully numerous manifestations. As dear *emo* has evinced. In the kind of environment that you radiate it has been fun to linearize the wrinkles of my thoughts, I am so lucky to have you!

Turku, Finland
June 2016

Jouni Smed
Harri Hakonen

1

Introduction

Let us play a little thought game. Get a pen and paper. Choose any game you know, and think about the elements required to make it work. Write down a list of these elements. Be as specific or indiscriminate as you want. Once you have finished, choose another game and think about it. Try to find items in the list of the first game that correspond to the second game and mark them. If there are features in the second game that the first one does not have, add them to the list. Repeat this procedure for two or three more games. Next, take the five most common items in your list and compare them to the following list. For each corresponding item you get one point.

The key elements of a game are:

- players who are willing to participate in the game;
- rules which define the limits of the game;
- goals which the players try to achieve during the game;
- opponents or opposing forces which prevent the player from achieving the goals;
- a representation of the game in the real world.

How many points did you score?

The five components we have listed seem to be present in every game, and the relationships between them form three aspects of a game, which are illustrated in Figure 1.1 (Smed and Hakonen 2003, 2005b):

(i) *Challenge*. Rules define the game and, consequently, the goal of the game. When players decide to participate in the game, they agree to follow the rules. The goal motivates the players and drives the game forward, because achieving a goal in the game gives the players enjoyment.

(ii) *Conflict*. The opponent (which can include unpredictable humans and random processes) obstructs the players from achieving the goal. Because the players do not have a comprehensive knowledge of the opponent, they cannot determine precisely the opponent's effect on the game.

(iii) *Play*. The rules are abstract but they correspond to real-world objects. This representation concretizes the game to the players.

The challenge aspect alone is not enough for a definition of a game, because games are also about conflict. For example, a crossword puzzle may be a challenge in its own right but there is hardly any conflict in solving it – unless someone erases the letters or changes the hints or keeps a record of the time to solve the puzzle. Obviously, the

Algorithms and Networking for Computer Games, Second Edition. Jouni Smed and Harri Hakonen.
© 2017 John Wiley & Sons Ltd. Published 2017 by John Wiley & Sons Ltd.

Figure 1.1 Components, relationships, and aspects of a game.

conflict arises from the presence of an opponent, which aims to obstruct the player from achieving the goal. The opponent does not have to be a human but it can be some random process (e.g. throw of dice or shuffling of the deck of cards). The main feature of the opponent is that it is non-deterministic to the player: because the player cannot predict exactly what another human being or a random process will do, outwitting or outguessing the opponent becomes an important part of the game.

Challenge and conflict aspects are enough for defining a game in an abstract sense. However, in order to be played the game needs to be concretized into a representation. This representation can be a board and plastic pieces as well as non-tactile words or three-dimensional graphics rendered on a computer screen. Even the players themselves can be the representation, as in the children's game of tag. Regardless of the representation there must exist a clear correspondence to the rules of the game.

Let us take the game of poker as an example. The players agree to follow the rules, which state (among other things) what cards there are in a deck, how many cards one can change, and how the hands are ranked. The rules also define the goal, having as good a hand as possible when the cards are laid on the table, which is the player's motivation. The other players are opponents, because they try to achieve a better hand to win – or, at least, to give such an impression. Also, the randomness of the deck caused by shuffling opposes the player, who cannot determine what cards will be dealt next. The game takes a concrete form in a deck of plastic-coated cards (or pixels on the screen), which represent the abstractions used in the rules.

One of the earliest written collection of games, *Libro de los juegos* ('Book of games'), commissioned by King Alfonso X of Castile, León and Galicia and completed in Toledo 1283, divides the games into three groups: games of skill (e.g. chess), games of chance (e.g. dice games) and games combining skill and chance (e.g. backgammon). This division reflects the conflict aspect and the type of the opponent.

Huizinga's definition of play from his classical work *Homo Ludens*, the playful human, captures most of the features we listed earlier:

> [Play] is an activity which proceeds within certain limits of time and space, in a visible order, according to rules freely accepted, and outside the sphere of necessity or material utility. The play-mood is one of rapture and enthusiasm, and is sacred or festive in accordance with the occasion. A feeling of exaltation and tension accompanies the action, mirth and relaxation follow. (Huizinga 1955, p. 132)

Moreover, Huizinga's idea of a magic circle tries to capture the complete game (or play) experience, which resides outside ordinary life.

Caillois (2001) builds upon Huizinga's work and divides games further into four forms:

- *agon* (competition) describes games where the aim is to beat the opponent and luck does not play a significant role (e.g. chess);
- *alea* (chance) describes games where luck or chance is the decisive factor on the outcome (e.g. Roulette);
- *mimicry* (role-play) describes games where the players go through an adventure with their characters in a game world (e.g. *Dungeons & Dragons*);
- *ilinx* (vertigo) describes games that affect the player's observations or movements (e.g. *Dance Dance Revolution*).

Games are usually a combination of the aforementioned forms. Moreover, Caillois notes that games form a continuum from structured, rule-governed games (*ludus*) to spontaneous, unstructured play (*paidia*).

Wittgenstein argues that it is impossible to define a game: 'For how is the concept of a game bounded? What still counts as a game and what no longer does? Can you give the boundary? No.' (Wittgenstein 2009, Aphorism 68). Suits responds to Wittgenstein's challenge directly by giving the following definition:

> To play a game is to attempt to achieve a specific state of affairs [prelusory goal], using only means permitted by rules [lusory means], where the rules prohibit use of more efficient in favour of less efficient means [constitutive rules], and where the rules are accepted just because they make possible such activity [lusory attitude]. I also offer the following simple and, so to speak, more portable version of the above: playing a game is the voluntary attempt to overcome unnecessary obstacles. (Suits 2014, p. 43)

Crawford (1984, Chapter 1) defines a game as 'a closed formal system that subjectively represents a subset of reality'. Accordingly, a game is self-sufficient, follows a set of rules, and has a representation in the real world. These observations are echoed by the definitions of Costikyan (2002, p. 24), who sees a game as 'an interactive structure of endogenous meaning that requires players to struggle toward a goal', and by Salen and Zimmerman (2004, p. 80), for whom a game is 'a system in which players engage in an artificial conflict, defined by rules, that results in a quantifiable outcome'. A widely known, practical definition of a game, attributed to the game designer Sid Meier, states that a game is a series of meaningful choices (Rollings and Morris 2000, p. 38). Schell (2015, p. 47) shares this point of view, defining a game as 'a problem-solving activity, approached with a playful attitude'.

Apart from formal features, the gameplay also includes subjective elements such as an immersion in the game world, a sense of purpose, and a sense of achievement from mastering the game. One could argue that the sense of purpose is essential for the immersion. What immerses us in a game (as well as in a book or a film) is the sense that there is a purpose or motive beneath the surface. In a similar fashion, the sense of achievement is essential for the sense of purpose (i.e. the purpose of a game is to achieve goals, points, money, recognition, etc.). From a human point of view, we get satisfaction in the process of nearing a challenging goal and finally achieving it – and then realizing that we can relive that feeling. These aspects, however, are outside the scope of our current discussion, and we turn our focus to a subset of games, namely computer games.

1.1 Anatomy of Computer Games

Computer games are a subset of games. To be more precise, let us define a computer game as a game that is carried out with the help of a computer program. This definition leaves us some leeway, since it does not imply that the whole game takes place in the computer. For example, a game of chess can be played on the screen or on a real-world board, regardless of whether the opponent is a computer program. Also, location-based games (see Chapter 11) further obscure the traditional role of a computer game by incorporating real-world objects into the game world.

In effect, a computer program in a game can act in three roles:

(i) coordinating the game process (e.g. realizing a participant's move in a chess game according to the rules);
(ii) illustrating the situation (e.g. displaying the chessboard and pieces on screen); and
(iii) participating as a fellow-player.

This role division closely resembles the *Model–View–Controller* (MVC) architectural pattern for computer programs. MVC was originally developed within the Smalltalk community (Krasner and Pope 1988) and was later adopted as a basis for object-oriented programming in general (Gamma et al. 1995). The basic idea is that the representation of the underlying application properties (Model) should be separated from the way it is presented to the user (View) and from the way the user interacts with it (Controller). Figure 1.2 illustrates the MVC components and the data flow in a computer game.

The Model part includes software components which are responsible for the coordination role (e.g. evaluating the rules and upholding the game state). The rules and basic entity information (e.g. physical laws) form the core structures. It remains unchanged while the state instance is created and configured for each game process. The core structures need not cover all the rules, because they can be instantiated. For example, the core structures can define the basic mechanism and properties of playing cards (e.g. suits and values) and the instance data can provide the additional structures required for a game of poker (e.g. ranking of the hands, staking, and resolving ties).

The View part handles the illustration role. A proto-view provides an interface into the Model. It is used for creating a synthetic view for a synthetic player or for rendering a view to an output device. The synthetic view can be preprocessed to suit the needs of the synthetic player (e.g. board coordinates rather than an image of the pieces on a board). Although rendering is often identified with visualization, it may also include audification and other forms of sensory feedback. The rendering can have some user-definable options (e.g. graphics resolution or sound quality).

The Controller part includes the components for the participation role. Control logic affects the Model and keeps up the integrity (e.g. by excluding illegal moves suggested by a player). The human player's input is received through an input device filtered by driver software. The configuration component provides instance data, which is used in generating the initial state for the game. The human player participates in the data flow by perceiving information from the output devices and performing actions through

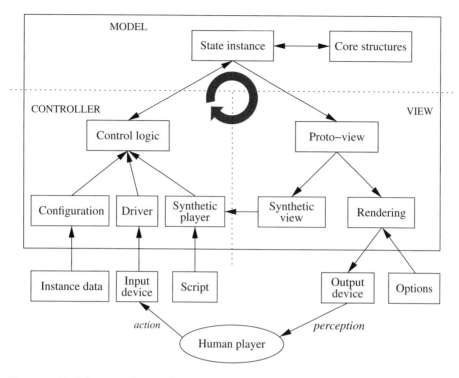

Figure 1.2 Model, View and Controller in a computer game.

the input devices. Although the illustration in Figure 1.2 includes only one player, naturally there can be multiple players participating in the data flow, each with their own output and input devices. Moreover, the computer game can be distributed among several computer nodes rather than residing inside a single node. Conceptually, this is not a problem since the components in the MVC can also be thought to be distributed (i.e. the data flows run through the network rather than inside a single computer). In practice, however, networked computer games provide their own challenges (see Section 1.4).

1.2 Game Development

In the game industry, the production process of games is called game development and the people participating in this process are collectively known as game developers. This group is diverse and houses talents with different skills and backgrounds, but typically the game industry recognizes seven professional disciplines (Novak 2007, pp. 302–321):

- *production* – managing the practical challenges of the game development process;
- *marketing* – raising and maintaining awareness of the game among the (potential) players;
- *testing and quality assurance* – ensuring the stability and playability of the game;
- *design* – handling the mechanics behind the rules and play of the game;
- *art* – creating the visual components of the game;

- *audio* – creating the sounds and aural environments for the game;
- *programming* – implementing the game in a digital form.

During game development, the producer and game designer play the pivotal roles. The game designer is the one with a vision of the game, which is to be carried from inception to conclusion. The producer is the counterpart who has to work with the realities – schedule, budget – to enable the project to materialize. They often work in tandem, the producer being the external link (e.g. to the customer or publisher) and the designer the internal link (i.e. to the rest of the development team). The artists (both visual and audio) design and create the assets that the game uses, and the programmers' task is to implement the game mechanics and the user interfaces. The game testers and quality assurance provide feedback to the development team by taking care that the game is playable, bug-free, enjoyable, and ready to be marketed to the customers.

A large commercial game project can take 2–4 years of work, throughout which the game development involves 50–150 people, possibly in several countries and production sites. For example, the production of *Grand Theft Auto V* took 5 years, involved over 300 people and cost £170 million. Requiring both technical and artistic expertise, even smaller projects require cooperation between several specialized professionals. Nevertheless, the finished game should be a cohesive whole, which delivers the vision of the game designer to the players.

From the game designer's perspective the game can be divided into the basic parts as illustrated in Figure 1.3 (Adams 2014). The three fundamental components are the player who plays the game, the user interface that presents the game to the player, and the core mechanics implementing the rules and the game artificial intelligence (AI). The core mechanics generates challenges that the user interface (through a camera model) converts to output for the player. Conversely, the player's input is conveyed through the user interface (based on the interaction model) and converted to actions for the core mechanics. Gameplay is then the challenges and actions, and together with the user interface they define the gameplay mode, of which a game can have several.

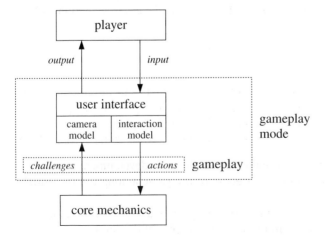

Figure 1.3 Basic design parts of a game.

1.2.1 Phases of development

Figure 1.4 illustrates the phases of a typical game development project (Novak 2007, pp. 334–346). In the concept phase, a game idea is concretized into a concept document, which is used (as a sales pitch) in order to raise funding for the production. If a publisher accepts the concept, the game idea will be refined in the pre-production phase, in which the game designer creates a game design document. This represents a

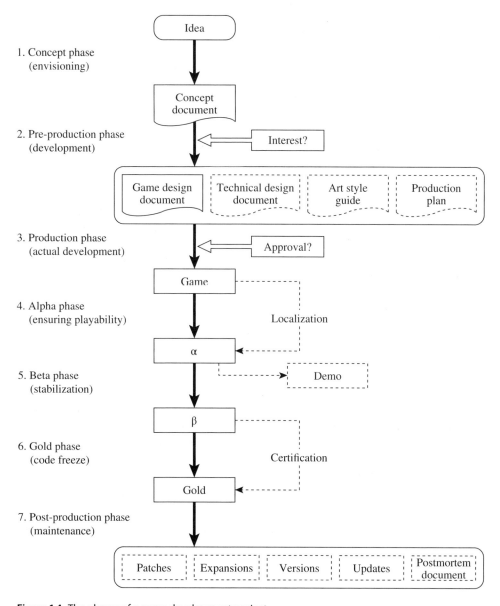

Figure 1.4 The phases of a game development project.

'blueprint' of the game for the production. Additionally, other documents such as a technical design document, an art style guide or a production plan can be generated during the pre-production phase.

After the pre-production phase, the project must get approval from the publisher before entering the production phase, where the actual game development takes place. Once the production phase is over, the game moves first to the alpha phase, which concentrates on ensuring playability, and then to the beta phase, where the aim is to stabilize the game by eliminating bugs. Finally, in the gold phase the game code and other assets are finalized before publishing. The game might also require certification from the publisher for market acceptance. At the same time, the game can be localized to other languages so that all the versions can be published simultaneously. In order to market the forthcoming game, playable demos can be made public before the final product is ready.

When the game has been published, it enters the post-production phase, where bugs and design flaws can be patched and the game can be updated according to possible new requirements. The game can be ported to other platforms or extended by creating new material for the players. Finally, the game developers can issue a postmortem document where they analyse the project.

Digital distribution and ideas from lean development have changed this model slightly into a more iterative process. Once the game has been published online, the development can revert back to production phase to include new content or even new game mechanisms based on feedback and metric data from players (more on this in Chapter 14). This means that the production process is not as heavy as in the traditional, game-as-a-product distribution model which aims to deliver a finished game. Lean and iterative production, which is common especially in mobile games, changes this into a game-as-a-service distribution model, where the game is never finished but continuously growing and transforming.

1.2.2 Documentation

To maintain the original vision a game development project is built upon game documents, which provide all the departments – from management to engineering and arts – with a single vision (Rouse 2004, pp. 206–319). Therefore, the documentation serves two purposes: it is a record of the design decisions, and it is a means of communication that conveys the game design to all participants in the project. The documentation can have any format suitable for the game production; for example, it can be, apart from text, a collection of thematic images, sounds, video and other items. The purpose is to compile and convey the business idea, product identity and value proposition of the game.

Figure 1.5 summarizes the typical documents created and used during a game development project (Schell 2015, pp. 425–432):

- *game design overview* – a short summary of the game written for the company's management;
- *game design document* – a detailed description of the game mechanics and interfaces;
- *story overview* – a description of the setting, characters, and actions that will take place in the game;
- *technical design document* – a specification of the technology used, for the engineering department;
- *pipeline overview* – instructions on how the art assets will be integrated into the game;

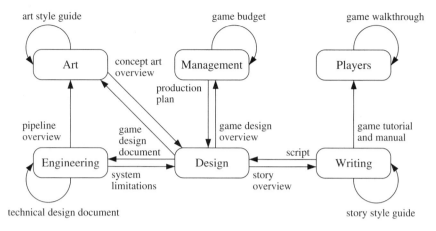

Figure 1.5 The game documents created and used in a game development project.

- *system limitations* – a summary of the technical limitations for the design department;
- *art style guide* – guidelines for the arts department to create a single, consistent look and feel;
- *concept art overview* – a summary of the outlook of the game;
- *game budget* – a spreadsheet for keeping track of costs;
- *production plan* – a schedule for the game project;
- *story style guide* – guidelines of the story-world for the writing department;
- *script* – dialogues for the game characters;
- *game tutorial and manual* – instructions on how to play the game;
- *game walkthrough* – a guide written by players to help other players to play the game.

The game design document (GDD) is the central written resource for the game design. It is typically a 50–200-page reference guide to the whole game development process (Novak 2007, pp. 368–370). It specifies the mechanics of the game, the rules of play, and the theme of the outlook (Chandler 2008, pp. 252–257). A GDD is not static but continually edited and updated by the designers and developers during the production phase. Nevertheless, the GDD should remain up to date even after the production phase because it will still be needed in localizing the game to new languages. If the game is ported to a new platform, the GDD provides a source of information for the (possibly third-party) team carrying out the conversion. Also, a GDD is a valuable asset when designing a follow-up or an extension to the original game.

1.2.3 Other considerations

Although defining what makes a game enjoyable is subjective, we can list some features that alluring computer games seem to have. Of course our list is far from complete and open to debate, but we want to raise certain issues which are interesting in their own right but which – unfortunately – fall outside the scope of this book.

- *Customization*. A good game has an intuitive interface that is easy to learn. Because players have their own preferences, they should be allowed to customize the user interface to their own liking. For example, the interface should adapt dynamically to the needs of a player so that in critical situations the player has more detailed control. If a player can personalize her avatar (e.g. customize the characteristics to correspond to her real-world persona), it can increase immersion in the game.

- *Tutorial.* The first problem a player faces is learning how the game works, which includes both the user interface and the game world. Tutorials are a convenient method for teaching the game mechanics to the player, where the player can learn the game by playing it in an easier and possibly assisted mode.
- *Profiles.* To keep the game challenging as the player progresses, it should support different difficulty levels which provide new challenges. Typically, this feature is implemented by increasing certain attributes of the enemies: their number, their accuracy, and their speed. The profile can also include the player's preferences of the type of game (e.g. whether it should focus on action or adventure).
- *Modifications.* Games gather communities around them, and members of the community start providing new modifications (or 'mods') and add-ons to the original game. A modification can be just a graphical enhancement (e.g. new textures) or can enlarge the game world (e.g. new levels). Also, the original game developers themselves can provide extension packs, which usually include new levels, playing characters, and objects, and perhaps some improvement of the user interface.
- *Replaying.* Once is not enough. We take pictures and videotape our lives. The same applies also to games. Traditionally, many games provide the option to take screen captures, but replays are also an important feature. Replaying can be extended to cover the whole game, and the recordings allow the players to relive and memorize the highlights of the game, and to share them with friends and the whole game community.

It is important to recognize beforehand what software development mechanisms are published to the players and with what interfaces. The game developers typically implement special software for creating content for the game. These editing tools are a valuable surplus to the final product. If the game community can create new variations of the original game, the longevity of the game increases. Furthermore, the inclusion of the developing tools is an inexpensive way – since they are already implemented – to enrich the contents of the final product.

Let us turn the discussion around and ask what makes a bad computer game. It can be summed up in one word: *limitation.* Of course to some extent limitation is necessary – we are, after all, dealing with limited resources. Moreover, the rules of the game are all about limitation, although their main function is to impose the goals for the game. The art of making games is to balance the means and limitations so that this equilibrium engrosses the human player. How do limitations manifest themselves in the program code? The answer is the lack of parameters: the more things are hard-coded, the lesser the possibilities to add and support new features. Rather than closing down possibilities, a good game – like any good computer program! – should be open and modifiable for both the developer and the player.

1.3 Synthetic Players

A synthetic player is a computer-generated actor in the game. It can be an opponent, a non-player character which participates in some limited way (like a supporting actor), or a *deus ex machina* which can control natural forces or godly powers and thus intervene or generate the game events.

Because everything in a computer game revolves around the human player, the game world is anthropocentric. Regardless of the underlying method for decision-making (see Chapter 9), the synthetic player is bound to show certain behaviour in relation to the human player, which can range from simple reactions to general attitudes and even complex intentions. As we can see in Figure 1.2, the data flow of the human player and the synthetic player resemble each other, which allows us to project human-like features onto the synthetic player.

We can argue that, in a sense, there should be no difference between the players whether they are humans or computer programs; if they are to operate on the same level, both should ideally have the same powers of observation and the same capabilities to cope with uncertainties (see Chapter 10). Ideally, the synthetic players should be in a similar situation to their human counterparts, but of course a computer program is no match for human ingenuity. This is why synthetic players rarely display real autonomy but appear to behave purposefully (e.g. in *Grand Theft Auto III* pedestrians walk around without any real destination).

The more open (i.e. the less restrictive) the game world is, the more complex the synthetic players are. This trade-off between the Model and the Controller software components is obvious: if we remove restricting code from the core structures, we have to reinstate it in the synthetic players. For example, if the players can hurt themselves by walking into fire, the synthetic player must know how to avoid it. Conversely, if we rule out fire as a permitted area, path finding (see Chapter 7) for a synthetic player becomes simpler.

Let us take a look at two external features that a casual player is most likely to notice first in a synthetic player: humanness and stance. These are also relevant to the design of the synthetic player by providing a framework for the game developers and programmers.

1.3.1 Humanness

The success of networked multiplayer games can be, at least in part, explained by the fact that the human players provide something that the synthetic ones still lack. This missing factor is the human traits and characteristics – flaws as much as (or even more than) strengths: fear, rage, compassion, hesitation, and emotions in general. Even minor displays of emotion can make the synthetic player appear more human. For instance, in *Half-Life* and *Halo* the synthetic players who have been taken by surprise do not act with superhuman coolness but show fear and panic appropriate to the situation; actually, the reaction time should be 0.2–0.4 seconds (Rabin 2015). We, as human beings, are quite apt to read humanness into the decisions even when there is nothing but naïve algorithms behind them. Sometimes a game, such as *NetHack*, even gathers around a community that starts to tell stories of the things that synthetic players have done and to interpret them in human terms.

A computer game comprising just synthetic players could be as interesting to watch as a movie or television show (Charles et al. 2002). In other words, if the game world is fascinating enough to observe, it is likely that it is also enjoyable to participate in – which is one of the key factors in games like *The Sims* and *Singles*, where the synthetic players seem to act (more or less) with a purpose and the human player's influence is, at best, only indirect.

There are also computer games that do not have human players at all. Already back in the 1980s *Core War* demonstrated that programming synthetic players to compete with each other can be an interesting game itself (Dewdney 1984). Since then some games have tried to use this approach, but, by and large, AI programming games have been only by-products of 'proper' games. For example, *Age of Empires II* includes the possibility of creating scripts for computer players, which allows games to be organized where programmers compete as to who creates the best AI script. The whole game is then carried out by a computer while the humans remain as observers. Although the programmers cannot affect the outcome during the game, they are more than just enthusiastic watchers: They are the coaches and the parents, and the synthetic players are the protégés and the children.

1.3.2 Stance

The computer-controlled player can have different stances (or attitudes) towards the human player. Traditionally, the synthetic player has been seen only in the role of an enemy. As an enemy the synthetic player must provide challenge and demonstrate intelligent (or at least purposeful) behaviour. Although the enemies may be omniscient or cheat when the human player cannot see them, it is important to keep the illusion that the synthetic player is at the same level as the human player.

When the computer acts as an ally, its behaviour must adjust to the human point of view. For example, a computer-controlled reconnaissance officer should provide intelligence in a visually accessible format rather than overwhelm the player with lists of raw variable values. In addition to accessibility, the human players require consistency, and even incomplete information (as long as it remains consistent) can have some value to them. The help can even be concrete operations as in *Neverwinter Nights* or *Star Wars: Battlefront* where the computer-controlled team-mates respond to the player's commands.

The computer has a neutral stance when it acts as an observer (e.g. camera director or commentator) or a referee (e.g. judging rule violations in a sports game) (Martel 2014; Siira 2004). Here, the behaviour depends on the context and conventions of the role. In a sports game, for example, the camera director program must heed the camera placements and cuts dictated by television programme practice. Refereeing provides another kind of challenge, because some rules can be hard to judge. Finally, synthetic players can be used to carry on the plot, to provide atmosphere, or simply to act as extras (de Sevin et al. 2015). Nevertheless, as we shall see next, they may have an important role in assisting immersion in the game world and directing the gameplay.

1.4 Multiplaying

What keeps us interested is – surprise. Humans are extremely creative at this, whereas a synthetic player can be lacking in humanness. One easy way to limit the resources dedicated to the development of synthetic players is to make the computer game a multiplayer game.

The first real-time multiplayer games usually limited the number of players to two, because the players had to share the same computer by dividing either the screen (e.g. *Pitstop II*) or the playtime among the participating players (e.g. *Formula One Grand Prix*). Also, the first networked real-time games connected two players over a modem (e.g. *Falcon A.T.*). Although text-based networked multiplayer games started out in the early 1980s with multi-user dungeons (Bartle 1990), real-time multiplayer games (e.g. *Quake*) became common in the 1990s as local area networks (LANs) and the Internet became more widespread. These two development lines were connected when online game sites (e.g. *Ultima Online*) started to provide real-time multiplayer games for a large number of players sharing the same game world.

On the technical level, networking in multiplayer computer games depends on achieving a balance between the consistency and responsiveness of a distributed game world (see Chapter 12). The problems are due to the inherent technical limitations (see Chapter 11). As the number of simultaneous players increases, scalability of the chosen network architecture become critical. Although related research work on interactive real-time networking has been done in military simulations and networked virtual environments (Smed et al. 2002, 2003b), the prevention of cheating is a unique problem for computer games due to the conflicting motivations and interests of the participants (see Chapter 13).

Nowadays, commercially published computer games are expected to offer a multiplayer option, and, at the same time, online game sites are expected to support an ever increasing number of users. Similarly, the new game console releases rely heavily on the appeal of online gaming, and a whole new branch of mobile entertainment has emerged with the intention to develop distributed multiplayer games for wireless applications.

The possibility of having multiple players enriches the game experience – and complicates the software design process – because of the interaction between the players, both synthetic and human. Moreover, the players do not have to be opponents but they can cooperate. Although more common in single-player computer games, it is possible to include a story-like plot in a multiplayer game, where the players are cooperatively solving the story (e.g. *No One Lives Forever 2* and *Neverwinter Nights*).

In the design of massively multiplayer online games, the two main game design approaches are called theme-park and playground – or, alternatively, rollercoaster and sandbox. A theme-park (or rollercoaster), such as *World of Warcraft*, provides the players with top-down generated challenges. The set-up and goal of a challenge are preconceived by the game designers, but there is much leeway as to how the players actually reach the goal. In contrast, a playground (or sandbox), such as *Eve Online*, relies on the emergence of player-originated stories and the social media connecting the game community. The game world is like a playground allowing all kinds of plays and events to unfold. The stories are then told by the community (retrospectively) the same way as reporters and historians do in the real world. Let us next look at storytelling from a broader perspective.

1.5 Interactive Storytelling

Storytelling is one of the oldest human activities. We learn from a very young age to use stories and narratives to communicate ideas and to think about possibilities. In the oral tradition of storytelling, a bard would adapt a story depending on the audience – even the structure of the story could vary within a certain confines. Only with the advent of the written media did storytelling become 'petrified' and come to mean the process of an author crafting a reproducible composition. 'Interactive storytelling' has taken the original meaning emphasizing the reactive and performative aspects of storytelling, where the aim is to generate dramatically compelling stories based on the user's input (Smed 2014).

Research on interactive digital storytelling (IDS) began in the 1980s with the seminal work of Brenda Laurel (1991). She took ideas from the world of theatre and applied them to computer interfaces in general and to IDS in particular. Formally put, an IDS application is 'designed for users (interactors) to take part in a concrete interactive experience, structured as a story represented in a computer' (Peinado and Gervás 2007).

The core question at the heart of interactive storytelling is the *narrative paradox*, in which the 'pre-authored plot structure conflicts with the freedom of action and interaction characteristics of the medium of real-time interactive graphical environment' (Aylett and Louchart 2007), causing a tension between the interactor's freedom and well-formed stories (Adams 2013). Simply put, the more freedom the interactor has, the less control the author has, and vice versa.

1.5.1 Approaches

The research on IDS has revolved around two distinct approaches. The *author-centric* approach likens IDS to theatre, where the author sets up the story-world and a computer-controlled drama manager directs its characters. A drama manager modifies how the computer-controlled characters react and tries to lead the story in a direction that the author has intended. It tries to change the situation so that the user is going in the direction of the intended story. This can be realized, for example, by limiting the stage and possible actions in the story-world such as in *Façade* where story happens in an apartment during a soirée involving an interactor and two characters having domestic problems (Mateas 2002).

The *character-centric* approach to IDS believes in emergence by allowing the characters in the story-world to be autonomous. Therefore, the key question is to model the mental factors that affect on how the characters act. The author's influence is limited in creating and setting up the story-world. After that, the story-world runs without the author's influence, and the story – hopefully – emerges from the interaction between the computer-controlled characters and the human interactor.

To compare the two approaches Riedl (2004, p.12–14) proposes two measures:

- plot coherence – the perception that the main events of a story are causally relevant to the outcome of the story;
- character believability – the perception that the events of a story are reasonably motivated by the beliefs, desires and goals of the characters.

Clearly, the author-centric approach allows us to have strong plot coherence, because of the drama manager's influence. The downside is, however, that character believability is weakened if the actions of the characters seem to be compelled to follow the author's will. The problem is then finding subtlety so that the influence does not feel too forced upon the user. In implementation, the main concern is that an IDS system must observe the reactions of the user as well as the situation in the story-world to recognize what pattern fits the current situation: is the story getting boring and should there be a surprise twist in the plot, or has there been too much action and the user would like to have a moment of peace to rest and regroup? Since we aim to tell a story to the human users, we must ensure that the world around them remains purposeful.

Conversely, the character-centric approach has (and requires) strong character believability. This means that plot coherence is weaker, because the story emerges from the bottom up from the characters' aspirations. Although the idea of emergent narrative of the character-centric approach seems to solve the narrative paradox, it is unlikely that it is enough for implementing a satisfying IDS system. Realistic actions are not necessarily dramatically interesting, if the characters have no dramatic intelligence. Therefore, the argument is that the author's presence is necessary, because without the author's artistic control we would end up having the chaos of everyday life.

Recently, the discussion has evolved to include a hybrid approach, where the characters are autonomous but they can communicate with one another outside of the story-world (Swartjes et al. 2008). These two modes of the character are called in-character (IC) and out-of-character (OOC). They are used, for example, in live action role-playing where the participants can act IC (i.e. within the role they are playing) or drop to OOC when they are being themselves. Also, in improvisational theatre the actors can convey OOC information using indirect communication (e.g. an actor can say 'Hello, son!', cuing the other actor to assume the role of son). For example, Weallans et al. (2012) present a hybrid approach called distributed drama management, where the characters act on an IC level and reflect on their actions on an OOC level. A character proposes a set of possible actions to a drama manager, which selects dramatically the best alternative. Here, the drama manager is no longer pushing the characters to follow its lead but supports their decision-making through OOC communication.

1.5.2 Storytelling in games

The International Game Developers Association (2004) says that '[a]ny game featuring both characters and a story in which one or more narrative aspects changes interactively can be considered an interactive story.' The simplest narrative aspect that can be interactive is the plot, which can vary in response to the player's actions. Another possibility is that the player's actions affect and change the non-player character's attitude and personality (e.g. if the player acts in a friendly manner, the non-player character also becomes more friendly and helpful towards the player). A third possibility is to have a varying theme, where the player's behaviour in the story-world trims the theme, making the story, for example, more romantic, thrilling or violent.

According to Costikyan (2002), a game is not a story: while a story progresses linearly, a game must provide an illusion of free will. Obviously, the player must have a range of actions to choose from at each stage. More formally, let us consider the story in a game as a directed graph where the episodes (or levels) are vertices and the possible transitions edges (Figure 1.6). This means that the greater the fan-out of a vertex is, the more freedom the player has in the story-world. The simplest game stories use a linear structure, where the story unfolds as an episodic sequence. A game may offer only a little room for the story to deviate – as in *Dragon's Lair* where, at each stage, the players can choose from several alternative actions of which all but one lead to certain

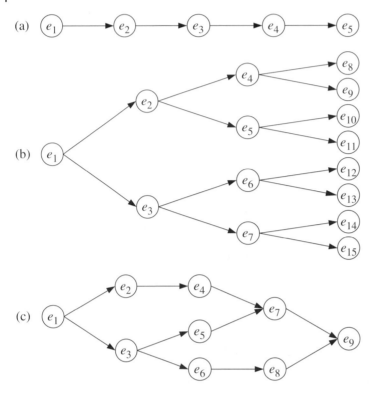

Figure 1.6 The story structure can be illustrated as a graph, where episodes (or levels) are represented as vertices and transitions as directed edges. (a) In a linear structure, the story always unfolds the same way. (b) In a branching structure, each transition leads to a unique episode. (c) In parallel paths, although the episodes can branch, they can also conjoin, limiting the number of episodes.

death. Nevertheless, this is the most commonly used structure to tell a story in computer games: An episode has a fixed starting point and ending point (e.g. a 'boss monster' at the end of the level) between which the player can proceed freely. For instance, in *Max Payne* or *Diablo II* the plot lines of the previous chapter are concluded at the transition point, and new alternatives are introduced for the next one. The episodes follow one another linearly in a pre-authored order, and they are linked, for example, by cut-scenes. Linear story structure is the cheapest to produce, which is why it is popular even today. The obvious drawback is that the player has no influence on how the story unfolds and the story can feel like it has been pasted over the game. In the worst case, the elaborate cut-scene videos and complex plot twists only bore the player who skips them in order to get right into the action.

In theory, branching structure would be optimal for IDS, because each decision has a unique outcome. However, combinatorial explosion prevents us from using it in practice. The only way to make it feasible is to have conjoining edges that bring two or more vertices (i.e. episodes) together, leading to a structure called parallel paths. The story is again presented in an episodic manner, but at the transition point, where the story of the previous episode is concluded, the player gets to choose from alternative paths for the next episode. Although the paths can take players to different routes, eventually they conjoin in a major story point. For example, given a task, a player can choose to fight to achieve his aims or to take a diplomatic path avoiding violence altogether. An early example of this is *Indiana Jones and the Fate of Atlantis*, where in mid-game the player has to choose one of three possible paths – team, wits or fists – which converge before the end. Although the paths could lead to the same outcome, the episodes leading there can be totally different. This of course means that the game will have content that a player cannot see in one play. For a game publisher this means that it seemingly gets less value for its investment, which is why there is a pressure for the game designers to limit the amount of parallel paths in a game. However, there are commercially successful games such as *Heavy Rain* and *The Walking Dead* as well as critically acclaimed games such as *80 Days* and *Her Story* using this approach.

1.6   Outline of the Book

The intention of our book is to look at the algorithmic and networking problems present in commercial computer games from the perspective of a computer scientist. As the title implies, this book divides into two parts: algorithms and networking. This emphasis in topic selection leaves out components of Figure 1.2 which are connected to the human-in-the-loop. Most noticeably we omit topics concerning graphics and human interaction – which is not to say that they are in any way less important or less interesting than the current selection of topics. Also, game design as well as ludological aspects of computer games fall outside the scope of this book.

The topics of the book are based on the usual problems that we have seen game developers encountering in game programming. We review the theoretical background of each problem and review the existing methods for solving them. The given algorithmic solutions are not provided in any specific programming language but in pseudocode format, which can be easily rewritten in any programming language and – more importantly – which emphasizes the algorithmic idea behind the solution. The algorithmic notation used is described in detail in Appendix A. We also present a practical approach to vectors and matrices in Appendix B.

We have also included examples from real-world computer games to clarify different uses for the theoretical methods. In addition, each chapter is followed by a set of exercises which go over the main points of the chapter and extend the topics by introducing new perspectives.

1.6.1   Algorithms

Part I of this book concentrates on typical algorithmic problems in computer games and presents solution methods. The chapters address the following questions:

- Chapter 2, 'Random Numbers': How can we achieve the indeterminism required by games using deterministic algorithms?
- Chapter 3, 'Noise': How can we make computation based on mathematics look more life-like?
- Chapter 4, 'Procedural Generation': How can we create game content using algorithms?

- Chapter 5, 'Tournaments': How we can form a tournament to decide a ranking for a set of contestants?
- Chapter 6, 'Game Trees': How can we build a synthetic player for perfect information games?
- Chapter 7, 'Path Finding': How can we find a route in a (possibly continuous) game world?
- Chapter 8, 'Group Movement': How can we steer a group of entities through the game world?
- Chapter 9, 'Decision-Making': How can we make a synthetic player act intelligently in the game world?
- Chapter 10, 'Modelling Uncertainty: How can we model the uncertainties present in decision-making?

1.6.2 Networking

Part II turns our attention to networking. Our aim is to describe the ideas behind different approaches rather than get too entangled in the technical details. The chapters address the following questions:

- Chapter 11, 'Communication Layers': What are the technical limitations behind networking?
- Chapter 12, 'Compensating Resource Limitations': How can we cope with the inherent communication delays and divide the network resources among multiple players?
- Chapter 13, 'Cheating Prevention': Can we guarantee a fair playing field for all players?
- Chapter 14, 'Online Metrics': What can we measure from the online player's behaviour?

1.7 Summary

All games have a common basic structure comprising players, rules, goals, opponents and representation. They form the challenge, play and conflict aspects of a game, which are reflected, for instance, in the Model–View–Controller software architecture pattern. The computer can participate in the game as a synthetic player, which can act in the role of an opponent or a team-mate or have a neutral stance. For example, the synthetic player must take the role of a story-teller, if we want to incorporate story-like features into the game. Multiplaying allows other human players to participate in the same game using networked computers.

Game development has matured from its humble beginnings and now resembles any other industrialized software project. Widely accepted software construction practices have been adopted in game development, and, at the same time, off-the-shelf components (e.g. 3D engines and animation tools) have removed the burden to develop all software components in-house. Moreover, modern game development tools such as CryEngine, Unity and Unreal Engine have democratized the development process and made it possible for people who are not so competent in programming to make games. This maturity, however, does not mean that there is no room for artistic creativity and technical innovations. There must be channels for bringing out novel and possibly radically different games, and, as in music and film industry, independent game publishing can act as a counterbalance to the mainstream. One could even argue that this liberation of the game industry has brought about a fresh evolution pool of ways to make business, already affecting the entertainment industry in the large.

Nevertheless, behind computer games are computer programs propelled by algorithms and networking. Let us see what they have in store for us.

Exercises

1-1 Take any simple computer game (e.g. *Pac-Man*) and discern what forms its challenge aspect (i.e. player, rules and goal), conflict aspect and play aspect.

1-2 A crossword puzzle is not a game (or is it?). What can you do to make it more game-like?

1-3 Why do we need a proto-view component in the MVC decomposition?

1-4 What kind of special skills and knowledge should game programmers have when they are programming
(a) the Model part of the software components,
(b) the View part of the software components, or
(c) the Controller part of the software components?

1-5 Let us look at a first-person shooter game (e.g. *Doom* or *Quake*). Discern the required software components by using the MVC. What kind of modelling does it require? What kind of View-specific considerations should be observed? How about the Controller part?

1-6 *Deus ex machina* (from Latin 'god from the machine') derives from ancient theatre, where the effect of the god's appearing in the sky, to solve a crisis by divine intervention, was achieved by means of a crane. If a synthetic player participates the game as a *deus ex machina*, what kind of role will it have?

1-7 What does 'anthropocentrism' mean? Are there non-anthropocentric games?

1-8 *The Sims* includes an option of free will. By turning it off, the synthetic players do nothing unless the player explicitly issues a command. Otherwise, they show their own initiative and follow, for example, their urges and needs. How much free will should a synthetic player have? Where it would serve best (e.g. in choosing a path or choosing an action)?

1-9 In the movie *Stranger Than Fiction* (2006), the protagonist realizes that his life is happening in a fictional novel, and when he refuses to obey the voiceover, the world tries to force him to follow the intended story. Does this represent an author-centric or character-centric approach to interactive storytelling?

1-10 Take your favourite game and decompose its storytelling. Does it always tell the same story or does it vary from one play instance to another? If the story does not respond to the player's actions, what could be done to make it more interactive?

1-11 Game development includes people with different talents (e.g. artists, programmers, designers and marketing people). What kind of communication problems might arise when they work together on the same game project? What is the role of a game programmer in a game project?

1-12 Consider the differences and similarities of Figures 1.4 and 1.5 for a triple-A game developed by hundreds of persons and an indie game developed by one person.

1-13 Because game documents are living documents that change on almost a daily basis, the biggest debate within the game industry is about the effectiveness of creating extensive game documentation during the pre-production phase. Usually many elements of the game change drastically during the production phase, and the documents cannot keep up with the pace of change. The problems encountered in game documentation can be classified into five categories: (Rouse 2004, pp. 374–379):

- Lack of content: The document does not provide enough reference material for the production phase.
- Misplaced focus: The document provides data (e.g. backstory) that is irrelevant to the production phase.
- Overspecification: The document goes too deeply into details, which will become clear only in the production phase.
- Infeasible content: The document contains design decisions that are impossible to realize in the game.
- Fossilization: The document is out of date and, subsequently, abandoned during production.

Game documentation often does not support but hinders the work, because there are no computer-aided tools for maintaining it. Instead, it comprises a bundle of text documents without a clear maintenance scheme. To complicate matters further, game documents – unlike, for example, film scripts – have no pre-defined formats (Rouse 2004, pp. 355–359). Although there are document templates, many game designers state that documents are different for every game and for every team. For example, Schell (2015, p. 426) says outright that a 'magic template [for game documents] does not exist'.

How could this problem be solved? Think about game documentation in terms of maintainability, accessibility and communicativeness. Also, take the concept of 'document medium' as sufficiently wide to cover, for example, a whiteboard or even an oral discussion.

1-14 Many games are variations of the same structure. Consider *Pac-Man* and Snake. Discern their common features and design a generic game which can be parameterized to be both games.

1-15 Judging rules can be difficult, even for an objective computer program. In football (or soccer as some people call it) the official rules say that the referee can allow play to continue if the team against which an offence has been committed has a chance of an immediate, promising attack (i.e. advantage), and penalize the original offence if the anticipated advantage does not ensue at that time (Fédération Internationale de Football Association 2016). How would you implement this rule? What difficulties are involved in it?

1-16 The progression in the lattice of mission groups in *Wing Commander* resembles the story structure shown in Figure 1.6(c). The player's performance in the missions branches in the story, and piling failures drive the player further away from the hope of a victory. However, with later successes it is still possible to get back to the path of victory.

With such second chances in mind, analyse the aspects of failure and failing in general in computer games. For example, in games like *Super Meat Boy* and *Dwarf Fortress* losing is an integral part of the game experience but, on the other hand, in *NetHack* death is permanent and the game feels intentionally brutally lost. How does the presence of failing define and complement the other features of a game?

Part I

Algorithms

2

Random Numbers

One of the most difficult problems in computer science is implementing a truly random number generator – even D.E. Knuth devotes a whole chapter of his *The Art of Computer Programming* to the topic (Knuth 1998b, Chapter 3). The difficulty stems partly from how we understand the word 'random', since no single number in itself is random. Hence, the task is not to simulate randomness but to generate a virtually infinite sequence of statistically independent random numbers uniformly distributed inside a given interval (Park and Miller 1988).

Because algorithms are deterministic, they cannot generate truly random numbers – except with the help of some outside device like processor-embedded circuits. Rather the numbers are generated with arithmetic operations, and, therefore, the sequences are not random but *appear* to be – hence, they are often called *pseudo-random*. It is quite easy to come up with methods like von Neumann's middle-square method, where we take the square of the previous random number and extract the middle digits; for example, if we are generating four-digit numbers, the sequence can include a subsequence:

$$r_i = 8269$$
$$r_{i+1} = 3763 \quad (r_i^2 = 68\underline{376}361)$$
$$r_{i+2} = 1601 \quad (r_{i+1}^2 = 14\underline{160}169)$$
$$\vdots$$

However, if we analyse this method more carefully, it will soon become clear why it is hardly satisfactory for the current purpose. This holds also for many other *ad hoc* methods, and Knuth sums up his own toils on the subject by exclaiming that 'random numbers should not be generated with a method chosen at random' (Knuth 1998b, p. 6).

Since every random number generator based on arithmetic operations has its in-built characteristic regularities, we cannot guarantee it will work everywhere. This problem is due to the fact that the pseudo-random number sequence produced is fixed and devised separately from its actual use contexts. Still, empirical testing and application-specific analysis can provide safety measures against deficiencies (Hellekalek 1998). The goal is to find such methods that produce sequences that are *unlikely* to get 'synchronized' to their contexts. Other aspects that may affect the design of random number generators are the speed of the algorithm, ease of implementation, parallelization, and portability across platforms.

Algorithms and Networking for Computer Games, Second Edition. Jouni Smed and Harri Hakonen.
© 2017 John Wiley & Sons Ltd. Published 2017 by John Wiley & Sons Ltd.

Before submerging into the wonderful world of pseudo-random numbers, let us take a small detour and acknowledge that sometimes we can do quite well without randomness. Most people will hardly consider the sequence $S = \langle 0, 1, 2, 3, 4, 5, 6, 7 \rangle$ random, because it is easy to come up with a rule that generates it: $S_{i+1} = (S_i + 1) \bmod m$. But how about the sequence $R = \langle 0, 4, 2, 6, 1, 5, 3, 7 \rangle$? There seems to be no direct relationship between two consecutive values, but as a whole the sequence has a structure: even numbers precede odd numbers. A bit-aware reader may soon realize that $R_i = \text{BIT-REVERSE}(i, 3)$ is a simple model that explains R. How about the sequence $Q = \langle 0, 1, 3, 2, 6, 7, 5, 4 \rangle$? It seems to have no general structure, but the difference between consecutive pairs is always one, which is typical for a binary-reflected Gray code. From these simple examples we can see that sequences can have properties that are useful in certain contexts. If these characteristics are not used or observed – or even discovered! – the sequence can *appear* to be random. To make a distinction, these random-like (or 'randomish') numbers are usually called *quasi-random numbers*. Quasi-randomness can be preferable to pseudo-randomness, for example, when we want to have a sequence that has a certain inherent behaviour or when we can calculate the bijection of a value and its index in the sequence.

2.1 Linear Congruential Method

At the turn of the 1950s D.H. Lehmer proposed an algorithm for generating random numbers. This algorithm is known as the *linear congruential method*, and since its inception it has quite firmly stood the test of time. The algorithm is simple to implement and requires only a rigorous choice of four fixed integer parameters:

$$
\begin{aligned}
\text{modulus:} \quad & m \quad (0 < m) \\
\text{multiplier:} \quad & a \quad (0 \leq a < m) \\
\text{increment:} \quad & c \quad (0 \leq c < m) \\
\text{starting value:} \quad & X_0 \quad (0 \leq X_0 < m)
\end{aligned}
$$

On the basis of these parameters, we can now obtain a sequence of random numbers by setting

$$X_{i+1} = (aX_i + c) \bmod m \quad (0 \leq i). \tag{2.1}$$

This recurrence produces a repeating sequence of numbers denoted by $\langle X_i \rangle_{i \geq 0}$. More generally, let us define

$$b = a - 1$$

and assume that

$$a \geq 2, \quad b \geq 1.$$

We can now generalize Equation (2.1) to

$$X_{i+k} = (a^k X_i + (a^k - 1)c/b) \bmod m \quad (k \geq 0, \ i \geq 0), \tag{2.2}$$

which expresses the $(i + k)$th term directly in terms of the ith term.

Algorithm 2.1 describes two implementation variants of the linear congruential method defined by Equation (2.1). The first one can be used when $a(m-1)$ does not exceed the largest integer that can be represented by the machine word. For example, if m is one-word integer, the product $a(m-1)$ must be evaluated within a two-word integer. The second variant can be applied when $(m \bmod a) \leq \lfloor m/a \rfloor$. The idea is to express the modulus in the form $m = aq + p$ to guarantee that the intermediate evaluations always stay within the interval $(-m, m)$. For a further discussion on implementation,

---

Algorithm 2.1 Linear congruential method for generating random integer numbers within the interval $[0, m)$.

RANDOM()
    out: random integer r $(0 \leq r \leq m-1)$
    constant: modulus m; multiplier a; increment c; starting value X_0 $(1 \leq m \wedge 0 \leq a, c, X_0 \leq m-1 \wedge a \leq i_{\max}/(m-1)$, where $i_{\max}$ is the largest possible integer value)
    local: previously generated random number x (initially $x = X_0$)
  1: $r \leftarrow (a \cdot x) \bmod m$
  2: $r \leftarrow$ MODULO-SUM(r, c, m)
  3: $x \leftarrow r$
  4: **return** r

RANDOM()
    out: random integer r $(0 \leq r \leq m-1)$
    constant: modulus m; multiplier a; increment c; starting value X_0 $(1 \leq m \wedge 0 \leq a, c, X_0 \leq m-1 \wedge (m \bmod a) \leq \lfloor m/a \rfloor)$
    local: previously generated random number x (initially $x = X_0$)
  1: $q \leftarrow m$ **div** a
  2: $p \leftarrow m \bmod a$
  3: $r \leftarrow a \cdot (x \bmod q) - p \cdot (x \text{ div } q)$
  4: **if** $r < 0$ **then**
  5:    $r \leftarrow r + m$
  6: **end if**
  7: $r \leftarrow$ MODULO-SUM(r, c, m)
  8: $x \leftarrow r$
  9: **return** r

MODULO-SUM(x, y, m)
    in: addends x and y; modulo m $(0 \leq x, y \leq m-1)$
    out: value $(x + y) \bmod m$ without intermediate overflows in $[0, m-1]$
  1: **if** $x \leq m - 1 - y$ **then**
  2:    **return** $x + y$
  3: **else**
  4:    **return** $x - (m - y)$
  5: **end if**

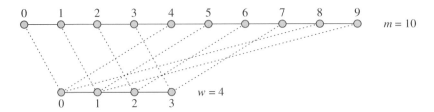

Figure 2.1 If $m = 10$ and $w = 4$, the Monte Carlo method does not provide a uniform distribution.

see Wichmann and Hill (1982), L'Ecuyer (1988), Park and Miller (1988), L'Ecuyer and Côté (1991), Bratley et al. (1983, pp. 201–202), and Knuth (1998b, Exercises 3.2.1.1-9 and 3.2.1.1-10).

Because computer numbers have a finite accuracy, m is usually set close to the maximum value of the computer's integer number range. If we want to generate random floating point numbers where U_i is distributed between zero (inclusive) and one (exclusive), we can use the fraction $U_i = X_i/m$ instead and call this routine RANDOM-UNIT().

What if we want a random integer number within a given interval of length w ($0 < w \le m$)? A straightforward solution would be to use the Monte Carlo approach and let $Y_i = X_i \bmod w$ or – to put it another way – to let $Y_i = \lfloor U_i w \rfloor$. The problem with this method is that the distribution is not guaranteed to be uniform (see Figure 2.1), but Monte Carlo methods allow the approximateness of the solution to be reduced at the cost of running time. In this case we could increase the range of the original random number, for example, by generating several random numbers and combining them, which would make the distribution more uniform but require more computation.

The Las Vegas approach guarantees exactness and gives a simple solution, a uniform distribution, to our problem. This method partitions the original interval

$$[0, m-1] = \bigcup_{i=0}^{w-1} \left[i \left\lfloor \frac{m}{w} \right\rfloor , (i+1) \left\lfloor \frac{m}{w} \right\rfloor - 1 \right] \cup \left[w \left\lfloor \frac{m}{w} \right\rfloor , m-1 \right],$$

where i gives the value in the new interval ($0 \le i \le w - 1$). The last interval (if it exists) is excess and considered invalid (see Figure 2.2). Algorithm 2.2 implements this partitioning by using integer division. If a generated number falls within the excess range, a new one is generated until it is valid. The obvious downside is that the termination

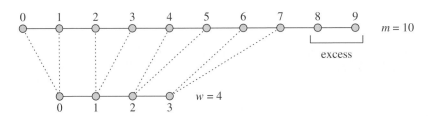

Figure 2.2 The Las Vegas method distributes the original interval uniformly by defining the excess area as invalid.

of the algorithm is not guaranteed. Nevertheless, if we consider the worst case where $w = \frac{m}{2} + 1$, the probability of not finding a solution after i rounds is of magnitude $1/2^i$.

Algorithm 2.2 Las Vegas method for generating random integer numbers within the interval $[\ell, u)$.

RANDOM-INTEGER(ℓ, u)
    in: lower bound ℓ $(0 \le \ell)$; upper bound u $(\ell < u \le \ell + m)$
    out: random integer r $(\ell \le r < u)$
    constant: modulus m used in RANDOM()
    local: the largest value w in the subinterval $[0, u - \ell] \subseteq [0, m - 1]$

  1: $w \leftarrow u - \ell$
  2: **repeat**
  3:   $r \leftarrow$ RANDOM() **div** (m **div** w)
  4: **until** $r < w$
  5: $r \leftarrow r + \ell$
  6: **return** r

2.1.1   Choice of parameters

Although the linear congruential method is simple to implement, the tricky part is choosing values for the four parameters. Let us have a look how they should be chosen and how we can analyse their effect.

The linear congruential method generates a finite sequence of random numbers, after which the sequence begins to repeat. For example, if $m = 12$ and $X_0 = a = c = 5$, we get the sequence

$$6, 11, 0, 5, 6, 11, 0, 5, \ldots$$

The repeating cycle is called a *period*, and, obviously, we want it to be as long as possible. Note that the values in the period of the linear congruential method are different, and it is impossible to have repetitions – unless, for example, we rescale the interval with RANDOM-INTEGER(ℓ, u) or combine multiple sequences into one (Wichmann and Hill 1982). However, a long period does not guarantee randomness: the longest period of length m can always be reached by letting $a = c = 1$ (but you can hardly call the generated sequence random). Luckily, there are other values which reach the longest period as the following theorem shows.

Theorem 2.1.1   *The linear congruential sequence defined by integer parameters m, a, c, and X_0 has period length m if and only if:*

  (i) *the greatest common divisor of c and m is 1,*
  (ii) *b is a multiple of each prime dividing m, and*
 (iii) *if m is a multiple of 4, then b is also a multiple of 4.*

We have denoted $b = a - 1$. For a proof, see Knuth (1998b, pp. 17–19).

Modulus

Since the period cannot have more than m elements, the value of m should be large. Ideally m should be $i_{max} + 1$, where i_{max} is the maximum value of the integer value range. For example, if the machine word is unsigned and has 32 bits, we let $m = (2^{32} - 1) + 1 = 2^{32}$. In this case the computation can eliminate the modulo operation completely. Similarly, if m is a power of 2, the modulo operation can be replaced by a quicker bitwise-and operation. Unfortunately, these m values do not necessarily provide us with good sequences, even if Theorem 2.1.1 holds.

Primes or Mersenne primes are much better choices for the value of m. A Mersenne prime is a prime of the form of $2^n - 1$; the first ten Mersenne primes have $n = 2, 3, 5, 7, 13, 17, 19, 31, 61, 89$. Quite conveniently, $2^{31} - 1$ is a Mersenne prime and thus is often used with 32-bit machine words.

Multiplier

The multiplier a should be chosen to produce a period of maximum length. From Theorem 2.1.1 it follows that if m is the product of distinct primes, only when $a = 1$ will we get a full period. However, if m is divisible by a high power of some prime, we have more choices for a. There is a fundamental problem with small a values: if X_i is small, X_{i+1} will probably also be small. As a rule of thumb, the multiplier a should reside between $0.01m$ and $0.99m$, and its binary representation should not have a simple, regular bit pattern. For example, multipliers of the form $a = 2^x + 1$ ($2 \leq x$) have a regular bit pattern and, therefore, tend to produce low-quality random sequences.

Increment

From Theorem 2.1.1 it also follows that the increment c can be chosen quite freely, as long as it does not have a common factor with m (e.g. $c = 1$ or $c = a$). In many implementations $c = 0$, because it allows the elimination of one operation and makes the processing a bit faster. However, as Theorem 2.1.1 indicates, this cuts down the length of the period. Also, when $c = 0$, we must guarantee that $X_0 \neq 0$.

Starting value

The starting value (or *seed*) X_0 determines from where in the sequence the numbers are taken. A common oversight in the initialization is to always use the same seed value, because it leads to the same sequence of generated numbers. Usually this can be avoided by obtaining the seed value from the built-in clock of the computer, the last value from the previous run, the user's mouse movements, previously handled keystrokes, or some other varying source.

2.1.2 Testing the randomness

Random number generators can be tested both empirically and theoretically. We omit the theoretical discussion and go through some rudiments of empirical tests; curious readers are referred to Knuth (1998b, Section 3.3). In most cases the following tests are based on statistical tests (e.g. χ^2 or Kolmogorov–Smirnov) and they aim to provide some quantitative measures for randomness, when choosing between different parameter settings. Nevertheless, one should bear in mind that although a random sequence might behave well in an existing test, there is no guarantee that it will pass a further test; each test gives us more confidence but can never banish our doubts.

Frequency test Are numbers distributed uniformly according to their frequencies?
Serial test Are pairs (triplets, quadruplets, etc.) of successive numbers uniformly distributed in an independent manner?
Gap test Given a range of numbers, what is the distribution of the gaps between their occurrences in the sequence?
Poker test Group the sequence into poker hands each comprising five consecutive integers. Are the hands distributed as random poker hands should be?
Coupon collector's test What is the length of sequence required to get a complete set of given integers?
Permutation test Divide the sequence into groups of a given size. How often do different permutations occur?
Run test How long are the monotone segments (run-ups or run-downs of consecutive numbers) of the sequence?
Collision test If numbers are categorized with a hash function, how many collisions occur?
Birthday spacings test If the numbers are hashed, how long are the spacings between them?
Spectral test If pairs (triplets, quadruples, etc.) of successive numbers are treated as points in a hypercube, how uniformly do they fill it?

The spectral test is an important (and yet quite intuitive) test for analysing linear congruential random number generators. Moreover, we can rest assured that all good generators will pass the test and bad ones are likely to fail it. Although it is an empirical test and requires computation, it resembles theoretical tests in the sense that it deals with the properties of the full period.

Suppose we have a sequence of period m and we take t consecutive numbers of the sequence so that we have a set of points

$$\{(X_i, X_{i+1}, \ldots, X_{i+t-1}) \mid 0 \le i < m\}$$

in t-dimensional space. For example, if $t = 2$ we can draw the points in a two-dimensional plane (see Figure 2.3). In this case one can easily discern the parallel lines into which the points fall. This is an inherent property of the linear congruential methods. When t increases, the periodic accuracy decreases as there are fewer hyperplanes where the points can reside. In contrast, a truly random sequence would have the same accuracy in all dimensions.

2.1.3   Using the generators

Although the programmer implementing a random number generator must understand the theory behind the method, the user also has responsibilities. If one does not know the assumptions behind the linear congruential method, it can easily become a random number 'degenerator'. To prevent this from happening, let us go through some common pitfalls lurking in pseudo-random numbers generated by Equation (2.1).

- If $X_0 \ne 0$, the largest range of multiplicative linear congruential method $X_{i+1} = aX_i \bmod m$ is $[1, m-1]$. However, the range of $U_i = X_i/m$ is not necessarily $(0, 1)$,

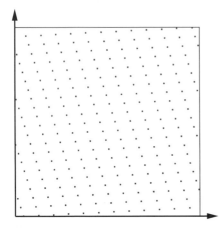

Figure 2.3 Two-dimensional spectral test results for the case where $m = 256$, $a = 21$, and $c = 11$.

if $1/m$ rounds to value 0.0 or $(m-1)/m$ rounds to value 1.0. In other words, when converting random integers to decimal values, the characteristics of floating point arithmetic such as rounding must be considered and documented.

- Even if the sequence $\langle X_i \rangle_{i \geq 0}$ is well tested and appears to be random, it does not imply that $\langle f(X_i) \rangle_{i \geq 0}$ is also random. For this reason, one should not extract bits from X_i and expect them to have random properties. In fact, in linear congruential generators the least significant bits tend to be less random than the most significant bits.
- The (pseudo-)randomness of a sequence $\langle X_i \rangle_{i \geq 0}$ does not imply any randomness for combinations (e.g. values in $\langle f(X_i, X_j) \rangle_{i,j \geq 0}$) or aggregations (e.g. pairs in $\langle (X_i, X_j) \rangle$). For example, if we take a bitwise exclusive-or of two pseudo-random numbers, the outcome can be totally non-random.
- If we select any subsequence of non-consecutive numbers from $\langle X_i \rangle_{i \geq 0}$, we cannot expect (without inspecting) this subsequence to have the same level of randomness. This is important especially when the same random number generator is shared among many subsystems.

What is common to all of these situations is the fact that when the user modifies the sequence produced, she takes the role of the supplier with its accompanying responsibilities.

Although the theoretical and test results concerning a pseudo-random sequence do not automatically apply to a sequence derived from it, in practice long continuous blocks behave similarly to the whole sequence. When we test the pseudo-randomness of a sequence, the local interrelationships are also measured and verified. This allows us define multiple *parallel random number generators* from a single generator. Assume that the original generator $R = \langle X_i \rangle_{i \geq 0}$ has a period of length p and we need k parallel generators S_j ($j = 0, \ldots, k-1$). If we require that the parallel generators S_j must be disjoint and with equal lengths, they can have at most $\ell = \lfloor p/k \rfloor$ numbers from R. Now, if we define

$$S_j = \langle X_{\ell j}, X_{\ell j+1}, \ldots, X_{\ell j+(\ell-1)} \rangle = \langle X_{\ell j+i} \rangle_{i=0}^{\ell-1}, \tag{2.3}$$

subsequence S_j can be produced with the same implementation as R just by setting the seed to $X_{\ell j}$. Common wisdom says that the number of values generated from a linear

Table 2.1 Seed values $X_{\ell j}$ of 12 parallel pseudo-random number generators S_j for five multiplicative linear congruential methods with multiplier a. The subsequences are $\ell = \lfloor (2^{31} - 2)/12 \rfloor = 178\,956\,970$ values apart from each other.

Block number j	Starting index ℓj	Multiplier a of the generator				
		16 807	39 373	41 358	48 271	69 621
0	0	1	1	1	1	1
1	178 956 970	1 695 056 031	129 559 008	289 615 684	128 178 418	1 694 409 695
2	357 913 940	273 600 077	1 210 108 086	1 353 057 761	947 520 058	521 770 721
3	536 870 910	1 751 115 243	881 279 780	1 827 749 946	1501 823 498	304 319 863
4	715 827 880	2 134 894 400	1 401 015 190	1 925 115 505	406 334 307	1 449 974 771
5	894 784 850	1 522 630 933	649 553 291	9 087 743	539 991 689	69 880 877
6	1 073 741 820	939 811 632	388 125 325	1 242 165 306	1 290 683 230	994 596 602
7	1 252 698 790	839 436 708	753 392 767	1 088 988 122	1 032 093 784	1 446 470 955
8	1 431 655 760	551 911 115	1 234 047 880	1 487 897 448	390 041 908	1 348 226 252
9	1 610 612 730	1 430 160 775	1 917 314 738	535 616 434	2 115 657 586	1 729 938 365
10	1 789 569 700	1 729 719 750	615 965 832	1 294 221 370	1 620 264 524	2 106 684 069
11	1 968 526 670	490 674 121	301 910 397	1 493 238 629	1 789 935 850	343 628 718

congruential method should not exceed one thousandth of p (Knuth 1998b, p. 185), and thus we can have $k \geq 1000$ parallel generators from only one generator. For example, if $p = 2^{31} - 2$, we can define one thousand consecutive blocks of length $\ell = 2\,147\,483$ each. However, there are dependencies both within a block and between the blocks. Although a single block reflects the random-like properties of the original sequence, the block-wise correlations remain unknown until they are tested (Entacher 1999).

Table 2.1 presents five well-tested multiplicative linear congruential methods and partitions them into 12 blocks of numbers. All of these generators have a Mersenne prime modulo $m = 2^{31} - 1 = 2\,147\,483\,647$, increment $c = 0$, and the same period length $p = 2^{31} - 2$. The multiplier $a = 16\,807 = 7^5$ is presented by Lewis et al. (1969), 39 373 by L'Ecuyer (1988), $41\,358 = 2 \cdot 3 \cdot 61 \cdot 113$ by L'Ecuyer et al. (1993), and both 48 271 and $69\,621 = 3 \cdot 23 \cdot 1009$ by Park and Miller (1988). All these generators can be implemented with the second variant of Algorithm 2.1. The blocks can be used as parallel generators, and we can draw about 2 million random numbers from each of them. For example, the seed of S_5 for the generator $X_{i+1} = 41\,358 \cdot X_i \bmod (2^{31} - 1)$ (where $X_0 = 1$) is $X_{894\,784\,850} = 9\,087\,743$. The values of Table 2.1 can also be used for verifying the implementations of these five generators.

2.2   Discrete Finite Distributions

Non-uniform random numbers are usually produced by combining uniform random numbers creatively (Knuth 1998b, Section 3.4). Distributions are usually described using a probability function of a random variable X. Assume the set of possible values of a variable X is $\{X_0, X_1, \ldots, X_{n-1}\}$ and the probability that binding $X = X_i$ occurs is known to be $p_i = P(X = X_i)$. If the constraint $\sum_{i=0}^{n-1} p_i = 1$ holds, the discrete probability distribution of X is well defined, and we call the function $P(X)$ having the values $p_0, p_1, \ldots, p_{n-1}$ a probability function of a discrete random variable X. The function $P(X)$ identifies the probability distribution and the ones that reappear most often are named along with their characteristic parameters.

Instead of listing the probabilities explicitly, a finite discrete distribution of events can be also defined by a formula. For example, suppose we have a trial where an event e occurs independently with probability p and does not occur with probability $1 - p$. Then we repeat this trial n times, fixing both n and p. To describe the probability that e happens exactly t times out of n, a random variable X can be introduced to count these occurrences; in other words, the possible values of X are $\{0, 1, \dots, n-1, n\}$. Now, it can be shown that the probability function is

$$p_t = P(X = t) = \binom{n}{t} p^t (1-p)^{n-t} = \frac{n! \, p^t (1-p)^{n-t}}{t!(n-t)!}$$

for $t = 0, 1, \dots, n$, with fixed $n \in \mathbb{N}$ and $p \in [0, 1]$. This is called the binomial distribution $\mathrm{Bin}(n, p)$ of X, also denoted by $X \sim \mathrm{Bin}(n, p)$.

Another fundamental discrete probability distribution is the Poisson distribution $\mathrm{Pois}(\mu)$ of X. This distribution is defined with respect to a fixed unit of some measurement such as a specific time interval, a certain area of a region or an observation of an attribute value. The disjoint events occur independently in this measurement unit and X counts the occurrences without an upper limit (i.e. $X \in \mathbb{N}$). The distribution parameter μ is the average number of events in each measurement unit, which means that the rate of events is also fixed. When we require also that the probability of an event is proportional to the size of the measurement unit and the events do not coincide, the probability function becomes

$$p_c = P(X = c) = \frac{\mu^c e^{-\mu}}{c!}$$

for $c \in \mathbb{N}$, with $0 < \mu \in \mathbb{R}$ per fixed measurement unit. To understand this better, suppose a mining colony operates on an asteroid and they can handle 12 haulers in one rotation period of the asteroid. The average number of haulers arriving is 7 per period. In this case the measurement unit is the rotation period, X is a counter for the haulers arriving on the period, and $\mu = 7$ assuming the haulers' routes are independent. The probability that there is at least one hauler orbiting on hold in a given period is

$$P(12 < X) = 1 - P(X \le 12) = 1 - \sum_{c=0}^{12} p_c = 1 - \sum_{c=0}^{12} \frac{7^c e^{-7}}{c!}$$

$$= 1 - \frac{14603038643}{13685760 e^7} \approx 1 - 0.9730 = 0.0270.$$

Algorithm 2.3 (Knuth 1998b, p. 137) generates a random value $X \sim \mathrm{Pois}(\mu)$ by simulating the occurrences of the events, given the rate μ. For this reason, the loop at lines 4–7 runs on average $\mu + 1$ times, making the algorithm quite feasible for $0 < \mu \lesssim 20$.

The combination of an abstract notion of a measurement unit and the independence of the events makes the Poisson distribution conveniently practical when we want to generate randomness. As an example, let us populate a bounded two-dimensional space $S = [0, \ell]^2$ with n points placed in uniformly random positions. Assume the space is attached with a fixed frame (i.e. the origin, x- and y-axes) so that each position can be referred to uniquely with Cartesian coordinates. The independence of the axes (e.g. the

---

Algorithm 2.3 A random count of events based on the Poisson distribution when there are on average μ independent events per a measurement unit.

RANDOM-POISSON(μ)
   in: average number of events μ ($0 < \mu \in \mathbb{R}$) for a unit of measurement
   out: number of pseudo-events n ($n \in \mathbb{N}$) for the measurement unit
   1: $t \leftarrow e^{-\mu}$ $\triangleright$ Termination limit value.
   2: $n \leftarrow -1$
   3: $p \leftarrow 1$ $\triangleright$ Accumulating product.
   4: **repeat** $\triangleright$ Simulation of the event occurrences.
   5:    $n \leftarrow n + 1$
   6:    $p \leftarrow p \cdot$ RANDOM-UNIT() $\triangleright$ Random unit value $\in [0, 1)$.
   7: **until** $p \leq t$
   8: **return** n

---

independence of their spatial properties such as density) allows us to generate a random coordinate in $[0, \ell]$ for both of the axes separately, and when these coordinates are combined the pair in $[0, \ell]^2$ is also uniformly random. This allocation is repeated for all n points, and Figure 2.4(a) illustrates one possible outcome when the space is a plane $[0, 600]^2$.

In this approach, the population of the space is grounded only after the last point has been placed. The uniform randomness is drawn from the whole range $[0, \ell]$ for both axes and the last point can land on any position within $[0, \ell]^2$. However, it can be shown that we can achieve this property of 'global' uniform randomness considering a space $\mathcal{U}$ of *any fixed size* as long as its properties are similar to the global one. It is especially worth noting that this applies to spaces $\mathcal{U}$ that are smaller than S, which means that the uniform randomness can be generated from decisions that are as 'local' as we want. These two approaches produce results with the same properties, the difference being that in the local one the subspaces can be populated independently, for example, in parallel or sequentially one by one.

The method relies on two features, and we utilize them here without further justification: the space has Cartesian coordinates and the Poisson distribution $X \sim \text{Pois}(\mu)$ has exactly the required properties. Now, let us fix the measurement unit to subspace $\mathcal{U}_0 = [0, \ell/6]^2 \subset S$ which is a $(6 \cdot 6)$th part of the whole space S. Because the population of n points in S is distributed uniformly randomly, on average there are $n/6^2$ points in $\mathcal{U}_0$ giving us $\mu = n/6^2$. Furthermore, since the points in $\mathcal{U}_0$ must also be uniformly random, we have the following population step. Generate a random number $X_0 \sim \text{Pois}(n/6^2)$. Then interpret the value of X_0 as a number of points, and place that many points uniformly randomly into $\mathcal{U}_0$. Repeat for all of the disjoint subspaces $\mathcal{U}_i$ of S so that their union covers the whole of S. To simplify the calculations, bookkeeping and the effort of partitioning S, the shapes of the subspaces $\mathcal{U}_i$ are often regular such as squares or cubes (but not necessarily equally sized). This is also convenient with the prerequisites of the Cartesian coordinate system.

Obviously, the result visualized in Figure 2.4(b) is similar to that in Figure 2.4(a), as well as that in Figure 2.4(c) where the subdivision has 900 parts and $\mu = n/30^2$.

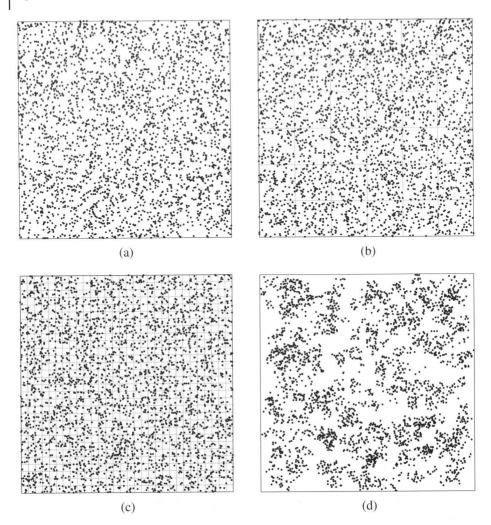

Figure 2.4 A plane of size 600 × 600 units consisting of *n* randomly generated points. (a) *n* = 3000 with discrete uniform distribution (DU) over the whole plane. (b) *n* = 3048 over the partition of 36 subplanes, each with DU of $X \sim \mathrm{Pois}(3000/(6 \cdot 6))$ points; *X* varies in [70, 107]. (c) *n* = 2977 over the 900 subplanes, each with DU of $X \sim \mathrm{Pois}(3000/(30 \cdot 30))$ points; *X* varies in [0, 11]. (d) *n* = 2994 in 400 uniformly randomly placed subplanes, each with DU of $X \sim \mathrm{Pois}(3000/(20 \cdot 20))$ points; *X* varies in [2, 16].

Actually, Figure 2.4(a) can also be considered as $X \sim \mathrm{Pois}(n)$ where by chance $X = n$. The cost of locality when generating the points is that the Poisson values $X_i \sim \mathrm{Pois}(\mu_i)$ must be calculated for each $\mathcal{U}_i$, and the actual total number of the points $\sum_i X_i$ cannot be predetermined to be exactly *n*. Fortunately, since the values X_i are independent it can be shown that

$$\left(\sum_i X_i \right) \sim \mathrm{Pois}\left(\sum_i \mu_i \right) = \mathrm{Pois}(n) \tag{2.4}$$

and, thus, $\sum_i X_i$ tends to be close to n. Equation (2.4) has another consequence as it justifies the fact that the points can also be generated in layers.

When uniform randomness of the whole is handled in parts, the generation process is simpler to parameterize. Parameterization can be used to change the uniformity into structural features, as illustrated in Figure 2.4(d): instead of tiling S regularly with $\mathcal{U}_i$, each square-shaped $\mathcal{U}_i$ is placed in a uniform random position in S without crossing the outer borders. Just randomizing the positions of randomness yields thinning or thickening in some regions. There are also other adjustment possibilities that can be triggered by some criterion. For example, the size of $\mathcal{U}_i$ or the μ attached to it can change on some regions of S. Also, there could be predetermined attractor or repeller positions for the placement of $\mathcal{U}_i$.

As we have seen so far, producing suitable random numbers for a specific situation can be a tedious task requiring formulation of a proper distribution and then devising an algorithm for it, or finding suitable parameters for an existing algorithm. Even listing the probabilities explicitly $\{p_0, p_1, \ldots, p_{n-1}\}$ and constraining them with $\sum_{i=0}^{n-1} p_i = 1$ is not always practical. For instance, if the probabilities are changing over time or if they are derived from separate calculations, the constraints can require an extra normalization step – but this can be avoided by relaxation: instead of a probability, each elementary event is given a weight value.

Algorithm 2.4 selects a random number r from a finite set $\{0, 1, \ldots, n-1\}$. Each possible choice is associated with a weight, and the value r is selected with the probability $W_r / \sum_{i=0}^{n-1} W_i$. For example, for a uniform distribution $DU(n)$ each choice has the probability $1/n$, which is achieved using weights $W = \langle c, c, \ldots, c \rangle$ for any positive integer c. A simple geometric distribution $\text{Geom}(\frac{1}{2})$, modelling the number of failures until the first success (where the success and failure are equiprobable), has probability $1/2^{r+1}$ for

---

Algorithm 2.4 Generating a random number from a distribution described by a finite sequence of weights.

RANDOM-FROM-WEIGHTS(W)

   in: sequence of n weights W describing the distribution ($W_i \in \mathbb{N}$ for $i = 0, \ldots, (n-1) \wedge 1 \leq \sum_{i=0}^{n-1} W_i$)

   out: randomly selected index r according to W ($0 \leq r \leq m - 1$)

  1: $|S| \leftarrow n$ ▷ Reserve space for n integers.

  2: $S_0 \leftarrow W_0$

  3: **for** $i \leftarrow 1 \ldots (n-1)$ **do**   ▷ Collect prefix sums.

  4:    $S_i \leftarrow S_{i-1} + W_i$

  5: **end for**

  6: $k \leftarrow$ RANDOM-INTEGER($1, S_{n-1} + 1$)   ▷ Random $k \in [1, S_{n-1}]$.

  7: **if** $k \leq S_0$ **then**

  8:    $r \leftarrow 0$

  9: **else**

  10:   $r \leftarrow$ smallest index i for which $S_{i-1} < k \leq S_i$ when $i = 1, \ldots, n-1$

  11: **end if**

  12: **return** r

---

a choice r, and it can be constructed using weights $W = \langle 2^{n-1}, 2^{n-2}, \ldots, 2^{n-1-r}, \ldots, 1 \rangle$. In general, W can be in any order and $W_i = 0$ denotes that i cannot be selected.

Because the sequence S in Algorithm 2.4 is non-descending, line 10 can be implemented efficiently using a binary search that favours the leftmost of equal values (i.e. the one with the smallest index). Furthermore, lines 8 and 10 can be collapsed into one line by introducing a sentinel $S_{-1} \leftarrow 0$. Conversely, we can speed up the algorithm by replacing the sequence S with a Huffman tree, which gives an optimal search branching (Knuth 1998a, Section 2.3.4.5). If speed is absolutely crucial and many random numbers are generated from the same distribution, Walker's alias method can provide a better implementation (Kronmal and Peterson 1979; Matias et al. 1993).

2.3 Random Shuffling

In random shuffling we want to generate a *random permutation*, where all permutations have a uniform random distribution. We can even consider random shuffling as inverse sorting, where we are not aiming for permutations fulfilling some sorting criterion but all permutations. Although methods based on card shuffling or other real-world analogues can generate random permutations, their distribution can be far from uniform. Hence, better methods are needed.

Suppose we have an ordered set $S = \langle s_1, \ldots, s_n \rangle$ to be shuffled. If n is small, we can enumerate all possible $n!$ permutations and obtain a random permutation quickly by generating a random integer between 1 and $n!$. Algorithm 2.5 produces all permutations of $\langle 0, \ldots, n-1 \rangle$. To optimize, we can unroll the while loop at lines 23–28, because it is entered at most twice. For $3 \leq n$, the body of the while loop at lines 18–22 is entered at most $n - 2$ times in every $2n$th iteration of the repeat loop. Also, line 29 is unnecessary when $n \geq 2$. For a further discussion and other solution methods, see Knuth (2011, Section 7.2.1.2) and Sedgewick (1977).

In most cases, generating all the permutations is not a practical approach (e.g. $9! > 2^{16}$, $13! > 2^{32}$ and $21! > 2^{64}$). Instead, we can shuffle S by doing random sampling without replacement. Initially, let an ordered set $R = \langle \, \rangle$. Select a random element iteratively from S and transfer it to R, until $S = \langle \, \rangle$. To convince ourselves that the distribution of the permutations generated is uniform, let us analyse the probabilities of element selections. Every element has a probability $1/n$ of being selected into the first position. The element selected cannot appear in any other position, and the subsequent positions are filled with the remaining $n - 1$ elements. Because the selections are independent, the probability of any generated ordered set is

$$1/n \cdot 1/(n-1) \cdot 1/(n-2) \cdot \ldots \cdot 1/1 = 1/n!.$$

Hence, the generated ordered sets have a uniform distribution, since there are exactly $n!$ possible permutations. Algorithm 2.6 implements this approach by constructing the solution in-place within the ordered set R.

Let us take a look at why the more 'naturalistic' methods often fail. Figure 2.5 illustrates a riffle shuffle, which is a common method when a human dealer shuffles playing cards. Knowledge about shuffling has been used by gamblers – which is why nowadays casinos use mechanisms employing other strategies, which, in turn, can turn out to be surprisingly inadequate (Mackenzie 2002) – and magicians in card tricks. Let us look at

Algorithm 2.5 Generating all permutations.

ALL-PERMUTATIONS(n)
    in: number of elements n $(1 \leq n)$
    out: sequence R containing all permutations of the sequence $\langle 0, 1, \ldots, (n-1) \rangle$
             ($|R| = n!$)
    local: index r of the result sequence

  1: $|R| \leftarrow n!$ ▷ Reserve space for $n!$ sequences.
  2: **for** $i \leftarrow 0 \ldots (n-1)$ **do**   ▷ Initialize C, O, and S of length n.
  3:    $C_i \leftarrow 0; O_i \leftarrow 1; S_i \leftarrow i$
  4: **end for**
  5: $r \leftarrow 0$
  6: **repeat**
  7:    $j \leftarrow n - 1$
  8:    $s \leftarrow 0$
  9:    $q \leftarrow C_j + O_j$

10:    **for** $i \leftarrow 0 \ldots (n-2)$ **do**
11:      $R_r \leftarrow$ **copy** $S; r \leftarrow r + 1$
12:      $\alpha \leftarrow j - C_j + s; \beta \leftarrow j - q + s$
13:      swap $S_\alpha \leftrightarrow S_\beta$
14:      $C_j \leftarrow q$
15:      $q \leftarrow C_j + O_j$
16:    **end for**
17:    $R_r \leftarrow$ **copy** $S; r \leftarrow r + 1$

18:    **while** $q < 0$ **do**
19:      $O_j \leftarrow -O_j$
20:      $j \leftarrow j - 1$
21:      $q \leftarrow C_j + O_j$
22:    **end while**
23:    **while** $q = (j + 1)$ **and** $j \neq 0$ **do**
24:      $s \leftarrow s + 1$
25:      $O_j \leftarrow -O_j$
26:      $j \leftarrow j - 1$
27:      $q \leftarrow C_j + O_j$
28:    **end while**
29:    **if** $j \neq 0$ **then**
30:      $\alpha \leftarrow j - C_j + s; \beta \leftarrow j - q + s$
31:      swap $S_\alpha \leftrightarrow S_\beta$
32:      $C_j \leftarrow q$
33:    **end if**
34:   **until** $j = 0$
35:   **return** R

Algorithm 2.6 Random shuffle

SHUFFLE(S)
  in: ordered set S
  out: shuffled ordered set R
  1: $R \leftarrow$ **copy** S
  2: **for** $i \leftarrow 0 \ldots (|R| - 2)$ **do**
  3:    $j \leftarrow$ RANDOM-INTEGER$(i, |R|)$
  4:    swap $R_i \leftrightarrow R_j$
  5: **end for**
  6: **return** R

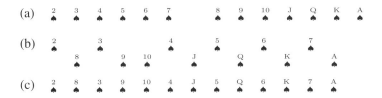

Figure 2.5 In riffle shuffle the deck is divided into two packets, which are riffled together by interleaving them.

a simplification of a card trick named 'Premo' (Bayer and Diaconis 1992). Suppose we have a deck of cards arranged in the following order:

2 3 4 5 6 7 8 9 10 J Q K A 2 3 4 5 6 7 8 9 10 J Q K A ♡ ♡ ♡ ♡ ♡ ♡ ♡ ♡ ♡ ♡ ♡ ♡ ♡ ◇ ◇ ◇ ◇ ◇ ◇ ◇ ◇ ◇ ◇ ◇ ◇ ◇

2 3 4 5 6 7 8 9 10 J Q K A 2 3 4 5 6 7 8 9 10 J Q K A ♣ ♣ ♣ ♣ ♣ ♣ ♣ ♣ ♣ ♣ ♣ ♣ ♣ ♠ ♠ ♠ ♠ ♠ ♠ ♠ ♠ ♠ ♠ ♠ ♠ ♠

A magician gives the deck to a spectator and asks her to give it two riffle shuffles. Next, the spectator is asked to remove the top (here the leftmost) card, memorize its value, and insert it into the pack. The magician has now a deck, which could look like this:

J 2 K Q A 3 2 K A A 3 4 2 2 4 5 K 3 3 5 4 4 6 6 5 5 ◇ ♡ ♡ ◇ ♣ ♡ ♠ ◇ ♡ ♡ ♠ ♡ ◇ ♣ ♠ ♡ ♣ ◇ ♣ ♠ ♡ ◇ ♡ ♠ ♣ ◇

7 7 6 8 8 6 7 9 8 7 9 10 9 8 10 J 10 Q J 9 J K Q 10 Q A ♡ ♠ ♣ ♠ ♡ ◇ ♣ ♠ ♣ ◇ ♡ ♠ ♣ ◇ ♡ ♠ ♣ ♠ ♣ ◇ ♡ ♠ ♣ ◇ ♡ ♠

Glancing at the deck, the magician can easily determine what is the chosen card.[1] After two shuffles the deck has four rising sequences of cards (hint: look at each suit), and the inserted card is very likely to break one such run. In fact, if the magician has only one guess, the probability of success is 0.997. The original Premo trick allows the spectator to do three riffle shuffles. If the magician has one guess, the probability of success is still as high as 0.839; with two guesses it increases to 0.943. However, if the spectator does four riffle shuffles, the probability of success with one and two guesses drops to 0.288 and 0.471, respectively. This is known as a cut-off phenomenon, where the 'randomness' of the deck suddenly increases at some point during the shuffling (Aldous and Diaconis 1986). How should one then shuffle? For a deck of 52 cards, the consensus is that at

---

[1] Answer: The king of clubs.

least seven riffle shuffles is enough for most purposes – assuming the players have mere human cognitive and computational skills.

2.4   Summary

If we try to generate random numbers using a deterministic method we end up generating pseudo-random numbers. The linear congruential method – which is basically just a recursive multiplication equation – is one of the simplest, oldest and most studied of such methods. Pseudo-randomness differs in many respects from true randomness, and common sense does not always apply when we are generating pseudo-random numbers. For example, a pseudo-random sequence cannot usually be modified and operated as freely as a true random sequence. Therefore, the design of a pseudo-random number generator must be done with great care – and this means that the user also has to understand the underlying limitations.

We can insert randomness to a deterministic algorithm to have a controlled variation of its output. This enables us, for example, to create game worlds that resemble the real world but still include randomly varying attributes. Moreover, we can choose a deterministic algorithm randomly, which can be a good decision-making policy when we do not have any guiding information on what the next step should be. A random decision is the safest choice in the long run, since it reduces the likelihood of making bad decisions (as well as good ones).

Exercises

2-1   A friend gives you the following random number generator:

MY-RANDOM()

out:　　　random integer r
constant: modulus m; starting value X_0
local:　　previously generated random number x (initially $x = X_0$)
1: **if** $x \bmod 2 = 0$ **then**
2: 　$r \leftarrow (x + 3) \cdot 5$
3: **else if** $x \bmod 3 = 0$ **then**
4: 　$r \leftarrow (x + 5) \boxplus 314159265$　　　　▷ Bitwise exclusive-or.
5: **else if** $x \bmod 5 = 0$ **then**
6: 　$r \leftarrow x^2$
7: **else**
8: 　$r \leftarrow x + 7$
9: **end if**
10: $r \leftarrow r \bmod m$; $x \leftarrow r$
11: **return** r

How can you verify how well (or poorly) it works?

2-2   In the design of random number generators (p. 27) parallelization and portability across platforms were mentioned. Why are they important issues?

2-3 The Las Vegas approach is not guaranteed to terminate. What is the probability that the **repeat** loop of Algorithm 2.2 continues after 100 rounds when $m = 100$ and $w = 9$?

2-4 An obvious variant to the linear congruential method is to choose its parameters randomly. Is the result of this new algorithm more random than the original?

2-5 Random number generators are as good as they perform on the tests. What would happen if someone came up with a test where the linear congruential method performs poorly?

2-6 Does the following algorithm produce a unit vector (i.e. with length 1) starting from the origin towards a random direction? Verify your answer by a writing program that visualizes the angle distributions with respect to x-axis.

MY-VECTOR()

    out: unit vector (x', y') towards a random direction
    1: $x \leftarrow 2 \cdot$ RANDOM-UNIT() $- 1$
    2: $y \leftarrow 2 \cdot$ RANDOM-UNIT() $- 1$
    3: $\ell \leftarrow \sqrt{x^2 + y^2}$ ▷ Distance from $(0, 0)$ to (x, y).
    4: **return** $(x/\ell, y/\ell)$ ▷ Scale to the unit circle.

2-7 Let us define functions c and s from domain $(0, 1) \times (0, 1)$ to codomain $\mathbb{R}$:

$$c(x, y) = \sqrt{-2 \ln x} \cos(2\pi y), \quad s(x, y) = \sqrt{-2 \ln x} \sin(2\pi y).$$

If we have two independent uniform random numbers $U_0, U_1 \in (0, 1)$, then $c(U_0, U_1)$ and $s(U_0, U_1)$ are independent random numbers from the standard normal distribution $N(0, 1)$, that is, with mean 0 and standard deviation 1 (Box and Muller 1958). In other words, if we aggregate combinations of independent uniform values, we have a normally distributed two-dimensional 'cloud' C of points around the origin:

$$C = \langle (c(U_{2i}, U_{2i+1}), s(U_{2i}, U_{2i+1})) \rangle_{i \geq 0}.$$

However, if we use any linear congruential method for generating these uniform values (i.e. $U_{2i} = X_{2i}/m$ and $U_{2i+1} = X_{2i+1}/m$), the independence requirement is not met. Curiously, in this case all the points in C fall on a single two-dimensional spiral and, therefore, cannot be considered normally distributed (Bratley et al. 1983). The effect can be analysed mathematically. To demonstrate how hard it is to recognize this defect experimentally, implement a program that draws the points of C using the linear congruential generator $a = 7^5, c = 0$, and $m = 2^{31} - 1$ (Lewis et al. 1969). How about the following example generators:
- $a = 799, c = 0$, and $m = 2^{11} - 9$ (L'Ecuyer 1999)
- $a = 137, c = 187$, and $m = 2^8$ (Knuth 1998b, p. 94)
- $a = 78, c = 0$, and $m = 2^7 - 1$ (Entacher 1999).

What can be learned from this exercise?

2-8 Suppose we are satisfied with the linear congruential method with parameter values $a = 799, c = 0$, and $m = 2039 = 2^{11} - 9$ (L'Ecuyer 1999). If we change the multiplier a to value 393, what happens to the sequence generated? Can you explain why? What does this mean when we test the randomness of these two generators?

2-9 Explain why parallel pseudo-random number generators such as that given in Equation (2.3) should not overlap.

2-10 Assume that we have a pseudo-random number sequence $R = \langle X_i \rangle_{i \geq 0}$ with a period of length p. We define k parallel generators S_j ($j = 0, \dots, k - 1$) of length $\ell = \lfloor p/k \rfloor$ from R:

$$S_j = \langle X_{\ell i + j} \rangle_{i=0}^{\ell - 1}.$$

Does S_j also have pseudo-random properties?

2-11 Let us call a die *phantom* if it produces the same elementary events – possibly with different probabilities – as an ordinary die. For example, if an ordinary hexahedral die gives integer values from $[1, 6]$, the expression $|x - y| + 1$ defines its phantom variant for integers $x, y \in [1, 6]$. The probability distribution of these phantom outcomes is depicted in Figure 2.6.

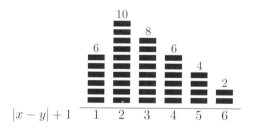

Figure 2.6 Probability distribution of a phantom die $|x - y| + 1$ when x and y are integers from $[1, 6]$.

In the game Phantom Cube Die a player can freely stack $6 \cdot 6 = 36$ tokens in six piles labelled with integers $[1, 6]$. The player casts two ordinary dice to determine the outcome e of the phantom die and removes one token from the pile labelled e. The game ends when the phantom die gives the label of an empty pile. The score is the number of phantom die throws.

The challenge is to place the tokens so that the player can continue casting the die as long as possible. It is worth noting that although Figure 2.6 represents the probability distribution of the phantom die, it does not give the optimal token placement. Find a better way to stack the tokens and explain this poltergeist phenomenon.

2-12 Interestingly, in the first edition of *The Art of Computer Programming* (1969) Knuth presents – albeit with some concern – Ulam's method, which simulates how a human shuffles cards. This was removed from subsequent editions, and

Knuth dismisses such methods as 'miserably inadequate' (Knuth 1998b, p. 145). Ulam's method for shuffling works as follows:

ULAM-SHUFFLE(S)

> **in:**   ordered set S
> **out:**   shuffled ordered set R
> **constant:** number of permutation generating subroutines p; number of repetitions r

> 1: $R \leftarrow$ **copy** S
> 2: **for** $i \leftarrow 1 \ldots r$ **do**
> 3:   **case** RANDOM-INTEGER$(1, p + 1)$ **of**
> 4:   1: $R \leftarrow$ PERMUTATION-1(R)
> 5:   2: $R \leftarrow$ PERMUTATION-2(R)
> 6: $\ldots$
> 7: p: $R \leftarrow$ PERMUTATION-$p(R)$
> 8:   **end case**
> 9: **end for**
> 10: **return** R

The method uses a fixed number (p) of subroutines, each of which apply a certain permutation to the elements. Shuffling is done by selecting and applying randomly one of these permutations and by repeating this r times.

What is the fundamental problem with this method?

2-13 The random points in Figure 2.4(a) are uniformly randomly placed in the bounded two-dimensional plane, positions in which are referred to with Cartesian coordinates. The placement method generates a uniform random coordinate for both of the x and y dimensions and then pairs them up without adjustments to give a two-dimensional coordinate. It can be shown that this process produces uniformly random two-dimensional placement.

Let us also apply this idea to the polar coordinate system. In this two-dimensional system, a position is defined by two measurements, the distance r from some fixed reference position $\mathfrak{p}$ and the angle θ from a fixed reference direction $\hat{a}$, counterclockwise. This gives polar coordinates of the form (r, θ) for all positions.

Polar coordinates can be converted to Cartesian coordinates by superimposing $\mathfrak{p}$ with the Cartesian origin $(0, 0)$ and $\hat{a}$ with the x-axis, and the mapping becomes $(r, \theta) \mapsto (r \cos \theta, r \sin \theta)$. Now, we are able to generate r and θ uniformly randomly, for example as follows:

MY-POSITION(r_{max})

> **in:** largest distance possible r_{max}
> **out:** a Cartesian coordinate $(x, y) \in \mathbb{R}^2$
> 1: $r \leftarrow$ RANDOM-UNIT$() \cdot r_{max}$ $\triangleright \in [0, r_{max})$.
> 2: $\theta \leftarrow$ RANDOM-UNIT$() \cdot 2\pi$ $\triangleright \in [0, 2\pi)$ radians.
> 3: **return** $(r \cos \theta, r \sin \theta)$

We then expect that the result is a uniformly randomly populated circle. Verify by experimentation whether the expectation agrees with the actual result. Speculate on the reasons for the outcome.

2-14 In Section 2.2, a discrete finite distribution is defined by listing the weight values W_r for each elementary event r. Obviously, W is not a unique representation for the distribution, because, for example, $W = \{1, 2, 3\}$ and $W' = \{2, 4, 6\}$ define the same distribution. This ambiguity can complicate, for example, equality comparisons. Design an algorithm CANONICAL-FORM-OF-WEIGHTS(W) which returns a unique representation for W.

2-15 When the number of elementary events n is small, we could implement line 10 in Algorithm 2.4 with a simple sequential search. The efficiency of the whole algorithm depends on how fast this linear search finds the smallest index i for which $S_{i-1} < k \leq S_i$. How would you organize the weight sequence W before the prefix sums are calculated? To verify your solution, implement a program that finds a permutation for the given weight sequence that minimizes the average number of sequential steps required (i.e. increments of i). Also try out different distributions.

2-16 In Algorithm 2.5 the result sequence R is formed in lines 10–17. This locality can be used when designing an iterator variant NEXT-PERMUTATION(S). Describe this algorithm, which returns the next sequence after the previously generated sequence S.

2-17 In a perfect shuffle a deck of cards is divided exactly in half, and the cards in each half are interleaved alternately together. This can be done two ways: in an *in-shuffle* the bottom half is interleaved on top (1234 5678 → 51627384); and in an *out-shuffle* the top half is interleaved on top (1234 5678 → 15263748).

   Take an ordinary deck of 52 cards and sort it into a recognizable order. Do consecutive out-shuffles for the deck and observe how the order changes (alternatively, if you feel more agile, write a computer program that simulates the shuffling). What happens eventually?

2-18 Casinos have devised different automated mechanical methods for shuffling cards. One such method divides the deck into seven piles by placing each card randomly either on the top or on the bottom of one pile (i.e. each card has 14 possible places to choose from). Then the piles are put together to form the shuffled deck.

   Is this a good method? Can a gambler utilize this information to his advantage?

3

Noise

The real world is rarely smooth, pretty and perfect, but objects wobble and hobble, have dents and stains, and the world is full of imperfections. On the other hand, mathematics provides a faultless world where everything follows the equations and everyone is in their place. For the observer, orderly boundaries, trajectories, transitions or arrangements can induce an undesirable ambiance of sterility. Despite the fact that mathematics can be used to model the world, a world built solely on mathematical precision does not look real enough!

To depart from the ideal presentation we can add smooth non-repetitive variations to the generation process to make it look more organic. This is a kind of magic trick, because the underlying computation does not vanish but is masked to resemble the real-world phenomena. One source for such variations are noise generators. Although the presence of noise in data is usually considered a problem and much effort is used to remove it (e.g. noise reduction functions), here we are actually aiming in the opposite direction: to add artificially generated noise to the data.

Let us assume a characteristic parameter c that produces some original true outcome $h(c)$. For example, c can be a world coordinate, a moment in time, the current velocity or a colour measurement, and, correspondingly, $h(c)$ can be a density, heading, the pitch of the wind passing by, or a colour correction or adjustment. Clearly, c can also be a composition of many measurements, and determining what kind of c would be beneficial is part of finding an ingenious application for the noise. Often the final result is based on many parameters c_i and the corresponding functions $h_i(c_i)$ need to be aggregated.

Noise generators can be grouped into methods independent of or dependent on $h(c)$. We can describe an independent generator simply as $n(c)$ and a dependent generator as $n(c, h(c))$. In other words, a noise generator is a proper function that always returns the same value for the same given input. There are several ways to combine the noise to the original true outcome, and, thus, we confine ourselves to generators of the form $n(c)$.

3.1 Applying Noise

When a true outcome $h(c)$ and a noise generator $n(c)$ are synthesized, the outcome generated is denoted $g(c)$ for each c. The simplest way to change the 'value' of $h(c)$ by the 'value' of $n(c)$ is a linear combination (i.e. addition and multiplication). Let us assume

Algorithms and Networking for Computer Games, Second Edition. Jouni Smed and Harri Hakonen.
© 2017 John Wiley & Sons Ltd. Published 2017 by John Wiley & Sons Ltd.

	horizontal		vertical	
translation				
left	$h(c + n(c))$	up	$h(c) + n(c)$	
right	$h(c - n(c))$	down	$h(c) - n(c)$	
scaling				
stretch	$h(c \cdot n(c))$		$h(c)/n(c)$	
shrink	$h(c/n(c))$		$h(c) \cdot n(c)$	

Table 3.1 Translation and scaling of $h(c)$ with $n(c)$. To describe how $n(c)$ affects the direction of change with respect to the original $h(c)$, we assume $0 < n(c) < 1$. Horizontal refers to the domain of $h(c)$ increasing to the left, and vertical to its codomain increasing in the upward direction. The changes are similar to the functions on the x- and y-axes of the Cartesian coordinates.

that these two operations and their inverse functions are well defined for the 'values' and also for c. Fitting the value domains and codomains of $h(c)$, $n(c)$, and c can require coercing and mapping, but the core intention is to preserve the smoothness of change in them (i.e. a small variation in the input causes relatively small effect on the output) by letting the noise generator determine the amount of the whole ripple from $h(c)$ to $g(c)$. To keep the notation simple, we assume from now on that those domains and codomains are already fitted, for example, into $\mathbb{R}$. This allows us to consider the basic function transformations (i.e. translation and scaling) as methods of synthesis.

Table 3.1 collects the fundamental transformations and their effects. The horizontal noise drifts the domain of $h(c)$ and the vertical noise the image of $h(c)$ within the codomain. Some details of Table 3.1 deserve further explanation:

- The horizontal translation $h(c + n(c))$ moves $h(c)$ to the *left*: in place of c, the value $c + n(c)$ on its right is used, meaning the function shifts in the opposite direction.
- Contracting c stretches $h(c)$ horizontally.
- Horizontal scaling preserves the y intercepts and vertical scaling the x intercepts.
- With negative multipliers, $-h(c)$ is a reflection of $h(c)$ in the x-axis and similarly $h(-c)$ in the y-axis.

The basic forms of Table 3.1 can be combined into a generic form as follows. Let a, p, f, and b represent the possible slots for the noise generators. Now,

$$g(c) = a \cdot h((c - p)f) + b \tag{3.1}$$

coalesces all the transformations. Although $g(c)$ is not necessarily periodic, the effects of the slots on $g(c)$ can be related to wave terminology: a corresponds to amplitude, f frequency, p phase shift, and b baseline shift. It is worth noting that we prefer here the positive noise values directed towards Cartesian Quadrant I, hence the subtraction in the term $(c - p)$.

From now on, we fix the codomain of $n(c)$ to $[-1, 1] \subset \mathbb{R}$, which means that the noise generators yield values that stay within the signed unit interval. This restriction – easily liftable by translation and scaling – makes the noise composable. In other words, the noise slots in Equation (3.1) now have well-defined contributions to $g(c)$, and we can anticipate the outcome if we adjust the $n(c)$ terms plugged in using similar function transformations. Figure 3.1 demonstrates an outcome of one such experiment.

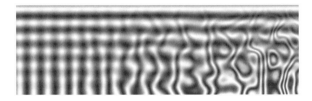

Figure 3.1 Application of noise to a regular recurrence with two perturbed sine functions. On the left, two perpendicular sine waves are merged by weighting them linearly. The amount of noise rippling the waves increases linearly to the right.

3.2   Origin of Noise

Since a noise generator $n(c)$ is a function, it depends solely on the information content of c. How, then, we can fabricate a variation on it using some fixed method? If variation means dissimilarity of $n(c)$ from nearby $n(c \pm \Delta c)$, perhaps randomization that stems from c would be useful, as long as $c \pm \Delta c$ produces a different result. To achieve this a random number r can be assigned for each c (e.g. with Algorithm 2.1), by inventing a mapping from c to the starting value X_0 of the random number generator. We denote the initialization of X_0 as routine SET-SEED($\bullet$).

As an aside, the random number generators utilized by the noise generators become degenerators as discussed in Section 2.1.3: because a random number generator is shared among all the references to c, each invocation of SET-SEED($\bullet$) resets the random sequence, possibly ruining the illusion of randomness. However, for a noise generator this is not a problem, because only the first number of the subsequence is consumed by each $n(c)$, making the situation similar to the case $(\ell = 1) \Rightarrow S_j = \langle X_j \rangle$ in Equation (2.3). Therefore, a suitable hash function would also suffice.

The next question is how to map c to X_0. With computers it is reasonable to assume that c can be converted to a sequence of integer numbers Z that represents c quite uniquely. Then the mapping in question is about aggregating Z to one integer k, but, at the same time, avoiding as much as possible any introduction of periodicity or other repeated patterns. The progress of these mappings from a characteristic parameter c to a random number r and, finally, to $n(c)$ can be summarized as

$$c \mapsto Z \mapsto k = X_0 \mapsto r \mapsto n(c) \in [-1, 1]. \tag{3.2}$$

Of course k can be used directly to represent the randomness r attached to c, provided it behaves as such. Here, we aggregate Z by calculating its *Morton code* (Morton 1966, Chapter 5). Simply put, a Morton code is a function that interleaves the bit representations of the integers in a sequence Z. For example, if $Z = \langle 10, 3 \rangle = \langle 1010_2, 0011_2 \rangle$, the code is $_01_00_11_10 = 01001110_2 = 78$. For non-negative integers, the most significant bits (MSBs) can be padded with 0-bits, as we did with the value 3. When negative integers are included, some sign representation must be selected, such as the prevailing two's complement where the MSBs of the negative numbers become padded with 1-bits.

Algorithm 3.1 converts a sequence Z to a Morton code. In addition to the parameter Z, it accepts a parameter b for controlling the number of the least significant bits interleaved from each integer of Z. The utility routine BITS-REQUIRED(n) determines the number of effective bits (i.e. the number of bits that are not considered as padding).

Algorithm 3.1 Morton code for interleaving a sequence of integers.

MORTON-CODE(Z, b)

   in: sequence Z of n integers $\in \mathbb{Z}$ (in two's complement representation); number of effective bits b ($0 \leq b$ or NIL)

   out: value $r \in \mathbb{Z}$ consisting of interleaved bits of the integers in Z (the least significant bits in Z are grouped to the least significant bits of the result)

   local: bit mask m; sequence S of bit shift amounts ($|S| = n$)

   1: $m \leftarrow 1$ ▷ Left-shifting bit mask.
   2: $|S| \leftarrow n$ ▷ Reserve space for n integers.
   3: **for** $i \leftarrow 0 \ldots (n-1)$ **do**
   4:     $S_i \leftarrow i$
   5: **end for**
   6: **if** $b =$ NIL **then**
   7:     **if** Z has negative values **then error** b cannot be NIL **end if**
   8:     $b \leftarrow \max \{$ BITS-REQUIRED($\min Z$), BITS-REQUIRED($\max Z$) $\}$
   9: **end if**
   10: $r \leftarrow 0$
   11: **for** $c \leftarrow 0 \ldots (b-1)$ **do**   ▷ Repeat b times (c not used).
   12:     **for** $i \leftarrow 0 \ldots (n-1)$ **do**
   13:        $r \leftarrow r \sqcup ((Z_i \sqcap m) \ll S_i)$
   14:        $S_i \leftarrow S_i + n - 1$
   15:     **end for**
   16:     $m \leftarrow m \ll 1$
   17: **end for**
   18: **return** r ▷ Integer of nb bits.

BITS-REQUIRED(n)

   in: integer $n \in \mathbb{Z}$

   out: number of effective bits required for n, assuming n is in two's complement representation

   1: **if** $n = 0$ **then return** 1 **end if**
   2: **if** $n < 0$ **then** $n \leftarrow -n$ **end if**
   3: **return** $1 + \lfloor \lg(n-1) \rfloor$

From now on, to simplify the presentation we concentrate on number sequences consisting of natural numbers instead of signed integers. In the context of noise generation, this is not such a restriction because the outcome is still similarly randomish and, if needed, the value intervals can be shifted along the number line.

Given a sequence N of natural numbers representing a characteristic parameter c, a straightforward realization of Equation (3.2) is given in Algorithm 3.2. If the noise $n(c)$ generated has artefacts, the outcome can be adjusted by assigning another value to the internal constant S_0.

Algorithm 3.2 A discrete-domain noise generator that returns a random value for the given sequence of natural numbers. The sequence specifies one data position.

Noise-Random(N)
 in: sequence N of natural numbers
 out: random floating point value $\in [-1, 1] \subset \mathbb{R}$
 constant: modulus m in Algorithm 2.1; adjustment seed S_0 of the noise generation
 1: Set-Seed(Morton-Code(N, nil) + S_0)
 2: $r \leftarrow$ Random() $\triangleright r \in [0, m - 1] \subset \mathbb{N}$.
 3: $s \leftarrow r/(m - 1)$ $\triangleright s \in [0, 1] \subset \mathbb{R}$, endpoints included.
 4: **return** $2s - 1$

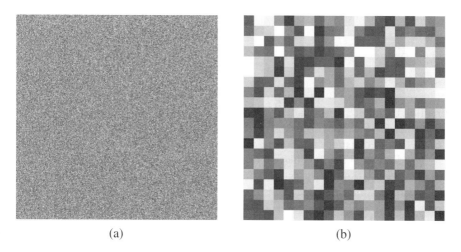

(a)   (b)

Figure 3.2 (a) The result of Noise-Random($\langle i, j \rangle$) where $0 \leq i, j \leq (640 - 1)$ with scaling $[-1, 1] \subset \mathbb{R}$ to the greyscale values $[0, 255] \subset \mathbb{N}$. (b) Detail from the top-left part of (a) zoomed in by magnification 32 revealing the individual pixels $[0, 19] \times [0, 19]$ on the discrete integer grid of image coordinates.

3.3 Visualization

The properties of noise generators are often visualized with two-dimensional greyscale images where the noise value -1 corresponds to black, 1 to white, and intermediate values are mapped linearly to grey tones.[1] In this context, c has the structure of a pixel coordinate $c = (i, j)$, where i is the row and j is the column index of the pixel $(i, j \in \mathbb{N})$. The coordinates can be rigged to Noise-Random(N) simply by mapping (i, j) to $N = \langle i, j \rangle$. Figure 3.2 depicts the typical features of Noise-Random($\langle i, j \rangle$). One of them is the unfortunate lack of coherence between neighbouring values, which can be seen in how the values $n(c)$ and $n(c \pm \Delta c)$ vary too randomly (see also the discussion on terrain

---

1 Exercise 3-6 demonstrates common pitfalls when converting a floating point interval into an integer interval.

generation in Section 4.1). However, there are two observations to be made that take us forward, and they are the core of noise generation.

Firstly, the problem in Figure 3.2(a) is it has too high a frequency and the image is a plain random shock of white noise that has such fine granularity that it does not present any structure. Figure 3.2(b) also has randomness, but because of zooming in on the pixel grid, it has much lower image frequencies and clear regions of equal greyness. At the very extreme, with a magnification of 640, we would be able to see only one pixel (at a time, when shifting over discrete rows and columns) and the frequency element would have disappeared totally; then the only variation is the randomness in a pixel value. The situation is similar to image processing: high-pass filtering emphasizes the edges and low-pass filtering blurs the image. This means the dominant frequencies of any noise must be within some useful bandwidth, preferably a rather narrow one.

Secondly, what if Figure 3.2(b) is not considered as a zoom-in of (a) but as a result of another noise generator producing a two-dimensional step function? Actually, such an image generator is trivial to describe:

1: **return** NOISE-RANDOM($\langle \lfloor i/32 \rfloor, \lfloor j/32 \rfloor \rangle$)

For example, recalling Table 3.1, the expression $\lfloor i/32 \rfloor = \lfloor i \cdot 1/32 \rfloor$ stretches the image in the i direction by collecting the values for the coordinates $i \in \{32k, 32k + 1, \ldots, 32k + 31\}$ from $32k$ only, for $k \in \mathbb{N}$. Moreover, Figure 3.2(b) can be seen as an instance of a step function that is defined also for all intermediate values, and, more generally, as a result of a simple two-dimensional interpolation over an integer grid.

Since many interpolation methods are known, there are multiple options for noise generation in n dimensions: take a regular integer grid of random numbers, zoom in to a suitable frequency bandwidth, and interpolate the intermediate values of the grid with a convenient method. Here, the core idea is to place the randomness onto the positions of the n-dimensional integer grid, and then interpolate the fractional parts with a suitable granularity. This makes interpolation elementary for the noise generation and, thus, we may go into the details.

3.4 Interpolation

Interpolation is a method that determines new values between given values. For example, if we know two values a_0 and a_1 and their positions x_0 and x_1, interpolation can be used to determine the values a_t when $x_t \in [x_0, x_1]$. In other words, interpolation defines a function $f(\bullet)$ that has the follows properties:

$$a_0 = f(x_0), \quad a_1 = f(x_1), \quad \text{and} \quad a_t = f(x_t) \quad \text{when} \quad x_t \in [x_0, x_1].$$

Naturally, these conditions are loose and there are infinitely many choices of $f(\bullet)$ and, consequently, to determine the intermediate values a_t.

Interpolation can be generalized to methods that consider further the known data positions beyond the nearest ones, but with noise generation we allow only the local surroundings to contribute to the position of interest. In other words, a noise is defined as a piecewise function over regular intervals $[x_i, x_{i+1}]$, and each piece alone is the domain utilized in an interpolation function one at a time. It turns out that the downsides of pre-ferring locality can be mitigated by selecting a suitable interpolation method together with aggregating more than one value from the neighbourhood into one. To achieve those compensations we first cover some interpolation methods, starting with elemen-tary utility routines for converting values, then introduce well-known one-dimensional interpolation curves $f(\bullet)$ and, finally, show how to apply them to yield two-dimensional curves $f(\bullet, \bullet)$. The step that generalizes interpolation to higher dimensions is similar but more laborious.

It is convenient to describe an interpolation method as a function $\varrho(t)$ confined to the unit square $[0, 1]^2 \subset \mathbb{R}^2$. The idea is to normalize the ends and the intermediate positions $x_t \in [x_0, x_1]$ to the unit interval $t \in [0, 1]$ and to define $\varrho(t) \in [0, 1]$ to be the proportion weight between the values $a_0 = f(x_0)$ and $a_1 = f(x_1)$ contributing to the value a_t at x_t. It is customary to interpret $\varrho(t)$ as the weight of x_1 over x_0, meaning that when $\varrho(t) = 0$ the value at x_t is a_0 and when $\varrho(t) = 1$ it is a_1. Furthermore, we require $\varrho(0) = 0$ and $\varrho(1) = 1$ to ensure $a_0 = f(x_0)$ and $a_1 = f(x_1)$. This whole set-up can be depicted as follow:

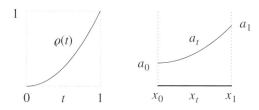

To simplify the value conversions involved, let us first describe the utility routines.

3.4.1 Utility routines for value conversions

Operating with the unit interval $[0, 1]$ is so established that there are some well-known utility routines for commonly occurring value conversions. Algorithm 3.3 introduces one way to define the concepts of *clamping, wrapping, stepping, rescaling,* and *lerping* a value both to and from the unit interval. In general, clamping restricts the given value x to a specified interval $I \subset \mathbb{R}$, wrapping returns the quotient of x modulo I, stepping classifies x to 0 or 1 by a fixed threshold, rescaling maps x linearly into I, and lerp-ing calculates fraction values linearly from I. As already mentioned, we have selected $I = [0, 1]$.

It is worth noting how UNIT-WRAP behaves with negative values. For example, UNIT-WRAP(-1.1) returns 0.9 because $\lfloor -1.1 \rfloor = -2$. If UNIT-WRAP is defined in terms of extracting the integer part of $x \in \mathbb{R}$, that is

$$\mathrm{int}(x) = \mathrm{sgn}(x) \lfloor |x| \rfloor,$$

the definition of routine UNIT-WRAP changes to

1: $x \leftarrow x - \mathrm{int}(x)$
2: **if** $x < 0$ **then** $x \leftarrow x + 1$ **end if**
3: **return** x

Algorithm 3.3 Utility routines for converting a value.

Unit-Clamp(x)
    in: value $x \in \mathbb{R}$
    out: $\min \{\max \{0, x\}, 1\} \in [0, 1]$
    1: **if** $x < 0$ **then return** 0 **else if** $1 < x$ **then return** 1 **else return** x **end if**

Unit-Wrap(x)
    in: value $x \in \mathbb{R}$
    out: fractional part $\in [0, 1)$ of x
    1: **return** $x - \lfloor x \rfloor$

Unit-Step(x)
    in: value $x \in \mathbb{R}$
    out: value 0 when $x \leq 0$, otherwise 1
    1: **return if** $0 < x$ **then return** 1 **else return** 0 **end if**

Unit-Rescale(x_{min}, x_{max}, x)
    in: value $x \in [x_{min}, x_{max}] \subset \mathbb{R}$ $(x_{min} < x_{max})$
    out: x linearly rescaled onto $[0, 1]$
    1: **return** $(x - x_{min})/(x_{max} - x_{min})$

Unit-Lerp(a_0, a_1, t)
    in: values $a_0, a_1 \in \mathbb{R}$; mixing weight $t \in [0, 1] \subset \mathbb{R}$
    out: linear interpolation between a_0 and a_1 by their mixing weight t, especially a_0
         when $t = 0$, and a_1 when $t = 1$
    1: **return** $a_0(1 - t) + a_1 t$

---

where line 2 compensates for the inequality of operations $\lfloor \bullet \rfloor$ and int($\bullet$) for the negative numbers. Obviously, if the values treated are always non-negative, this distinction is not needed.

The routines of Algorithm 3.3 can be used to derive generalizations. For example, Step(x, x_t) can be defined as

    1: **return** Unit-Step($x - x_t$)

and scaling $x \in [x_{min}, x_{max}]$ linearly onto $[x'_{min}, x'_{max}]$ can be computed as

    1: **return** Unit-Lerp(x'_{min}, x'_{max}, Unit-Rescale(x_{min}, x_{max}, x))

which we can name Rescale($x'_{min}, x'_{max}, x_{min}, x_{max}, x$). Curiously, the lerp interpolation within the unit interval is its own generalization with respect to parameter t:

for values $t \in \mathbb{R} \setminus [0,1]$ it linearly *extrapolates* x along the line via the data positions (x_0, a_0) and (x_1, a_1). When the prerequisite $t \in [0,1]$ is relaxed to $x \in \mathbb{R}$, UNIT-LERP is aliased to LERP. The extensions CLAMP and WRAP are discussed in Exercises 3-9 and 3-10.

These utility routines are useful because they replace simple and often used control structures by data-oriented routine signatures, and the definitions using them become more declarative. In other words, the data that affect the outcome have clear entry points in the descriptions at appropriately high level. However, as with all conceptualizations, they have advantages only when one is familiar with them. To demonstrate the effect, consider Algorithm 3.4 which generates the black-and-white image in Figure 3.3.

Algorithm 3.4 A method for generating Figure 3.3. Primitive routine *pixel* is used to assign a greyscale colour into the given image.

GRID-OF-DISTORTIONS(*img*)
  in: empty pixel image *img* of h rows and w columns
  out: filled greyscale image *img*, 0 for black and 255 for white colour
  1: **for** $i \leftarrow 0 \dots (h-1)$ **do**
  2:   **for** $j \leftarrow 0 \dots (w-1)$ **do**
  3:     $r \leftarrow i/h$; $c \leftarrow j/w$ $\triangleright$ Normalize to $\in [0,1) \subset \mathbb{R}$.
  4:     $w_r \leftarrow$ WRAP$(0, 0.194, r)$
  5:     $w_c \leftarrow$ WRAP$(0, 0.250, c)$
  6:     $d_r \leftarrow$ UNIT-LERP$(-0.02, 0,$ STEP$(0.1, w_c))$
  7:     $d_c \leftarrow$ UNIT-LERP$(\ \ 0.02, 0,$ STEP$(0.1, w_r))$
  8:     $v_r \leftarrow$ STEP$(w_r, 0.05 + d_r) -$ STEP$(w_r, 0.2 + d_r)$
  9:     $v_c \leftarrow$ STEP$(w_c, 0.05 + d_c) -$ STEP$(w_c, 0.2 + d_c)$
  10:    $v \leftarrow$ UNIT-STEP$(1 - v_r v_c) \cdot 255$ $\triangleright v \in \{0, 255\}$
  11:    *pixel*(*img*, i, j) $\leftarrow v$ $\triangleright$ Set pixel colour into row i, column j.
  12:   **end do**
  13: **end do**

Figure 3.3 A grid of distorted squares inside a square-sized image, generated with Algorithm 3.4.

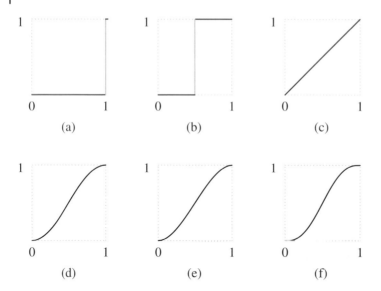

Figure 3.4 Simple interpolation functions $\varrho(t)$ for $t \in [0,1] \subset \mathbb{R}$: (a) value-hold 0, (b) nearest-neighbour STEP$(t, \frac{1}{2})$, (c) linear t, (d) cosine $\frac{1}{2}(1 - \cos(\pi t))$, (e) smoothstep $-2t^3 + 3t^2$, and (f) smootherstep $6t^5 - 15t^4 + 10t^3$.

3.4.2 Interpolation in a single parameter

Figure 3.4 illustrates well-known interpolation functions described as variants of the function $\varrho(t)$ over $t \in [0, 1]$. The value-hold function in Figure 3.4(a), considered from left to right, replicates the held value a_0 till the next one, a_1, is encountered. This is the interpolation that is implicitly used when a noise image is zoomed in, as with Figure 3.2(b). The effect is due to the floor function $\lfloor \bullet \rfloor$.

Since the value-hold is almost function STEP$(t, 1)$, the nearest-neighbour function in Figure 3.4(b) is almost just a translation of it by displacement $\frac{1}{2}$ and, correspondingly, the effect resembles the rounding of a value. When a noise is derived from a uniform integer grid, the interpolation gives a Voronoi diagram of squares with the known data values at the midpoints.

Figure 3.4(c) represents the identity function $\varrho(t) = t$ weighting linearly the mixing of a_0 and a_1 for a_t (i.e. $a_t = $ UNIT-LERP(a_0, a_1, t)). This observation gives us the general mapping from any $\varrho(t)$ to its corresponding $a_t = f(x_t)$:

$$a_t = \text{UNIT-LERP}\,(a_0, a_1, \varrho(t)) \tag{3.3}$$

where the parameter $t \in [0, 1]$ is equal to UNIT-RESCALE (x_0, x_1, x_t). Observe that the function $f(\bullet)$ is *defined* by Equation (3.3), making it only an alias notion. The endpoints are given as x_0 and x_1 with their values a_0 and a_1, respectively. The interpolation positions $x_t \in [x_0, x_1]$ are mapped to $t \in [0, 1]$ and then $\varrho(t)$ determines the mix of values a_0 and a_1 to value a_t for x_t. Algorithm 3.5 shows how this idea can be used to interpolate one-dimensional noise.

Algorithm 3.5 A noise generator over the unit-length intervals $[n, n+1] \subset \mathbb{R}$ ($n \in \mathbb{N}$) that interpolates the random noise values placed at the integer positions n and $n+1$.

NOISE-INTERPOLATION-1(x_t)
  in: position $0 \le x_t \in \mathbb{R}$
  out: interpolated noise value $\in \mathbb{R}$
  1: $x_w \leftarrow \lfloor x_t \rfloor$ ▷ Integer ('wholes') part of x_t.
  2: $x_f \leftarrow x_t - x_w$ ▷ Fractional part $\in [0, 1)$ of x_t.
  3: $a_0 \leftarrow$ NOISE-RANDOM($\langle x_w \rangle$)
  4: $a_1 \leftarrow$ NOISE-RANDOM($\langle x_w + 1 \rangle$)
  5: **return** VALUE-INTERPOLATION-1(a_0, a_1, x_f)

VALUE-INTERPOLATION-1(a_0, a_1, t)
  in: reference values $a_0, a_1 \in \mathbb{R}$; mixing weight $t \in [0, 1] \subset \mathbb{R}$
  out: interpolated value $\in [a_0, a_1]$
  local: an interpolation function $\varrho : [0, 1] \mapsto \mathbb{R}$ (e.g. one of in Figure 3.4)
  1: **return** UNIT-LERP($a_0, a_1, \varrho(t)$)

To have a nonlinear but continuous $\varrho(t)$ the rate of change must decrease and increase. If flatness of the values is needed near the endpoints and steepness in the middle region, the cosine function can be adjusted by horizontal and vertical shrinking and codomain reversion for this purpose (see Figure 3.4(d)).

A cubic Hermite spline has a basis function similar to the cosine interpolation function, as can be seen by comparing Figure 3.4(e) to Figure 3.4(d). Their difference is at most only slightly more than 1% for $t \in [0, 1]$. Because this function is a simple cubic polynomial and it can be calculated with three multiplications and one subtraction, it has been given the widely known nickname 'smoothstep'.

The smootherstep function in Figure 3.4(f) has more curvature near the endpoints, and the maximum difference from the cosine interpolation is about 4% and from the smoothstep about 5%. It can be calculated with five multiplications, one addition, and one subtraction.

We can compare and rank the interpolation functions by their continuity. The rationale is that since in our case the given datapoints are random, the relevant randomness does not disappear when an interpolation yields continuous results. Also, to avoid deficiencies the seam between the interpolation intervals should be smooth (i.e. the derivatives of the piecewise interpolations should match at the known data positions). Because the changes in the interpolation values are driven by $\varrho(t)$, we can require that, for instance, functions at $\varrho(1)$ and $1 - \varrho(0)$ match smoothly when they are adjacent.

The 'value-hold' and 'nearest-neighbour' functions are discontinuous on $[0, 1]$ causing jumps in the resulting data, and for this reason they are rarely used intentionally. The 'linear' function is continuous and gives a linear ramp of values. However, at the endpoints it is not smooth in general, because the constant derivatives of the adjacent intervals can differ, causing sudden changes between the interpolation intervals. The sharp edges themselves are not necessarily a problem, but in this case they occur regularly, which breaks the illusion of noise.

The 'cosine', 'smoothstep', and 'smootherstep' functions have first derivative equal to 0 at both endpoints, matching them over the adjacent intervals. Despite this, the cosine and smoothstep interpolations can have visible bends at the interval boundaries because the changes in the changes – their second derivatives – do not match. Smootherstep has both first and second derivatives equal to 0, and this is why it is suggested when smoothness is critical (Perlin 2002).

3.4.3 Interpolation in two parameters

An interpolation over a two-dimensional integer grid can be constructed from a one-dimensional interpolation $\varrho(\bullet)$. Let us consider four values $a_{(0,0)}$, $a_{(1,0)}$, $a_{(1,1)}$, and $a_{(0,1)}$ at the corner positions of the unit square $[0, 1]^2 \subset \mathbb{R}^2$. We want to interpolate a value $a_{(x,y)}$ at (x, y) when $0 \le x, y \le 1$. The idea is to calculate two $\varrho(\bullet)$-interpolated values, for instance, in the direction of the x-axis, and then take their $\varrho(\bullet)$-interpolation in the direction of the y-axis. One actual arrangement of this is

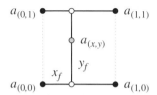

where x_f is the fractional part of x, and y_f of y. Of course in the unit square $x_f = x$ and $y_f = y$, but we introduce this notation here for more general situations. The white circles are the horizontal interpolations of the values at the corners with mixing weight x_f and the grey circle is the vertical interpolation with weight y_f.

Algorithm 3.6 connects this method to two-dimensional noise generation. The routine VALUE-INTERPOLATION-1 defined in Algorithm 3.5 utilizes any of the one-dimensional interpolation functions $\varrho(\bullet)$.

Algorithm 3.6 A noise generator over the unit-sized intervals $[m, m+1] \times [n, n+1] \subset \mathbb{R}^2$ $(m, n \in \mathbb{N})$ that interpolates the random noise values placed at the integer positions (m, n), $(m + 1, n)$, $(m + 1, n + 1)$, and $(m, n + 1)$.

NOISE-INTERPOLATION-2(x, y)
 in: position $(x, y) \in \mathbb{R}^2$ in the Cartesian Quadrant I $(0 \le x, y)$
 out: interpolated noise value $\in \mathbb{R}$
 1: $x_w \leftarrow \lfloor x \rfloor$; $x_f \leftarrow x - x_w$ ▷ Integer and fractional parts of x
 2: $y_w \leftarrow \lfloor y \rfloor$; $y_f \leftarrow y - y_w$ ▷ . . . and y.
 3: $a_{00} \leftarrow$ NOISE-RANDOM$(\langle x_w \quad , y_w \quad \rangle)$
 4: $a_{10} \leftarrow$ NOISE-RANDOM$(\langle x_w + 1, y_w \quad \rangle)$
 5: $a_{11} \leftarrow$ NOISE-RANDOM$(\langle x_w + 1, y_w + 1 \rangle)$
 6: $a_{01} \leftarrow$ NOISE-RANDOM$(\langle x_w \quad , y_w + 1 \rangle)$
 7: $a_{\square 0} \leftarrow$ VALUE-INTERPOLATION-1(a_{00}, a_{10}, x_f)
 8: $a_{\square 1} \leftarrow$ VALUE-INTERPOLATION-1(a_{01}, a_{11}, x_f)
 9: **return** VALUE-INTERPOLATION-1$(a_{\square 0}, a_{\square 1}, y_f)$

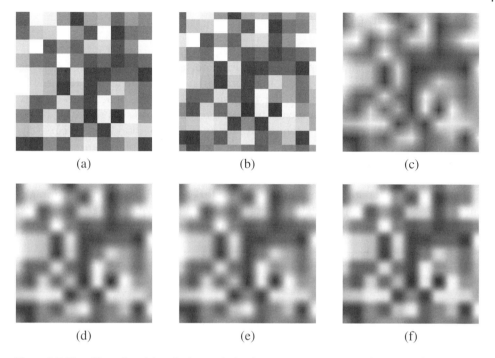

(a)   (b)   (c)

(d)   (e)   (f)

Figure 3.5 The effect of applying the interpolation functions in Figure 3.4 to the noise values placed on an integer grid. The grid is generated by Algorithm 3.2 (see also Figure 3.2) and then zoomed in by magnification 64: (a) value-hold, (b) nearest-neighbour, (c) linear, (d) cosine, (e) smoothstep, and (f) smootherstep.

Figure 3.5 visualizes the two-dimensional outcome of Algorithm 3.6 using each of the one-dimensional interpolation functions in Figure 3.4. The discrete-domain noise generator for the integer grid values is NOISE-RANDOM, which we also used for Figure 3.2. For this reason, Figure 3.5(a) depicting the value-hold function is the same as the upper-left quarter of Figure 3.2(b), and it can be used as the base image for comparisons. However, note that all the images in Figure 3.5 are on $\mathbb{R}^2_{\geqslant 0}$ whereas Figure 3.2(b) is a zoom-in of $\mathbb{N}^2$.

The method that generalizes one-dimensional interpolation of noise to two dimensions can also be applied for three dimensions and beyond. In three dimensions, we have a unit cube and the interpolation process has three phases – one for each dimension – and in total seven one-dimensional value interpolations.

3.5 Composition of Noise

The overall variation of randomness in Figure 3.5(f) is continuous but it can still have regions that are – or at least seem to be – flat. For a noise, it is too smooth and calls for random variations that form the details. In nature, variations tend to present themselves recursively at different scales (see also the discussion on L-systems in Section 4.3). This idea can also be copied into noise generation: an interpolated noise is scaled to different layers and then the layers are composed into one. This method forms recursively self-similar features in the noise, making it more useful, for example, when zooming in towards the integer grid.

Algorithm 3.7 defines one way to compose a number of nesting layers ℓ of a noise for the given characteristic parameter c. The noise for each layer is drawn from a single generator, A-NOISE(c), so that a layer has its own particular frequency f and amplitude a. This generator can use any method that yields proper noise for c.

Algorithm 3.7 Composition of the values of a noise generator by varying both amplitude and frequency with exponentiation.

NOISE-COMPOSITION(c, ℓ, a_0, f_0)
in: characteristic parameter c; number of nesting layers ℓ ($1 \leq \ell$); initial amplitude $a_0 \in \mathbb{R}$; initial frequency $f_0 \in \mathbb{R}$
out: composed noise value $\in [-1, 1] \subset \mathbb{R}$
local: largest cumulative amplitude r_{max} possible
1: $r \leftarrow 0$ ▷ Result accumulator.
2: $r_{max} \leftarrow 0$
3: **for** $i \leftarrow 0 \ldots (\ell - 1)$ **do**   ▷ The base noise is $i = 0$.
4:    $a \leftarrow a_0^i$
5:    $f \leftarrow f_0^i$
6:    $r \leftarrow r + a \cdot$ A-NOISE($c \cdot f$)   ▷ Any noise generator returning $\in [-1, 1]$.
7:    $r_{max} \leftarrow r_{max} + a$ ▷ $r \in [-r_{max}, r_{max}]$.
8: **end for**
9: **return** r / r_{max}

The change in f and a is defined as a geometric progression starting from parameters f_0 and a_0. Since the layers are combined together simply with an addition operation, the composition result can be accumulated during the generation of the layers.

Although the parameters of NOISE-COMPOSITION have quite liberal domains, in practice $\ell \in [3, 7] \subset \mathbb{N}$ layers suffice. Also, it is common that the higher the frequency, the lower the amplitude, meaning $1 < f_0$ and $0 < a_0 < 1$. In some application contexts, it is advantageous if the features between the layers match. In such a case, f_0 can be chosen so that the geometric progression produces multiples; for example, when $f_0 = 2$, the frequencies of the layers meet recursively at the factors of 2. If such a resonance is unwanted, f_0 can be an irrational number (e.g. $\sqrt{5}$).

Algorithm 3.7 has a variant that produces composite noise with discontinuous edges at each noise layer, forming gnarly-like features. Its definition is as Algorithm 3.7 but with the following replacement lines:

6: $r \leftarrow r + |a \cdot \text{A-Noise}(c \cdot f)|$
7: $r_{\max} \leftarrow r_{\max} + |a|$

9: **return** $2(r/r_{\max}) - 1$

Perlin (1985) calls this composition variant *turbulence*, which is why we call it Noise-Turbulence(c, ℓ, a_0, f_0). Figure 3.6 depicts these compositions when $c = (x, y)$ is a position in Cartesian Quadrant I. The noise generator with the frequency and amplitude adjustments is $a \cdot \text{Noise-Interpolation-2}(x \cdot f, y \cdot f)$. Note that when the parameters

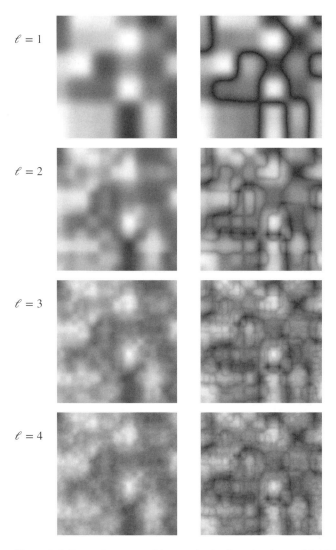

$\ell = 1$

$\ell = 2$

$\ell = 3$

$\ell = 4$

Figure 3.6 Two noise composition methods of nesting layers ℓ, initial amplitude $a_0 = \frac{1}{2}$, and initial frequency $f_0 = 2$. The left column is by Noise-Composition and the right one by Noise-Turbulence. The noise generator is Noise-Interpolation-2 with the one-dimensional smootherstep interpolation function.

ℓ, a_0, and f_0 are fixed, the noise composition methods have the signature of the noise generators.

3.6 Periodic Noise

So far our goal has been noise generation without periodicity. However, there are situations where the noise ought to be generated only once and then stored for later use or cached for frequent access. To achieve this only a subset $\mathcal{R}$ of all the possible values C of characteristic parameter c must be selected. In other words, the noise $n(c)$ is defined only for a specific region

$$\mathcal{R} = \text{(the preselected characteristics)} \subset C$$

that creates crisp boundaries. Unfortunately, this also limits the usability of the noise since the control logic structures accessing the noise must be confined to $\mathcal{R}$.

In this case, the technique of modular arithmetic becomes valuable. As discussed with Equation (3.2), c often has a numeric representation $c \mapsto \ldots \mapsto k$ $(k \in \mathbb{N} \subset \mathbb{Z})$ that allows us to refine $\mathcal{R}$ as

$$\mathcal{R}' = \{ (c \mapsto k) \bmod k_0 \mid k_0 = \text{(preselected value} \in \mathbb{N} \setminus \{0\}) \}$$

for *all* possible $c \in C$, avoiding the abrupt boundaries. Now, only the noise results for the values $\in [0, k_0 - 1] \subset \mathbb{N}$ need to be calculated and the whole space of the characteristic parameter becomes tiled by the noise determined by $\mathcal{R}'$.

As an example, let us consider a two-dimensional case where $c = (x, y)$ is a position on a plane $(x, y \in \mathbb{R}_{\geq 0})$. First, we adapt the idea of $\mathcal{R}'$ directly to the generation of the underlying integer grid of random values by wrapping NOISE-RANDOM of Algorithm 3.2 with NOISE-TILED-RANDOM of Algorithm 3.8. Then this discrete tiling generator can be used by an noise interpolator (e.g. NOISE-INTERPOLATION-2) that feeds a noise compositor (e.g. NOISE-TURBULENCE). This results in periodic noise as illustrated in Figure 3.7.

Algorithm 3.8 A discrete-domain noise generator that returns a random value for the given integer position (i, j). Primitive routine *cached* is used as a memento storage for the already calculated noise values.

NOISE-TILED-RANDOM(i, j)
    in: position $(i, j) \in \mathbb{N}^2$ in the Cartesian Quadrant I $(0 \leq i, j)$
    out: random floating point value $\in [-1, 1] \subset \mathbb{R}$
    constant: region boundaries $i_\ell, j_\ell \in \mathbb{N} \setminus \{0\}$; adjustment offsets $i_0, j_0 \in \mathbb{N}$
    1: $i' \leftarrow (i + i_0) \bmod i_\ell$
    2: $j' \leftarrow (j + j_0) \bmod j_\ell$
    3: $r \leftarrow cached(\langle i', j' \rangle)$
    4: **if** $r \neq$ NIL **then return** r **end if**
    5: $r \leftarrow$ NOISE-RANDOM$(\langle i', j' \rangle)$
    6: $cached(\langle i', j' \rangle) \leftarrow r$
    7: **return** r

Figure 3.7 Tiling of a plane with a periodic noise.

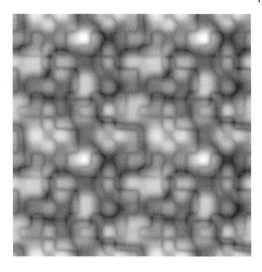

Another method for generating periodic noise would be to map some already generated noise to its periodic variant. In particular, the opposite edges of the region of interest are matched together. For instance, suppose the region is the unit square $[0, 1]^2 \subset \mathbb{R}^2$. Then we could select the noise values on the edges $(0, 0)(1, 0)$ and $(0, 0)(0, 1)$ as the reference values towards which the noise near the opposite sides $(0, 1)(1, 1)$ and $(1, 0)(1, 1)$, respectively, is coerced by a suitable interpolation function. This approach produces a new generation of noise, where the structures on the opposite edges are morphed together and the region can be tiled. However, this approach has at least two complexities. Firstly, it is tricky to match the second derivatives over the edges. Secondly, the interpolation can introduce artefacts not present in the original source of the noise. To summarize, it is much easier to create periodicity than to reconstruct it.

3.7 Perlin Noise

Noise generated from a discrete integer grid of random numbers is called *value noise*. However, as Ken Perlin shows in his seminal papers (Perlin 1985, 2001, 2002; Perlin and Hoffert 1989), which have planted and cultivated the field of noise generation, value noise is not always sufficient. One inherent problem with value noise functions is that their local minimum and maximum are always at the positions of the integer grid. The noise compositions break this regularity by adding detail, but they do not mitigate the effect on the low frequencies as can be seen in Figure 3.6.

One of Perlin's fundamental ideas is to improve the properties of the generated noise by embedding more information into the process. Instead of filling the positions of the integer grid with plain random numbers, we use random unit vectors. These vectors represent directed unit gradients that affect the interpolation of the values between the integer grid. For this reason, the outcome of this kind of approach is called *gradient noise*, one type of which is *Perlin noise*.

To define Perlin noise, we first need a method for generating uniformly random n-dimensional unit vectors. These can be constructed from the data returned by the utility routine RANDOM-ON-UNIT-SPHERE(n) in Algorithm 3.10, which in turn requires random numbers from the standard normal distribution $N(0, 1)$. To generate them we utilize Marsaglia's polar method because it provides convenient intermediate data for this task, in addition to two random numbers, with one invocation. Hence, the routine for generating numbers from $N(0, 1)$ is called RANDOM-NORMAL-01-PAIR, which is split into two parts in Algorithm 3.9. The rationale for the actual calculations in these two algorithms is discussed by Brown (1956, p. 302), Box and Muller (1958), Marsaglia (1962), Marsaglia and Bray (1964) and Knuth (1998b, pp. 135–136).

Algorithm 3.9 Marsaglia's Polar method for generating a pair of independent random numbers from the standard normal distribution $N(0, 1)$.

RANDOM-NORMAL-01-PAIR()
  out: sequence of two numbers $X_0, X_1 \in \mathbb{R}$ both of which are independent
       random numbers from the standard normal distribution $N(0, 1)$ ($X_0 \sim$
       $N(0, 1), X_1 \sim N(0, 1)$)
1: $\langle x, y, s \rangle \leftarrow$ POSITION-IN-UNIT-CIRCLE()
2: **if** $s \approx 0$ **then** $\triangleright$ Is s so near 0 that $1/s$ is too large?
3:   **return** $\langle 0, 0 \rangle$
4: **end if**
5: $c \leftarrow \sqrt{-2 \cdot \ln(s)/s}$
6: $X_0 \leftarrow x \cdot c$; $X_1 \leftarrow y \cdot c$
7: **return** $\langle X_0, X_1 \rangle$

POSITION-IN-UNIT-CIRCLE()
  out: sequence of three numbers $x, y, s \in \mathbb{R}$ so that position (x, y) is in a particular
       way random inside the unit circle, and $s = x^2 + y^2$ ($0 < s < 1$)
1: **repeat**
2:   $x \leftarrow 2 \cdot$ RANDOM-UNIT() $- 1$ $\triangleright \in [-1, 1)$.
3:   $y \leftarrow 2 \cdot$ RANDOM-UNIT() $- 1$
4:   $s \leftarrow x^2 + y^2$
5: **until** $0 < s$ **and** $s < 1$
6: **return** $\langle x, y, s \rangle$

The foundations of Perlin noise are analogous to those of value noise. A discrete grid determines the positions of the randomly generated data that are then utilized to interpolate the intermediate values. That is, similarly to NOISE-RANDOM(N) in Algorithm 3.2, routine NOISE-RANDOM-VECTOR(N, n) in Algorithm 3.11 is able to populate each position, determined by sequence N, by an n-dimensional uniformly random unit vector. Here, we prefer column vectors and, consequently, in the algorithms the vectors $\vec{v}$ are of the form $[v_1 \quad v_2 \quad \dots \quad v_n]^\mathsf{T}$. These unit vectors are the source of randomness for each intermediate position inside the grid's regions.

Algorithm 3.10 Las Vegas approach for generating a uniformly random position *on* the n-dimensional unit sphere. For a uniformly random position *in* the sphere, map the result as $R_i \mapsto R_i \cdot \sqrt[n]{\text{RANDOM-UNIT}()}$.

RANDOM-ON-UNIT-SPHERE(n)
   in: number of dimensions n ($1 \leq n \in \mathbb{N}$)
   out: sequence of n numbers $R = \langle R_0, R_1, \ldots, R_{n-1} \rangle$ ($R_i \in \mathbb{R}$) so that position
          $(R_0, R_1, \ldots, R_{n-1})$ is uniformly random on the surface of the n-dimensional
          unit sphere
   local: total sum of the squares of the normal deviates $\varsigma = R_0^2 + R_1^2 + \ldots + R_{n-1}^2$ (here
          the R_i values are not yet scaled to the final ones)

1: $d \leftarrow n$ ▷ Number of dimensions remaining.
2: $|R| \leftarrow n$ ▷ Reserve space for n numbers $\in \mathbb{R}$.
3: $\varsigma \leftarrow 0$
4: **while** $2 \leq d$ **do**   ▷ Traverse two dimensions at a time.
5:    $d \leftarrow d - 2$
6:    $\langle x, y, s \rangle \leftarrow$ POSITION-IN-UNIT-CIRCLE()
7:    **if** $s \approx 0$ **then**   ▷ Is s so near 0 that $1/s$ is too large?
8:      $R_d \leftarrow 0$; $R_{d+1} \leftarrow 0$
9:    **else**
10:     $q \leftarrow -2 \cdot \ln(s)$ ▷ $q = R_d^2 + R_{d+1}^2$.
11:     $\varsigma \leftarrow \varsigma + q$
12:     $c \leftarrow \sqrt{q/s}$
13:     $R_d \leftarrow x \cdot c$; $R_{d+1} \leftarrow y \cdot c$ ▷ Polar method by Marsaglia.
14:    **end if**
15: **end while**
16: **if** $d = 1$ **then**   ▷ The given n is such an odd number.
17:    $\langle x, y, s \rangle \leftarrow$ POSITION-IN-UNIT-CIRCLE()
18:    **if** $s \approx 0$ **then**   ▷ Is s so near 0 that $1/s$ is too large?
19:     $R_0 \leftarrow 0$
20:    **else**
21:     $R_0 \leftarrow x \cdot \sqrt{-2 \cdot \ln(s)/s}$ ▷ Polar method by Marsaglia.
22:     $\varsigma \leftarrow \varsigma + R_0^2$ ▷ The final one, R_0^2.
23:    **end if**
24: **end if**
25: **if** $\varsigma \approx 0$ **then**   ▷ Is s so near 0 that $1/\sqrt{\varsigma}$ is too large?
26:    **return** RANDOM-ON-UNIT-SPHERE(n)   ▷ Las Vegas approach.
27: **end if**
28: **for** $i \leftarrow 0 \ldots (n-1)$ **do**   ▷ Scaling of R onto the surface.
29:   $R_i \leftarrow R_i / \sqrt{\varsigma}$
30: **end for**
31: **return** R

Algorithm 3.11 A discrete-domain noise generator that returns an n-dimensional random vector for the given sequence of natural numbers. The sequence specifies one data position.

NOISE-RANDOM-VECTOR(N, n)
   in: sequence N of natural numbers; number of dimensions n ($1 \leq n \in \mathbb{N}$)
   out: uniformly random n-dimensional unit vector
   constant: adjustment seed S_0 of the noise generation
   1: SET-SEED(MORTON-CODE(N, NIL) $+ S_0$)
   2: $R \leftarrow$ RANDOM-ON-UNIT-SPHERE(n)
   3: **return** $[\ R_0 \quad R_1 \quad \ldots \quad R_{n-1}\ ]^\top$ ▷ Interpret R as a vector.

To visualize Perlin noise we concretize it in two-dimensional space. The purpose of this simplification, however, is to demonstrate the ideas involved. The algorithm consists of simple vector manipulations and an interpolation phase. The basic vector operations, discussed in detail in Appendix B, are well defined in any dimension – excluding the cross product. Thus, the effort of generalization of the algorithm to higher dimensions is concerned solely with the interpolation step (see Section 3.4).

As in Section 3.3, we fit the position (i, j) of the two-dimensional discrete grid $\mathbb{N}^2$ to the routine NOISE-RANDOM-VECTOR(N, n) by mapping (i, j) to $N = \langle i, j \rangle$. Also, we set $n = 2$ because we are operating on a plane with two-dimensional vectors.

In general, the Perlin algorithm treats each region of the integer grid in the same way, after a particular region of interest has been identified. For this reason, on a plane, it is sufficient to consider the unit square only. Figure 3.8 exemplifies how the Perlin algorithm proceeds. The goal is to interpolate a noise value $d_{(x,y)}$ for the position $(x, y) \in [0, 1]^2$ with respect to the data at the 'corners' of the square. First, the integer grid is filled by the uniformly random unit vectors that are generated with NOISE-RANDOM-VECTOR. We denote these four vectors by $\hat{a}_{(\square,\square)}$ where $\square$ symbolizes values in $\{0, 1\}$. Then the given position (x, y) is represented as four vectors $\vec{v}_{(\square,\square)}$, each having initial point at the corresponding corner position $(\square, \square)$ and terminal point at (x, y). Next, we consider a corner (i, j) ($i, j \in \{0, 1\}$) and the two vectors attached to it. These vectors are converted to a scalar value by the dot product $d_{(i,j)} = \vec{v}_{(i,j)} \bullet \hat{a}_{(i,j)}$, which turns the situation into the ordinary interpolation task discussed in Section 3.4. As a result we have the noise value $d_{(x,y)}$ specific to the position (x, y).

Now, what is the codomain of $d_{(x,y)}$? Remembering that we require all noise values to stay in $[-1, 1] \subset \mathbb{R}$, let us analyse the values of Perlin noise in more detail. Equation (B.1) in Appendix B gives us the following development for the corner values:

$$d_{(i,j)} = \vec{v}_{(i,j)} \bullet \hat{a}_{(i,j)} = \|\vec{v}_{(i,j)}\| \, \|\hat{a}_{(i,j)}\| \cos \theta = \|\vec{v}_{(i,j)}\| \cos \theta$$

where $i, j \in \mathbb{N}$, the notation $\| \ \|$ can be considered as the length of a vector and θ as the angle between two vectors. The codomain of the cosine function is $[-1, 1] \subset \mathbb{R}$ and $\|\vec{v}_{(i,j)}\| \in [0, \sqrt{2}]$. But if $\|\vec{v}_{(i,j)}\| = \sqrt{2}$, the position of interest (x, y) must be at one of the corners. Without loss of generality we can assume that the corner is $(0, 0)$ (i.e. $x = 0$ and $y = 0$). Now $\vec{v}_{(0,0)} = \vec{0}$, from which it follows that $d_{(0,0)} = 0$. In other words, when (x, y) is on the integer grid, its noise value $d_{(x,y)} = 0$.

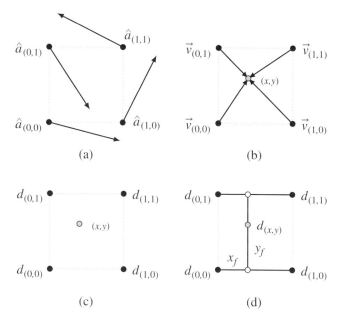

Figure 3.8 The phases of a Perlin noise generator in the unit square $[0, 1]^2 \subset \mathbb{R}^2$. The positions at the integer grid are (0, 0), (1, 0), (1, 1), and (0, 1). The position of interest is (x, y) for which we want to determine a noise value. (a) The grid positions are populated with uniformly random unit vectors $\hat{a}_{(\square,\square)}$. These vectors are fixed for their positions. (b) Position (x, y) is used to define vectors $\vec{v}_{(\square,\square)}$ that together are unique to it. (c) The noise values $d_{(i,j)} = \vec{v}_{(i,j)} \bullet \hat{a}_{(i,j)}$ are calculated for the grid positions. These values are specific to (x, y) in this particular grid region. (d) The values $d_{(\square,\square)}$ are interpolated to the resulting noise value $d_{(x,y)}$.

This kind of regularity would be alarming in value noise generators, but with gradient noise it is barely distinguishable: The unit vectors $\hat{a}_{(\square,\square)}$ turn the gradients affecting the interpolation in random directions breaking the regular patterns. Actually, for a Perlin noise generator, this result shows that the noise keeps a baseline and there is the possibility of a narrow bandwidth.

Let us return to the codomain of $d_{(x,y)}$. Since all the positions in the integer grid give $d_{(x,y)} = 0$, the terminal point $(x, y)^*$ of $\vec{v}_{(i,j)}$ yielding the maximal $\|\vec{v}_{(i,j)}\|$ must be inside the grid's region, in the middle of it. This can be thought of as follows. If $(x, y)^*$ were somewhere else, then it would be located asymmetrically with respect to the grid. Then, if the maximal value exists, the asymmetry must be caused by favouring some direction or measurement over another, which cannot be the case.

Consequently, the distance from $(\square, \square)$ to $(x, y)^*$ is $\sqrt{2}/2 = 1/\sqrt{2}$, and $\|\vec{v}_{(i,j)}\| \in [0, 1/\sqrt{2}]$ from which $d_{(x,y)} \in [-1/\sqrt{2}, 1/\sqrt{2}]$. In n-dimensional space, the maximizing point is always on the longest diagonal, in the middle of the hypercube. Because the length of the diagonal is $\sqrt{n}$, we have, in general,

$$\text{codomain of Perlin method in } \mathbb{R}^n = \left[-\frac{\sqrt{n}}{2}, \frac{\sqrt{n}}{2} \right]. \qquad (3.4)$$

Algorithm 3.12 Perlin noise generator over the unit-sized intervals $[m, m + 1] \times [n, n + 1] \subset \mathbb{R}^2$ ($m, n \in \mathbb{N}$) that interpolates the random noise vectors placed at the integer positions (m, n), $(m + 1, n)$, $(m + 1, n + 1)$, and $(m, n + 1)$.

NOISE-PERLIN-2(x, y)

in: position $(x, y) \in \mathbb{R}^2$ in Cartesian Quadrant I ($0 \leq x, y$)

out: interpolated noise value $\in \mathbb{R}$

constant: codomain scaler s for two-dimensional space ($s = \sqrt{2}$), see Equation (3.4)

1: $x_w \leftarrow \lfloor x \rfloor$; $x_f \leftarrow x - x_w$ $\triangleright$ Integer and fractional parts of x
2: $y_w \leftarrow \lfloor y \rfloor$; $y_f \leftarrow y - y_w$ $\triangleright$ ... and y.
3: $\hat{a}_{00} \leftarrow$ NOISE-RANDOM-VECTOR$(\langle x_w \quad , y_w \quad \rangle, 2)$
4: $\hat{a}_{10} \leftarrow$ NOISE-RANDOM-VECTOR$(\langle x_w + 1, y_w \quad \rangle, 2)$
5: $\hat{a}_{11} \leftarrow$ NOISE-RANDOM-VECTOR$(\langle x_w + 1, y_w + 1 \rangle, 2)$
6: $\hat{a}_{01} \leftarrow$ NOISE-RANDOM-VECTOR$(\langle x_w \quad , y_w + 1 \rangle, 2)$
7: $\vec{p} \leftarrow \begin{bmatrix} x & y \end{bmatrix}^\mathsf{T}$
8: $\vec{v}_{00} \leftarrow \vec{p} - \begin{bmatrix} x_w & y_w \end{bmatrix}^\mathsf{T}$
9: $\vec{v}_{10} \leftarrow \vec{p} - \begin{bmatrix} x_w + 1 & y_w \end{bmatrix}^\mathsf{T}$
10: $\vec{v}_{11} \leftarrow \vec{p} - \begin{bmatrix} x_w + 1 & y_w + 1 \end{bmatrix}^\mathsf{T}$
11: $\vec{v}_{01} \leftarrow \vec{p} - \begin{bmatrix} x_w & y_w + 1 \end{bmatrix}^\mathsf{T}$
12: $d_{00} \leftarrow \vec{v}_{00} \cdot \hat{a}_{00}$
13: $d_{10} \leftarrow \vec{v}_{10} \cdot \hat{a}_{10}$
14: $d_{11} \leftarrow \vec{v}_{11} \cdot \hat{a}_{11}$
15: $d_{01} \leftarrow \vec{v}_{01} \cdot \hat{a}_{01}$
16: $d_{\square 0} \leftarrow$ VALUE-INTERPOLATION-1(d_{00}, d_{10}, x_f)
17: $d_{\square 1} \leftarrow$ VALUE-INTERPOLATION-1(d_{01}, d_{11}, x_f)
18: **return** VALUE-INTERPOLATION-1$(d_{\square 0}, d_{\square 1}, y_f) \cdot s$

Thus, the values the Perlin method yields are scaled by multiplying them by $2/\sqrt{n}$. Algorithm 3.12 defines a routine NOISE-PERLIN-2(x, y) for this process. It is worth noting its similarities with the routine NOISE-INTERPOLATION-2(x, y) in Algorithm 3.6. Figure 3.9 collects assorted variations of Perlin noise. Observe how irregular the gradient noise in Figure 3.9(a) seems compared to the value noise in Figure 3.6(a).

The actual implementations of Perlin noise generators are often extremely optimized, and they can utilize, for example, elaborate array arrangements and permutations of precomputed unit vectors. Moreover, there are many kinds of Perlin noise. We have discussed here the so-called classic Perlin noise, but there is also a more sophisticated method called simplex noise (see Perlin 2001).

3.8 Worley Noise

Any source of randomness can be utilized by a noise generator, but it is the refining method of the generator that determines the characteristics of the noise. From the perspective of noise generation, individual random numbers are inherently 'local' and it

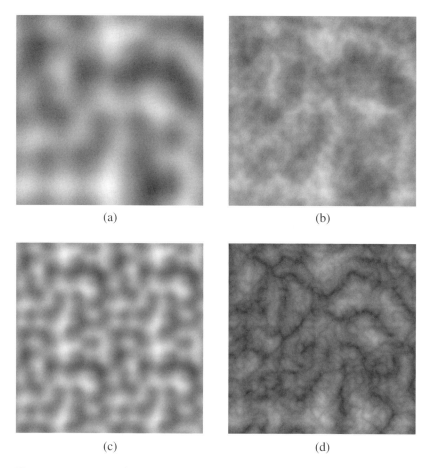

(a)

(b)

(c)

(d)

Figure 3.9 Variations of Perlin noise on a plane: (a) the original zoomed in to a region of 5×5 integer grid positions; (b) composed ($\ell = 3, a_0 = \frac{1}{2}, f_0 = \sqrt{5}$); (c) periodic based on the original with 10×10 grid positions; and (d) turbulenced ($\ell = 3, a_0 = \frac{1}{2}, f_0 = \sqrt{5}$).

requires effort to account for their surrounding data. To tackle this the gradient noise methods process random vectors and spread their randomness around regularly pre-fixed reference positions. Consequently, compared to value noises, gradient noises have quite different properties. But to enrich the field of noise generation, are there other ways we can define randomness with effects beyond the local region? As a continuation of this line of thought, the fixed positions that are beyond the nearest ones – from the given input position – become interesting. However, locality has been the key ingredient for both the feasibility of the calculations and the applicability of the noise.

Worley noise generators try to respond to these challenges. The core idea in Worley's approach is to distil variation from the randomly pre-located points in a multidimensional space. This has turned out to be a versatile method with a wide spectrum of diverse outputs. For this reason, we introduce only some of its properties; for a deeper view, we refer the reader to Worley (1996) and Ebert et al. (2002).

Given a position p, Worley's method considers the distances from p to the n closest pre-generated points in a multidimensional space. These pre-fixed points are called *feature points* and the distances between those and the position of interest p are denoted $f_i(p)$ for $1 \leq i \leq n$; that is, $f_1(p)$ is the distance of the closest feature point to p, $f_2(p)$ of the second closest, and so on. Clearly, it follows from the definition of $f_i(p)$ that the nonstrict inequalities $0 \leq f_1(p) \leq f_1(p) \leq \ldots \leq f_n(p)$ always hold. When the $f_i(p)$ values are calculated for p, the noise generator phase of the method maps some composition of these $f_i(p)$ values onto $[-1, 1] \subset \mathbb{R}$ as the noise outcome.

The purpose of defining and setting n is a practical one, because it is used to limit the regions of interest that need to be analysed for the noise generation. In other words, the parameter n allows us to confine the search for the near feature points to a bounded area. This is directly connected to the way Worley's method generates the fixed feature points: the space is divided into regular unit-sized regions and each region is filled with c uniformly random points, where $c \sim \text{Pois}(\mu)$. The parameter μ is the average number of points we want in each region. Since routines such as RANDOM-POISSON(μ) in Algorithm 2.3 can be slow, Worley (1996) recommends that $c \leq 9$.

To fix a feature point into its location, the region of the point is uniquely identified by its lowest integers: a point at the position (x, y) belongs to the region $(\lfloor x \rfloor, \lfloor y \rfloor)$. The region identity is used as the seed for the randomization that places the points. Now the feature points can be generated independently for each region as needed. The reason why this works is discussed in Section 2.2; see also Figure 2.4. Additionally, if c is replaced by $\max\{1, c\}$, each region has at least one feature point. When the feature points are searched to determine the $f_i(p)$ values for small n, it always suffices to consider only the nearest regions of the region where the point p resides. The codomain restrictions of c can be combined into CLAMP($1, 9, c$) when the Poisson random number generator cannot be modified.

It is possible to enforce the locality without much loss from the principal properties in Worley noise. To simplify the discussion, let us assume from now on that we are generating Worley noise in two-dimensional space, which is only a limitation of the presentation. As an introduction to ensuring the locality, let us consider position $p = (x, y) = (2 + \epsilon, 2 + \epsilon)$, $0 < \epsilon \ll 1$, which is located at the unit-sized region identified uniquely by $(\lfloor x \rfloor, \lfloor y \rfloor) = (2, 2)$. All the feature points in that region are within distance $\sqrt{2}(1 - \epsilon)$ from p, since the diagonal has length $\sqrt{2}$:

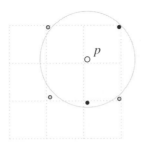

In other words, $f_1(p) < \sqrt{2}(1 - \epsilon)$. However, at least when

$$1 + 2\epsilon < \sqrt{2}(1 - \epsilon) \quad \Longleftrightarrow \quad \epsilon < \frac{\sqrt{2} - 1}{\sqrt{2} + 2} \approx 0.12,$$

it is possible that the closest feature point to p is, for instance, $(2 + \epsilon, 1 - \epsilon)$ of region $(2, 0)$ (i.e. it is the neighbour region of a neighbour of p, stressing the search of the nearest feature points). In this situation, we think in terms of practicality and declare that this case has such an insignificant effect on the outcome that we can ignore it completely. Hence, Worley's method considers only the immediate neighbour regions of the region where the position of interest is. On a plane it is possible to determine the distances through $f_9(p)$ without the need to analyse the regions further away. This is sufficient in most cases since the interesting variations occur already in $n \lesssim 4$ (Worley 1996).

Routine NOISE-WORLEY-2(x, y, n, μ) in Algorithm 3.13 generates Worley noise. Utility routine NEIGHBOURS-2(x, y, n, μ) orchestrates the walkthrough of the regions and

---

Algorithm 3.13 Worley noise generator over a plane (continues in Algorithm 3.14).

NOISE-WORLEY-2(x, y, n, μ)

> **in:**　　　position (x, y) in Cartesian Quadrant I $(0 \leq x, y \in \mathbb{R})$; nth closest point
> 　　　　　　$(1 \leq n \in \mathbb{N})$; average number of points μ in a region $(0 < \mu \in \mathbb{R})$
> **out:**　　　interpolated noise value $\in [-1, 1] \subset \mathbb{R}$
> **constant:** effective value range of the generated values $[\,v_{min}, v_{max}]$ (this range depends on n and μ)

1: $x_s \leftarrow x + 2\,;\, y_s \leftarrow y + 2$ 　　　　$\triangleright$ Enforce the neighbourhoods inside $\mathbb{R}^2_{\geq 0}$.
2: $N \leftarrow$ NEIGHBOURS-2(x_s, y_s, n, μ) 　　$\triangleright$ At most n feature points around (x_s, y_s).
3: $v \leftarrow generator(N)$ 　　　　　　　　　$\triangleright$ Determine the noise value.
4: **return** RESCALE$(-1, 1, v_{min}, v_{max},$ CLAMP$(v_{min}, v_{max}, v))$

NEIGHBOURS-2(x, y, n, μ)

> **in:**　　as in NOISE-WORLEY-2
> **out:**　sequence of the nearest feature points around (x, y) (at most n)
> **local:** identification of the current region $(x_w, y_w) \in \mathbb{N}^2$; the longest distance d_{max}
> 　　　　from (x, y) within the nth feature point can reside

1: $x_w \leftarrow \lfloor x \rfloor$ 　　　　　　　　$\triangleright$ Integer ('wholes') part of x.
2: $y_w \leftarrow \lfloor y \rfloor$ 　　　　　　　　$\triangleright$ …and of y.
3: $d_{max} \leftarrow 4 \cdot radius()$ 　　　　　$\triangleright$ Cover all the neighbours in all cases.
4: $R \leftarrow$ GRID-NEIGHBOURS-2$(x, y, n, \mu, d_{max}, x_w, y_w)$
5: **if** $n \leq |R|$ **then** 　　　　　　$\triangleright$ Shrink the circle of interest?
6: 　$d_{max} \leftarrow distance(R_{n-1})$
7: **end if**
8: **for** $i \leftarrow -1 \dots 1$ **do** 　　　　$\triangleright$ All the possible neighbour regions…
9: 　**for** $j \leftarrow -1 \dots 1$ **do** 　　　$\triangleright$ …in all directions…
10: 　　**if** $i \neq 0$ **and** $j \neq 0$ **then** 　$\triangleright$ …but not our own one, (x_w, y_w).
11: 　　　$R \leftarrow R \,\|\,$ GRID-NEIGHBOURS-2$(x, y, n, \mu, d_{max}, x_w + i, y_w + j)$
12: 　　　$R \leftarrow sub(sorted(R), 0, \min\{n, |R|\})$
13: 　　　**if** $n \leq |R|$ **then** 　　　$\triangleright$ Shrink the circle of interest?
14: 　　　　$d_{max} \leftarrow distance(R_{n-1})$
15: 　　　**end if**
16: 　　**end if**
17: 　**end for**
18: **end for**
19: **return** R

Algorithm 3.14 Worley noise generator over a plane (continued from Algorithm 3.13).

GRID-NEIGHBOURS-2$(x, y, n, \mu, d_{max}, x_w, y_w)$

    in: as in NOISE-WORLEY-2 ; maximum distance from (x, y) that needs to be
                considered d_{max} ; region identification $(x_w, y_w) \in \mathbb{N}^2$

    out: as in NEIGHBOURS-2 but only for this region (x_w, y_w)

    constant: adjustment seed S_0 of the noise generation

  1: $R \leftarrow \langle \, \rangle$

  2: $p \leftarrow (x, y)$ ▷ The position of interest.

  3: $m \leftarrow (x_w + \frac{1}{2}, y_w + \frac{1}{2})$ ▷ Midposition of the region.

  4: **if** $d_{max} + radius() < distance(p, m)$ **then**

  5:   **return** R ▷ This region does not contribute.

  6: **end if**

  7: SET-SEED(MORTON-CODE($\langle x_w, y_w \rangle$, NIL) $+ S_0$)

  8: $c \leftarrow$ RANDOM-POISSON(μ) ▷ Algorithm 2.3, reset for (x_w, y_w).

  9: $c \leftarrow$ CLAMP$(1, 9, c)$ ▷ A practical simplification.

10: **for** $i \leftarrow 1 \dots c$ **do**   ▷ Generate c feature points on-the-fly.

11:   $x_s \leftarrow$ RANDOM-UNIT() ; $y_s \leftarrow$ RANDOM-UNIT()

12:   $q \leftarrow (x_w + x_s, y_w + y_s)$ ▷ A random ghost in the shell.

13:   **if** $distance(p, q) < d_{max}$ **then**

14:     $r \leftarrow$ create an entity that represents the relationship between p and q

15:     $distance(r) \leftarrow distance(p, q)$

16:     $feature(r) \leftarrow q$ ▷ Example: piggyback the feature point.

17:     $R \leftarrow R \parallel \langle r \rangle$

18:   **end if**

19: **end for**

20: **return** $sub(sorted(R), 0, \min\{n, |R|\})$

---

routine GRID-NEIGHBOURS-2$(x, y, n, \mu, d_{max}, x_w, y_w)$ in Algorithm 3.14 generates and selects the feature points in the given region. On a higher level, the process works as follows, assuming we are interested only in the distances to the nth feature points:

1. Define the region of the position of interest (x, y) as $\xi = (\lfloor x \rfloor, \lfloor y \rfloor)$.
2. Reset the seed of the underlying random number generator to ξ.
3. Generate the random feature points in the region ξ, which are fixed to the region.
4. Find all the n closest points (or as many as possible) in ξ.
5. Query the neighbouring regions of ξ in a similar fashion.
6. Concatenate the results, select the nth closest (or, if none, the furthest) and output the distance.

The Worley algorithm has many details and possibilities for adjustment, such as the following:

- Since the Worley noise generator has parameters n and μ, it actually describes a family of algorithms. Furthermore, the method is parameterized by the distance metric $distance(\bullet, \bullet)$ which is used when the nearest points are searched. For example, $distance$ can be:

$$euclidean(p, q) = \sqrt{(p_1 - q_1)^2 + \ldots + (p_n - q_n)^2} = \sqrt{\sum_{i=1}^{n}(p_i - q_i)^2};$$

$$manhattan(p, q) = |p_1 - q_1| + \ldots + |p_n - q_n| = \sum_{i=1}^{n}|p_i - q_i|;$$

$$maximum(p, q) = \max\{\,|p_1 - q_1|, \ldots, |p_n - q_n|\,\} = \max_{i=1}^{n}|p_i - q_i|.$$

- The primitive routine $radius()$ returns the radius length of the unit-sized region for the $distance(\bullet, \bullet)$ used. For $euclidean$ it is $1/\sqrt{2}$, for $manhattan$ 1, and for $maximum$ $\frac{1}{2}$.
- The neighbourhood N consists of entities r_i ($0 \le i < |N|$) that represent the relationship between the position $p = (x, y)$ and the feature point that is located distance $f_i(p)$ away. The idea is that entity r_i piggybacks all the data needed when the noise is generated in NOISE-WORLEY-2. For this reason, the entity r_i has at least attribute $distance(\bullet)$ that stores the value $f_i(p)$. Because there are many ways Worley's method can derive the actual noise values, r_i is adjusted and annotated if necessary.
- Apart from the position, a feature point can have other attributes, such as an identity or a random number, which can be used as an additional data source, when the r_i entities are created and their attributes are assigned. This practice is common with Worley's method because it allows the inclusion of new noise properties.
- The primitive routine $generator(N)$ composes the r_i entities into an appropriate value in $[v_{min}, v_{max}]$. This codomain interval depends on the parameters n and μ and it must be determined with a separate calibration phase. Suppose $N = \langle r_1, r_2, r_3 \rangle$. Then a generator can map N, for example, as $N \mapsto distance(r_1)$ or $N \mapsto distance(r_2) - distance(r_1)$. In these cases, the source of the outcome can also be denoted by $f_1(\bullet)$ or $f_2(\bullet) - f_1(\bullet)$, respectively.
- The operation $\|$ concatenates the sequences, $sorted$ arranges the sequence of r_i entities in a non-descending order by $distance(\bullet)$, and $sub(\bullet, 0, n)$ extracts n items from the beginning of the given sequence.
- There are two simple optimizations in the routine GRID-NEIGHBOURS-2. First, the neighbour regions that are too far away from the point of interest are filtered out in lines 3–6. This selection could also be handled by NEIGHBOURS-2, but that would need a separate filtering phase that would hinder parallelized implementations. Second, the value d_{max} is utilized to skip far away feature points (see line 13). To give a rough estimate of the efficacy of these filters with distance metric $euclidean$:

when determining	$f_1(\bullet)$	$f_2(\bullet)$	$f_3(\bullet)$	when $\mu = 3$,
about	62%	45%	33%	of regions are filtered out and
from the remaining regions	65%	61%	54%	of feature points are skipped.

- The Worley noise generator presented here has many optimization points. For example, the for loop in routine GRID-NEIGHBOURS-2 can be speeded up with a fixed sized min-heap, together with the one-liner $sub(sorted(R), 0, \min\{\,n, |R|\,\})$.

$f_1(\cdot)$

$f_2(\cdot)$

$f_3(\cdot)$

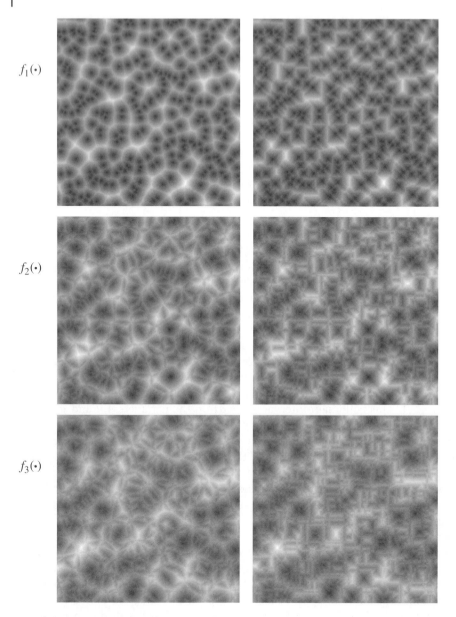

Figure 3.10 Worley noise generated from the feature distance $f_i(\cdot)$, $i = 1, 2, 3$, with $n = 3$ and $\mu = 3$. The left column is by distance metric *euclidean* and the right one by *maximum*.

As a demonstration of the diverse outcomes of the Worley noise generator, Figure 3.10 depicts the outcome when primitive routine *generator*(N) maps N to the noise value by taking into account $f_i(\cdot)$, $i = 1, 2, 3$. Because the feature points are the same for all the images, the noise spaces resemble each other. The top-left image of Figure 3.10 is the reason why Worley noise is considered to be a model representative of *cell noise*. Figure 3.11 presents how Worley noise can be manipulated and mixed.

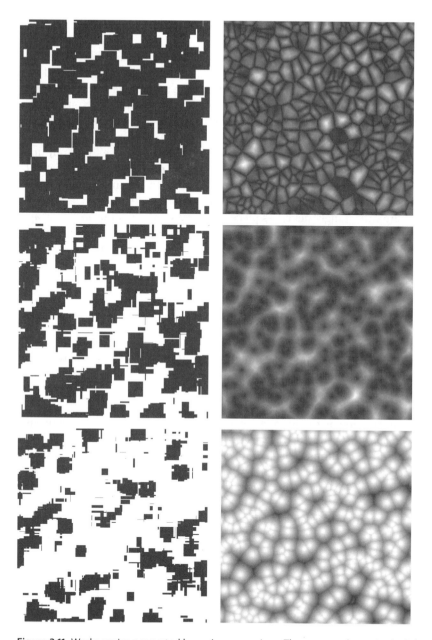

Figure 3.11 Worley noise generated by various mappings. The source values v in the left column are the right column in Figure 3.10, modified by RUNG$(1, -1, -\frac{1}{2}, v)$. In the right column the distance metric is *euclidean*; the top image is generated from $f_2(\bullet) - f_1(\bullet)$, the middle from $f_2(\bullet) \cdot f_1(\bullet)$, and the bottom with turbulence ($\ell = 3, a_0 = 0.03, f_0 = 1.97$) from generator $f_2(\bullet)$ ($n = 3, \mu = 3$).

3.9 Summary

Real-world events usually include noise due to various factors present in the situation. Using mathematical methods alone can make the game world to look too sterile and too machine-like. The introduction of noise helps us to create an organic surface to mask the underlying perfectness of the computations – to make it more life-like. Noise can be applied almost everywhere and the methods can be used in making abstract decisions as well as in generating graphical assets.

Noise generation can be based on random numbers (i.e. value noise), random unit vectors (i.e. gradient noise such as Perlin noise) or randomly pre-located points (i.e. cell noise such as Worley noise). Regardless of the approach chosen, the implementation of a noise generator often requires a high level of optimization. More often than not, the techniques used are intriguingly delicious pieces of 'nerd chocolate', but in this chapter our goal has been to give a presentation that separates the concepts, encouraging modification and twisting of the algorithms. Once a method fits its purpose it can be optimized to the limits of pessimization.

Exercises

3-1 Equation (3.1) demonstrates some basic ways to utilize noise generators. Consider also other functions and their function compositions such as square roots, exponents and logarithms. What are their domains and codomains? How do they affect $h(c)$?

3-2 Generate images similar to Figure 3.1. Hint: Suppose the image is $h \times w$ pixels, the zoom-in factor is s, and the noise is $n(i/s, j/s) \in [-1, 1] \subset \mathbb{R}$ for pixel (i, j), i for the rows and j the columns. Let $p(i, j) = lerp(0, n(i/s, j/s), j/w)$ be the amount of perturbance at (i, j). Also, denote $a(i, j) = \sin(i/(s + p(i, j)))$ and $b(i, j) = \sin(j/(s + p(i, j)))$. Now we can define $g(i, j) = lerp(a(i, j), b(i, j), i/h)$.

3-3 Equation (3.2) summarizes an approach for attaching the randomness to c via a random number generator. However, hash functions in general can provide a similar effect. Experiment with various hash functions over the sequence of natural numbers. For further details, see Cormen et al. (2001) and Knuth (1998c).

3-4 Invent some simple $h(c)$-dependent noise generators $n(c, h(c))$ and try them out, for example, on a chequered pattern.

3-5 Assume that we have two original true outcomes $h_0(c)$ and $h_1(c)$ of a characteristic parameter c. They can be blended linearly by

$$g(c) = h_0(c)(1 - w) + h_1(c)w$$

where $w \in [0, 1]$ weights the share between $h_0(c)$ and $h_1(c)$. Instead of keeping w constant it can be defined as a function of noise $n(c)$: $w_c = (n(c) + 1)/2$. Apply this idea to ruin mazes (see Section 4.2). What does c represent? How does the frequency of $n(c)$ affect the generated outcome $g(c)$?

3-6 If $x \in [-1, 1] \subset \mathbb{R}$ is a uniform random value, *none* of the following conversions produce a uniformly random value $\in [0, 255] \subset \mathbb{N}$. What is wrong with them?

(a) $\left\lfloor \dfrac{x+1}{2} \cdot 255 \right\rfloor$ (c) $\left\lfloor \dfrac{\lfloor x + \frac{1}{2} \rfloor + 1}{2} \cdot 255 \right\rfloor$

(b) $\left\lfloor \dfrac{x+1}{2} \cdot 256 \right\rfloor$ (d) $\left\lfloor \left\lfloor \dfrac{x+1}{2} + \dfrac{1}{2} \right\rfloor \cdot 255 \right\rfloor$ (e) $\left\lfloor \dfrac{x+1}{2} \cdot 255 + \dfrac{1}{2} \right\rfloor$

Devise a proper conversion and try it out. Hint: There are two common approaches – one utilizes a small floating point value such as 10^{-9}, and the other makes an explicit check with **if**. What if the target interval has also negative values (e.g. it is $[-128, 127] \subset \mathbb{Z}$)?

3-7 With images the characteristic parameter c is often defined as pixel coordinates (i, j), $0 \le i, j$. Assume the coordinates are merged into one value with the function $s_k(i, j) = ki + j$, where k is a fixed constant (e.g. 2^{10}). Next, $s_k(i, j)$ is used to generate the noise value $n(i, j)$. What properties does $n(i, j)$ have? To visualize your answer, sketch a plane graph showing the regions of interest in the generated noise.

3-8 The bit manipulations in Algorithm 3.1 can be fine-tuned, especially when $|Z|$ is a constant or has a known upper bound. Consider alternatives for gathering the bits and interleaving them, and ponder on their practicality when $|Z|$ is fixed (e.g. to 2, 3, or 8).

3-9 Although the routines in Algorithm 3.3 are simple, they can be generalized easily and their combined use tends to streamline many control structures of conditional selections. For instance:

(a) Given $x, x_{min}, x_{max} \in \mathbb{R}$ so that $x_{min} < x_{max}$, utilize UNIT-CLAMP to define a routine CLAMP(x_{min}, x_{max}, x) which returns $\min\{\max\{x_{min}, x\}, x_{max}\} \in [x_{min}, x_{max}]$. Hint: conversion to the unit interval and back.

(b) Express the following selection logic as a one-liner with UNIT-LERP and UNIT-STEP:

```
1: if x_t < x then
2:    return a_1
3: else
4:    return a_0
5: end if
```

Note that this gives us a generalization for STEP(x, x_t) – let us just call it RUNG(a_0, a_1, x, x_t).

(c) Graph the following function for $x \in \mathbb{R}$, when $a, x_0, x_1 \in \mathbb{R}$ and $x_0 \le x_1$:

$$a \cdot (\text{UNIT-STEP}\,(x - x_0) - \text{UNIT-STEP}\,(x - x_1))$$

What if $x_1 \le x_0$?

(d) Suppose we have a function $f(t)$ for $t \in [0, 1]$ for which $f(0) = f(1)$. What kind of a function is

$$f(\text{UNIT-WRAP}(x))$$

when $x \in [-\frac{3}{2}, \frac{3}{2}]$? How it could be scaled along the x-axis?

3-10 Given $x, x_0, x_1 \in \mathbb{R}$, we can generalize UNIT-WRAP in Algorithm 3.3 to the routine WRAP as follows (adapted from Graham et al. 1994, p. 82):

WRAP(x_0, x_1, x)

    in: values $x_0, x_1, x \in \mathbb{R}$ ($x_0 < x_1$)
    out: fractional part $\in [x_0, x_1)$ of x
    1: $\ell \leftarrow x_1 - x_0$ ▷ Length of the target interval.
    2: $x' \leftarrow x - x_0$ ▷ Map $[x_0, x_1]$ to $[0, \ell]$.
    3: $i \leftarrow \lfloor x'/\ell \rfloor \cdot \ell$ ▷ "Integer" amount of x' modulo ℓ.
    4: $r \leftarrow x' - i$ ▷ $r = (x' \mod \ell)$.
    5: **return** $r + x_0$ ▷ Map $[0, \ell]$ to $[x_0, x_1)$.

(a) Is the prerequisite $x_0 < x_1$ imperative or could it be relaxed to $x_0 \neq x_1$?
(b) Does this one-liner define the same outcome:

    1: **return** UNIT-WRAP(UNIT-RESCALE(x_0, x_1, x)) $\cdot (x_1 - x_0) + x_0$

If there is a difference, what could cause it?

3-11 The routine UNIT-LERP(a_0, a_1, t) in Algorithm 3.3 evaluates the expression $a_0(1 - t) + a_1 t$ which is equal to $a_0 + (a_1 - a_0)t$. However, with floating point values these expressions do not always result in equal values because of rounding errors. Also, due to floating point calculations before calling the routine, the input parameter t can be outside the unit interval, and then the indented interpolation turns into an accidental extrapolation.
(a) Find some concrete floating point values when $a_0 + (a_1 - a_0)t$ is not within $[a_0, a_1]$ for $t \in [0, 1]$. Does this problem happen with $a_0(1 - t) + a_1 t$?
(b) Devise another definition for UNIT-LERP(a_0, a_1, t) that clamps both t and the result value inside their proper intervals.

3-12 Algorithm 3.6 utilizes two one-dimensional $\varrho(t)$-interpolations in the x-axis direction and then joins those results by $\varrho(t)$-interpolating them in the y-axis direction ($t \in [0, 1]$).
(a) Show that when $\varrho(t)$ is a linear interpolation t, the interpolation result $a_{(f_x, f_y)}$ inside the unit square ($0 \leq f_x, f_y \leq 1$) equals

$$a_{(f_x, f_y)} = \begin{bmatrix} 1 - f_x & f_x \end{bmatrix} \begin{bmatrix} a_{(0,0)} & a_{(0,1)} \\ a_{(1,0)} & a_{(1,1)} \end{bmatrix} \begin{bmatrix} 1 - f_y \\ f_y \end{bmatrix}.$$

This generalizes linear interpolation to two dimensions and is called *bilinear interpolation*. The term 'bilinear' refers to the linear sub-interpolations in the x and y directions, but the total outcome is *nonlinear*.

(b) If the directions of the interpolations are swapped (i.e. the y-direction is interpolated first and then the x-direction) does the outcome change? With any $\varrho(t)$? Why or why not?

(c) How about Perlin noise in Algorithm 3.12: is it invariant with respect to the x- and y-directions?

3-13 Algorithm 3.7 can be varied in many ways, for example:

(a) Instead of exponentiation at lines 4–5, the ith amplitude and frequency in the iteration can be drawn from some functions $a(i)$ and $f(i)$. Experiment with various value combinations, for example, by implementing $a(i)$ and $f(i)$ as arrays or lambda functions of a programming language of your choice. How does the outcome differ when $a(i)$ values are ascending or descending?

(b) Using only one noise generator A-NOISE may introduce interference artefacts to the composed noise values. One way to tackle this is to generate each nesting layer from a different noise generator A-NOISE $_i$. To experiment with this, let $\ell = 2$, choose two generators A-NOISE $_0$ and A-NOISE $_1$, and generate the noise image for each of the four combinations of nesting.

(c) The **for** loop terminates when all the nesting layers are generated, independently of the development of the amplitudes and frequencies. Modify the algorithm so that it terminates when $a < \delta$ or $1/f < \gamma$ for given parameters $\delta, \gamma \in \mathbb{R}$. Why is $1/f$ a sensible expression for the termination condition on frequency f?

3-14 Since Algorithm 3.7 returns a noise value in $[-1, 1]$ for each c, it can be used as a noise generator, for instance, by defining NOISE-FROM-COMPOSITION(c) as NOISE-COMPOSITION($c, 4, \frac{1}{2}, 2$). Speculate as to what kind of noise is produced when that generator is used as A-NOISE in another NOISE-COMPOSITION. Then experiment. What happens to the noise when this idea of 'defining a new noise generator from a noise compositor' is repeated a few times? Tens of times? Hundreds? What if ℓ is decreased along the dependency/invocation chain of these algorithms (i.e. the chain ends for $\ell = 0$ and A-NOISE is returned without any compositions)?

3-15 The routine NOISE-TILED-RANDOM in Algorithm 3.8 forms a periodic noise from NOISE-RANDOM(N). Define a new routine NOISE-TILED-RANDOM-VECTOR that does the same to NOISE-RANDOM-VECTOR(N, n).

3-16 Modify the routine GRID-NEIGHBOURS-2 in Algorithm 3.14 so that Worley noise becomes tiled.

3-17 Select any two-dimensional noise, fix a position p in it, and imagine a spiral centred at p. Take the noise values along the spiral and consider them as the height modifiers of the horizon in some horizontal scenery. Since the noise is in the interval $[-1, 1]$, the level of the horizon is kept by noise value 0. Consider a pleasant theme and examine ways to decorate the landscape. How would you make the scenery tileable?

3-18 *Minecraft* generates the game world with a three-dimensional noise generator that resembles the Perlin noise method. The noise value specifies, for instance, features that relate to the density in the world. Discuss other uses for n-dimensional noise generation where $3 \leq n$.

3-19 Let us generate a Minecraftian cave system on a plane. We begin as in Exercise 3-17, but place a line segment randomly in the two-dimensional noise space. The noise values along the line are interpreted, sequentially one at a time, as the variation in the direction we are caving a small line segment of length $\ell \sim \text{Pois}(\mu)$, where μ is the average length of the corridors. The cave ends when the values in the line segment in the noise space are exhausted.

(a) Craft an algorithm from the description above. Apply the concepts discussed in this chapter. For example, the line segments can be walked by *lerping*.

(b) How can this two-dimensional method be to generalized to three dimensions? Hint: More than half of the problem is already solved.

(c) This method has a fundamental flaw, not necessarily in its outcome, but in its usability. What is the drawback? Devise another caving algorithm that does not have the same problem.

4

Procedural Generation

Procedural generation refers to the creation of content algorithmically with or without the user's assistance (Roden and Parberry 2004; Smith 2015). Such content can be, for example, a level that is unique and has not been defined by a human designer completely in advance, as in *NetHack*, or even a universe comprising hundreds of planets with individual attributes, as in *Elite*. Although procedural generation has been used widely in games since the 1980s, the related research has increased only recently (Togelius et al. 2011, 2016). This increasing popularity of procedural generation has many explanations. From the player's perspective, it improves and enlivens the design by creating (possibly perpetually) new content for them to enjoy. From the developer's perspective, it saves time and money in the development, especially when creating graphical assets for the game. Lastly, it increases the longevity of the game as it provides new content even for experienced players.

Procedural generation can used in various places. By randomizing the personality models we can create new, interesting combinations of character traits. Moreover, it allows us to make each character unique, possibly with a unique history and backstory. And more than just individual character histories, it can be used to create even complex histories of the game world. In level design, procedural generation allows the creation of new, surprising and continuously entertaining levels, such as in *Spelunky*. Now, instead of mastering the levels of a game, the players get into mastering a set of rules creating the levels. Automatic creation of content also allows a novelty of exploration, which is eminent in the procedurally generated game worlds of *Age of Empires*. This variation and freshness can be nearly infinite; for example, *No Man's Sky* offers a procedurally generated universe with over 1.8×10^{19} planets with their unique features. However, the plethora of game assets should be accompanied by dependencies that root their meaning and impact and, thus, make them engaging.

In this chapter, we will present methods from various areas. The terrain generation methods of Section 4.1 imitate the way terrains form or look in the real world. In Section 4.2 we focus on creating mazes by converting the task into a graph problem and solving it using different methods. Section 4.3 describes the idea behind L-systems, which can be used in creating various, often nature-related, patterns but also for producing human-made artefacts and landscapes. Finally, we broaden the perspective to creating complete game worlds procedurally in Section 4.4.

Algorithms and Networking for Computer Games, Second Edition. Jouni Smed and Harri Hakonen.
© 2017 John Wiley & Sons Ltd. Published 2017 by John Wiley & Sons Ltd.

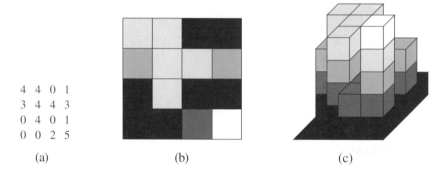

$$
\begin{matrix}
4 & 4 & 0 & 1 \\
3 & 4 & 4 & 3 \\
0 & 4 & 0 & 1 \\
0 & 0 & 2 & 5
\end{matrix}
$$

(a)   (b)   (c)

Figure 4.1 A height map divides the terrain into a grid: (a) the height values in a matrix; (b) the corresponding greyscale picture; (c) the corresponding oblique greyscale picture.

4.1 Terrain Generation

Random numbers can be used to generate the terrain for a game world. To simplify this process, let us divide the terrain into discrete points (e.g. using a grid; see Section 7.1.1), each of which has a value representing the height of the terrain at that position. These points form a *height map*, which is a matrix comprising the height values (see Figure 4.1). Height maps are often illustrated with greyscale pictures, where brightness is associated with the height (i.e. darker pixels represent lower and brighter pixels higher ground).

Algorithm 4.1 gives a straightforward implementation where a randomly generated number is assigned to each point in the height map. Unfortunately, the resulting terrain is too noisy to resemble any landscape in the real world, as we can see in Figure 4.2(a). To smoothen the terrain we can set a range within which the random value can vary (see Algorithm 4.2). Since the range depends on the already assigned heights (i.e. the neighbours to the west and north), the terrain generated has diagonal ridges going to the south-east, as illustrated in Figure 4.2(b).

Algorithm 4.1 Generating simple random terrain.

SIMPLE-RANDOM-TERRAIN()
    out: height map H (H is rectangular)
    constant: maximum height h_{max}
  1: **for** $x \leftarrow 0 \dots (columns(H) - 1)$ **do**
  2:   **for** $y \leftarrow 0 \dots (rows(H) - 1)$ **do**
  3:     $H_{x,y} \leftarrow$ RANDOM-UNIT() $\cdot h_{max}$ $\triangleright H_{x,y} \in [0, h_{max})$.
  4:   **end for**
  5: **end for**
  6: **return** H

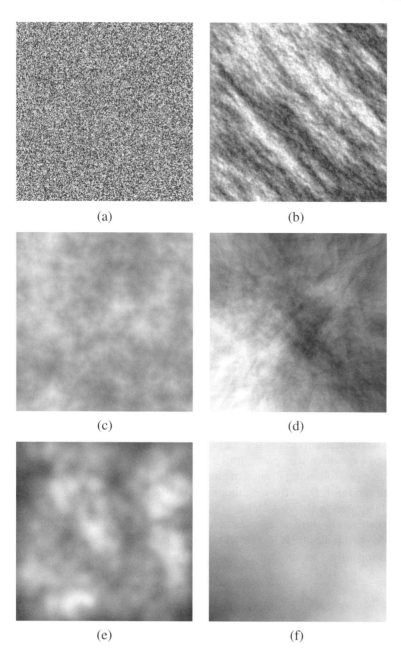

(a)

(b)

(c)

(d)

(e)

(f)

Figure 4.2 Randomly generated terrains where $h_{max} = 256$. (a) Simple random terrain. (b) Limited random terrain where $d_{max} = 64$. (c) Particle deposition terrain where $m = 10^7$, $i = 1$ and $b = 4$. (d) Fault line terrain where $f = 1000$ and $c = 2$. (e) Circle hill terrain where $c = 400$, $r = 32$ and $s = 16$. (f) Midpoint displacement terrain using diamond-square where $d_{max} = 128$ and $s = 1$.

Algorithm 4.2 Generating limited random terrain.

LIMITED-RANDOM-TERRAIN()
 out: height map H (H is rectangular)
 local: average height of northern and western neighbours a; height h
 constant: maximum height h_{max}; maximum height difference d_{max}
 1: **for** $x \leftarrow 0 \ldots (columns(H) - 1)$ **do**
 2: **for** $y \leftarrow 0 \ldots (rows(H) - 1)$ **do**
 3:   **if** $x \neq 0$ **and** $y \neq 0$ **then**
 4:    $a \leftarrow \left(H_{(x-1),y} + H_{x,(y-1)} \right) / 2$
 5:   **else if** $x \neq 0$ **and** $y = 0$ **then**
 6:    $a \leftarrow H_{(x-1),y}$
 7:   **else**
 8:    $a \leftarrow$ RANDOM-UNIT() $\cdot h_{max}$
 9:   **end if**
 10:   $h \leftarrow a + d_{max} \cdot ($RANDOM-UNIT() $- 1/2)$
 11:   $H_{x,y} \leftarrow \max\{0, \min\{h, h_{max}\}\}$ $\triangleright H_{x,y} \in [0, h_{max}]$.
 12: **end for**
 13: **end for**
 14: **return** H

Instead of generating random height values we can randomize the process of formation. In the *particle deposition* method 'grains' are dropped randomly on to the terrain
and allowed to pile up (see Algorithm 4.3). The height difference between neighbouring
points is limited. If the dropped grain causes the height difference to exceed this limit,
the grain falls down to a neighbouring point until it reaches an equilibrium (see Figure
4.3). The grains are dropped following Brownian movement (or motion), where the next
drop point is selected randomly from the neighbourhood of the current drop point. The
resulting terrain is illustrated in Figure 4.2(c).

Random numbers can also be used to select *fault lines* in the terrain. The height difference between the sides of a fault line is increased as shown in Figure 4.4. Algorithm 4.4
gives an implementation where we first randomly select two points (x_0, y_0) and (x_1, y_1).

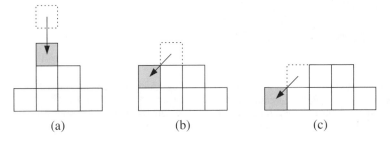

   (a)   (b)   (c)

Figure 4.3 In particle deposition, each dropped grain falls down until it reaches an equilibrium. If the
threshold $b = 1$, the grey grain moves downwards until its height difference with respect to its
neighbourhood is at most b.

Algorithm 4.3 Generating particle deposition terrain.

PARTICLE-DEPOSITION-TERRAIN(m)
  in: number of movements m
  out: height map H (H is rectangular)
  1: $p \leftarrow \langle$RANDOM-INTEGER$(0, columns(H))$, RANDOM-INTEGER$(0, rows(H))\rangle$
  2: **for** $i \leftarrow 1 \ldots m$ **do**
  3:   $\langle p', i' \rangle \leftarrow$ INCREASE(H, p) ▷ Increase i' if $H_{p'}$ can still grow.
  4:   $H_{p'} \leftarrow H_{p'} + i'$
  5:   $p \leftarrow$ BROWNIAN-MOVEMENT(H, p)
  6: **end for**
  7: **return** H

BROWNIAN-MOVEMENT H, p)
  in: height map H; position p
  out: neighbouring position of p
  1: **case** RANDOM-INTEGER$(0, 4)$ **of**
  2:   0 : **return** EAST-NEIGHBOUR(H, p)
  3:   1 : **return** WEST-NEIGHBOUR(H, p)
  4:   2 : **return** SOUTH-NEIGHBOUR(H, p)
  5:   3 : **return** NORTH-NEIGHBOUR(H, p)
  6: **end case**

INCREASE(H, p)
  in: height map H; position p
  out: pair $\langle$position, increase$\rangle$
  constant: increase i; maximum height h_{max}
  1: $i' \leftarrow \min\{h_{max} - H_p, i\}$ ▷ Proper amount for increase.
  2: $n \leftarrow$ UNBALANCED-NEIGHBOUR(H, p, i')
  3: **if** $n =$ NIL **then return** $\langle p, i' \rangle$
  4: **else return** INCREASE(H, n)
  5: **end if**

UNBALANCED-NEIGHBOUR(H, p, i')
  in: height map H; position p; increase i' if H_p can still grow
  out: neighbour of p which exceeds b or otherwise NIL
  constant: height difference threshold b
  1: $e \leftarrow$ EAST-NEIGHBOUR(H, p); $w \leftarrow$ WEST-NEIGHBOUR(H, p)
  2: $s \leftarrow$ SOUTH-NEIGHBOUR(H, p); $n \leftarrow$ NORTH-NEIGHBOUR(H, p)
  3: **if** $H_p + i' - H_e > b$ **then return** e
  4: **if** $H_p + i' - H_w > b$ **then return** w
  5: **if** $H_p + i' - H_s > b$ **then return** s
  6: **if** $H_p + i' - H_n > b$ **then return** n
  7: **return** NIL

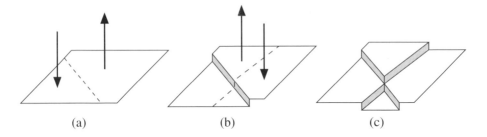

       (a)   (b)   (c)

Figure 4.4 Fault lines are selected randomly. The terrain is raised on one side of the fault line and lowered on the other.

To calculate the fault line going through these points we form a vector $\vec{v}$ with components $\vec{v}_x = x_1 - x_0$ and $\vec{v}_y = y_1 - y_0$. After that, for each point (x, y) in the terrain, we can form a vector $\vec{w}$ for which $\vec{w}_x = x - x_0$ and $\vec{w}_y = y - y_0$. When we calculate the cross product $\vec{u} = \vec{v} \times \vec{w}$, we know depending on the sign of $\vec{u}_z$ whether to lower or lift the terrain at the point (x, y):

$$\vec{u}_z = \vec{v}_x \vec{w}_y - \vec{v}_y \vec{w}_x.$$

An example of the fault line terrain can be seen in Figure 4.2(d).

Algorithm 4.4 Generating fault line terrain.

Fault-Line-Terrain()
   out: height map H (H is rectangular)
   constant: maximum height h_{max}; number of fault lines f; fault change c
   1: $H \leftarrow$ Level-Terrain($h_{max}/2$)   ▷ Initialize the terrain to flat.
   2: **for** $i \leftarrow 1 \ldots f$ **do**
   3:   $x_0 \leftarrow$ Random-Integer(0, *columns*(H))
   4:   $y_0 \leftarrow$ Random-Integer(0, *rows*(H))
   5:   $x_1 \leftarrow$ Random-Integer(0, *columns*(H))
   6:   $y_1 \leftarrow$ Random-Integer(0, *rows*(H))
   7:   **for** $x \leftarrow 0 \ldots (columns(H) - 1)$ **do**
   8:     **for** $y \leftarrow 0 \ldots (rows(H) - 1)$ **do**
   9:     **if** $(x_1 - x_0) \cdot (y - y_0) - (y_1 - y_0) \cdot (x - x_0) > 0$ **then**
  10:       $H_{x,y} \leftarrow \min\{H_{x,y} + c, \, h_{max}\}$
  11:     **else**
  12:       $H_{x,y} \leftarrow \max\{H_{x,y} - c, \, 0\}$
  13:     **end if**
  14:   **end for**
  15: **end for**
  16: **end for**
  17: **return** H

Instead of fault lines, we can use *hills* to simulate real-world terrain formation. Random numbers can be used to select locations for the hills. Algorithm 4.5 gives a simple method, where every hill is in a circle with the same diameter and the height increase is based on the cosine function. The resulting terrain is shown in Figure 4.2(e).

Algorithm 4.5 Generating circle hill terrain.

CIRCLE-HILL-TERRAIN()
    out: height map H (H is rectangular)
    constant: maximum height h_{max}; number of circles c; circle radius r; circle height
                    increase s
    local: centre of the circle (x', y')
  1: **for** $i \leftarrow 1 \dots c$ **do**
  2:   $x' \leftarrow$ RANDOM-INTEGER$(0, columns(H))$
  3:   $y' \leftarrow$ RANDOM-INTEGER$(0, rows(H))$
  4:   **for** $x \leftarrow 0 \dots (columns(H) - 1)$ **do**
  5:     **for** $y \leftarrow 0 \dots (rows(H) - 1)$ **do**
  6:     $d \leftarrow (x' - x)^2 + (y' - y)^2$
  7:     **if** $d < r^2$ **then**
  8:       $a \leftarrow (s/2) \cdot (1 + \cos(\pi d / r^2))$
  9:       $H_{x,y} \leftarrow \min\{H_{x,y} + a, \; h_{max}\}$
 10:    **end if**
 11:    **end for**
 12: **end for**
 13: **end for**
 14: **return** H

The random *midpoint displacement* method, introduced by Fournier et al. (1982), starts by setting heights for the corner points of the terrain. Then it subdivides the region inside iteratively in two steps (see Figure 4.5):

(i) Diamond step: Taking a square of four corner points, generate a random value at the diamond point (i.e. the centre of the square), where the two diagonals meet. The value is calculated by averaging the four corner values and by adding a random displacement value.

(ii) Square step: Taking each diamond of four corner points, generate a random value at the square point (i.e. the centre of the diamond). The value is calculated by averaging the corner values and adding a random displacement value.

Variations on these steps are presented by Miller (1986) and Lewis (1987).

To make the implementation easier we limit the size of the height map to $n \times n$, where

$$n = 2^k + 1$$

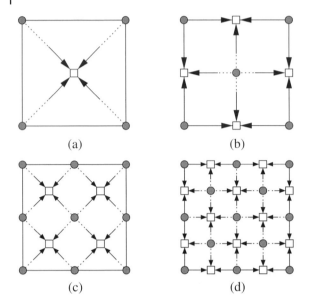

Figure 4.5 Midpoint displacement method consists of the diamond step, shown in (a) and (c), and the square step, shown in (b) and (d). The circles represent the values calculated.

when the integer $k \geq 0$. Algorithm 4.6 gives an implementation, where the subroutine DISPLACEMENT(H, x, y, S, d) returns the height value for position (x, y) in height map H,

$$d + \frac{1}{4} \cdot \sum_{i=0}^{3} H_{(x+S_{2i}),(y+S_{2i+1})},$$

in which S defines the point offsets from (x, y) in the square or diamond, and d is the current height displacement.

In addition to the methods described here, there are approaches such as fractal noise (Perlin 1985) and stream erosion (Kelley et al. 1988) for terrain generation. Moreover, existing height maps can be modified using image processing methods (e.g. sharpening and smoothing).

4.2 Maze Algorithms

Labyrinths and mazes have intrigued humans since ancient times. The most famous labyrinth is recorded in the myth of the Minotaur living at the centre of a labyrinth designed by Daedalus and his son Icarus by order of King Minos of Crete. Although the terms 'labyrinth' and 'maze' are sometimes used interchangeably, they differ in their meaning (Gazzard 2013, p. 25–34): a *labyrinth* has a unicursal path (i.e. there is one path from the beginning to the end), whereas a *maze* has a multicursal path (i.e. it offers choices for the path), as illustrated in Figure 4.6. A labyrinth is, therefore, a special case of a maze, which is why we will use the term 'maze' in the rest of this section.

Algorithm 4.6 Generating midpoint displacement terrain.

MIDPOINT-DISPLACEMENT-TERRAIN()
    out: height map H $(columns(H) = rows(H) = n = 2^k + 1$ when $k \geq 0)$
    constant: maximum displacement d_{max}; smoothness s
  1: initialize $H_{0,0}$, $H_{column(H)-1,0}$, $H_{0,row(H)-1}$ and $H_{column(H)-1,row(H)-1}$
  2: $m \leftarrow (n-1); c \leftarrow 1; d \leftarrow d_{max}$
  3: **while** $m \geq 2$ **do**
  4:   $w \leftarrow m/2; x \leftarrow w$
  5:   **for** $i \leftarrow 0 \ldots (c-1)$ **do**   ▷ Centres.
  6:     $y \leftarrow w$
  7:     **for** $j \leftarrow 0 \ldots (c-1)$ **do**
  8:       $H_{x,y} \leftarrow$ DISPLACEMENT$(H, x, y, \langle -w, -w, -w, +w, +w, -w, +w, +w \rangle, d)$
  9:       $y \leftarrow y + m$
10:     **end for**
11:     $x \leftarrow x + m$
12:   **end for**
13:   $x \leftarrow x - w; t \leftarrow w$
14:   **for** $p \leftarrow 0 \ldots (c-1)$ **do**   ▷ Borders.
15:     $H_{0,t} \leftarrow$ DISPLACEMENT$(H, 0, t, \langle\ \ 0, -w,\ \ \ 0, +w, +w,\ \ \ 0, +w,\ \ \ \ 0 \rangle, d)$
16:     $H_{t,0} \leftarrow$ DISPLACEMENT$(H, t, 0, \langle -w,\ \ \ \ 0, +w,\ \ \ 0,\ \ \ 0, +w,\ \ \ 0, +w \rangle, d)$
17:     $H_{t,x} \leftarrow$ DISPLACEMENT$(H, t, x, \langle -w,\ \ \ \ 0, +w,\ \ \ 0,\ \ \ 0, -w,\ \ \ 0, -w \rangle, d)$
18:     $H_{x,t} \leftarrow$ DISPLACEMENT$(H, x, t, \langle\ \ 0, -w,\ \ \ 0, +w, -w,\ \ \ 0, -w,\ \ \ \ 0 \rangle, d)$
19:     $t \leftarrow t + m$
20:   **end for**
21:   $x \leftarrow m$
22:   **for** $i \leftarrow 0 \ldots (c-2)$ **do**   ▷ Middle horizontal.
23:     $y \leftarrow w$
24:     **for** $j \leftarrow 0 \ldots (c-1)$ **do**
25:       $H_{x,y} \leftarrow$ DISPLACEMENT$(H, x, y, \langle -w, 0, +w, 0, 0, -w, 0, +w \rangle, d)$
26:       $y \leftarrow y + m$
27:     **end for**
28:     $x \leftarrow x + m$
29:   **end for**
30:   $x \leftarrow w$
31:   **for** $i \leftarrow 0 \ldots (c-1)$ **do**   ▷ Middle vertical.
32:     $y \leftarrow m$
33:     **for** $j \leftarrow 0 \ldots (c-2)$ **do**
34:       $H_{x,y} \leftarrow$ DISPLACEMENT$(H, x, y, \langle -w, 0, +w, 0, 0, -w, 0, +w \rangle, d)$
35:       $y \leftarrow y + m$
36:     **end for**
37:     $x \leftarrow x + m$
38:   **end for**
39:   $m \leftarrow m/2; c \leftarrow c \cdot 2; d \leftarrow d \cdot 2^{-s}$
40: **end while**
41: **return** H

(a)   (b)

Figure 4.6 Comparison of a labyrinth and a maze: (a) a labyrinth has only one path from *s* to *r*, whereas (b) a maze offers choices along the way.

In computer games, mazes have two functions (Gazzard 2013, pp. 38–41). First, they can make the space appear larger by having multiple paths restricting the movement. For example, in *Pac-Man* the structure of the level is formed by a maze and the player has to follow it when moving around. Second, if a maze offers generative or emergent paths, it can lead to differences from play to play. For example, the randomly appearing fruits in *Pac-Man* create emergent paths for the player to follow.

Although there is a wide variety of methods for creating mazes such as genetic algorithms (Ashlock et al. 2011) and cellular automata (LifeWiki 2014), we focus here on methods based on graphs. There is a natural connection between graphs and mazes. Possible connections can be presented as a graph $G = (V, E)$, where the vertices V represent the cells (or rooms) and the edges E all the possible connections between the cells (see Figure 4.7). Since a graph models the connections, not the actual placement of vertices nor rendering, considering a maze as a graph allows us to segregate visualizations into another phase.

A maze algorithm returns a set $W \subseteq E$ which includes all the connections blocked by walls (i.e. the remaining connections in the maze form the set $M = E \setminus W$). The outcome of a maze-generating algorithm can be affected in three ways, for example, to have open spaces or to reserve areas for special use. First, the generator does not consider vertices or edges that are not in the given parameter G. In other words, the paths in the generated mazes pass through the given vertices only. Second, the resulting set of walls W can

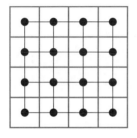
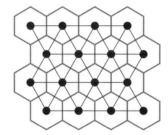

Figure 4.7 A square and hexagonal grid as a graph.

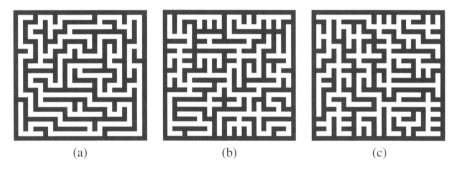

(a)   (b)   (c)

Figure 4.8 Procedurally created mazes: (a) depth-first algorithm; (b) randomized Kruskal's algorithm; and (c) randomized Prim's algorithm.

be post-processed. Removing a wall creates – in addition to more space – more paths, whereas adding a wall can prevent any walk into a sub-maze. Third, the algorithms can be guided towards certain structures by providing a pre-planned random number generator or modifying the method to take into account weighted vertices or edges.

In the following we present three variants based on depth-first search, Kruskal's algorithm, and Prim's algorithm. The generation of mazes is based on the idea of *removing* the walls from the path; at the beginning all the possible passage locations are blocked by walls. A path is generated by selecting a chain of walls to be removed. Figure 4.8 illustrates examples of mazes created with these methods. For a more detailed discussion on maze algorithms, we recommend the book by Buck (2015).

4.2.1 Depth-first algorithm

A natural candidate for creating mazes is depth-first search which, can be implemented iteratively or recursively. In the iterative variant (see Algorithm 4.7), we use a stack as a data structure for holding a backtrack of vertices along the path. At the beginning, we select an arbitrary cell (i.e. vertex) as the current one and mark it visited. Then we randomly select an unvisited cell from its neighbourhood and remove the wall between the current cell and the selected neighbour. The algorithm will move next to the selected neighbour and the current cell is pushed into the stack. If, at some point, the current cell has only visited neighbours, we have reached a dead-end and have to backtrack by retrieving a cell from the stack. This is iterated until all the cells have been visited.

In practice, the depth-first algorithm creates a randomly twisting tunnel until it reaches a dead-end. Then it backtracks the cells along the tunnel until it can start constructing a new tunnel in another direction. The resulting maze has a low branching factor because the tunnels tend to be long, as illustrated in Figure 4.8(a).

We can easily modify the algorithm to handle a given initial situation by removing walls from the set W beforehand. These removed walls can represent open spaces or can be regarded as areas reserved for special use.

4.2.2 Randomized Kruskal's algorithm

From the perspective of graph theory, mazes can be viewed as spanning trees. A spanning tree T of a graph G is an acyclic connected subgraph of G that includes all the

---

Algorithm 4.7 Generating a maze using depth-first algorithm.

DEPTH-FIRST-MAZE(G)
   in: undirected connection graph $G = (V, E)$
   out: walls $W \subseteq E$
   local: unvisited cells $C \subseteq V$; sequence S used as a stack for backtracking
  1: $C \leftarrow$ **copy** V $\triangleright$ All the cells are unvisited.
  2: $W \leftarrow$ **copy** E $\triangleright$ All the connections have walls.
  3: $S \leftarrow \langle \, \rangle$ $\triangleright$ Empty stack.
  4: select $c \in C$ randomly
  5: $C \leftarrow C \setminus \{c\}$ $\triangleright$ Mark visited.
  6: **repeat**
  7:   $N \leftarrow neighbourhood(c) \cap C$ $\triangleright$ Exclude the already visited cells.
  8:   **if** $N = \emptyset$ **then** $\triangleright$ Dead-end, select another cell.
  9:    **if** $|S| \geq 1$ **then**
 10:     $c \leftarrow$ STACK-POP(S)
 11:    **end if**
 12:   **else**
 13:    select $n \in N$ randomly
 14:    $W \leftarrow W \setminus \{(c, n)\}$ $\triangleright$ Remove the wall.
 15:    STACK-PUSH(S, c)
 16:    $c \leftarrow n$
 17:    $C \leftarrow C \setminus \{n\}$ $\triangleright$ Mark visited.
 18:   **end if**
 19: **until** $C = \emptyset$ $\triangleright$ All the cells have been visited.
 20: **return** W

---

vertices of G. If the edges have weights, a minimum spanning tree (MST) connects the vertices with a minimum total weight of the edges. There are many methods for finding MSTs, one of earliest being a greedy algorithm presented by J.B. Kruskal (1956). Simply put, the idea of it is to iteratively choose the edge with the minimum weight (solving ties arbitrarily). If the edge connects two subtrees (i.e. it does not create a cycle), it is added to the MST.

We can simplify Kruskal's algorithm to create mazes by omitting the weights and choosing the next edge randomly (or by assigning random values to the edges). This randomized Kruskal's algorithm (see Algorithm 4.8) goes randomly through the set of walls. If the cells that the selected wall divides belong to distinct sets (i.e. sub-mazes), the wall is removed and the two sets are combined (i.e. the sub-mazes are merged together). This is continued until the algorithm has gone through all the walls.

Figure 4.8(b) illustrates a labyrinth created by a randomized Kruskal's algorithm. It tends to create fairly easily solvable mazes with regular patterns. The randomized Kruskal's algorithm also allows mazes to be created using initial patterns that are then connected (Buck 2015, pp. 166–171).

Algorithm 4.8 Generating a maze using randomized Kruskal's algorithm.

RANDOMIZED-KRUSKAL-MAZE(G)
  in: undirected connection graph $G = (V, E)$
  out: walls $W \subseteq E$
  local: set of sets of connected cells M
  1: $W \leftarrow \mathbf{copy}\ E$ ▷ All the connections have walls.
  2: $M \leftarrow \varnothing$
  3: **for all** $c \in V$ **do**
  4:   $M \leftarrow M \cup \{\{c\}\}$ ▷ Initially all cells are isolated.
  5: **end for**
  6: **for all** $w \in W$ **do**
  7:   $(c_1, c_2) \leftarrow w$ ▷ The ends of the edge.
  8:   find $S_1 \in M$ such that $c_1 \in S_1$
  9:   find $S_2 \in M$ such that $c_2 \in S_2$
  10:   **if** $S_1 \neq S_2$ **then**   ▷ Are the cells disconnected?
  11:     $W \leftarrow W \setminus \{w\}$ ▷ Remove the wall.
  12:     $M \leftarrow M \setminus \{S_1, S_2\}$
  13:     $M \leftarrow M \cup \{S_1 \cup S_2\}$ ▷ Combine the sets.
  14:   **end if**
  15: **end for**
  16: **return** W

4.2.3   Randomized Prim's algorithm

MSTs are also the basis for a method presented by R.C. Prim (1957). The method starts with an arbitrary vertex and adds it to a set of visited vertices. Then the algorithm chooses among the neighbouring cells of the visited vertices an unvisited vertex with the lowest connecting edge weight. The edge is added to the MST and the selected vertex is added to the set of visited vertices. This is repeated until all the vertices have been visited.

Again, the algorithm can be simplified to create mazes by omitting the weights (or assigning them randomly) and making random selections (see Algorithm 4.9). The mazes created by this randomized Prim's algorithm are stylistically similar to those created by Kruskal's algorithm as illustrated in Figure 4.8(c).

4.3 L-Systems

An L-system, named after its inventor A. Lindenmayer (1968a,b), is a string rewriting system, where complex objects are defined by successively replacing parts of a simple object using a set of rules. In an L-system, the rules (or productions) are applied in parallel and simultaneously replacing all the symbols, whereas in formal grammars the production is applied sequentially (Prusinkiewicz and Lindenmayer 1990).

Algorithm 4.9 Generating a maze using randomized Prim's algorithm.

RANDOMIZED-PRIM-MAZE(G)

  in: undirected connection graph $G = (V, E)$

  out: walls $W \subseteq E$

  local: visited cells $C \subseteq V$; set of walls to check out L

  1: $C \leftarrow \emptyset$ ▷ All the cells are unvisited.

  2: $W \leftarrow$ **copy** E ▷ All the connections have walls.

  3: $L \leftarrow \emptyset$

  4: select $c \in V$ randomly

  5: **for all** $w \in W$ **do**   ▷ Initialize L with the neighbours of c.

  6:   **if** $c \in ends(w)$ **then**

  7:     $L \leftarrow L \cup \{w\}$

  8:   **end if**

  9: **end for**

10: **while** $L \neq \emptyset$ **do**

11:   select $\ell \in L$ randomly

12:   **if** $|ends(\ell) \cap C| \leq 1$ **then**   ▷ Both ends not already visited.

13:     $C \leftarrow C \cup ends(\ell)$

14:     $W \leftarrow W \setminus \{\ell\}$ ▷ Remove the wall.

15:     **for all** $w \in W$ **do**

16:       **if** $ends(w) \cap ends(\ell) \neq \emptyset$ **then**

17:         **if** $w \notin W$

18:           $L \leftarrow L \cup \{w\}$ ▷ Add the neighbouring walls.

19:         **end if**

20:       **end if**

21:     **end for**

22:   **end if**

23:   $L \leftarrow L \setminus \{\ell\}$

24: **end while**

25: **return** W

Formally, let V denote an alphabet, V^* the set of all words over V, and V^+ the set of non-empty words. Now, an L-system is an ordered triplet $G = \langle V, \omega, P \rangle$ where

- V is the alphabet (i.e. a set of symbols),
- $\omega \in V^+$ is the axiom (i.e. start or initiator), and
- $P \subset V \times V^*$ is a finite set of production rules.

A rule $(a, \chi) \in P$ can be written $a \rightarrow \chi$, where a is called the predecessor and χ the successor. If there is no rule for a given predecessor $a \in V$, then we assume an identity production $a \rightarrow a$. If $a \in V$ is not on the left-hand side of any of the rules in P, then a is said to be a constant (or terminal).

An L-system can be defined to be context-free, where the rules refer only to individual symbols, or context-sensitive. A context-free L-system is deterministic, if there is only one production rule $a \rightarrow \chi$ for each symbol $a \in V$. If there are multiple rules for a symbol, the L-system is stochastic and we can map a probability distribution to the rules. These probabilities are then used to choose the production rule, which allows a stochastic L-system to create variations while keeping the general features intact.

4.3.1   Examples

Let us assume the following deterministic, context-free L-system:

$$\begin{cases} V = \{0, 1\} \\ \omega = 1 \\ P = \{(0 \rightarrow 1), (1 \rightarrow 10)\} \end{cases}$$

For the sake of argument, we can call the symbol 0 a new pair of rabbits and 1 a mature pair. The rules then mean that in the next iteration a new pair becomes a mature pair, and a mature pair remains mature and produces a new pair of rabbits.

The L-system begins with the axiom 1, and in the first iteration it applies the production $1 \rightarrow 10$ to it. In the second iteration, we can apply the same rule to the leading 1 and the rule $0 \rightarrow 1$ to the trailing 0. The first seven iterations of the L-system generate the following sequences:

$$S_0 = 1$$
$$S_1 = 10$$
$$S_2 = 101$$
$$S_3 = 10110$$
$$S_4 = 10110101$$
$$S_5 = 1011010110110$$
$$S_6 = 10110101101010110101$$
$$S_7 = 1011010110110101101011011010110110$$

In this case, the L-system generates *Fibonacci words*, where the number of 0-bits in the sequence S_n equals the Fibonacci number F_n, the number of 1-bits equals F_{n+1}, and the length of the sequence $|S_n| = F_{n+2}$. To illustrate the sequences generated we can use the fractal formulation by Monnerot-Dumaine (2009) shown in Figure 4.9:

```
1: for i ← 0 … |S_n| do
2:   if (S_n)_i = 1
3:     if even(i) then TURN-RIGHT
4:     if odd(i) then TURN-LEFT
5:   end if
6:   DRAW-SEGMENT
7: end for
```

Lindenmayer's motivation for creating L-systems was biological: to capture cell division in multicellular organisms. Various kinds of images and models can be created by using L-systems such as models and textures of plants, plant-like arabesques and other ornaments.

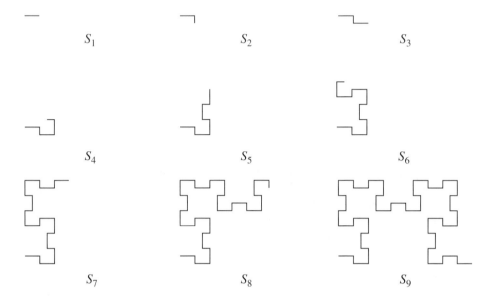

Figure 4.9 Fibonacci words as fractals.

Although the definition of L-system does not specify a data structure, we can represent them as strings with brackets to limit the branching (Prusinkiewicz and Lindenmayer 1990, pp. 24–27):

- [pushes the current position and direction to the stack, and
-] pops the position and direction from the stack.

Figure 4.10 illustrates the L-system

$$
\begin{cases}
V = \{x, f, +, -, [,]\} \\
\omega = x \\
P = \{(x \to f[+f]f[-x] + x), f \to ff\}
\end{cases}
$$

When generating the graphical representation, the symbols $+$ and $-$ mean a turn of 25 degrees to the right or left, respectively, and the symbols x and f refer to drawing a line segment.

4.3.2 City generation

Many games include a large-scale three-dimensional environment, whose manual generation process by level designers and game artists – taking into account modern graphical requirements – is a long and expensive process. Procedural generation is often the

Figure 4.10 Plant created with an L-system after eight iterations.

most cost-effective solution allowing the game environments first to be generated procedurally and then to be refined and polished manually (Watson et al. 2008).

Kelly and McCabe (2006) list the following criteria for procedural city generation techniques:

- How realistic are the generated cities in comparison to real cityscapes?
- Is the generated content in the scale of a city?
- Does the generation method provide variation?
- What input is required from the user?
- What is the computational efficiency of the method?
- How much control does the user have to influence the city generation?
- Does the method work in real time or offline only?

Typical methods for city generation are based on grid and geometric primitives, architectural templates, L-systems, agent-based systems, and split grammars (Wang and Hua 2006; Kelly and McCabe 2006). L-systems are ranked among the most flexible, their only downside being the computational requirements, because as the iteration increases, the number of variables to be replaced, and thus the complexity, increases exponentially.

Parish and Müller (2001) in their seminal work present an L-system for creating urban environments based on a hierarchical set of comprehensible and extendable rules. The approach follows the general pattern of Kelly and McCabe (2007) who divide procedural city generation into three stages:

- primary road generation (based on the main traffic flow),
- secondary road generation (in areas closed by the primary roads), and
- building generation (in areas closed by the primary and secondary roads).

The idea is that the primary roads are based on the user's input, after which the secondary roads are generated automatically. Then the areas are subdivided into lots where

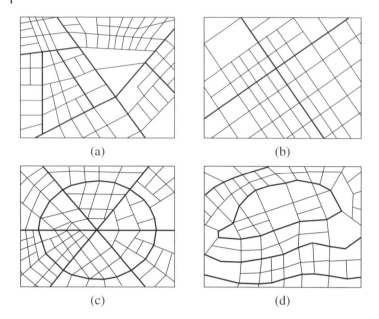

Figure 4.11 Road patterns: (a) basic rule; (b) New York rule; (c) Paris rule; (d) San Francisco rule.

the buildings are placed. The input includes geographic (e.g. elevation and land type) and sociostatistical (e.g. population density) influence maps (see Section 9.3). The city generation is carried out by using two L-systems, one for creating the streets and another for creating the buildings.

The road and street network generation is a context-sensitive L-system, which takes into account the existing land shapes and the influence maps. The rule set includes global goals to create initial, tentative road segments, and local constraints which are used in refinement. Stretches of road are drawn first to meet the global goals, and, next, these interim plans are finalized to follow the local constraints (e.g. roads going around bodies of water and connecting and intersecting roads).

The global goals follow one of the following four road patterns (see Figure 4.11):

1. Basic rule: there is no superimposed pattern but the roads follow the population density, which is typical of older cities.
2. New York rule: the roads follow a global and local angle (i.e. chequered pattern) and the blocks reside within given maximum and minimum lengths.
3. Paris rule: the roads follow a radial track around a centre.
4. San Francisco rule: the main roads follow the least elevation, connected by short smaller streets following the steepest elevation.

The local constraints grow the roads together and forms loops. These constraints ensure that there is a crossing when two streets intersect, or if a road ends close to an existing crossing, it is extended to the crossing.

The second L-system creates allotments for buildings. It includes modules for transformation (scale, move), extrusion, branching, termination, and geometric templates. The shape of a building is created by dividing it into sections resting on top of one

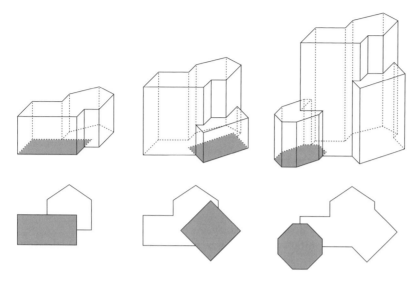

Figure 4.12 Creating buildings by extruding.

another. The top section of a building is given a geometrically simple form, and the three-dimensional form is made by extruding it downwards (see Figure 4.12). At the beginning of the next section of the building, the geometric shape changes, and the extrusion process is continued until all sections have been created.

4.4 Hierarchical Universe Generation

Suppose we have a two-dimensional galaxy which we want to populate with stars (see Figure 4.13). Moreover, suppose the galaxy is finite and discrete, where each position (x, y) can represent either a star or void space. Let d be the density of the galaxy (i.e. the ratio between stars and void). We can now enumerate each position, for example, row by row, starting from the origin: $(0, 0)$, $(0, 1)$, ..., $(0, y_{max})$, $(1, 0)$, $(1, 1)$, ..., (x_{max}, y_{max}). By

Figure 4.13 The positions in a two-dimensional galaxy are enumerated row by row, starting from the origin.

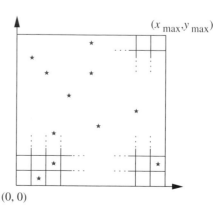

(x_{max}, y_{max})

$(0, 0)$

using this order we generate a random number from the interval $[0, 1)$ for each position. If the generated number is greater than the density, the position is empty; otherwise, it is populated with a star and we generate a random number for it. This method is illustrated in the first part of Algorithm 4.10, which assumes that we have a function SET-SEED(v) for (re)setting the seed value used in Algorithm 2.1 (i.e. after the call $x = v$). If we want to conserve memory (as always, with the cost of computation time), we could use Equation (2.2) to generate a random number for a given position immediately without the need to generate the whole galaxy at once.

Algorithm 4.10 Methods for generating stars and planets.

CREATE-STARS(v)
    in: seed value v of the galaxy
    out: matrix G of seed values for the stars
    constant: maximum horizontal value x_{max}; maximum vertical value y_{max}; density
               d $(0 \le d \le 1)$

  1: $rows(G) \leftarrow x_{max} + 1$ ▷ Rows for the x-axis.
  2: $columns(G) \leftarrow y_{max} + 1$ ▷ Columns for the y-axis.
  3: SET-SEED(v)
  4: **for** $x \leftarrow 0 \dots x_{max}$ **do**
  5:   **for** $y \leftarrow 0 \dots y_{max}$ **do**
  6:     **if** RANDOM-UNIT() $< d$ **then**
  7:       $G_{x,y} \leftarrow$ RANDOM()   ▷ Create a star.
  8:     **else**
  9:       $G_{x,y} \leftarrow$ NIL   ▷ Void space.
10:     **end if**
11:   **end for**
12: **end for**
13: **return** G

CREATE-PLANETS(v)
    in: seed value v of the star system
    out: ordered set P of seed values for the planets
    constant: minimum number of planets p_{min}; maximum number of planets p_{max}
    local: number of planets p
  1: SET-SEED(v)
  2: $p \leftarrow$ RANDOM-INTEGER($p_{min}, p_{max} + 1$)
  3: **for** $i \leftarrow 0 \dots (p - 1)$ **do**
  4:   $P_i \leftarrow$ RANDOM()
  5: **end for**
  6: **return** P

Each star is now associated with a random number, which is used as a new seed value when creating star-related characteristics such as name, size, and composition (see Figure 4.14). These characteristics can be extended to the planets in the star

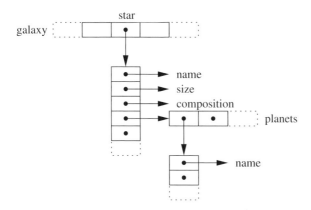

Figure 4.14 The seed value is used to create the characteristics of the star including the rest of the star system.

system, as the second part of Algorithm 4.10 illustrates. We could continue refining this hierarchy into smaller and smaller details (from a planet to continents to states to towns to citizens, etc.), always using a seed value generated on the upper level as a basis for the next level (Lecky-Thompson 1999).

If we have constructed a galaxy in this way, we can compress it down to the initial seed value, which is then stored for later use. Since the pseudo-random numbers are deterministic, we can create the very same galaxy, down to the smallest details, time and again from this one number.

4.5   Summary

Procedural generation is akin to data decompression where we expand the compressed information until we have achieved the required level of detail. However, in contrast to compression, we usually do not have the detailed information at the beginning but it is hidden inside the algorithm and the initial values. There are two ways to get out this hidden information:

- *Teleological algorithms* attempt to simulate the physical processes which result in the desired procedural output (Barr 1991).
- *Ontogenetic algorithms* attempt to duplicate the end result of a physical process without emulating the intermediate steps (Ebert et al. 2002).

Obviously, teleological algorithms – such as L-systems – have the benefit that their parameters can easily be tweaked to create new, emergent results that maintain the original design intent. This, however, comes at the cost of extra processing time. Ontogenetic algorithms – such as the terrain generation methods – are faster in achieving the result, but require much more fine-tuning and are not so robust to parameter variations.

In the end, what matters is how the player perceives the procedurally generated content. Realism might not be the only factor but – as always – ensuring playability remains the main concern.

Exercises

4-1 What possible drawbacks does procedural generation have? How does it affect the game design process?

4-2 In Algorithm 4.3 the routine UNBALANCED-NEIGHBOUR favours the neighbours in the order east, west, south and north. Randomize the scanning order of the neighbourhood.

4-3 The midpoint displacement method limits the size of the terrain to $n \times n$, where $n = 2^k + 1$ when $k \geq 0$. How we can use it to generate arbitrary sized terrains?

4-4 In Algorithm 4.6 the 'middle horizontal' and 'middle vertical' double loops have similar loop indices (the ranges and the initial values differ only slightly). Collapse these loops together by introducing two extra loops with range $i = 0, \ldots, (c - 1)$. Then collapse these two extra loops to include the 'borders' loop. Implement these two variants and compare their running times.

   The 'centres' double loop generates every index pair in the matrix H. If the positions $H_{i,j}$ and $H_{j,i}$ are updated together and the diagonal of H is traversed separately, the range of the inner loop of 'centres' can be cut to $j = 0, \ldots, i - 1$. Also, the diagonal loop can be embedded into the 'borders' loop. Implement this third variant (with great care). Are these optimizations worth the effort? Continue this code tweaking until it becomes code pessimization. After that, give the fastest variant to your friends and let them ponder what it does.

4-5 The difference between a labyrinth and a maze is that a labyrinth has only one way through whereas a maze offer a choice of paths. If there is only one path in a labyrinth, how can you get lost in it? Where can you use labyrinths in a computer game?

4-6 What happens if you add portals to a maze? A portal allows the player to jump from one cell to another even if they are not connected or even if there is a wall between them. From the player's perspective, what do portals add to the challenge of a maze?

4-7 Algorithm 4.7 creates a depth-first maze iteratively. Rewrite the algorithm to use recursion instead.

4-8 What if you were to use breadth-first search to create a maze. What kind of mazes it would create and why they would not be useful?

4-9 In the graph-based maze algorithms, only a graph is given as parameter. Why it is not necessary to give any entry nor exit vertices?

4-10 The maze algorithms presented do not produce cycles. Modify the algorithms so that mazes have cycles. Consider various ways to control the distribution of the walls punctured with holes in the mazes.

4-11 What is the benefit of using stochastic L-systems in procedural generation?

4-12 Implement an L-system using brackets and re-create Figure 4.10. Make changes in the production rules governing the outcome and observe the results. How much pre-thought is required in creating natural looking plants?

4-13 Is the list of criteria for city generation techniques in Section 4.3.2 sufficient? How would you prioritize the criteria?

4-14 Take a terrain generated with a method from Section 4.1 and apply one of the road patterns illustrated in Figure 4.11 to it. You can also use an influence map (see Section 9.3) as a starting point.

4-15 In 1984 David Braben and Ian Bell released a computer game on interstellar trading. In addition to the trading system and three-dimensional space simulation, they managed to fit eight galaxies filled with hundreds of stars, each with unique characteristics, into the 32 kB memory of a BBC Micro computer. The game is called *Elite*, and it uses procedural generation quite cleverly to compress the whole game world.

Algorithm 4.11 presents the name generation algorithm used in *Elite*. Study how it works, when we call it with the original hexadecimal parameter values for the first galaxy. (Hint: The eighth name in the sequence should be Lave, where the game begins.)

Algorithm 4.11 Name generation of *Elite*.

ELITE-NAMES(D, w_0, w_1, w_2, m)
   in: digram sequence D; seed values $w_0, w_1, w_2 \in \mathbb{B}^{16}$; amount of generated
        names m
  out: sequence of names P
1: $|P| \leftarrow m$
2: **for** $i \leftarrow 0 \ldots m$ **do**
3:    $\ell \leftarrow w_0 \sqcap 0040_{16} \neq 0$ $\triangleright$ Is bit 6 set?
4:    $R \leftarrow \langle\,\rangle$
5:    **for** $n = 0 \ldots 3$ **do**
6:      $q \leftarrow (w_2 \gg 8) \sqcap 001F_{16}$
7:      **if** $(D_q \neq \text{NIL and } (n < 3 \text{ or } \ell))$ **then**
8:        $R \leftarrow R \parallel D_q$
9:      **end if**
10:     $t \leftarrow (w_0 + w_1 + w_2) \textbf{ mod } 10000_{16}$
11:     $w_0 \leftarrow w_1; w_1 \leftarrow w_2; w_2 \leftarrow t$
12:    **end for**
13:    $P_m \leftarrow R$
14: **end for**
15: **return** P

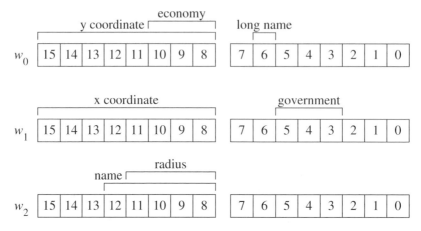

Figure 4.15 Generation of numbers in *Elite*.

$$D = \{\text{NIL, LE, XE, GE, ZA, CE, BI, SO, US, ES, AR, MA, IN, DI, RE, A,}$$
$$\text{ER, AT, EN, BE, RA, LA, VE, TI, ED, OR, QU, AN, TE, IS, RI, ON}\}$$
$$w_0 = \text{5A4A}_{16}$$
$$w_1 = \text{0248}_{16}$$
$$w_2 = \text{B753}_{16}$$
$$m = 255$$

The generation uses a Pisano period (i.e. Fibonacci numbers taken modulo 10000_{16}) to generate the values. In addition to generating its name, the values are used to generate different attributes of the planet such as its coordinates, radius, economy and government type (see Figure 4.15).

4-16 Random numbers can be used to create names. Instead of creating random strings of characters, names usually follow certain rules. Select a set of real-world names (e.g. from J.R.R. Tolkien's world or from an atlas) and devise a set of rules that they follow. Design and implement a method that creates new names based on the set of rules and random numbers.

4-17 The starmap generation of Algorithm 4.10 creates a static galaxy. How would you implement a dynamic galaxy where every planet orbits around its star and rotates around its axis (i.e. at a given global startime the planet has a position and orientation)? What if we have an even more dynamic galaxy, where existing heavenly bodies can die and new ones can be born?

5

Tournaments

The seven brothers of Jukola – Juhani, Tuomas, Aapo, Simeoni, Timo, Lauri and Eero – have decided to find out who is best at the game of Kyykkä. To do this the brothers need a series of matches, a *tournament*, and have to set down the rules for the form of the tournament (see Figure 5.1). They can form a scoring tournament, where everybody has one match against everybody else, in total 21 matches. To determine their relative order, a ranking, the brothers can agree to aggregate the match outcomes together by awarding two points to the winner and no points for the loser of a match, or one point each if the result is even and the match is a tie. When all the matches have been played, the brother with the most points will be the champion.

Another possibility is that they organize the event as a cup (or single elimination) tournament of three rounds and six matches, where the loser of each match (ties are resolved by arm-wrestling) is dropped from the competition, until there is only one contestant left. Apart from the champion, the rankings of the other players are not so obvious. Also, if the number of contestants is not a power of 2, the incomplete pairing has to be handled fairly in the first round. Should the brothers have a ranking from the last year's tournament, the pairing can be organized so that the best-ranked players can meet only at the later stages of the tournament.

The brothers can settle the championship with a hill-climbing tournament, where the reigning champion from the previous year's tournament has to defend his title in a series of six matches. If he loses a match, the winner becomes the new reigning champion and continues the series. The winner of the last match is crowned the champion of the whole tournament. Obviously, the previous year's champion has the hard task of maintaining the title, because that requires six consecutive wins, whereas the last man in line can become champion by winning just one match.

Although the application area of tournament algorithms seems to be confined to sports games only, they provide us with a general approach to determining a partial order between the participants and, therefore, we can apply them to a much wider range of problems. The (possibly incomplete) ranking information can be used, for instance, in game balancing (e.g. testing synthetic players by putting them in a duel, or adjusting point award schemes), in heuristic search (e.g. selecting suboptimal candidates for a genetic algorithm or an evolving system), in group behaviour (e.g. modelling the pecking order in a flock), and in learning player characteristics (e.g. managing overall history knowledge about strengths and weaknesses).

Algorithms and Networking for Computer Games, Second Edition. Jouni Smed and Harri Hakonen.
© 2017 John Wiley & Sons Ltd. Published 2017 by John Wiley & Sons Ltd.

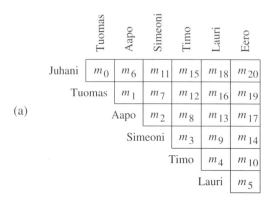

(a)

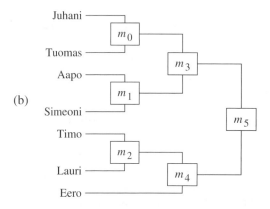

(b)

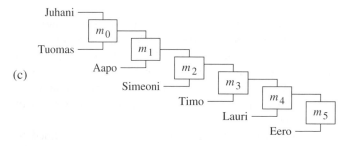

(c)

Figure 5.1 Tournaments for the seven brothers. (a) In a scoring tournament, everybody has one match against everybody else. (b) In an elimination tournament (or a cup), the players are paired and only the winners get to the next round. (c) In a hill-climbing tournament, the reigning champion defends the title against players who have not yet had the possibility of becoming the champion.

Formally put, a tournament is a competition where the players have one-on-one matches to resolve their relative fitnesses. Here, 'player' is a general term and can refer to an individual or a team. The result of a tournament is an ordering of the players' relative fitnesses. This information is often simplified into a *ranking* of the players, where the players are assigned a ranking number, and the smaller the rank, the better the player.

Ranking can also be partial, which means that only some of the players can be ordered in comparison to the others. Even in these incomplete rankings, the result usually includes the player with the smallest rank, the *champion*, who is sometimes called – especially by scholars – the king.

Planning and organizing a tournament in the real world involves many constraints concerning costs, venue bookings, the time spent travelling to the tournament sites, risk management, and other limited resources (Smith et al. 2006). In this chapter we omit these practical concerns and limit our focus to scheduling the players of a tournament into matches of two players, which is called *pairing*.

As we saw earlier with the seven brothers' tournament, depending on how one match relates to the other matches, tournaments can be divided into three main categories:

- In a *rank adjustment tournament* (i.e. challenge or extended tournament), a match is a challenge for a rank exchange and is quite independent of the other challenges.
- In an *elimination tournament*, the purpose of a match is to eliminate one player from the upcoming matches.
- In a *scoring tournament*, a player gets a reward if she succeeds in a match.

This categorization, however, is not strict, because these characterizing features are often combined together. For example, a season-wide ranking list can be used for assigning players either to preliminary qualifying rounds (i.e. elimination matches) or directly into the actual point-awarding matches. For an analysis of the predictive power of the tournament formats, see Ryvkin and Ortmann (2008).

But before getting into the details of these tournaments, a few words about the notation we use in this chapter. Let us denote the set of n players in a tournament by P. We can label these players with indices $p_0, p_1, \ldots, p_{n-1}$, and player p_i can be referred to simply as player i. If player i has a rank, we denote it by $rank(i)$, and the ranks are enumerated consecutively starting from 0. The set of players having the same rank r is denoted with $rankeds(P, r)$, or $rankeds(r)$ if the set of players is clear from the context. If this set is a singleton (i.e. $rankeds(P, r) = \{p\}$), we simply use the notation $ranked(r)$ to refer to p directly. A match (or a duel) between players i and j, denoted with $match(i, j)$, has the outcomes i, j or TIE for the cases where i wins, j wins, or there is no winner or loser, respectively. The *match* function itself does not change the ranks of the players, because the ranking rules are specific to the tournament. Furthermore, we assume that winning is transitive: if player q wins against player r and p wins against q, then by our definition p also wins against r. This indirect winning allows us to have different kinds of matching structures, especially in elimination tournaments.

5.1 Rank Adjustment Tournaments

In a rank adjustment tournament, we have a set of players, who already have a ranking, and we want to organize a tournament, where this ranking is adjusted according to the match outcomes. Since the ranking can be updated immediately after each match, this kind of tournament suits ongoing (i.e. seasonless) competitions, and the player pairings do not have to be coordinated in any specific way. A round in a rank adjustment tournament can have $0, 1, \ldots, \lfloor n/2 \rfloor$ independent matches at the same time. This makes it possible to insert or remove a tournament player without ruining the intuitiveness of the rank order.

We can set up the initial ranking of the players in P by using a ranking structure S (see Algorithm 5.1). The ranking structure S has size $m = |S|$, which defines the number of different ranks, $0, 1, \ldots, m - 1$. The value S_i indicates how many players have the same rank i in the tournament. In other words, in a proper ranking $S_i = |rankeds(i)|$.

Algorithm 5.1 Constructing initial ranking in rank adjustment tournaments.

INITIAL-RANK-ADJUSTMENT(P, S)

    in: set P of n unranked players in the tournament; sequence S of m non-negative integers in which S_i defines the number of players that have the same rank i
           ($\sum_{i=0}^{m-1} S_i = n$)

    out: set R of ranked players having the ranking structure S

    local: match sequences M and M' of players

    1: $R \leftarrow$ **copy** P
    2: $M \leftarrow enumeration(R)$ $\triangleright$ Order R to M in some way.
    3: **for** $i \leftarrow 0 \ldots (S_0 - 1)$ **do**
    4:   $rank(M_i) \leftarrow 0$ $\triangleright$ Declare M_i an initial champion.
    5: **end for**
    6: $c \leftarrow S_0$
    7: **for** $r \leftarrow 1 \ldots (m - 1)$ **do**
    8:   $W \leftarrow rankeds(R, r - 1)$ $\triangleright$ The runners-up.
    9:   $M' \leftarrow enumeration(W)$
  10:   **for** $i \leftarrow 0 \ldots (S_r - 1)$ **do**
  11:     $rank(M_{c+i}) \leftarrow r$
  12:     $j \leftarrow i$ **mod** $|M'|$
  13:     **if** $rank(M'_j) \neq r$ **then**
  14:       $R \leftarrow$ LADDER-MATCH(R, M'_j, M_{c+i}) $\triangleright$ Update ranks of M'_j and M_{c+i}.
  15:     **end if**
  16:   **end for**
  17:   $c \leftarrow c + S_r$
  18: **end for**
  19: **return** R

Algorithm 5.1 uses routine *enumeration* to define some order on the given set, which can be, for example, a random order generated by function SHUFFLE described in Algorithm 2.6. The algorithm also uses LADDER-MATCH described in Algorithm 5.2 to join the next subset of players into an existing rank structure (i.e. among the least successful players ranked so far). A new player exchanges rank with an already ranked opponent only if she wins the match. Because Algorithm 5.1 lets the players compete for the initial ranking, it is one of the simplest fair initialization methods. If fairness is unnecessary,

Algorithm 5.2 Match in a ladder tournament.

LADDER-MATCH(P, p, q)

    in: set P of players in the ladder structure; players p and q ($p, q \in P \land 1 \leq rank(q) - rank(p) \leq 2$)

   out: set R of players after p and q have had a match

1: $m \leftarrow match(p, q)$
2: **if** $m =$ TIE **or** $m = p$ **then**   ▷ Nothing changes.
3:    **return** P
4: **else**   ▷ Rank exchange.
5:    $R \leftarrow P \setminus \{p, q\}$
6:    $p' \leftarrow$ **copy** p ; $q' \leftarrow$ **copy** q
7:    $rank(p') \leftarrow rank(q)$
8:    $rank(q') \leftarrow rank(p)$
9:    **return** $R \cup \{p', q'\}$
10: **end if**

the body of the algorithm becomes even simpler. For example, we can assign each player a random rank from structure S:

1: $R \leftarrow$ SHUFFLE(P)
2: $c \leftarrow 0$
3: **for** $r \leftarrow 0 \ldots (m - 1)$ **do**
4:    **for** $i \leftarrow 0 \ldots (S_r - 1)$ **do**
5:     $rank(R_{c+i}) \leftarrow r$
6:    **end for**
7:    $c \leftarrow c + S_r$
8: **end for**
9: **return** R

Ladder tournaments

In a ladder tournament, a player can improve her rank by winning against another player who is ranked higher. A general ladder tournament orders the players P into a single chain according to their ranks: the first player in the chain, $ranked(0)$, is the champion, player $ranked(1)$ is the first runner-up, and so forth. Algorithm 5.2 describes the re-ranking rule LADDER-MATCH for a given pair of players. A match can be arranged only between players whose ranks differ by one or two. Also, the possible rank exchange affects only the two players participating in the match. We can relax these two properties to allow less localized changes in the tournament ranking: the rank difference can be greater, or when a better-ranked player p loses to a worse-ranked player q, it also affects the ranks between them (i.e. the players $ranked(rank(p))$, $ranked(rank(p) + 1)$, ..., $ranked(rank(q))$). To realize this generalized re-ranking we can use, for example, list update techniques (Albers and Mitzenmacher 1998; Bachrach and El-Yaniv 1997).

Hill-climbing tournament

A hill-climbing tournament – which is sometimes called a top-of-the-mountain tournament or a last man standing tournament – is a special ladder tournament, where the reigning champion defends the title against challengers. The tournament has $n - 1$ rounds each having one match as described in Algorithm 5.3, which sequences the players and arranges a match between the reigning champion and the next player who has not yet participated. In other words, the matches obey the following invariant: after round $i = 0, \ldots, (n - 1) - 1$ we know that the player $ranked((n - 1) - i - 1)$ has won (directly or indirectly) against the players with ranks less than or equal to $(n - 1) - i$. This reigning champion can be seen as a 'hill climber' among the other players.

Algorithm 5.3 Hill climbing tournament.

HILL-CLIMBING-TOURNAMENT(P)
   in: set P of n unranked players $(1 \leq n)$
   out: set R of ranked players which has a champion $ranked(R, 0)$
   local: ranking structure S; reigning champion c
   1: $S \leftarrow \langle 1, 1, \ldots, 1 \rangle$ ▷ Initialize n values.
   2: $R \leftarrow$ INITIAL-RANK-ADJUSTMENT(P, S)
   3: $c \leftarrow ranked(R, n - 1)$ ▷ The tailender in R.
   4: **for** $r' \leftarrow 0 \ldots (n - 2)$ **do**
   5:    $r \leftarrow (n - 2) - r'$ ▷ For each rank from the bottom to the top.
   6:    $R \leftarrow$ LADDER-MATCH($R, ranked(R, r), c$)
   7:    $c \leftarrow ranked(R, r)$
   8: **end for**
   9: **return** R

Algorithm 5.3 assumes that the players are unranked and the initial order is generated using Algorithm 5.1. However, there are other ways to arrange the players into the match sequence. For example, we can produce a uniformly distributed random permutation SHUFFLE($\langle 0, 1, \ldots, n - 1 \rangle$) and use it for the initial ranks. Alternatively, the initial ranking can be based on ranks from previous competitions. If the players are then arranged in a descending rank order, the reigning champion has only one match, the last one, whereas the bottom-ranked player has to win against all the other players to clear her way to the championship match. Conversely, an ascending rank order requires that the reigning champion wins all $(n - 1)$ matches to keep the title. In short, we can set the reactivity of the championship race by initialization: descending order is conservative, random order is democratic, and ascending order is challenging.

Pyramid tournaments

A general pyramid tournament relaxes the ladder tournament by allowing players to share the same rank. Assume that the ranks are $0, \ldots, m - 1$ and $m \leq n = |P|$. The pyramid ranking usually has a structure where

$$1 = |rankeds(0)| < |rankeds(1)| < \ldots < |rankeds(m - 1)|$$

and

$$\sum_{i=0}^{m-1} |rankeds(i)| = n.$$

In this case, there is only one champion, and the set of ranked players grows as the rank index increases. Algorithm 5.4 defines re-ranking rule PYRAMID-MATCH for two players participating in a match. There are two kind of matches. In a peer match both players have the same rank, and the winner gets the status *peerWinner*. A rank challenge match requires that the challenger has the *peerWinner* status; otherwise, the match is similar to LADDER-MATCH in Algorithm 5.2, with the difference that the rank difference is exactly one.

Algorithm 5.4 Match in a pyramid tournament.

PYRAMID-MATCH(P, p, q)
    in: set P of players in the pyramid structure; players p and q ($p, q \in P \wedge$
            $((rank(p) = rank(q) \wedge \neg peerWinner(q)) \vee (rank(p) = rank(q) - 1 \wedge$
            $peerWinner(q))))$
    out: set R of players after p and q have had a match
    local: match outcome m

  1: $R \leftarrow P \setminus \{p, q\}$
  2: $m \leftarrow match(p, q)$
  3: **if** $rank(p) = rank(q)$ **then**   ▷ Peer match.
  4:   **if** ($m = p$ **and not** $peerWinner(p)$) **or**
              (($m = q$ **or** $m = $ TIE) **and** $peerWinner(p)$) **then**
  5:     $p' \leftarrow$ **copy** p
  6:     $peerWinner(p') \leftarrow (m = p)$
  7:   **else**
  8:     $p' \leftarrow p$
  9:   **end if**
 10:   **if** $m = q$ **then**
 11:     $q' \leftarrow$ **copy** q
 12:     $peerWinner(q') \leftarrow$ TRUE
 13:   **else**
 14:     $q' \leftarrow q$
 15:   **end if**
 16:   **return** $R \cup \{p', q'\}$
 17: **else**   ▷ Rank challenge match.
 18:   $q' \leftarrow$ **copy** q
 19:   $peerWinner(q') \leftarrow$ FALSE
 20:   **if** $m = p$ **or** $m = $ TIE **then**   ▷ No rank changes.
 21:     **return** $R \cup \{p, q'\}$
 22:   **else**   ▷ Rank exchange.
 23:     $p' \leftarrow$ **copy** p
 24:     $peerWinner(p') \leftarrow$ FALSE
 25:     $rank(p') \leftarrow rank(q)$
 26:     $rank(q') \leftarrow rank(p)$
 27:     **return** $R \cup \{p', q'\}$
 28:   **end if**
 29: **end if**

King-of-the-hill tournament

A king-of-the-hill tournament specializes the general pyramid tournament in the same way as the hill-climbing tournament specializes the general ladder tournament. Assume that the m-level pyramid has the form $|rankeds(i)| = 2^i$ for all $i \in [0, m-1]$, and $m \leq n$. This means that the number of player pairings at level $i + 1$ is equal to the number of players at the level i. Algorithm 5.5 describes how the matches are organized into $2(m-1)$ rounds. There are two rounds of matches for each pyramid level, except for the champion level 0. At level $(i + 1)$, 2^i matches are held to find the peer winners. Then these winners face the players at level i in a rank challenge match.

Algorithm 5.5 King of the hill tournament.

KING-OF-THE-HILL-TOURNAMENT(P)
    in: set P of n unranked players $(1 \leq n \wedge (n + 1)$ is a power of two)
    out: set R of ranked players which has a champion $ranked(R, 0)$
    constant: number of pyramid levels m $(m = \lg(n + 1))$
    local: ranking structure S; match sequences M and M' of players
  1: $S \leftarrow \langle 2^0, 2^1, 2^2, \ldots, 2^{m-1} \rangle$ ▷ Initialize m values.
  2: $R \leftarrow$ INITIAL-RANK-ADJUSTMENT(P, S)
  3: **for** $r' \leftarrow 1 \ldots (m-1)$ **do**
  4:   $r \leftarrow (m-1) - (r' - 1)$ ▷ From the bottom to the first runner-up.
  5:   $M \leftarrow enumeration(rankeds(R, r))$ ▷ Arrange the set into an order.
  6:   $\ell \leftarrow |M|$
  7:   **for** $i \leftarrow 0 \ldots (\ell/2 - 1)$ **do**   ▷ Determine the peer winners.
  8:     $peerWinner(M_{2i}) \leftarrow$ FALSE
  9:     $peerWinner(M_{2i+1}) \leftarrow$ FALSE
 10:     $R \leftarrow$ PYRAMID-MATCH(R, M_{2i}, M_{2i+1})
 11:   **end for**
 12:   $M \leftarrow$ all peer winner players in $rankeds(R, r)$
 13:   $M' \leftarrow enumeration(rankeds(R, r - 1))$ ▷ Arrange the set into an order.
 14:   **for** $i \leftarrow 0 \ldots (\ell/2 - 1)$ **do**   ▷ Determine the rank exchanges.
 15:     $R \leftarrow$ PYRAMID-MATCH(R, M'_i, M_i)
 16:   **end for**
 17: **end for**
 18: **return** R

5.2 Elimination Tournaments

In an elimination tournament (or a knockout tournament) the loser of a match is eliminated from the tournament and the winner continues to the next round. This means that the match cannot end in a tie but must always have a winner and a loser, which can be decided by an extra tiebreak competition such as overtime play and penalty kicks in football, or a re-spotted black ball in snooker. Also, multiple matches can be combined into a best-of-m match series (when m is odd), where the winner is the first one to win $(m + 1)/2$ matches.

Random selection tournament

The simplest elimination tournament is the random selection tournament, where a randomly selected player is declared champion without any matches being played. The random selection is drawn from a distribution that can be given as a weight sequence for Algorithm 5.6 (for details on assigning weight sequences, see Section 2.2).

Algorithm 5.6 Random selection tournament.

RANDOM-SELECTION-TOURNAMENT(P, W)
in: sequence P of n unranked players ($1 \leq n$); sequence W of player weights
          ($|W| = n \wedge W_i \in \mathbb{N}$ for $i = 0, \ldots, n-1 \wedge 1 \leq \sum_{k=0}^{n-1} W_k$)
out: set R of ranked players which has a champion $ranked(R, 0)$ and the rest of the
          players have rank 1
1: $R \leftarrow$ **copy** P
2: $k \leftarrow$ RANDOM-FROM-WEIGHTS(W)
3: $c \leftarrow R_k$
4: $rank(c) \leftarrow 0$
5: **for all** $p \in (R \setminus \{c\})$ **do**
6:   $rank(p) \leftarrow 1$
7: **end for**
8: **return** R

Random pairing tournament

In a random pairing tournament the champion is decided by randomly selecting one of the first round winners. This is implemented in Algorithm 5.7, which uses Algorithm 5.6 for random drawing.

Algorithm 5.7 Random pairing tournament.

RANDOM-PAIRING-TOURNAMENT(P)
in: set P of n unranked players ($1 \leq n$)
out: set R of ranked players which has a champion $ranked(R, 0)$ and the rest of the
          players have a rank 1
local: match sequence M of players
1: $W \leftarrow \langle 0, 0, \ldots, 0 \rangle$ ▷ Initialize n values.
2: $M \leftarrow enumeration(P)$ ▷ Order P to M in some way.
3: **for** $i \leftarrow 0 \ldots ((n \text{ div } 2) - 1)$ **do**
4:   $m \leftarrow match(M_{2i}, M_{2i+1})$
5:   $W_m \leftarrow 1$ ▷ Set the winner's weight to 1.
6: **end for**
7: $R \leftarrow$ RANDOM-SELECTION-TOURNAMENT(M, W)
8: **return** R

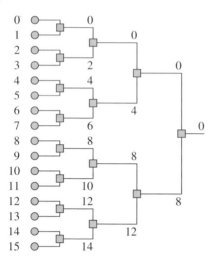

Figure 5.2 A bracket for an elimination tournament with 16 players (circles), which has 15 matches (squares).

Single elimination tournament

A single elimination tournament – which is perhaps better known as a *cup tournament* – resembles a complete binary tree: leaf nodes represent the players and the internal nodes represent the matches. The winner of a match proceeds to the parent of the corresponding internal node (i.e. to the next match). The organization of the matches can be visualized with a diagram called a *bracket*, which illustrated in Figure 5.2. By observing the binary tree structure we have the following properties:

- For $n = 2^x$ players, where $x = 0, 1, \ldots$, we have $n - 1$ matches organized into $\lg n = x$ rounds.
- If the rounds are indexed from 0, then round i has $2^{x-1-i} = n/2^{i+1}$ matches.
- After each round the number of participants remaining is halved.

Round $x - 3$, which has four matches, is called the *quarter-final*, round $x - 2$ with two matches is the *semifinal*, and the last round $x - 1$ having only one match is the *final*.

If the number of players n is not a power of 2, we cannot pair the players in every round. This means that some players may proceed to the next round without a match, and such a player is said to receive a *bye*. If we handle the byes by adding them as virtual players that automatically lose their matches, we can increase n to the nearest higher power of 2 by including $2^{\lceil \lg n \rceil} - n$ byes in the tournament bracket.

Due to the hierarchical organization of matches, the future player pairings depend strongly on the initial pairings. For instance, if the players are assigned to the matches as in Figure 5.2, it is not possible to have both *match*(0, 2) and *match*(1, 3). This inherent property of the single elimination tournament becomes a problem, if we have some *a priori* knowledge about the player strengths and expect that it is possible for all of the t top-ranked players to reach round $\lg (n/t)$. To analyse this reachability criterion we must first consider how initial pairing is done.

The process of assigning the players into the initial match pairs is called *seeding* (Groh et al. 2012). We can formulate it as follows. Given a bracket with consecutively indexed placeholders for the n players, the seeding is an arrangement of player indices $\{0, 1, \ldots, n-1\}$ into a sequence R so that player R_i is put into the bracket position i. The bracket positions define the first round matches to be $match(R_{2i}, R_{2i+1})$ for $i \in [0, n/2 - 1]$. Now we can analyse the reachability criterion by setting the player index to be equal to the player's rank.

When the pre-tournament ranking cannot be estimated, we can use a random seeding. Hence, the probability that the two best players are able to reach the final is $\frac{1}{2} \cdot \frac{n}{n-1}$. A simple implementation for RANDOM-SEEDING(n) is

1: **return** SHUFFLE($\langle 0, 1, \ldots, n-1 \rangle$)

Table 5.1 presents the three most commonly used deterministic seedings for 16 player ranks, which fulfil the reachability criterion (i.e. the top-ranked players have the best possibilities of proceeding to the next round). The first column contains the place index in the bracket (as a decimal number and a binary radix). The *standard seeding* is bijective (i.e. $S_{S_i} = i$) and can be generated with Algorithm 5.8. In the *ordered standard seeding*, the mapping sequence of the standard seeding is sorted such that it is in ascending order as far as possible without violating the reachability criterion. Quite surprisingly, Algorithm 5.9 produces this sequence with a simple control flow. Both of these standard seedings reward past success by pairing the top-ranked players with the bottom-ranked ones: the initial matches are $match(ranked(i), ranked(n-1-i))$ for $i \in [0, n/2 - 1]$. If this is considered to be unfair play, Algorithm 5.10 provides a method for *equitable seeding*, where each initial match has the same rank difference $n/2$. Bit enthusiasts may appreciate the observation that this sequence can be generated easily by reversing the bits of the placeholder indices – perhaps this property could be called 'bitectivity'.

Table 5.1 Three common deterministic seeding types for an elimination tournament of 16 players. Instead of player indices the seedings are defined by predetermined ranks.

Placeholder index	Standard	Ordered standard	Equitable
0 (0000)	0	0	0 (0000)
1 (0001)	15	15	8 (1000)
2 (0010)	8	7	4 (0100)
3 (0011)	7	8	12 (1100)
4 (0100)	4	3	2 (0010)
5 (0101)	11	12	10 (1010)
6 (0110)	12	4	6 (0110)
7 (0111)	3	11	14 (1110)
8 (1000)	2	1	1 (0001)
9 (1001)	13	14	9 (1001)
10 (1010)	10	6	5 (0101)
11 (1011)	5	9	13 (1101)
12 (1100)	6	2	3 (0011)
13 (1101)	9	13	11 (1011)
14 (1110)	14	5	7 (0111)
15 (1111)	1	10	15 (1111)

Algorithm 5.8 Standard seeding for an elimination bracket.

STANDARD-SEEDING(n)

   in: number of players n ($2 \leq n \wedge n$ is a power of 2)

   out: sequence R of n ranks indicating the initial match pairings between players
         $ranked(R_{2i})$ and $ranked(R_{2i+1})$, when $i = 0, \ldots, n/2 - 1$

  1: $R \leftarrow \langle 0, -1, -1, \ldots, -1 \rangle$ ▷ Initialize n values.

  2: **return** INTERNAL-STANDARD-SEEDING($R, 2, 0, n - 1$)

INTERNAL-STANDARD-SEEDING(R, n', α, ω)

   in: sequence R of n ranks; number of players n' at the current bracket level ($1 \leq n' \wedge n'$ is a power of 2); interval $[\alpha, \omega]$ of R under construction ($0 \leq \alpha \leq \omega < |R|$)

   out: sequence of ranks R

  1: **if** $\alpha = \omega$ **then return** R **end if**

  2: **if** $R_\alpha = -1$ **then**

  3:   $R_\alpha \leftarrow (n' - 1) - R_\omega$

  4: **else**

  5:   $R_\omega \leftarrow (n' - 1) - R_\alpha$

  6: **end if**

  7: $\mu \leftarrow (\omega - \alpha - 1)/2$

  8: $R \leftarrow$ INTERNAL-STANDARD-SEEDING($R, 2 \cdot n', \alpha, \alpha + \mu$)

  9: $R \leftarrow$ INTERNAL-STANDARD-SEEDING($R, 2 \cdot n', \alpha + \mu + 1, \omega$)

 10: **return** R

Algorithm 5.9 Ordered standard seeding for an elimination bracket.

ORDERED-STANDARD-SEEDING(n)

   in: number of players n ($2 \leq n \wedge n$ is a power of 2)

   out: sequence R of n ranks indicating the initial match pairings between players
         $ranked(R_{2i})$ and $ranked(R_{2i+1})$, when $i = 0, \ldots, n/2 - 1$

  1: $|R| \leftarrow n$ ▷ Reserve space for n integers.

  2: $R_0 \leftarrow 0$

  3: **return** INTERNAL-ORDERED-STANDARD-SEEDING($R, 2, 0, n - 1$)

INTERNAL-ORDERED-STANDARD-SEEDING(R, n', α, ω)

   in: sequence R of n ranks; number of players n' at current bracket level ($1 \leq n' \wedge n'$ is a power of 2); interval $[\alpha, \omega]$ of R under construction ($0 \leq \alpha \leq \omega < |R|$)

   out: sequence of ranks R

  1: **if** $\alpha = \omega$ **then return** R **end if**

  2: $\mu \leftarrow (\omega - \alpha - 1)/2$

  3: $R \leftarrow$ INTERNAL-ORDERED-STANDARD-SEEDING($R, 2 \cdot n', \alpha, \alpha + \mu$)

  4: $R_{\alpha+\mu+1} \leftarrow (n' - 1) - R_\alpha$

  5: $R \leftarrow$ INTERNAL-ORDERED-STANDARD-SEEDING($R, 2 \cdot n', \alpha + \mu + 1, \omega$)

  6: **return** R

Algorithm 5.10 Equitable seeding for an elimination bracket.

EQUITABLE-SEEDING(n)
  in: number of players n ($2 \leq n \wedge n$ is a power of 2)
  out: sequence R of n ranks indicating the initial match pairings between players
        $ranked(R_{2i})$ and $ranked(R_{2i+1})$, when $i = 0, \ldots, n/2 - 1$
  1: $w \leftarrow 1 + \lfloor \lg(n-1) \rfloor$ ▷ Bits required for the value $(n-1)$.
  2: $|R| \leftarrow n$ ▷ Reserve space for n integers.
  3: **for** $i \leftarrow 0 \ldots (n-1)$ **do**
  4:     $R_i \leftarrow$ BIT-REVERSE(i, w)
  5: **end for**
  6: **return** R

BIT-REVERSE(x, w)
  in: λ-bit integer value x with bit representation $b_{\lambda-1} \ldots b_1 b_0$; number of the lower-most bits w ($0 \leq w \leq \lambda$)
  out: integer value in which the w lowermost bits are reversal of the w lowermost
        bits in x
  1: **return** λ-bit integer value $0 \ldots 0 b_0 b_1 \ldots b_{w-1}$

The allocation of byes in the elimination bracket is another possible source of unfairness. There are two practical suggestions:

(i) The byes should have the bottom ranks (i.e. they are paired with the best players).
(ii) The byes should be restricted to the first round (i.e. the number of players in the second round is a power of 2).

While this seems sensible for both of the standard seedings, realizing it in the equitable seeding turns out to be different, because the $\ell = 2^{\lceil \lg n \rceil} - n$ byes should have ranks $n/2, \ldots, n/2 + \ell - 1$.

Let us return to the single elimination tournament, which is implemented in Algorithm 5.11. It assumes that the players P are already ranked, and the function call A-SEEDING produces a rank ordering, for example, by applying one of the four seeding algorithms described earlier. Although the players have initially unique ranks, the only outcome of the tournament is the champion. It is clear why the runners-up are hard to decide; for instance, the first runner-up has lost to the champion (not necessarily the final). To sort the runners-up we would have to organize a mini-tournament of $\lg n$ players before we know the silver medallist. Naturally, we can give the players a score for each match won, which is then used to adjust the already existing ranking, especially if there are many tournaments in a season.

In real-world sports games, a fair assessment of ranks for all players before the tournament can be too demanding a task. To compensate and to reduce the effect of seeding we can introduce a random element into the pairing. For example, if we are able to determine the best four players (regardless of their relative ranking), we can place them in

---

Algorithm 5.11 Single elimination tournament.

Single-Elimination-Tournament(P)

   in: sequence P of n ranked players ($1 \leq n \wedge n$ is a power of 2 $\wedge$ P is a permutation of $\langle 0, 1, \ldots, n-1 \rangle$)

   out: set R of ranked players which has a champion $ranked(R, 0)$ and the rest of the players have rank 1; attribute $wins(i)$ indicates the number of wins for player i

   local: sequence S of initial match indices

  1: $R \leftarrow$ **copy** P
  2: $S \leftarrow$ A-Seeding(n) $\triangleright$ Seeding as a rank order.
  3: $|M| \leftarrow n$ $\triangleright$ Reserve space for n players.
  4: **for** $i \leftarrow 0 \ldots (n-1)$ **do** $\triangleright$ Assign the initial order.
  5:   $M_i \leftarrow ranked(R, S_i)$ $\triangleright$ The player with rank S_i.
  6: **end for**
  7: **for** $r \leftarrow 0 \ldots ((\lg n) - 1)$ **do** $\triangleright$ For each round.
  8:   $|M'| \leftarrow n/2^{r+1}$ $\triangleright$ Reserve space for the winners.
  9:   **for** $i \leftarrow 0 \ldots (n/2^{r+1} - 1)$ **do** $\triangleright$ For each match.
10:     $M'_i \leftarrow match(M_{2i}, M_{2i+1})$
11:   **end for**
12:   **for all** $p \in (M \setminus M')$ **do** $\triangleright$ The runners-up.
13:     $rank(p) \leftarrow 1$
14:     $wins(p) \leftarrow r$
15:   **end for**
16:   $M \leftarrow M'$
17: **end for**
18: $p \leftarrow$ the single value in M
19: $rank(p) \leftarrow 0$ $\triangleright$ The champion.
20: $wins(p) \leftarrow \lg n$
21: **return** R

---

the sub-brackets of the tournament according to a deterministic seeding, after which the rest of the (unranked) players are seeded randomly to the whole bracket. Another possibility is to re-seed the players before each round, the rationale being that wins provide us with information on the players' current strength.

    When the players are equally matched (i.e. there is not much difference in their level of fitness), the single elimination tournament has the disadvantage that the match outcomes are susceptible to mistakes, relapses, accidents and other unpredictable mishaps. To compensate for this 'randomness' the players can of course have multiple matches (e.g. a best-of-m match series) but there are also variants of the elimination tournament that provide a more robust result. In a *double elimination tournament* the player is eliminated from the competition after lost two matches. The matches are organized into a winners' bracket and a losers' bracket (or a consolation bracket) – naturally there are specific rules for assigning a loser to the losers' bracket. The brackets are then used as in the single elimination tournament, and the winner of each bracket gets to the final.

5.3 Scoring Tournaments

Instead of adjusting the ranking directly, the ranks can be decided based on a scoring table. Points are awarded to the winner of a match, while the loser gets none, and in a tie the points are shared by both players. These scoring tournaments measure the overall fitness among the players better, and the matches are less dependent on one another. We can even arrange for the same pairs to have multiple matches during the season, which, in the long run, should make the ranking reflect the true fitness order of the players better. This, however, can present the problem of unimportant matches, which are expected to have no influence on the tournament outcome (Scarf and Shi 2008), or even dead rubbers that are completely meaningless.

Scoring can be included in any tournament type and provides an easy way to combine different tournament types into one, hybrid tournament. For example, in the preliminary matches the players can be grouped into 16 disjoint *pools* where they play three random pairing tournaments. Players receive one point for a win and half a point for a tie. If several players have the highest score in a pool, the pool champion is selected randomly. The preliminary champions are then seeded into an elimination tournament, which decides the champion of the whole tournament.

Let us begin with the *round robin tournament*, which is the basis for many scoring tournaments. The round robin tournament itself does not impose any specific scoring mechanism but describes how to organize the matches such that every player meets the other players exactly once with a minimum number of rounds. To describe the idea behind the algorithm we convert the match allocation to a graph problem.

An undirected graph $G = (V, E)$ with vertices V and edges E is called *complete* if every vertex is connected to another vertex by an edge and no vertex has a loop. In other words, for all $v \in V$ we have $|neighbourhood(v)| = |V| - 1 \wedge (v, v) \notin E$. A complete graph with n vertices is called a *clique* and is denoted by K_n. Without loss of generality, we can place the vertices on the perimeter of a circle so as to have a polygonal representation of the graph and enumerate the vertices clockwise as in Figure 5.3. Let us identify a vertex with its number. If we set a vertex to be a player and an edge to be a match, K_n represents all the match pairings in a round robin tournament for n players.

Figure 5.3 A clique graph representation of the matches in a round robin tournament with seven players.

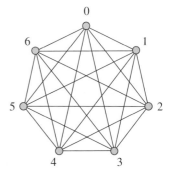

Because the players are allowed to participate in at most one match at a time, we still have to schedule the matches into the rounds. If n is odd, the edges E of K_n can be partitioned into $(n-1)/2$ disjoint sets. Let us define a perimeter distance π of the edge (p, q) as $\pi(p, q) = \min\{|p - q|, n - |p - q|\}$. If we define a subset of undirected edges with a perimeter distance i as

$$\Pi(V, i) = \{(p, q) \mid \pi(p, q) = i \wedge p, q \in V\}, \tag{5.1}$$

the edge set of K_n becomes a disjoint union

$$E = \bigcup_{i=1}^{(n-1)/2} \Pi(V, i), \tag{5.2}$$

where each $\Pi(V, i)$ has exactly n members. In other words, if n is odd, Equation (5.2) provides us with a convenient way to partition all the $n(n - 1)/2$ possible pairings into n rounds with $(n - 1)/2$ matches each. When assigning matches for a round, we select only the unused pairings with different perimeter distances. Because a player faces the other players exactly once and each player 'rests' for one match (i.e. has a bye for one round), this scheduling gives a solution with a minimum number of rounds.

We have some leeway when selecting the unused player pairings for a round. We can partition the sets $\Pi(V, i)$ into n rounds as illustrated in Figure 5.4. In round $r \in [0, n-1]$, the player with the index r is given a bye, and the matches for the round are

$$match((r + k) \bmod n, (r + n - k) \bmod n) \tag{5.3}$$

for $k \in [1, (n - 1)/2]$ (note that k is just a match enumeration, not a perimeter length). As Figure 5.4 illustrates, each edge belongs to one round only and every edge gets selected to some round. Table 5.2 lists the whole schedule round by round for seven players. The 'resting' column shows the player with the bye, and, as already mentioned, it equals the round index.

The observant reader might already have noticed that the presented method does not work at all, if the number of players is even. Fortunately, we can easily transform the

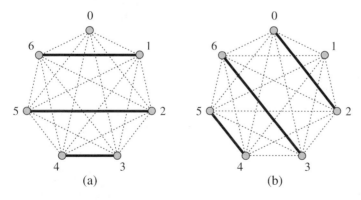

Figure 5.4 A partition of the matches into two rounds of a round robin tournaments with seven players: (a) the matches for the initial round; (b) the matches for the next round.

Table 5.2 A straightforward organization of matches in a round robin tournament with seven players.

Round	Matches			Resting
0	1 − 6	2 − 5	3 − 4	0
1	2 − 0	3 − 6	4 − 5	1
2	3 − 1	4 − 0	5 − 6	2
3	4 − 2	5 − 1	6 − 0	3
4	5 − 3	6 − 2	0 − 1	4
5	6 − 4	0 − 3	1 − 2	5
6	0 − 5	1 − 4	2 − 3	6

scheduling problem with an even n to a problem with an odd n. If n is even, we divide the set of players $P = \{p_0, p_1, \ldots, p_{n-1}\}$ into two sets

$$P = S \cup P' \tag{5.4}$$

where S is a singleton and set P' equals $P \setminus S$. We can always let $S = \{p_{n-1}\}$. Because set P' has an odd number of players, Equation (5.3) schedules their matches. The resting player of P' is then paired with the player in S. For example, to determine the matches for eight players, we pair the eighth player p_7 with the resting player in Table 5.2.

Algorithm 5.12 returns the matches in a round robin tournament, when the round index and the number of players is given. The resulting sequence R consists of $\lfloor n/2 \rfloor$ pairs of player indices that define the matches. If n is odd, the sequence also includes an extra entry R_{n-1} for the resting player.

Algorithm 5.12 Straightforward pairings for a round robin tournament.

SIMPLE-ROUND-ROBIN-PAIRINGS(r, n)
   in: round index r ($0 \le r \le 2 \cdot \lfloor (n-1)/2 \rfloor$); number of players n ($1 \le n$)
   out: sequence R of n player indices indicating the match pairings between players
             R_{2i} and R_{2i+1}, when $i = 0, \ldots, \lfloor n/2 \rfloor - 1$; if n is odd, R_{n-1} indicates the resting
             player
  1: $|R| \leftarrow n$ ▷ Reserve space for n player indices.
  2: $R_{n-1} \leftarrow r$ ▷ The resting player when n is odd.
  3: $n' \leftarrow n$
  4: **if** n is even **then**
  5:    $R_{(n-1)-1} \leftarrow n - 1$ ▷ The player in the singleton set.
  6:    $n' \leftarrow n - 1$ ▷ Transform the problem to 'n is odd'.
  7: **end if**
  8: **for** $k \leftarrow 1 \ldots ((n' - 1)/2)$ **do**
  9:    $i \leftarrow 2(k - 1)$
10:    $R_i \leftarrow (r + k) \bmod n'$
11:    $R_{i+1} \leftarrow (r + n' - k) \bmod n'$
12: **end for**
13: **return** R

Round	Matches			Resting	Modulo
0	1 − 6	2 − 5	3 − 4	0	0
1	5 − 3	6 − 2	0 − 1	4	1
2	2 − 0	3 − 6	4 − 5	1	2
3	6 − 4	0 − 3	1 − 2	5	3
4	3 − 1	4 − 0	5 − 6	2	4
5	0 − 5	1 − 4	2 − 3	6	5
6	4 − 2	5 − 1	6 − 0	3	6

Table 5.3 A normalized organization of matches in a round robin tournament with seven players.

If the players face each other once, the round robin tournament has $n(n-1)/2$ matches in total. For instance, if $n = 100$, a full tournament requires 4950 matches. Instead of generating and storing the match pairings into a data structure, it would be more convenient to have a combination rule linking the player indices and the round index. Based on this rule, we could answer directly questions such as:

(i) Who is the resting player (i.e. the opponent of the player in the singleton set in Equation (5.4)) in the given round?

(ii) Given two players, in which round they will face one another?

Since Algorithm 5.12 is based on Equation (5.3), we have a simple invariant for a round r: the sum of the player indices equals $2r \bmod n$ whenever n is odd. Unfortunately, this regularity does not seem to give a direct answer to question (ii) (e.g. if $n = 7$, the sums are $0, 2, 4, 6, 1, 3, 5$ for rounds $0, 1, \ldots, 6$, respectively). However, we can use the sum to define the match organization. For example, sorting the rounds listed in Table 5.2 according to the sum of player indices modulo n gives us Table 5.3. Let us call this match schedule *normalized round robin pairings*.

Algorithm 5.13 describes a method for generating pairings for a round in a normalized round robin tournament. Also, it defines a function RESTING that gives an answer to question (i), and a function ROUND answering question (ii).

An algorithm generating the match pairings is in key position in the algorithm that organizes the round robin tournament. The concept of the *sorted sequence of kings* approximates the player rankings in a round robin tournament without having to resort to a scoring mechanism (Wu and Sheng 2001). Nevertheless, it is quite common to reward players when they excel in their matches, and Algorithm 5.14 realizes such a tournament. The algorithm uses a function A-ROUND-ROBIN-PAIRINGS which can be any method that generates proper pairings (e.g. Algorithms 5.12 and 5.13).

5.4 Summary

Tournaments compare the participants to rank them in a relative order or, at least, to find out who is best. The comparison of two competitors is carried out in a match, and its outcome contributes in a specified way to the rankings. Since there are no regulations

---

Algorithm 5.13 Normalized pairings for a round robin tournament.

NORMALIZED-ROUND-ROBIN-PAIRINGS(r, n)
  in: round index r ($0 \leq r \leq 2 \cdot \lfloor (n-1)/2 \rfloor$); number of players n ($1 \leq n$)
  out: sequence R of n player indices indicating the match pairings between players
         R_{2i} and R_{2i+1}, when $i = 0, \ldots, \lfloor n/2 \rfloor - 1$; if n is odd, R_{n-1} indicates the resting
         player
  1: $|R| \leftarrow n$ ▷ Reserve space for n player indices.
  2: $s \leftarrow$ RESTING(r, n)   ▷ The resting player when n is odd.
  3: $R_{n-1} \leftarrow s$
  4: $n' \leftarrow n$
  5: **if** n is even **then**
  6:   $R_{(n-1)-1} \leftarrow n - 1$ ▷ The player in the singleton set.
  7:   $n' \leftarrow n - 1$ ▷ Transform the problem to 'n is odd'.
  8: **end if**
  9: **for** $k \leftarrow 1 \ldots ((n'-1)/2)$ **do**
 10:   $i \leftarrow 2(k-1)$
 11:   $R_i \leftarrow (s + k) \bmod n'$
 12:   $R_{i+1} \leftarrow (n - (s+k) + r) \bmod n'$
 13: **end for**
 14: **return** R

RESTING(r, n)
  in: round index r ($0 \leq r \leq 2 \cdot \lfloor (n-1)/2 \rfloor$); number of players n ($1 \leq n$)
  out: index of the resting player (when n is odd) or the opponent of the singleton
         player (when n is even)
  1: **return** $(r \cdot ((n+1) \textbf{ div } 2)) \bmod n$

ROUND(p, q, n)
  in: player indices p and q ($0 \leq p, q \leq n - 1 \wedge p \neq q$); number of players n ($1 \leq n$)
  out: index of the round in where the players p and q have a match
  1: **if** n is even **and** ($p = n - 1$ **or** $q = n - 1$) **then**
  2:   $o \leftarrow p + q - (n-1)$ ▷ Opponent of the singleton player.
  3:   **return** $(2o) \bmod (n-1)$
  4: **else**
  5:   $t \leftarrow 2 \cdot ((n-1) \textbf{ div } 2) + 1$ ▷ Number of rounds.
  6:   **return** $(p + q) \bmod t$
  7: **end if**

---

on how the matches and ranks should affect each other, we are free to compose a tournament that suits our needs. However, if we want both a simple tournament structure and an effective comparison method, we can choose from three different approaches: rank adjustment, competitor elimination, and point scoring. In practice, a tournament event often combines these concepts so that consecutive rounds have a justifiable assignment of one-to-one matches.

Algorithm 5.14 Round robin tournament including a scoring for the match results.

ROUND-ROBIN-TOURNAMENT(P)

    in: sequence P of n players ($1 \leq n$)
    out: sequence R of n players with attribute $score(i)$
    constant: score points for a winner w, for a loser ℓ, for a tie t
    local: number of rounds t

1: $R \leftarrow$ **copy** P
2: **for all** $p \in R$ **do**
3:   $score(p) \leftarrow 0$
4: **end for**
5: **if** n is even **then**
6:   $t \leftarrow n - 1$
7: **else**
8:   $t \leftarrow n$
9: **end if**
10: **for** $r \leftarrow 0 \ldots (t - 1)$ **do**
11:   $M \leftarrow$ A-ROUND-ROBIN-PAIRINGS(r, n)
12:   **for** $i \leftarrow 0 \ldots ((n \textbf{ div } 2) - 1)$ **do**
13:     $p \leftarrow M_{2i}$
14:     $q \leftarrow M_{2i+1}$
15:     $m \leftarrow match(R_p, R_q)$
16:     **if** $m = p$ **then**
17:       $score(p) \leftarrow score(p) + w$
18:       $score(q) \leftarrow score(q) + \ell$
19:     **else if** $m = q$ **then**
20:       $score(p) \leftarrow score(p) + \ell$
21:       $score(q) \leftarrow score(q) + w$
22:     **else**
23:       $score(p) \leftarrow score(p) + t$
24:       $score(q) \leftarrow score(q) + t$
25:     **end if**
26:   **end for**
27:   **if** n is odd **then**
28:     player R_{n-1} receives a bye
29:   **end if**
30: **end for**
31: **return**

In a rank adjustment tournament, a match is seen as a challenge where the winner gets a better rank than the looser. Because ranks are persistent, this approach suits the case where the rank order must be upheld constantly, the set of participants changes often, and there are no competition seasons. In an elimination tournament, a match win provides entrance to the next round, while the loser goes out of the tournament. The tournament structure can include random elements, for instance, in making the initial pairings or the final drawings. Because the participants can be ordered only partially, the

Table 5.4 Characteristic features of tournaments for n players. The matches for initial rank adjustments are not taken into account. However, we assume that the single elimination tournament is set up by a standard seeding order. In general, we assume $2 \leq n$, except that for the king-of-the-hill tournament we require that $n + 1$ is a power of 2. The round index i is from the interval $[0, r - 1]$.

	Hill climbing	King of the hill	Single elimination	Round robin
all matches	$n - 1$	$n - 1$	$n - 1$	$n(n-1)/2$
all rounds $(= r)$	$n - 1$	$2(\lg(n+1) - 1)$	$\lceil \lg n \rceil$	n if n is odd; $n - 1$ otherwise
matches of the champion	$\in [1, r]$	$\in [1, r]$	$\in [r - 1, r]$	$n - 1$
matches in round i	1	$2^{\lfloor (r-1-i)/2 \rfloor}$	$n - 2^{\lceil \lg n \rceil - 1}$ if $i = 0$; $2^{\lceil \lg n \rceil - (i+1)}$ if $i \geq 1$	$\lfloor n/2 \rfloor$

purpose of the event is often only to determine the champion. A scoring tournament makes the matches more independent of one another by accumulating the outcomes using a points system. Since the participants are ranked according to their point tallies, we can balance the number of the matches and the fairness of the final ordering.

Table 5.4 summarizes the characteristic properties of four tournament types. Their overall structure can be measured in terms of the total number of matches, the number of rounds required to determine the champion, the number of matches before one can become the champion, and the number of matches in a given round. The hill-climbing tournament is the simplest due to the linear scheduling of the matches. The king-of-the-hill and the elimination tournament are based on a tree-like structure and, thus, have a logarithmic number of rounds with respect to the number of players. The round robin tournament is the most demanding by all measures because every player has a match with every other player.

Although tournaments are often associated with sports games, they can be used in any context that evaluates a set of objects against each other. These methods have intuitive consequences, they are very customizable, and they have an inherent property of managing partial ordering.

Exercises

5-1 Draw a bracket for a hill-climbing tournament (see Algorithm 5.3) and for a king-of-the-hill tournament (see Algorithm 5.5).

5-2 Algorithm 5.3 organizes a hill-climbing tournament and ranks the players. If we only want to find the champion, the algorithm can be simplified by unfolding the function calls INITIAL-RANK-ADJUSTMENT and LADDER-MATCH and by removing the unnecessary steps. Implement these changes and name the algorithm SIMPLE-HILL-CLIMBING-TOURNAMENT(P).

5-3 Draw a bracket of match pairings for SIMPLE-HILL-CLIMBING-TOURNAMENT(P) when $|P| = 8$ (see Exercise 5-2).

5-4 Algorithm 5.5 uses routine *enumeration* to arrange the players into some order so that they can be paired to the matches. If the order is random, the operation resembles RANDOM-SEEDING (see p. 124). Rewrite Algorithm 5.5 by substituting *enumeration* with RANDOM-SEEDING.

5-5 Algorithm 5.5 defines the king-of-the-hill tournament. Simplify the algorithm for finding the champion only (see Exercise 5-2). Call this new algorithm SIMPLE-KING-OF-THE-HILL-TOURNAMENT(P).

5-6 Draw a bracket for SIMPLE-KING-OF-THE-HILL-TOURNAMENT(P) when $|P| = 15$ (see Exercise 5-5).

5-7 In the real world, a player p can decline a rank adjustment tournament match with a less ranked player q. After d rejections the player p is considered to lose to q. We have considered only the case where $d = 0$. Generalize Algorithm 5.2 for the case $d > 0$.

5-8 In a rank adjustment tournament the number of revenge matches r is usually limited. This means that a player cannot face the same player more than r times in a row. We considered only the case where $r = \infty$. Generalize Algorithm 5.2 to account for finite r values.

5-9 Removing a player p from a rank adjustment tournament empties the rank $rank(p)$. Invent at least three different strategies to handle the empty slots in a ranking structure.

5-10 A ladder tournament L can be split into two separate ladder tournaments L' and L'' by assigning each player either to L' or L''. The new ranks of the players are adjusted so that they do not contradict the relative rankings in L. However, there are many ways to define the inverse operation, joining two tournaments of disjoint players. Design an algorithm JOIN-LADDER-TOURNAMENTS(L', L'') that gives both tournaments equal value. This means, for example, that the joining does not force the champion of L'' to compete against the worst players in L' before she can have a match with the champion of L'.

5-11 Exercise 5-10 tackles the problem of splitting and joining ladder tournaments. How can these operations be defined in an elimination tournament?

5-12 In the pyramid tournament the player status *peerWinner* can be seen as a token that is assigned to player p, and it can only be lost in a match. If the players' ranks change often, this tokenization can be unfair: if p competes only occasionally, he keeps the *peerWinner* status even if all the other peer players have been re-ranked. Devise a better strategy for controlling *peerWinner* status in such situations.

5-13 Solving the organization of the matches of a tournament resembles the (parallel) selection algorithms. For example, the structure of the hill-climbing tournament is similar to searching for a maximum of n values sequentially (see Exercise 5-2).

Algorithm 5.15 describes how to search for a maximum value in parallel. What tournament structure does it resemble?

Algorithm 5.15 Maximum value in parallel.

PARALLEL-MAX(P)
    in: sequence P of n values $(1 \leq n)$
    out: maximum value of P
    local: amount of pairs h
  1: **if** $n = 1$ **then**
  2:   **return** P_0
  3: **else**
  4:   $h \leftarrow n$ **div** 2
  5:   **if** n is odd **then**   ▷ Reserve space for Q.
  6:     $|Q| \leftarrow h + 1$
  7:     $Q_h \leftarrow P_{n-1}$
  8:   **else**
  9:     $|Q| \leftarrow h$
10:   **end if**
11:   **for** $i \leftarrow 0 \ldots (h-1)$ **do**   ▷ In parallel for each i.
12:     $Q_i \leftarrow \max\{P_{2i}, P_{2i+1}\}$
13:   **end for**
14:   **return** PARALLEL-MAX(Q)
15: **end if**

5-14 In a best-of-m match series between two players (e.g. p and q) the winner is the first one to win $\lceil (m+1)/2 \rceil$ matches. Suppose we have in total n players ranked uniquely from $[0, n-1]$ so that $ranked(0)$ is the champion and $ranked(n-1)$ is the tail-ender. If we define that for one match

$$P(match(p,q) = p) = \frac{1}{2} \cdot \left(1 + \frac{rank(q) - rank(p)}{n}\right)$$

when $rank(p) < rank(q)$, what is the probability that p wins the best-of-m series?

5-15 The random selection tournament (see Algorithm 5.6) and the random pairing tournament (see Algorithm 5.7) provide similar types of results. However, the latter method seems to be under-defined because the pairwise matches provide us with information about the relative strengths between the players. Should we rephrase the output as follows: 'set R of ranked players which has a champion $ranked(R, 0)$, the initial match winners with rank 1, and the rest of the players with rank 2'?

5-16 If you answered 'yes' to Exercise 5-15, redesign the elimination tournament algorithms presented. In particular, remove attribute $wins(\bullet)$ from Algorithm 5.11. If you answered 'no', complement all the elimination tournament algorithms with attribute *wins*($\bullet$). Finally, give the opposite answer to Exercise 5-15 and redo this exercise.

5-17 The three common deterministic seeding methods – standard seeding, ordered standard seeding, and equitable seeding – for an elimination tournament are listed in Table 5.1. To prevent the same matches from occurring in successive tournaments (and to introduce an element of surprise), we can apply these seeding methods only partially. The $t = 2^x$ top players are seeded as before, but the rest are placed randomly. Refine the deterministic seeding algorithms to include the parameter t.

5-18 In a single elimination tournament (see Algorithm 5.11) the seeding initializes the match pairs for the first round. Design an algorithm SINGLE-ELIMINATION-SEEDING-TOURNAMENT(P) where the seeding is applied before every round. Analyse and explain the effects of different seeding methods.

5-19 In the bracket of a single elimination tournament we have allocated the players to the initial matches by labelling the player placeholders by player indices or equivalently by ranks (see Figure 5.2 and Table 5.1). In practice it would be convenient to also identify the matches. Design an algorithm that gives a unique label for each match in the bracket so that the label is independent of the actual players in the match.

5-20 Design and describe a general *m-round winner tournament*, ROUND-WINNER-TOURNAMENT(P, m), for players P, where in each round $0, 1, \ldots, m-1$ the players are paired randomly and the winners continue to the next round. After round $m-1$ the champion is selected randomly from the remaining players. Interestingly, this tournament structure has the following special cases: $m = 0$ is a random selection tournament, $m = 1$ is a random pairing tournament, and $m = \lg |P|$ is a single elimination seeding tournament as in Exercise 5-18.

5-21 Assume that a single elimination tournament has $n = 2^x$ players and the number of rounds is x. How many single elimination tournaments must we have so that the total number of matches equals the number of matches in a round robin tournament?

6

Game Trees

Many classical games such as chess, draughts and Go are *perfect information games*, because the players can always see all the possible moves. In other words, there is no hidden information among the participants but they all know exactly what has been done in the previous turns and can devise strategies for the next turns from equal grounds. In contrast, poker is an example of a game in which the players do not have perfect information, since they cannot see the opponents' hands. Random events are another source of indeterminism: although there is no hidden information in backgammon, dice provide an element of chance which changes the nature of information from perfect to probabilistic. Because perfect information games can be analysed using combinatorial methods, they have been widely studied and were the first games to have computer-controlled opponents.

This chapter concentrates on two-player perfect information zero-sum games. A game has the *zero-sum* property when one player's gain equals another player's loss, whereas in a non-zero-sum game one player gains more than the other loses. All possible plays of a perfect information game can be represented in a *game tree*: the root node is the initial position, its successors are the positions the first player can reach in one move, their successors are the positions resulting from the second player's responses, and so forth. Alternatively, a game position can be seen as a state from the set of all legal game positions, and a move defines the transition from one state to another. The leaves of the game tree represent terminal positions where the outcome of the game – win, loss, or draw – can be determined. Each path from the root to a leaf node represents a complete play instance of the game. Figure 6.1 illustrates a partial game tree for the first two moves of noughts and crosses.

In two-player perfect information games, the first player of the round is commonly called MAX and the second player MIN. Hence, a game tree contains two types of nodes, MAX nodes and MIN nodes, depending on which player must make a move in the given situation. A *ply* is the length of the path between two nodes (i.e. the number of moves required to get from one node to another). For example, one round in a two-player game equals two plies in a game tree. Considering the root node, MAX nodes have even plies and MIN nodes odd plies. Due to notational conventions the root node has no ply number (i.e. the smallest ply number is 1), and the leaves, despite having no moves, are still labelled as MAX or MIN nodes. In graphical illustrations MAX nodes are often represented with squares and MIN nodes with circles. Nevertheless, we have chosen to illustrate MAX

Algorithms and Networking for Computer Games, Second Edition. Jouni Smed and Harri Hakonen.
© 2017 John Wiley & Sons Ltd. Published 2017 by John Wiley & Sons Ltd.

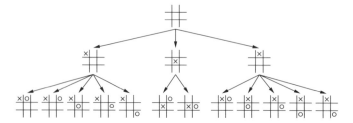

Figure 6.1 Partial game tree for the first two moves of noughts and crosses. The tree has been simplified by removing symmetrical positions.

and MIN nodes with triangles $\triangledown$ and $\triangle$, because these glyphs bear a resemblance to the equivalent logical operators $\vee$ and $\wedge$.

Having touched upon the fundamentals, we are now ready for the problem statement. Given a node v in a game tree, find a winning strategy for player MAX (or MIN) from node v, or, equivalently, show that MAX (or MIN) can force a win from node v. To tackle this problem we review in the following sections the minimax method, which allows us to analyse both whole and partial game trees, and alpha-beta pruning, which often reduces the number of nodes expanded during the search for a winning strategy. Monte Carlo tree search reduces the search space even more radically by using random sampling. Finally, we look at how we can include random elements in a game tree to model games of chance.

6.1 Minimax

Let us start by thinking of the simplest possible subgame, where we have a MAX node v whose children are all leaves. We can be sure that the game ends in one move if the game-play reaches node v. Since the aim is (presumably) to win the game, MAX will choose the node that leads to the best possible outcome from his perspective: if there is a leaf leading to a win position, MAX will select it and win the game; if a win is not possible but a draw is, he will choose it; otherwise, MAX will lose no matter what he does. Conversely, due to the zero-sum property, if v belongs to MIN, she will do her utmost to minimize MAX's advantage. We know now the outcome of the game for the nodes one ply above the leaves, and we can analyse the outcome of the plies above that recursively using the same method until we reach the root node. This strategy for determining successive selections is called the *minimax* method, and the sequence of moves which minimax deduces to be optimal for both sides is called the *principal variation*. The first move in the principal variation is the best decision for the player who is assigned to the root of the game tree.

We can assign numeric values to the nodes: let a win for MAX be assigned $+1$, a win for MIN -1, and a draw 0. Because we know the outcome of the leaves, we can immediately assign values to them. Then minimax propagates the value up the tree according to the following rules:

(i) If the node is labelled MAX, assign the maximum value of its children to it.
(ii) If the node is labelled MIN, assign the minimum value of its children to it.

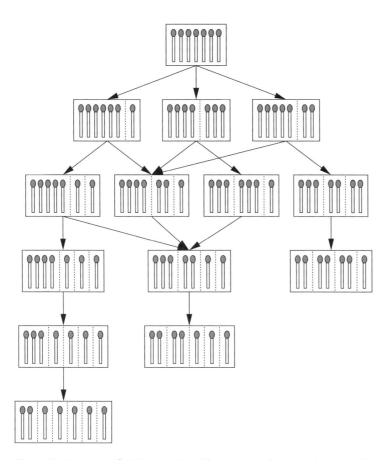

Figure 6.2 Game tree for Division Nim with seven matches. To reduce size, identical nodes in a ply have been combined.

The assigned value indicates the value of the best outcome that a player can hope to achieve – assuming the opponent also uses minimax.

As an example let us look at a simplification of the game of Nim called Division Nim. Initially, there is one heap of matches on the table. On each turn a player must divide one heap into two non-empty heaps that have different numbers of matches (e.g. for a heap of six matches the only allowed divisions are 5–1 and 4–2). The player who cannot make a move loses the game. Figure 6.2 illustrates the complete game tree for a game with seven matches.

Figure 6.3 illustrates the same game tree but now with values assigned. The two leaves labelled MIN are assigned to +1, because in those positions MIN cannot make a move and loses; conversely, the only MAX leaf is assigned to −1, because it represents a position where MAX loses. By using the aforementioned rules, we can assign values to all internal nodes, and, as we can see in the root node, MAX, who has the first move, loses the game because MIN can always force the game to end in the MAX leaf node.

The function that gives a value to every leaf node is called a *utility function* (or pay-off function). In many cases, this value can be determined solely from the properties of the

MAX

MIN

MAX

MIN

MAX

MIN

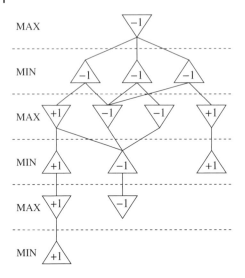

Figure 6.3 Complete game tree with valued nodes for Division Nim with seven matches.

leaf. For example, in Division Nim if the leaf's ply from the root is odd, its value is $+1$; otherwise, the value is -1. However, as pointed out by Michie (1966), the value of a leaf can also depend on the nodes preceding it up to the initial root. When assigning values to a leaf node v_i, we take MAX's perspective and assign a positive value to a win by MAX, negative for a loss, and zero for a draw. Let us denote this function by $value(v_i)$. Now, the minimax value for a node v can be defined with a simple recursion

$$minimax(v) = \begin{cases} value(v), & \text{if } v \text{ is a leaf,} \\ \min_{u \in children(v)} \{minimax(u)\}, & \text{if } v \text{ is a MIN node,} \\ \max_{u \in children(v)} \{minimax(u)\}, & \text{if } v \text{ is a MAX node,} \end{cases} \quad (6.1)$$

where $children(v)$ gives the set of successors of node v. Algorithm 6.1 implements this recurrence by determining backed-up values for the internal nodes after the leaves have been evaluated.

Both Equation (6.1) and its implementation in Algorithm 6.1 have almost similar sub-parts for the MIN and MAX nodes. Knuth and Moore (1975) give a more compact formulation for the minimax method called *negamax*, where both node types are handled identically. The idea is first to negate the values assigned to the MIN nodes and then to take the maximum value as in the MAX nodes. Algorithm 6.2 gives an implementation for the negamax method.

6.1.1 Analysis

When analysing game tree algorithms, some simplifying assumptions are made about the features of the game tree. Let us assume that each internal node has the same branching factor (i.e. number of children), and we search the tree to some fixed depth before which the game does not end. We can now estimate how much time the minimax (and negamax) method uses, because it is proportional to the number of expanded nodes. If

---

Algorithm 6.1 Minimax.

MINIMAX(v)
  in: node v
  out: utility value of node v
  1: **if** $children(v) = \varnothing$ **then**   ▷ v is a leaf.
  2:   **return** $value(v)$
  3: **else if** $label(v)$ = MIN **then**   ▷ v is a MIN node.
  4:   $e \leftarrow +\infty$
  5:   **for all** $u \in children(v)$ **do**
  6:     $e \leftarrow \min\{e, \text{MINIMAX}(u)\}$
  7:   **end for**
  8:   **return** e
  9: **else**   ▷ v is a MAX node.
10:   $e \leftarrow -\infty$
11:   **for all** $u \in children(v)$ **do**
12:     $e \leftarrow \max\{e, \text{MINIMAX}(u)\}$
13:   **end for**
14:   **return** e
15: **end if**

Algorithm 6.2 Negamax.

NEGAMAX(v)
  in: node v
  out: utility value of node v
  1: **if** $children(v) = \varnothing$ **then**   ▷ v is a leaf.
  2:   $\ell \leftarrow value(v)$
  3:   **if** $label(v)$ = MIN **then** $\ell \leftarrow -\ell$ **end if**
  4:   **return** ℓ
  5: **else**   ▷ v is a MAX or MIN node.
  6:   $e \leftarrow -\infty$
  7:   **for all** $u \in children(v)$ **do**
  8:     $e \leftarrow \max\{e, -\text{NEGAMAX}(u)\}$
  9:   **end for**
10:   **return** e
11: **end if**

---

the branching factor is b and the depth is d, the number of expanded nodes (the initial node included) is

$$1 + b + b^2 + \ldots + b^d = \frac{1 - b^{d+1}}{1 - b} = \frac{b^{d+1} - 1}{b - 1}.$$

Hence, the overall running time is $O(b^d)$.

There are two ways to speed up the minimax method: we can try to reduce b by pruning the game tree, which is the idea behind alpha-beta pruning described in Section 6.2, or we can try to reduce d by limiting the search depth, which we shall study next.

6.1.2 Partial minimax

The minimax method gives the best zero-sum move available for the player at any node in the game tree. This optimality is, however, subject to the utility function used in the leaves and the assumption that both players utilize the same minimax method for their moves. In practice, the game trees are too large for computing the perfect information from the leaves up, and we must limit the search to a *partial game tree* by stopping the search and handling internal nodes as if they were leaves. For example, we can stop after sequences of n moves and guess how likely it is for the player to win from that position. This depth-limiting approach is called an *n-move look-ahead* strategy, where n is the number of plies included in the search.

In a *partial minimax* method, such as n-move look-ahead, the internal nodes where the node expansion is stopped are referred to as *frontier nodes* (or horizon nodes or tip nodes). Because the frontier nodes do not represent the final positions of the game, we have to estimate whether they lead to a win, loss or draw by using a heuristic *evaluation function* (or static evaluation function or estimation function). Naturally, it can use more than the values $+1$, 0, -1 to imply the likelihood of the outcome. After the evaluation, the estimated values are propagated up the tree using minimax. At best, the evaluation function correctly estimates the backed-up utility function values and the frontier node behaves as a leaf node. Unfortunately, this is rarely the case and we can end up selecting non-optimal moves.

Evaluation function

Devising an appropriate evaluation function is essential for the partial minimax method to be of any use. First, it implants domain-specific information into the general search method by assigning a merit value to a game state. This means that the range of the evaluation function must be wide enough so that we can distinguish relevant game situations. Second, theoretical analysis of the partial minimax shows that errors in the evaluation function start to dominate the root value when the look-ahead depth n increases, and to tackle this the evaluation function should be derived using a suitable methodology for the problem. Also, static evaluation functions often analyse just one game state at a time, which makes it hard to identify strategic issues and to maintain consistency of consecutive moves, because strategy is about setting up goals with different time scales.

We can also define an evaluation function for the leaf nodes. This can be accomplished simply by including the utility function in the evaluation function (and possibly rescaling the range of the utility function). An evaluation function $e(s, p)$ for a player p is usually formed by combining numerical measurements $m_i(s, p)$ of the most important properties in the game state s. These measurements define terms $t_k(s, p)$ that often have one of the following substructures:

- A single measurement $m_i(s, p)$ alone defines a term value. These are mainly derived from a game state, but nothing prevents us from using the move history as a measurement. For example, the ply number of the game state can be used to emphasize the effect of a measurement for more offensive or defensive play.

Figure 6.4 Evaluation function $e(\bullet)$ in noughts and crosses. (a) MAX (crosses) has six possible winning lines, whereas MIN (noughts) has five: $e(\bullet) = 6 - 5 = 1$. (b) MAX has four possible winning lines and MIN has five $e(\bullet) = 4 - 5 = -1$. (c) Forced win by MAX, hence $e(\bullet) = +\infty$

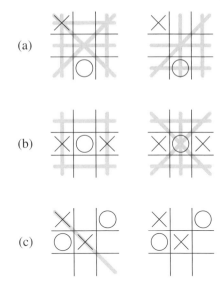

(a)

(b)

(c)

- The difference between measurements $m_i(s,p) - m_j(s,q)$ is used to estimate opposing features between players p and q, and often the measure is about the balance of the same property (i.e. $i = j$). For example, if $m_i(s,p)$ gives the centre of mass of p's pieces, the term $|m_i(s,p) - m_i(s,q)|$ reflects the degree of conflicting interests in the game world. In noughts and crosses, the evaluation function can estimate the number of win nodes in the non-leaf subtrees of the current node (see Figure 6.4).
- The ratio of measurements $m_i(s,p)/m_j(s,q)$ combines properties that are not necessarily conflicting, and the term often represents some form of advantage over the other player. In draughts, for example, a heuristic can consider the piece advantage, because it is likely that having more pieces than your opponent will lead to a better outcome.

The evaluation function aggregates these terms, maintaining the zero-sum property: $e(s, \text{MAX}) = -e(s', \text{MIN})$ where s' is a state which resembles state s but where the MIN and MAX roles are reversed. For example, A.L. Samuel's classical heuristic for draughts (Samuel 1959) evaluates board states with a weighted sum of 16 heuristic measures (e.g. piece locations, piece advantage, centre control, and piece mobility). An evaluation function in the form of a weighted linear sum

$$e(s,p) = \sum_k w_k t_k(s,p) \tag{6.2}$$

best suits the cases where the terms are independent. In practice, such terms are hard to devise, because a state can present many conflicting advantages and disadvantages at the same time. Samuel (1959, 1967) describes different ways to handle terms that are dependent, interacting, nonlinear, or otherwise combinational.

Apart from the selection of measurements and terms, evaluation functions akin to Equation (6.2) pose other questions:

- How many terms should we have? If there are too few terms, we can fail to recognize some aspects of the play leading to strategic mistakes. On the other hand, too many terms can result in erratic moves, because a critical term can be overrun by a group of irrelevant ones.

- What magnitude should the weights have? Samuel (1959) reduces this problem to determining how to orient towards the inherent goals and strategies of the game. The terms that define the dominant game goals (e.g. winning the game) should have the largest weights. A medium weight indicates that the term relates to subgoals (e.g. capturing enemy pieces). The smallest weights are assigned to terms which guide the search towards achieving intermediate goals (e.g. moving pieces to opportunistic positions).
- Which weight values lead to the best outcome? Determining the weights can be seen an optimization problem for the evaluation function over all possible game situations. For simple games, assigning the weights manually can lead to satisfactory evaluation, but more complex games require automatized weight adjusting as well as proper validation and verification strategies.
- How can the loss of 'tendency' information be avoided? For example, in turn-based games the goodness or badness of a given game situation depends on whose turn it is. This kind of information is easily lost when the evaluation function is based on a weighted sum of terms.

The partial minimax method assumes that game situations can be ranked by giving them a single numeric value. In the real world decision-making is rarely this simple. Humans are – at least in their favourite expertise domain – apt to ponder on multidimensional 'functions' and can approximately grade and compare the pros and cons of different selections. Moreover, humans tend to consider the positional and material advantages and their balance. Moves that radically change both of these measurements are hard to evaluate and compare using any general single-value scheme. For example, losing the queen in chess usually weakens winning possibilities radically, but in certain situations sacrificing the queen can lead to a better endgame.

Controlling the search depth

Evaluation to a fixed ply depth can be seriously misleading, because a heuristically promising path can lead later on to an unfavourable situation. This is called the *horizon effect*, and a usual way to counteract it is to do a *staged search*, where we search several plies deeper from nodes that look exceptionally good (one should always look a gift horse in the mouth).

If the game has often-occurring game states, the time used in the search can be traded for larger memory consumption by storing triples ⟨state, state value, best move from state⟩ in a *transposition table*. Transposition tables implement one of the simplest learning strategies, *rote learning*. If the frontier node's value is already stored, the effective search depth is increased without extra stage searches. Transposition tables also give an efficient implementation for *iterative deepening*, where the idea is to apply n-move look-ahead with increasing values for $n = 1, 2, \ldots$ until time or memory constraints are exceeded.

The look-ahead depth need not be the same for every node, but it can vary according to the phase of the game or the branching factor. A chain of unusually narrow subtrees is easier to follow deeper, and they often relate to tactical situations that do not allow mistakes. Moreover, games can be divided into phases (e.g. opening, midgame and endgame) that correlate to the number of pieces and their positions on the board. The strategies employed in each phase differ somewhat, and the search method should adapt to these different requirements.

No matter how cleverly we change the search depth, it does not entirely remove the horizon effect – it only widens the horizon. Another weakness of the look-ahead approach is that the evaluations that take place deep in the tree can be biased by their very depth: we want an estimate of minimax but, in reality, we get a minimax of estimates. Also, the search depth introduces another bias, because the minimax value for the root node gets distorted towards win in odd plies and towards loss in even plies, which is caused by errors in the evaluation function. A survey of other approaches to cope with the horizon effect – including identification of quiescent nodes and using null moves – is presented by Abramson (1989).

At first sight, it seems that the deeper partial minimax searches the game tree, the better it performs. Perhaps counter-intuitively, the theory derived for analysing the partial minimax method warns that this assumption is not always justified. Assume that we are using an n-move look-ahead heuristic in a game tree that has a uniform branching factor b and depth d, and the leaf values are generated from a uniform random distribution. Now, we have three theorems about the partial search, which can be summarized as follows:

- *Minimax convergence theorem.* As n increases, it is likely that the root value converges to only one value that is given by a function of b and d.
- *Last player theorem.* The root values backed up from odd and even n frontiers cannot be compared with each other. In other words, values from different plies can be compared only if the same player has made the last move.
- *Minimax pathology theorem.* When n increases, the probability of selecting a non-optimal move increases. This result seems to be caused by the combination of the uniformity assumptions on branching, depth and leaf value distribution. Removing any of these assumptions seems to result in non-pathology. Fortunately, this is often the case in practice.

Although the partial minimax method is easy to derive from the minimax method just by introducing one count-down parameter into the recursion, theoretical results show that these two methods differ considerably. Theory also cautions us not to assume too much, and the development of partial minimax methods belongs more to the area of experimentation, verification and hindsight.

6.2   Alpha-Beta Pruning

When we are expanding a node in minimax, we already have available more information than the basic minimax uses due to the depth-first search order. For example, if we are expanding MIN's node, we know that in order to end up in this node, MAX has to choose it in the previous ply. Assume that the MAX node in the previous ply has already found a choice that provides a result of 4 (see Figure 6.5). Therefore, the MIN node we are currently expanding will not be selected by MAX if its result is less than 4. With this in mind, we descend to its children, and because we are expanding a MIN node, we want to find the minimum among them. If at any point this minimum becomes smaller than

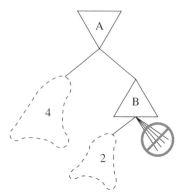

Figure 6.5 Pruning the game tree. MAX node A has the maximum value 4 when it expands node B. If the minimum value of node B gets below 4, node B can be discarded from the search and unexpanded children can be omitted.

or equal to 4, we can stop immediately and prune this branch of the game tree. Why? Because in the previous ply MAX has a choice that leads to at least as good a result, this part of the tree will not be selected. Thus, by removing branches that do not offer good move candidates we can reduce the actual branching factor and the number of expanded nodes.

Alpha-beta pruning is a search method that keeps track of the best move for each player while it proceeds in a depth-first fashion in the game tree. During the search it observes and updates two values, alpha and beta. The alpha value is associated with MAX and can never decrease; the beta value is associated with MIN and can never increase. If in a MAX node alpha has value 4, it means that MAX does not have to consider any of the children that have a value less than or equal to 4; alpha is the worst result that MAX can achieve from that node. Similarly, a MIN node that has a beta value of 6 can omit children that have a value of 6 or more. In other words, the value of a backed-up node is not less than alpha and not greater than beta. Moreover, the alpha value of a node is never less than the alpha value of its ancestors, and the beta value of a node is never greater than the beta value of its ancestors.

The alpha-beta method prunes subtrees off the original game tree, observing the following rules:

(i) Prune below any MIN node having a beta value less than or equal to the alpha value of any of its MAX ancestors.
(ii) Prune below any MAX node having an alpha value greater than or equal to the beta value of any of its MIN ancestors.

Algorithm 6.3 describes a minimax method which employs alpha-beta pruning. Initially, the algorithm is called with the parameter values $\alpha = -\infty$ and $\beta = +\infty$. Algorithm 6.4 describes a variant of alpha-beta pruning using negamax instead.

Let us go through an example, which is illustrated in Figure 6.6. First, we recurse through nodes A and B passing the initial values $\alpha = -\infty$ and $\beta = +\infty$, until for MAX node C we get values -3 and -2 from the leaves. We return $\alpha = -2$ to B, which calls D with parameters $\alpha = -\infty$ and $\beta = -2$. Checking the first leaf gives $\alpha = +5$, which fulfils the pruning condition $\alpha \geq \beta$. We can prune all other leaves of node D, because we know MIN will never choose D when it is in node B. In node B, $\beta = -2$ which is returned to node A as a new α value. Second, we call node E with parameters $\alpha = -2$ and $\beta = +\infty$. The leaf value -5 below node F has no effect, and F returns -2 to node E, which fulfils

Algorithm 6.3 Alpha-beta pruning using minimax.

MINIMAX-ALPHA-BETA(v, α, β)
   in: node v; alpha value α; beta value β
   out: utility value of node v
   1: **if** $children(v) = \varnothing$ **then**   ▷ v is a leaf.
   2:   **return** $value(v)$
   3: **else if** $label(v) = $ MIN **then**   ▷ v is a MIN node.
   4:   **for all** $u \in children(v)$ **do**
   5:     $e \leftarrow$ MINIMAX-ALPHA-BETA(u, α, β)
   6:     **if** $e < \beta$ **then**
   7:        $\beta \leftarrow e$
   8:     **end if**
   9:     **if** $\beta \leq \alpha$ **then**
  10:        **return** β ▷ Prune.
  11:     **end if**
  12:   **end for**
  13:   **return** β
  14: **else**   ▷ v is a MAX node.
  15:   **for all** $u \in children(v)$ **do**
  16:     $e \leftarrow$ MINIMAX-ALPHA-BETA(u, α, β)
  17:     **if** $\alpha < e$ **then**
  18:        $\alpha \leftarrow e$
  19:     **end if**
  20:     **if** $\beta \leq \alpha$ **then**
  21:        **return** α ▷ Prune.
  22:     **end if**
  23:   **end for**
  24:   **return** α
  25: **end if**

---

the pruning condition $\beta \leq \alpha$. Third, we recurse nodes leaving from G with $\alpha = -2$ and $\beta = +\infty$. In node H, we update $\alpha = +1$, which becomes the β value for G. Because the first leaf node of I fulfils the pruning condition, we can prune all other branches leaving it. Finally, node G returns the β value to the root node A, which becomes its α value and $+1$ is the result for the whole tree.

6.2.1   Analysis

The efficiency of alpha-beta pruning depends on the order in which the children are expanded. Preferably, we would like to consider them in non-decreasing value order in MIN nodes and in non-increasing order in MAX nodes. If the orders are reversed, it is possible that alpha-beta cannot prune anything and reduces to plain minimax.

Reverting to the best case, let us analyse, using the negamax variant, how many nodes alpha-beta pruning expands. Suppose that at depth $d - 1$ alpha-beta can prune as often as possible so that each node at depth $d - 1$ needs to expand only one child at depth

---

Algorithm 6.4 Alpha-beta pruning using negamax.

Negamax-Alpha-Beta(v, α, β)

   in: node v; alpha value α; beta value β

   out: utility value of node v

  1: **if** $children(v) = \emptyset$ **then**   ▷ v is a leaf.

  2:   $\ell \leftarrow value(v)$

  3:   **if** $label(v) = $ MIN **then** $\ell \leftarrow -\ell$ **end if**

  4:   **return** ℓ

  5: **else**   ▷ v is a MAX or MIN node.

  6:   **for all** $u \in children(v)$ **do**

  7:     $e \leftarrow -$Negamax-Alpha-Beta($u, -\beta, -\alpha$)

  8:     **if** $\beta \leq e$ **then**

  9:       **return** e ▷ Prune.

10:     **end if**

11:     **if** $\alpha < e$ **then**

12:       $\alpha \leftarrow e$

13:     **end if**

14:   **end for**

15:   **return** α

16: **end if**

---

d before the rest get pruned away. The only exception are the nodes belonging to the principal variation (or the optimum path), but we leave them out in our analysis. At depth $d - 2$ we cannot prune any nodes, because no child returns a value less than the value of beta it was originally passed, which at $d - 2$ is negated and becomes less than or equal to alpha. Continuing upwards, at depth $d - 3$ all nodes (except the principal variation) can be pruned, at depth $d - 4$ no nodes can be pruned, and so forth.

If the branching factor of the tree is b, the number of nodes increases by a factor of b at half of the plies of the tree and stays almost constant at the other half. Hence, the total amount of expanded nodes is $\Omega(b^{d/2}) = \Omega(\sqrt{b^d})$. In other words, in the best case alpha-beta allows the number of branches to be reduced to the square root of its original value and lets minimax search twice the original depth in the same time.

6.2.2   Principal variation search

For alpha-beta pruning to be more effective the interval (α, β) should be as small as possible. In *aspiration search*, we limit the interval artificially and are ready to handle cases where the search fails and we have to revert to the original values. The search fails at internal node v if all of its subtrees have their minimax values outside the assumed range (α', β') (i.e. every subtree value $e \notin (\alpha', \beta')$). Because the minimax (and negamax) method with alpha-beta pruning always returns values within the search interval, the out-of-range value e can be used to recognize a failed search. As noted by Fishburn (1983), we can add a *fail-soft* enhancement to the search by returning a value e that gives the best possible estimate of the actual alpha-beta range (i.e. e is as close as possible to it with respect to the information gathered in the failed search).

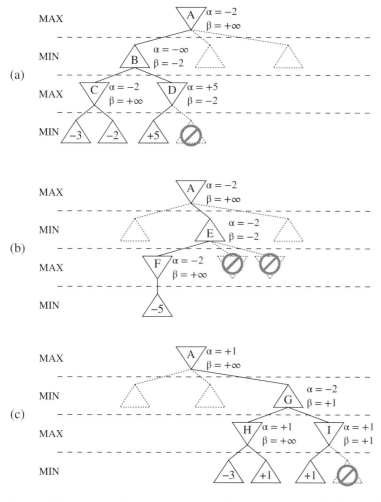

Figure 6.6 An example of alpha-beta pruning: (a) searching subtree B; (b) searching subtree E; (c) searching subtree G. The values of α and β represent the situation when a node has been searched.

Principal variation search–introduced by Finkel and Fishburn (1982) and renamed by Marsland and Campbell (1982) – does the search even more intelligently. A node in a game tree belongs to one of the following types:

(i) α-node where every move has $e \leq \alpha$ and none of them gets selected;
(ii) β-node where every move has $e \geq \beta$;
(iii) principal variation node where one or more moves has $e > \alpha$ but none of them has $e \geq \beta$.

Principal variation search assumes that whenever we find a principal variation move when searching a node, we have a principal variation node. This assumption means that we will not find a better move for the node in the remaining children. Simply put, once we have found a good move (i.e. which is between α and β), we search the rest of the moves assuming that they are all bad, which can be done much more quickly than searching for a good move among them. This can be verified by using a narrow alpha-beta interval $(\alpha, \alpha + \varepsilon)$, which is called a *null window*. The value ε is selected so that the values encountered cannot fall inside the interval $(\alpha, \alpha + \varepsilon)$. If this principal variation assumption fails and we find a better move, we have to re-search it normally without assumptions, but this extra effort is often compensated by the savings gained. Algorithm 6.5 concretizes this idea.

Algorithm 6.5 Principal variation search using negamax.

PRINCIPAL-VARIATION-SEARCH(v, α, β)
    in: node v; alpha value α; beta value β
    out: utility value of node v
    local: value t for null-window test
  1: **if** $children(v) = \emptyset$ **then**   ▷ v is a leaf.
  2:   $\ell \leftarrow value(v)$
  3:   **if** $label(v) = $ MIN **then** $\ell \leftarrow -\ell$ **end if**
  4:   **return** ℓ
  5: **else**   ▷ v is a MAX or MIN node.
  6:   $w \leftarrow$ some node $w' \in children(v)$
  7:   $e \leftarrow -$PRINCIPAL-VARIATION-SEARCH($w, -\beta, -\alpha$)
  8:   **for all** $u \in children(v) \setminus \{w\}$ **do**
  9:     **if** $\beta \leq e$ **then**
10:       **return** e ▷ Prune.
11:     **end if**
12:     **if** $\alpha < e$ **then**
13:       $\alpha \leftarrow e$
14:     **end if**
15:     $t \leftarrow -$PRINCIPAL-VARIATION-SEARCH($u, -(\alpha + \varepsilon), -\alpha$)
16:     **if** $e < t$ **then**
17:       **if** $t \leq \alpha$ **or** $\beta \leq t$ **then**
18:         $e \leftarrow t$
19:       **else**   ▷ Not a principal variation node.
20:         $e \leftarrow -$PRINCIPAL-VARIATION-SEARCH($u, -\beta, -t$)
21:       **end if**
22:     **end if**
23:   **end for**
24:   **return** e ▷ Fail-soft enhancement.
25: **end if**

6.3 Monte Carlo Tree Search

Classic game tree algorithms rely on the definition of an evaluation function used for estimating the utility values of the nodes in the game tree (i.e. how each node relates to the outcome of the game instance). If the evaluation is heuristic – as it is in most practical situations – its accuracy is crucial for both the feasibility of the calculations and the usability of the outcomes. This accuracy is pursued by uncovering and aggregating as much information as possible from the problem itself and the game situation at hand. For this reason, each problem becomes attached to a domain-specific evaluation function, and tailoring it can be considered as an art form of inventive data and control structures.

However, as observed by Abramson (1987), the unbiased value of a game instance itself is known at the end of the game, at the leaf node, and the internal nodes of the game tree can be seen as a model of the probability distribution of the consequences among the possible choices during gameplay. In other words, evaluating a node is about calculating the expected value of all the leaf nodes reachable from it. Consequently, since there are probability distributions involved, random sampling is one general approach that can be considered when estimating those values.

Applying randomization and statistics to a game tree avoids the problem of defining an explicit evaluation function – instead it can be approximated by repeating gameplay trials and collecting statistical values from the outcomes until some criterion terminates the sampling. To guide the upcoming value probing, the game tree is used for bookkeeping what moves (i.e. transitions from the nodes to their child nodes) have been tried out. Moreover, the tree nodes store the calculated value estimates for the moves and, hence, also for the move sequences. This makes the game tree partial with respect to the possible moves in the game: the frontier consists of the nodes that have only untried moves. It is worth noting that these frontier nodes can be internal nodes or leaf nodes of the whole game tree.

The most important goal is to gather evidence to weed out the poor moves from the beneficial ones. By repeating the sampling, the estimates in the partial game tree become more accurate and the tree of tried-out moves grows gradually in the best-first search manner. The convergence of the value assessments can be accelerated by incorporating domain-specific features, but that is an optimization refinement not a prerequisite. When the method is terminated, the result is the most valued move from the root node.

These and certain other ideas, supported by theoretical developments, have led to a family of algorithms that are known as *Monte Carlo tree search* (MCTS); see Coulom (2007) and Browne et al. (2012). At a high level, all these methods consist of the following main phases:

1. *Selection.* Descend from root node v_r of the game tree to a node v_d that preferably does not terminate the game (i.e. it is not a leaf in the whole game tree) and has at least one move that has not yet been tried.

   Node v_d can be an internal node or a frontier node, and it is used for collecting more information about the moves from v_r to v_d and, thus, it expands the partial game tree. If v_d is a leaf, the bookkeeping is updated and a new iteration can be started.

   The descent is driven by a suitable selection method such as a uniformly random one or a more refined one. If the selection favours some nodes over others, the game tree tends to become asymmetric, which may even reveal properties in the problem itself with respect to the selection method.

2. *Expansion.* Select an untried move of v_d and insert the corresponding node v_n as a new child of v_d.

   Node v_n is always a frontier node since none of its moves have been tried out. It is also possible to expand multiple untried moves at once. The selection of a move can be random or it can be based on, for example, some domain-specific information.

Also, if the game has states that can be arrived from many different sources, this phase can access a memento storage that caches the situations already evaluated.

3. *Simulation.* Run the game starting from the game situation corresponding to node v_n to the end. Determine a reward value e for the outcome of the terminated game from MAX's perspective (since MAX starts the game).

   The value e can be of any applicable type, for instance, $\{-1, 0, +1\}$, $[0, 1] \subset \mathbb{R}$, $\mathbb{R}$, or even a vector. The gameplay is simulated outside the MCTS game tree by some method, for example, by generating random but valid moves or using a domain-specific game logic.

   Because the intention is to assess v_n, many gameplays can be run from it and their outcomes composed. However, the estimates of the nodes near the root – which are the ones we are most interested in – already become refined when the frontier moves further away from the root.

4. *Backpropagation.* Update the statistical bookkeeping data of all the nodes in the path between v_n and v_r to reflect the new information gained from the outcome e.

   The next iteration loop utilizes this updated information to gather more evidence on what are the favourable moves. Depending on the problem, the length of the game, $length(v_r \rightsquigarrow v_n) +$ (number of iterations in the simulation phase), can affect the accuracy of e. For instance, the longer plays can have more uncertainties than the shorter ones. This can be taken into account in the backpropagation.

5. *Termination.* Stop the iteration when some condition is met, for instance, when time or memory limits are exceeded.

   Each repetition of phases (1)–(4) improves the estimations stored in the continuously growing partial game tree and the results are usable after each iteration. Determining the most valuable outcome depends on the problem.

The selection and expansion phases together are often called as the *tree policy* and the simulation phase is called the *default policy*.

One of the most popular variants of MCTS algorithms is *upper confidence bounds applied to trees* (UCT) by Kocsis and Szepesvári (2006). This variant is defined for the selection phase of MCTS. There are two opposing forces in the selection of a node v. To obtain a precise value estimate for v we must run many simulations for it. Nevertheless, to ensure the selection does not ignore some other good alternative v' by favouring v, we must also estimate the other nodes in the partial game tree.

The balance between the currently suboptimal and currently optimal choices is referred to as the *exploration–exploitation dilemma* and its properties are studied by formulating the dilemma in terms of so-called *bandit problems*. One of these problems has a solution method UCB1 (Auer et al. 2002), which has greatly influenced UCT and explains its current popularity. One of the central observations is that no matter how many iterations are run, UCB1 does not fix on a subset of the nodes but keeps on exploring. This property is also inherited by UCT, meaning it finds the most valuable nodes eventually. Moreover, it can be proven that UCT converges to minimax given enough time and memory (Kocsis and Szepesvári 2006), and this proof of convergence does not assume domain knowledge in UCT.

To understand and appreciate the key ingredient in UCT we next introduce the multi-armed bandit problem and UCB1. Then we go on to describe UCT itself.

Multi-armed bandit problem

Suppose we are in a situation where we have to choose from k independent actions, and then we perform the one selected and measure the outcome. Unfortunately the outcomes are generated by some unknown process that we are not able to discover. Next, we iterate the same procedure until some termination condition is triggered.

The outcomes have the same codomain so we can aggregate them into one cumulative sum and strive to maximize it. Since we do not know the underlying process producing the outcomes, we have to balance between repeating the most rewarding actions found so far and experimenting with the actions that are carried out less frequently. Why? Because we are unable to distinguish the optimal actions from the suboptimal ones, and this leads to inevitable estimation errors, especially in the early iterations. Now, we have to gather more information and hone our decision-making on the forthcoming iterations. The properties of this kind of dilemma can be defined and analysed in the form of various bandit problems. Here we describe one of these.

A multi-armed bandit problem can be defined as follows. A gambler has exclusive access to k slot-machines – each a one-armed bandit – that work independently but do not necessarily yield the same winnings. The gambler's objective is to maximize the earnings when the slot-machines are operated one at a time.

More formally, the ith slot-machine $(0 \le i < k)$ represents a random variable ${}^{i}X$ of an unknown distribution D_i with an unknown expectation μ_i. Pulling the lever of the ith bandit the jth time $(1 \le j)$ yields reward ${}^{i}X_j$. This also means that we have already received the rewards $\langle {}^{i}X_1, {}^{i}X_2, \ldots, {}^{i}X_{j-1} \rangle$ from machine i at some point, possibly interleaved with the rewards from the other machines. All the machines and the rewards are independent of each other.

The gambler's decision-making can be modelled as algorithm $\mathcal{A}$, which forms over time a sequence of chosen machines together with their rewards. This sequence of specific ${}^{i}X_j$ values is the information that is available when choosing the next machine to be tried. Assume n plays have been completed and let $T_i(n)$ denote the number of times the ith machine has been played by $\mathcal{A}$ during those n plays. Clearly, $\sum_{i=0}^{k-1} T_i(n) = n$. The objective of algorithm $\mathcal{A}$ is to minimize the gambler's *regret* r_n,

$$\min_{n \in \mathbb{N}} r_n = n \cdot \mu^* - \sum_{i=0}^{k-1} (\mathrm{E}[T_i(n)] \cdot \mu_i), \tag{6.3}$$

of not being able to have the most lucrative cumulative reward due to the hidden distributions D_i. The best possible expected reward from a single machine is $\mu^* = \max\{\mu_0, \mu_1, \ldots, \mu_{k-1}\}$ and the expected number of plays of machine i during the n plays is $\mathrm{E}[T_i(n)]$.

Since the actual reward distributions are unknown for $\mathcal{A}$, choosing the next machine to play is difficult. However, Auer et al. (2002) have shown that Algorithm 6.6 is one method that can be applied when allocating the actions to the machines. They present also other methods, but UCB1 is the one that has inspired the development of UCT.

Line 7 of Algorithm 6.6 selects some machine i that maximizes the given expression. Note how the exploitation of the profitable machine is encouraged by R_i/T_i: The better

---

Algorithm 6.6 Algorithm UCB1 for the multi-armed bandit problem. Primitive routine *play(i)* returns a reward of the machine i ($0 \leq i < k$), which can change in each invocation.

UCB1(k, n_{max})
    in: number of machines k ($1 \leq k \in \mathbb{N}$); number of plays n_{max} ($k \leq n_{max} \in \mathbb{N}$)
    out: total reward after n_{max} plays (depending on the use context any information
              gathered could be returned, e.g. a sequence of average rewards $\bar{w}_i = R_i/T_i$)
    local: number of plays n so far ($n \in \mathbb{N}$); sequence T of counters for the number of
              times each machine has been played ($\sum_{i=0}^{k-1} T_i = n$); sequence R of cumulative
              reward counters for each machine

1: $|T| \leftarrow k$; $|R| \leftarrow k$ ▷ Reserve space for k values in T and R.
2: **for** $i \leftarrow 0 \ldots (k-1)$ **do**   ▷ Initialize T and R by playing each machine once.
3:     $T_i \leftarrow 1$
4:     $R_i \leftarrow play(i)$
5: **end for**
6: **for** $n \leftarrow (k+1) \ldots n_{max}$ **do**   ▷ Play n_{max} times in total.
7:     $i \leftarrow \arg\max_{0 \leq j < k} \left((R_j/T_j) + \sqrt{(2 \cdot \ln n)/T_j} \right)$
8:     $T_i \leftarrow T_i + 1$
9:     $R_i \leftarrow R_i + play(i)$
10: **end do**
11: **return** $\sum_{i=0}^{k-1} R_i$

---

the reward R_j the more it is utilized, but, at the same time, the more it is selected the less inviting it is. The exploration aspect is reinforced by the term $\sqrt{(2 \cdot \ln n)/T_i}$ which steadily increases the attraction of all the machines that are not played. For a detailed rationalization of the form of the whole expression, see Auer et al. (2002).

UCT variant of Monte Carlo tree search

It is up to the selection phase of MCTS to find a node v_d that reveals more information about the moves from the root node v_r. To descend from a node one of its child nodes must be chosen over the other ones. UCT considers this situation as a multi-armed bandit problem where the moves to the child nodes are the lever pulls and the outcome of the subsequent simulation is the received reward. However, there is one significant difference, the underlying probability distribution D_i of move i changes when it is on the backpropagation path. Fortunately, this drift can be compensated for by slightly modifying the expression at line 7 of Algorithm 6.6, as proved by Kocsis and Szepesvári (2006):

$$\frac{R_i}{T_i} + \sqrt{\frac{2 \cdot \ln n}{T_i}} \quad \xrightarrow[\text{to}]{\text{changes}} \quad \frac{R_i}{T_i} + w \cdot \sqrt{\frac{\ln n}{T_i}}, \tag{6.4}$$

where w ($0 < w \in \mathbb{R}$) is an appropriate constant that balances the exploitation and exploration terms. The actual value of w depends on the problem and the codomain of the rewards. The derivation of Equation (6.4) is based on certain assumptions that can be considered valid in most circumstances.

UCT is defined in Algorithm 6.7, which continues in Algorithm 6.8. The description of the method is based on the following details:

Algorithm 6.7 UCT variant of Monte Carlo tree search. The details are discussed in the body text, including the possibility of a division by zero in UCT-CHILD. Continues in Algorithm 6.8.

UCT-MONTE-CARLO-TREE-SEARCH(v_r)
  in: root node v_r
  out: the most valued node v^* representing the best move found
  1: **while** *continue*() **do**   ▷ Resources still available?
  2:   $v_d \leftarrow$ UCT-SELECTION(v_r)
  3:   $v_n \leftarrow$ UCT-EXPANSION(v_d)
  4:   $e \leftarrow$ UCT-SIMULATION(v_n)
  5:   UCT-BACKPROPAGATION(e, v_n)
  6: **end while**
  7: **return** UCT-TERMINATION(v_r)   ▷ Determine v^* from the root node.

UCT-SELECTION(v)
  in: node v
  constant: exploration constant c ($c \in \mathbb{R}_{>0}$), depends on the problem and the codomain of the reward values, for example, $c \approx \sqrt{2}$ satisfies certain theoretical considerations when $value(\cdot) \in [0, 1] \subset \mathbb{R}$
  1: $u \leftarrow v$
  2: **while** *children*(u) $\neq \emptyset$ **do**   ▷ Is u playable?
  3:   **if** *untrieds*(u) $\neq \emptyset$ **then**   ▷ Is at least one move untried in u?
  4:     **return** u
  5:   **else**
  6:     $u \leftarrow$ UCT-CHILD(u, c)   ▷ Descend in the game tree.
  7:   **end if**
  8: **end while**
  9: **return** u ▷ Game is ended at u.

UCT-CHILD(v, w)
  in: node v (*children*(v) $\neq \emptyset$) ; exploration weight w ($0 < w \in \mathbb{R}$)
  out: a child node of v that maximizes the given function, and if there are many such child nodes a uniformly random one of those
  1: $n \leftarrow visits(v)$
  2: **if** *label*(v) = MAX **then**
  3:     **return** $\underset{u \in children(v)}{\arg\max} \left(\dfrac{value(u)}{visits(u)} + w \cdot \sqrt{\dfrac{\ln n}{visits(u)}} \right)$
  4: **else**   ▷ v is MIN node.
  5:     **return** $\underset{u \in children(v)}{\arg\min} \left(\dfrac{value(u)}{visits(u)} - w \cdot \sqrt{\dfrac{\ln n}{visits(u)}} \right)$
  6: **end if**

Algorithm 6.8 Continued from Algorithm 6.7.

UCT-EXPANSION(v)

  in: node v

  out: a node $v_n \in children(v)$ to be tried ($untrieds(v_n) = children(v_n)$) or the given v
       if such node does not exist

  1: **if** $children(v) = \emptyset$ **or** $untrieds(v) = \emptyset$ **then**

  2:   **return** v ▷ No (untried) moves at v.

  3: **end if**

  4: $v_n \leftarrow$ some node $\in untrieds(v)$ ▷ Choose an untried move.

  5: $untrieds(v) \leftarrow untrieds(v) \setminus \{v_n\}$ ▷ Move from v to v_n.

  6: $visits(v_n) \leftarrow 0$

  7: $value(v_n) \leftarrow 0$

  8: **return** v_n

UCT-SIMULATION(v)

  in: node v

  out: value of v obtained by a simulated gameplay

  1: $u \leftarrow v$

  2: **while** $children(u) \neq \emptyset$ **do**   ▷ Is u playable?

  3:   $u \leftarrow$ some node $\in children(u)$ ▷ Choose any valid move.

  4: **end while**

  5: $e \leftarrow value(u)$ ▷ On MAX's perspective.

  6: **return** e ▷ Game is ended at u with value e.

UCT-BACKPROPAGATION(e, v)

  in: value e ; node v

  1: $u \leftarrow v$

  2: **repeat**   ▷ From v to the root node.

  3:   $visits(u) \leftarrow visits(u) + 1$

  4:   $value(u) \leftarrow value(u) + e$

  5:   $u \leftarrow parent(u)$

  6: **until** $v =$ NIL

UCT-TERMINATION(v)

  in: node v ($children(v) \neq \emptyset$)

  out: the most valued node from v

  1: **return** UCT-CHILD($v, 0$)

- The selection of the best move – the most valued child node – is part of the algorithm. For this reason the routine UCT-MONTE-CARLO-TREE-SEARCH returns a child node of the root node v_r, not the utility value of v_r.
- The method constructs a partial game tree that is grown iteratively until the condition *continue*() fails. The attribute *label*($\bullet$) discerns the MAX and MIN nodes in the tree; MAX has the first turn.

- The attribute *children*(*v*) is a set of nodes such that $u \in children(v)$ exactly when *v* has a move that leads to *u*. Also, the moves in *v* precede all the moves of the nodes in *children*(*v*). The nodes represent the possible states in the game.
- The partial game tree partitions the moves into those that have already been tried by UCT and those that are still untried. This separation is bookkept by the set *untrieds*(*v*) $\subseteq$ *children*(*v*): membership $u \in untrieds(v)$ means that node *v* has a move leading to *u* that has not yet been considered.

  For the frontier nodes v_n of the partial tree, $untrieds(v_n) = children(v_n)$. When all the moves from *v* have been handled at least once, then $untrieds(v) = \emptyset$.
- Each node *v* has also two attributes for bookkeeping the data UCT collects from the simulations for ranking the nodes: *visits*(*v*) counts how many times *v* has been considered and *value*(*v*) accumulates the estimations made.

Note that at line 3 and 5 of UCT-CHILD the maximization and minimization are over all the child nodes of *v*, including $u \in untrieds(v)$ for which $visits(u) = 0$ (or NIL when *v* is on the frontier). There are options to resolve this undefined issue. For instance, the situation can be interpreted to yield the result $+\infty$ for MAX's *v* (and $-\infty$ for MIN's), which enforces all the nodes in *children*(*v*) so that they are considered before descending to their child nodes. Alternatively, the undefined case can be evaluated for some other value that results in an effective selection of the nodes.

To sum up, UCT has many adjustment possibilities to fit it to a particular problem:

- the termination condition *continue*();
- the exploration constant *w* that depends on the problem and the codomain of *value*(•);
- the prioritization of the available moves in UCT-EXPANSION;
- the method that plays the game to the end in UCT-SIMULATION;
- the determination of the best result in UCT-TERMINATION.

These and other enhancements and variations are discussed by Browne et al. (2012) along with an introduction to assorted applications. The MCTS methods, including UCT in particular, are versatile algorithms and they have demonstrated their feasibility when solving hard problems such as Go (Gelly and Silver 2011). This approach has provided us with a way to trade rigorous domain specificity against blind consumption of runtime resources, allowing us to seek out new ways to balance between those extremes and, at the same time, to learn more about the problems themselves.

6.4 Games of Chance

Diced noughts and crosses is a generalization of ordinary noughts and crosses. The game is played on an $m \times m$ grid with a die of *n* equally probable sides. The player who has ℓ tokens in a row is the winner. In each turn a player first selects a subset *S* of empty squares on the grid and then distributes *n* 'reservation marks' on them. The number of marks in an empty square *s* is denoted by *marks*(*s*). Next, the player casts the die for each $s \in S$. Let us assume that the outcome of the die is *d*. The player places her token on *s* if $d \leq marks(s)$. In other words, each mark on a square increases the probability of capturing it by $1/n$, and if $marks(s) = n$, the capture is certain. By way of comparison, in noughts and crosses a legal move is always certain, but in diced noughts and crosses a

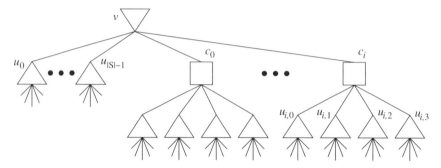

Figure 6.7 An extract from a general game tree for copper noughts and crosses consists of a MAX node (the labile triangle), MIN nodes (the stable triangles) and CHANCE nodes (the squares).

move is only a player's suggestion that can be rejected with probability $1 - d/marks(\bullet)$. We get ordinary noughts and crosses with parameters $m = \ell = 3$ and $n = 1$. The variant where $n = 2$ can be played using a coin and we name it copper noughts and crosses.

Due to non-deterministic moves, the game tree of copper noughts and crosses cannot be drawn as a *minimax tree* as in Figure 6.1. However, the outcome of a random event can be calculated by considering its expected value. This idea can be used to generalize the game trees by introducing *chance nodes* (Michie 1966). Figure 6.7 illustrates how to evaluate a move in copper noughts and crosses from the perspective of MAX. Suppose that the grid has $|S|$ empty squares. The player can select $|S|$ certain moves $u_0, \ldots, u_{|S|-1}$ that can be evaluated as in an ordinary minimax tree. Coin tossing is used when the player's marks m_0 and m_1 are on different squares. Because we do not have to care about the identity of the marks, there are $|S|(|S| - 1)/2$ combinations to consider. A chance node c_i ($i \in [0, \ldots, |S|(|S| - 1)/2 - 1]$) has four possible outcomes: the token can be placed on both marks, only on m_0, only on m_1, or both marks are void. Because each of these events happen with probability $\frac{1}{4}$, the value of c_i can be calculated by $\frac{1}{4} \cdot (e(u_{i,0}) + e(u_{i,1}) + e(u_{i,2}) + e(u_{i,3}))$, where $e(\bullet)$ represents the utility value of the subtree.

Game trees resembling Figure 6.7 are called *∗-minimax trees* (Ballard 1983). Their utility value is given by

$$
emm(v) = \begin{cases}
value(v), & \text{if } v \text{ is a leaf,} \\
\min_{u \in children(v)} \{emm(u)\}, & \text{if } v \text{ is a MIN node,} \\
\max_{u \in children(v)} \{emm(u)\}, & \text{if } v \text{ is a MAX node,} \\
\sum_{u \in children(v)} (P(u) \cdot emm(u)), & \text{if } v \text{ is a CHANCE node,}
\end{cases} \tag{6.5}
$$

which is a generalization of Equation (6.1). Here, $emm(\bullet)$ is an abbreviation for the *expectiminimax* value. The chance nodes often cause a combinatorial explosion in the branching factor of the game trees, which prevents us from implementing Equation (6.5) similarly to Algorithm 6.1. Because the chance nodes do not affect the evaluation of MIN and MAX nodes, the evaluation method can use alpha-beta pruning, but even this observation does not help much if the chance nodes have the largest branching factor.

Interestingly, it is also possible to utilize the information gathered by the depth-first search order in the chance nodes. To do this we assume that for the leaf nodes $value(\bullet)$ can be bounded within a constant interval $[\ell_{min}, \ell_{max}]$ (Ballard 1983). Suppose we are calculating the value of a chance node c within the given interval (α, β) and we are about to descend to its child node u_i. In other words, we have already evaluated the child nodes $u_0, \ldots, u_{i-1}$, and nodes $u_{i+1}, \ldots$ will be evaluated later. Node c will not be selected by its parent, if either of the following inequalities holds:

$$\sum_{k=0}^{i-1}(P(u_k) \cdot emm(u_k)) + P(u_i) \cdot emm(u_i) + \ell_{max} \cdot \left(1 - \sum_{k=0}^{i} P(u_k)\right) \leq \alpha, \qquad (6.6)$$

$$\sum_{k=0}^{i-1}(P(u_k) \cdot emm(u_k)) + P(u_i) \cdot emm(u_i) + \ell_{min} \cdot \left(1 - \sum_{k=0}^{i} P(u_k)\right) \geq \beta. \qquad (6.7)$$

The first term of the summation is already known, the middle term is to be calculated next, and the last one gives the worst estimate for the remaining nodes. By reorganizing the terms we get the inequalities

$$emm(u_i) \leq \frac{\alpha - \sum_{k=0}^{i-1}(P(u_k) \cdot emm(u_k)) - \ell_{max} \cdot \left(1 - \sum_{k=0}^{i} P(u_k)\right)}{P(u_i)}, \qquad (6.8)$$

$$emm(u_i) \geq \frac{\beta - \sum_{k=0}^{i-1}(P(u_k) \cdot emm(u_k)) - \ell_{min} \cdot \left(1 - \sum_{k=0}^{i} P(u_k)\right)}{P(u_i)}. \qquad (6.9)$$

respectively, and due to the direction of these inequalities the expressions on the right-hand side can be used as alpha-beta values for the node u_i. The alpha-beta values for the child nodes can be calculated incrementally from the following recurrences:

$$\begin{cases} E_0 = 0 \\ E_k = E_{k-1} + P(u_{k-1}) \cdot emm(u_{k-1}) \end{cases} \qquad \begin{cases} D_0 = 1 - P(u_0) \\ D_k = D_{k-1} - P(u_k) \end{cases}$$

In other words, for child node u_i we get the interval bounds

$$\alpha_i = \frac{\alpha - E_i - \ell_{max} \cdot D_i}{P(u_i)}, \qquad (6.10)$$

$$\beta_i = \frac{\beta - E_i - \ell_{min} \cdot D_i}{P(u_i)}. \qquad (6.11)$$

Note that $E_k + P(u_k) \cdot emm(u_k)$ also gives the final result of c at the last child node u_k. Algorithm 6.9 implements this alpha-beta pruning for every node in a $*$-minimax tree with the fail-soft enhancement.

The drawback of Algorithm 6.9 is that it expects the worst from the unvisited children of the chance nodes and, thus, the alpha-beta pruning begins to have an effect only later in the evaluation. However, in practice these children tend to have the same properties. This is why Ballard (1983) considers Algorithm 6.9 as a starting point (called Star1) and presents various effective sampling (or probing) strategies for the child nodes that supplement the depth-first idea and lead to narrower alpha-beta intervals. Hauk et al. (2005) provide further insights into the topic.

Algorithm 6.9 Expectiminimax using alpha-beta pruning and fail-soft enhancement.

EXPECTI-ALPHA-BETA(v, α, β)
    in: node v; alpha value α; beta value β
    out: utility value of node v
    constant: the range of $value(\cdot)$ for a leaf node is $[\ell_{min}, \ell_{max}]$
  1: **if** $children(v) = \emptyset$ **then**   ▷ v is a leaf.
  2:   **return** $value(v)$
  3: **else if** $label(v) = $ CHANCE **then**   ▷ v is a CHANCE node.
  4:   $d \leftarrow 1$
  5:   $s \leftarrow 0$
  6:   **for all** $u \in children(v)$ **do**
  7:     $d \leftarrow d - P(u)$
  8:     $\alpha' \leftarrow \max\{\ell_{min}, (\alpha - s - \ell_{max} \cdot d)/P(u)\}$
  9:     $\beta' \leftarrow \min\{\ell_{max}, (\beta - s - \ell_{min} \cdot d)/P(u)\}$
10:     $e \leftarrow$ EXPECTI-ALPHA-BETA(u, α', β')
11:     $s \leftarrow s + P(u) \cdot e$
12:     **if** $e \leq \alpha$ **then**
13:       **return** $s + \ell_{max} \cdot d$
14:     **end if**
15:     **if** $\beta \leq e$ **then**
16:       **return** $s + \ell_{min} \cdot d$
17:     **end if**
18:   **end for**
19:   **return** s
20: **else if** $label(v) = $ MIN **then**   ▷ v is a MIN node.
21:   $e \leftarrow +\infty$
22:   **for all** $u \in children(v)$ **do**
23:     **if** $e < \beta$ **then** $\beta \leftarrow e$ **end if**
24:     $t \leftarrow$ EXPECTI-ALPHA-BETA(u, α, β)
25:     **if** $t < e$ **then** $e \leftarrow t$ **end if**
26:     **if** $e \leq \alpha$ **then return** e **end if**
27:   **end for**
28:   **return** e
29: **else**   ▷ v is a MAX node.
30:   $e \leftarrow -\infty$
31:   **for all** $u \in children(v)$ **do**
32:     **if** $\alpha < e$ **then** $\alpha \leftarrow e$ **end if**
33:     $t \leftarrow$ EXPECTI-ALPHA-BETA(u, α, β)
34:     **if** $e < t$ **then** $e \leftarrow t$ **end if**
35:     **if** $\beta \leq e$ **then return** e **end if**
36:   **end for**
37:   **return** e
38: **end if**

6.5 Summary

In zero-sum perfect information games, the minimax method provides us with the optimal gameplay. However, if we cannot build the whole game tree for the game, we have to reduce its size either by limiting the search depth or cutting the branches. In a partial game tree, the depth is reduced artificially by making the internal nodes leaves. This can be done using a heuristic to estimate their outcome, which of course can lead to suboptimal results. The branching factor can be reduced with alpha-beta pruning, which cuts off nodes that cannot provide a better outcome than the current best result. If we set tighter limits for the pruning (as in principal variation search), we can improve the running even further. With Monte Carlo tree search we can reduce the search space considerably without an evaluation function. A game tree can also include probabilistic elements, which can be handled by modelling them as chance nodes.

Game trees can be used in many classical board games, and they have been studied widely. There are many game-specific improvements that allow, for example, the opening and closing moves to be chosen from a set of precalculated alternatives. Nevertheless, in the middle of the gameplay where the number of possible situations is much greater, the methods revert back to building game trees to find the best move for the next round.

Exercises

6-1 The most famous non-zero-sum game is prisoner's dilemma, where two prisoners (i.e. players), accused of the same crime, have two possible moves:
  • cooperate with the other prisoner and keep silent during the interrogation;
  • defect and rat on the other prisoner.
The moves have the following pay-offs:

	You cooperate	*You defect*
I cooperate	6 months' imprisonment	10 years' imprisonment
I defect	Freedom	5 years' imprisonment

Not knowing the opponent's move, each prisoner must now select a move and face the consequences.

In iterated prisoner's dilemma these encounters are repeated, and the players try to minimize the sum of the prison sentences. The players remember all previous encounters. Devise a strategy for iterated prisoner's dilemma. Try out both egoistic and altruistic approaches.

6-2 Assume we have the game trees of Figures 6.8 and 6.9, where player MAX has the first move. Show how to solve the winner of the games using the minimax method. Illustrate how the algorithm operates with the given game trees.

6-3 In practice we are interested not only in the evaluation value of the root node but also in the best move from it. Devise a simple method that extends the game tree algorithms presented to support this.

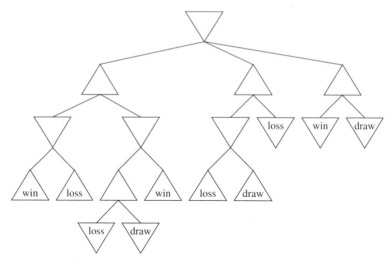

Figure 6.8 A game tree with three possible outcomes (from the perspective of MAX): win, draw, loss.

6-4 In the game tree algorithms presented, the moves are generated implicitly by the statement $u \in children(v)$. Concretize these algorithms by introducing a primitive routine $child(v)$ that iterates all the nodes in $children(v)$ one by one and returns NIL when they are exhausted.

6-5 In Exercise 6-4 we concretize the game tree algorithms with an iterator abstraction. In this exercise use the following state changing functions instead:

$move(v)$	Iterates all the possible moves from node v of player $label(v)$ and returns NIL when they are exhausted.
$apply(v, m)$	Returns the successor node of v for move m.
$cancel(u, m)$	Yields the parent node of u when move m is taken back.

You can assume that a move is reversible (i.e. $v = cancel(apply(v, m), m)$).

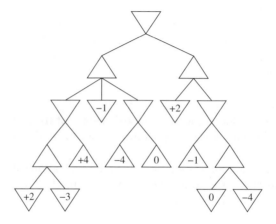

Figure 6.9 A game tree with outcomes in the range $[-4, +4]$.

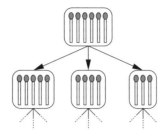

Figure 6.10 Partial game tree for One-Two-Three Nim.

6-6 Draw a complete game tree for Division Nim with eight matches. Analyse the outcome using minimax.

6-7 In Division Nim the heap cannot be divided into equal halves. Factor Division Nim relaxes this constraint by allowing a heap of $2n$ matches to be divided into two heaps of n matches, if n has a common prime factor with the player's turn number. The turns are numbered consecutively starting from zero. Give a complete game tree for Factor Division Nim with seven matches and assign the values 'win', 'loss', and 'draw' to the nodes.

6-8 One-Two-Three Nim is another simplification of Nim. It starts with a heap of n matches and on each turn a player removes one, two or three matches from the heap. The player to pick the last match wins. Draw a complete game tree and analyse the outcome using minimax for this variant of Nim when $n = 6$ (see Figure 6.10).

6-9 Extend the game tree of Exercise 6-8 for $n = 9$. Observe how wins and losses behave in MAX and MIN nodes. Can you design an evaluation function that gives for each node a perfect estimate of the utility function? If so, how does this affect playing One-Two-Three Nim?

6-10 In Nim proper, there are initially several heaps of matches. On each turn a player selects one heap and removes at least one match from that heap. The player to pick the last match wins. Draw a complete game tree and analyse the outcome using minimax for Nim with three heaps having 1, 2 and 3 matches (see Figure 6.11).

6-11 Poker is an imperfect information game. Why is it that the minimax method cannot be used to solve it?

6-12 Minimax assumes that the players are rational and try to win. If this is not true, does the method still work?

6-13 When searching a game tree, which would be preferable situation: having a large d or a large b (i.e. having a deep or a wide game tree)?

6-14 Minimax can expand $(b^{d+1} - 1)/(b - 1)$ nodes in a game tree with a branching factor b and depth d. Obviously, the branching factor depends on the game: in

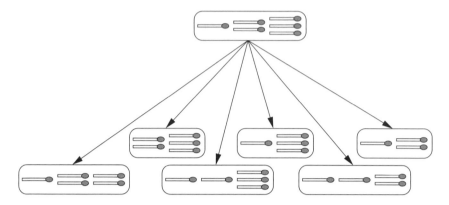

Figure 6.11 Partial game tree for Nim with heaps of size 1, 2 and 3.

draughts each position has on average three possible moves, in chess about 30, and in Go there are hundreds of possible moves. Assume that expanding a node takes 1 ms of computation time. How long does it take to evaluate a game tree when $b \in \{3, 30, 300\}$ and $d \in \{2, 4, 8, 16\}$?

6-15 Equation (6.1) defines the minimax value for a node as a recursive function. Give a similar definition for negamax.

6-16 Assume that in noughts and crosses MIN (playing noughts) is using a one-move look-ahead heuristic with the evaluation function of Figure 6.4. Player MAX has made the first move by putting a cross in a corner (see the left subtree in Figure 6.1), and MIN has to select one of the five possible moves by estimating the outcome of the next ply. What move does MIN select and why?

   If on the next turn MAX puts a cross in the opposite corner, what is MIN's next move? How does the game end and why?

6-17 A compact transposition table does not include redundant game state information. Design an algorithm that normalizes the game states of noughts and crosses so that rotations and mirror images are represented only by one game state as in Figure 6.1.

6-18 Some turn-based games allow the same state (e.g. the same board situation) to occur many times. How would you make them unique so that they can be differentiated in the game tree algorithms?

6-19 Show how alpha-beta pruning works on the game tree of Figure 6.9. Does the expanding order of nodes in the first ply from the root affect the overall number of pruned nodes?

6-20 In the expansion phase of MCTS, it is possible to consider multiple untried moves of the selected node at once. For example, one could bundle similar moves and observe whether their outcomes are also similar. On the other hand, the results of the different moves cover the decision space more. Consider situations or problems where expanding many moves at once would be useful.

6-21 The simulation phase of MCTS can be driven, for instance, by choosing the moves randomly or by utilizing some domain-specific method. Ponder the following aspects:

(a) The problem with random play is that the evaluations of the outcomes are inaccurate, a player rarely chooses a random move and an opponent hardly ever passes up the opportunity to benefit from such a move. However, with enough repetitions estimation becomes more accurate without the need for domain knowledge.

(b) An intelligent playing method yields inherently more accurate estimations since it utilizes information about the problem domain. But still the result can be biased because of a poor move at the beginning of the trial game, and if such moves are systematic the repetitions do not refine the results – on the contrary.

In general, 'either/or' thinking tends to have 'both/and' as a viable alternative. Devise a method that incorporates both of these simulation approaches.

6-22 Assume the unknown distributions D_i associated with Equation (6.3) are equal, that is, $D = D_i$ and $\mu = \mu_i$ ($0 \le i < k$). What can be said about r_n?

6-23 Algorithm 6.6 defines the routine UCB1 that simulates the choices in the multi-armed bandit problem. Let us define another routine NON-UCB1 that replaces line 7 with a random selection:

> 7: $i \leftarrow$ RANDOM-INTEGER$(0, k)$ ▷ Random $i \in [0, k-1]$.

Implement both of these methods and compare their outcomes with various distributions generated, for example, by Algorithm 2.4.

6-24 The multi-armed bandit problem is described from the human point of view: there are machines acting randomly and we want to learn their possible dissimilarities and benefit from them. Let us turn the tables. If a computer, identified as C-64, had consciousness, it would arguably consider the humans to act even more randomly.

(a) Thus, C-64 could see a sequence of humans as a row of bandits, and when C-64 acts, the values of the humans' responses are drawn from some unknown distribution. The objective is of the form 'who likes this thing'.

(b) Alternatively, if there is only one petty human, the bandits would be the types of actions towards that human. Then the hidden distributions are the human's likings of C-64's various actions. The objective is of the form 'which of these things is liked'.

Assume that C-64 has k consumption items that can be thrown to a player, supporting different play styles in a game. The reward for the action could be measured, for instance, by how soon the player uses that particular item.

Ponder situations where this kind of turned-table approach could work and where it would not. Invent more applications for the bandit problem.

6-25 The UCT method defined in Algorithms 6.7 and 6.8 can have a slightly more compact presentation. Try out different ways to reorganize the control logic into routines.

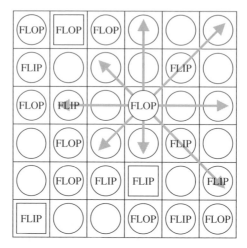

Figure 6.12 An example of n^2-Pile Flipflop where $n = 6$. Round pieces represent the tokens for FLIP, FLOP or empty pieces for NEUTRAL; square pieces represent the fixed tokens. When a FLOP token is added to a pile, all the piles along the marked lines are reversed. The reversing line ends at another FLOP token, at a fixed FLIP token, or at the end of the board.

6-26 The two-player game n^2-Pile Flipflop is played on an $n \times n$ board. Initially, each square of the board has a token with the value NEUTRAL. Player Flip has $5n$ FLIP tokens and $\lceil \sqrt{n} \rceil$ fixed FLIP tokens, and player Flop has $5n$ FLOP tokens and $\lceil \sqrt{n} \rceil$ fixed FLOP tokens. Player Flip starts the game. On each turn, a player can put one token on top of any pile that does not yet have a fixed token. The topmost token of a pile is said to control the pile. When a token is added, all piles on the two horizontal, two vertical, and four diagonal lines starting from the added token are reversed (i.e. the undermost token is turned up to be the topmost and controls the pile). The reversing line ends at the player's other control token, at the opponent's fixed token, or at the end of the board (see Figure 6.12). The game ends when either of the players has run out of tokens or cannot add a token to the board. The player controlling more piles at the end is the winner.

Write a program that plays n^2-Pile Flipflop. If $n = 1$, player Flip wins. Is there a winning strategy for other n values?

6-27 Simplify Algorithm 6.9 by assuming that the event probabilities in a chance node are uniform. In other words, each chance node c has n children u_i for which $P(u_i) = 1/n$.

6-28 In copper noughts and crosses all the chance moves are marked and fixed before the coin is tossed for both of them. Let us change this rule. First, the player makes a mark in an empty square and then the coin is used to resolve the capture. Then the second mark is handled in the same way. Draw a simple game tree for this variant.

7

Path Finding

As in the real world, finding a path from one place to another is a common – if not the most common – algorithmic problem in computer games. Although the problem can seem fairly simple to us humans (most of the time), a surprising amount of the total computation time in many commercial computer games is spent in solving path-finding problems. The reasons for this are the ever-increasing complexity of game world environments and the number of entities that must be calculated. Moreover, if the environment changes dynamically (e.g. old paths becomes blocked and new ones are opened), routes cannot be solved beforehand but only reactively on the spot as the game progresses. Real-time interaction imposes even further constraints, because the feedback to the human player should be almost instant and the path must be found before he gets too impatient to wait any longer.

The problem statement of path finding is simple: given a starting point s and a goal point r, find a path from s to r minimizing a given criterion. Usually this cost function is travelling time, which can depend on the distance, the type of terrain, or the mode of travel. We can think of path finding either as a search problem – find a path that minimizes the cost – or as an optimization problem – minimize the cost subject to the constraint of the path. Consequently, graph search methods can be seen as optimization methods, where the constraints are given implicitly in the form and weights of the graph. Although we can use general optimization methods such as simplex, they lose the graph-like qualities of the path-finding problem, which is why we mainly focus on the search problem throughout this chapter.

In an ideal case, we would do path finding in a continuous game world and solve the route from s to r straightforwardly. Unfortunately, this is rarely a realistic option, since the search space gets too complex. Instead, we discretize the search space by restricting the possible *waypoints* into a finite set and reducing the paths to *connections* between them. In other words, we form a graph where the vertices are the waypoints and the edges are the connections. We have thus reduced the original problem to finding a path in a graph (see Figure 7.1). The idea resembles travelling in the real world: move to the closest waypoint (airport, bus stop, underground station, harbour, etc.), go through waypoints until closest to the destination, exit the final waypoint, and proceed to the destination.

This approach gives us a three-step method. First, we show how the game world can be discretized. On the basis of the discretization we can form a graph, and the path-finding problem is transformed into finding the minimum path in the graph. Although there

Algorithms and Networking for Computer Games, Second Edition. Jouni Smed and Harri Hakonen.
© 2017 John Wiley & Sons Ltd. Published 2017 by John Wiley & Sons Ltd.

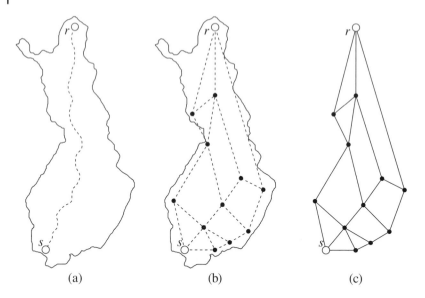

(a)   (b)   (c)

Figure 7.1 Real-world path finding is reduced to a graph problem by discretizing the search space into waypoints. The waypoints are the vertices and the connections between them the edges of the graph.

are several algorithms to solve this problem, we concentrate on A* algorithm, which uses a heuristic estimate function to enhance the search. Finally, when the minimum path in the graph has been found, it has to be realized as movements in the game world considering how realistic the movements look to the human observing them.

7.1 Discretization of the Game World

The first step in solving the path-finding problem in a continuous world is to discretize it. The type of game world usually gives an indication of how this discretization should be done. We can immediately come up with intuitive choices for waypoints: doorways, centres of the room, along the walls, corners, and around the obstacles (Tozour 2003). Once the waypoints have been selected, we establish whether there is a connection between them based on the geometry of the game world. The connection can be associated with cost based on the distance or type of environment, and this cost is set to be the weight of the edge.

Although the waypoints can be laid down manually during the level design, it should preferably be an automatic process. Two common approaches to achieve this are to superimpose a grid on the game world, or to use a navigation mesh which observes the underlying geometry.

7.1.1 Grid

We can place a grid, which is a tiling of polygons (i.e. tessellation), over the game world. To simplify, we consider only grids where each tile shares at most one edge with a neighbouring tile (see Figure 7.2). Now, the centre of a tile represents a waypoint, and its

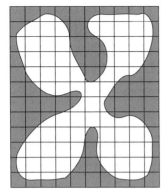 

Figure 7.2 A square grid is laid over the game world. If the majority of the world inside a tile is open, the tile is included in the waypoints.

neighbourhood, composed of the adjacent tiles, forms the possible connections to other waypoints. The world inside the tile defines whether it is included in the waypoints and what are its connections to other waypoints (Uras and Koenig 2015).

Grids usually support random-access lookup, because each tile should be accessible in a constant time. The drawback of this approach is that a grid does not pay attention to the actual geometry of the game world. For instance, some parts of the world may get unconnected if the granularity of the grid is not fine enough. Also, storing the grid requires memory, but we can reduce this requirement, for example, by using hierarchical lookup tables (van der Sterren 2003).

There are exactly three regular tessellations, composed of either equilateral triangles, squares or regular hexagons (see Figure 7.3). When we are defining a neighbourhood for triangular and square grids, we must first decide whether we consider only the tiles adjacent to the edges of a tile or also the tiles which share a corner point with the tile. Figure 7.4 illustrates the situation in a square grid: in the former case we have four-connectivity (i.e. a tile has at most four neighbours), and in the latter case eight-connectivity. An obvious problem of eight-connectivity is that diagonal moves are longer than vertical or horizontal ones, which should be taken into account in distance calculations. Because hexagonal grids allow only six-connectivity and the neighbours are equidistant, they are often used in strategy and role-playing games (Jahn and Loviscach 2008).

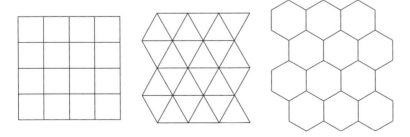

Figure 7.3 The square grid, triangular grid, and hexagonal grid are the only regular two-dimensional tessellations.

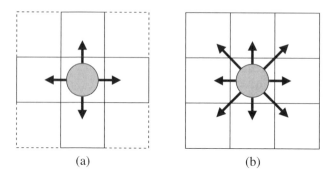

(a)   (b)

Figure 7.4 A square grid allows (a) four-connectivity and (b) eight-connectivity.

Instead of assigning the waypoints to the centre of the tiles, we can use the corners of the tiles. Now the neighbourhood is determined along the edges and not over them. However, these two waypoint assignments are dual to each other, since they can be converted in both directions. For the regular tessellations the conversion is simple, because we can consider the centre of a tile as a corner point of the dual grid and vice versa, and – as we can see in Figure 7.3 – the square grid is the dual shape of itself and the triangular and hexagonal grids are dual shapes of each other.

7.1.2 Navigation mesh

A navigation mesh is a convex partitioning of the game world geometry. In other words, it is a set of convex polygons that covers the game world, where all adjacent polygons share only two points and one edge, and no polygon overlaps another polygon. Each polygon (or shared edge) represents a waypoint that is connected to the adjacent polygons (see Figure 7.5). Convexity guarantees that we can move in a straight line inside a

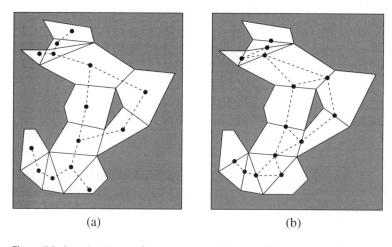

(a)   (b)

Figure 7.5 A navigation mesh is a convex partitioning of the game world geometry. (a) The waypoints have been placed in the middle of each polygon. (b) The centre of each shared edge is a waypoint.

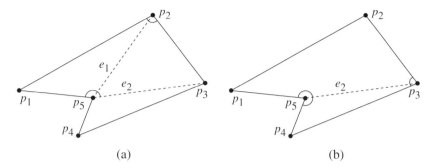

Figure 7.6 After triangulation, the Hertel–Mehlhorn method begins to remove non-essential edges to form a convex partition. (a) Edge e_1 is non-essential, because it divides only convex angles at points p_2 and p_5. If it is removed, the resulting polygon $\langle p_1, p_2, p_3, p_5 \rangle$ will be convex. (b) When e_1 has been removed, edge e_2 becomes essential and cannot be removed, because it divides a concave angle at point p_5.

polygon (e.g. from the current position to the first waypoint, and from the final waypoint to the destination) and from one polygon to another.

By using dynamic programming we can solve the convex partition problem (i.e. minimize the number of convex polygons needed to cover the original polygon) optimally in $O(r^2 n \log n)$ time, where n is the number of points (i.e. vertices) and r the number of notches (i.e. points whose interior angle is concave; $r \leq n - 3$) (Keil 1985). The Hertel–Mehlhorn heuristic finds a convex partition in $O(n + r \log r)$ time, and the resulting partition has at most four times the number of polygons as the optimum solution (Hertel and Mehlhorn 1985). The method, described in Algorithm 7.1, first triangulates the original polygon. Although a simple polygon can be triangulated in $O(n)$ time (Chazelle 1991), Seidel's algorithm provides a simpler randomized algorithm with expected $O(n \log^* n)$ running time (Seidel 1991). After triangulation, the Hertel–Mehlhorn removes non-essential edges between convex polygons (see Figure 7.6).

Algorithm 7.1 Hertel–Mehlhorn method for convex partition.

CONVEX-PARTITION(P)
  in: polygon P
  out: convex partition R
  1: $R \leftarrow$ TRIANGULATE(P)
  2: **for all** $e \in E(R) \setminus E(P)$ **do**   ▷ Edges added by triangulation.
  3:   **if not** e divides a concave angle in R **then**
  4:     $E(R) \leftarrow E(R) \setminus \{e\}$
  5:   **end if**
  6: **end for**
  7: **return** R

7.2 Finding the Minimum Path

After the game world has been discretized, the problem of path finding has been transposed into that of path finding in a finite graph. The waypoints are the vertices of the graph, the connections are the edges, and if each connection is associated with a cost (e.g. travelling time), this is assigned to the weight of the edge.

We have a set of well-known graph algorithms for solving the shortest path problem (let $|V|$ be the number of vertices and $|E|$ the number of edges); for details, see Cormen et al. (2001).

- *Breadth-first search.* Expand all vertices at distance k from the start vertex before proceeding to any vertices at distance $k + 1$. Once this frontier has reached the goal vertex, the shortest path has been found. The running time is $O(|V| + |E|)$.
- *Depth-first search.* Expand an undiscovered vertex in the neighbourhood of the most recently expanded vertex, until the goal vertex has been found. The running time is $\Theta(|V| + |E|)$.
- *Dijkstra's algorithm.* Find the shortest paths from a single start vertex to all other vertices in a directed graph with non-negative weights. A straightforward implementation yields a running time $O(|V|^2)$, which can be improved to $O(|V| \log |V| + |E|)$ with a proper choice of data structure.

We can improve the methods by guiding the search heuristically so that as few vertices as possible are expanded during the search. For instance, *best-first search* orders the vertices in the neighbourhood of a vertex according to a heuristic estimate of their closeness to the goal. Despite the use of a heuristic, best-first returns the optimal solution because no vertex is discarded. Naturally, we can decrease the running time if we give up optimality: *beam search* is based on best-first search but it expands only the most promising candidates in the neighbourhood, thus allowing suboptimal solutions (see Figure 7.7).

In the remainder of this section we consider the properties of a heuristic evaluation function used in guiding the search. Also, we describe and analyse the A* algorithm,

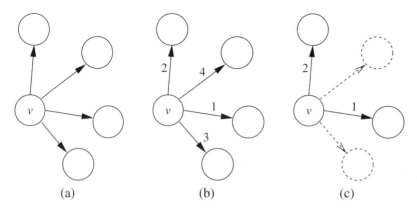

Figure 7.7 Expanding the vertices in the neighbourhood. (a) Breadth-first search does not consider the order in which the neighbourhood of vertex *v* is expanded. (b) Best-first search uses a heuristic function to rank the neighbours but does not exclude any of them. (c) Beam search expands only a subset of the neighbourhood.

which is the *de facto* method for path finding in commercial computer games. The basic graph notation used in this section is introduced in Appendix A. The cost of moving (i.e. the sum of weights along a path) from vertex v to vertex u is stored in $g(v \rightsquigarrow u)$. Also, we need two distinguished vertices: a start vertex $s \in V$ and a goal vertex $r \in V$. Obviously, we are interested in the cases where $s \neq r$, and we want to find a path minimizing $g(s \rightsquigarrow r)$.

7.2.1 Evaluation function

The vertex chosen for expansion is always the one minimizing the evaluation function

$$f(v) = g(s \rightsquigarrow v) + h(v \rightsquigarrow r), \tag{7.1}$$

where $g(s \rightsquigarrow v)$ estimates the minimum cost from the start vertex s to vertex v, and $h(v \rightsquigarrow r)$ is a heuristic estimate of the cost from v to the goal vertex r. Hence, $f(v)$ estimates the minimal cost of the path from the start vertex to the goal vertex passing through vertex v.

Let $g^*(s \rightsquigarrow v)$ denote the exact cost of the shortest path from s to v, and $h^*(v \rightsquigarrow r)$ the exact cost of the shortest path from v to r. Now, $f^*(v) = g^*(s \rightsquigarrow v) + h^*(v \rightsquigarrow r)$ gives the exact cost of the optimal path from s to r through vertex v. Ideally, we would use the function f^* in our algorithm, because then we would not have to expand any unnecessary vertices. Unfortunately, for most search problems, such an oracle function h^* does not exist or is too costly to compute.

The value of the cost function $g(s \rightsquigarrow v)$ is calculated as the actual cost from the start vertex s to vertex v along the cheapest path found so far. If the graph G is a tree, $g(s \rightsquigarrow v)$ will give the exact cost, because there is only one path leading from s to v. In general graphs, the cost function $g(s \rightsquigarrow v)$ can err only in overestimating the minimal cost, and its value can be adjusted downwards if a cheaper path to v is found. If we let the evaluation function $f(v) = g(s \rightsquigarrow v)$ and assume a cost of one unit for each move, we get breadth-first search, because shorter paths will be preferred over the longer ones; instead, if we let $f(v) = -g(s \rightsquigarrow v)$, we get depth-first search, since vertices deeper in the graph will now have a lower cost.

The heuristic function h carries information which is usually based on knowledge from outside the graph. It can be defined in any way appropriate to the problem domain (see Figure 7.8). Obviously, the closer the heuristic estimate is to the actual cost, the less our algorithm will expand superfluous vertices. If we disregard h and our search is based solely on the value of g, we have cheapest-first search, where the algorithm will always choose the vertex nearest to the start vertex. Conversely, an algorithm using only the function h gives us best-first search.

7.2.2 Properties

Let us define Algorithm A – a name due to tradition – as a best-first search using the evaluation function of Equation (7.1). A search algorithm is *admissible* if it is guaranteed to find a solution path of minimal cost if any solution path exists (e.g. breadth-first search is admissible). If Algorithm A uses the optimal evaluation function f^*, we can prove that it is admissible. In reality, however, the heuristic function h is an estimate. Let us define Algorithm A* as Algorithm A which uses such an estimate. It can be proven that Algorithm A* is admissible if it satisfies the following condition: the value of $h(v \rightsquigarrow r)$

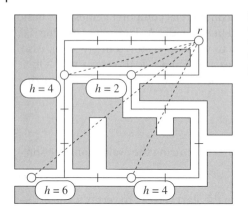

Figure 7.8 An example of a heuristic function. If the weight of an edge is the distance between the vertices using Manhattan metric, a heuristic function h can estimate them with truncated Euclidean distances.

must not overestimate the cost of getting from vertex v to the goal vertex r. In other words,

$$\forall v \in V : h(v \rightsquigarrow r) \le h^*(v \rightsquigarrow r). \tag{7.2}$$

If the heuristic is locally admissible, it is said to be *monotonic*. In this case, when the search moves through the graph, the evaluation function f will never decrease, since the actual cost is not less than the heuristic cost. Obviously, any monotonic heuristic is also admissible. If Algorithm A* is monotonic, it finds the shortest path to any vertex the first time it is expanded. In other words, if the search rediscovers a vertex, we know that the new path will not be shorter than the one found previously. This allows us to significantly simplify the implementation of the algorithm, because we can omit the closed list employed by general search strategies.

Let us state an *optimality* result for Algorithm A*:

Theorem 7.2.1 *The first path from start vertex s to goal vertex r found by monotonic Algorithm A* is optimal.*

Proof: We use a proof by contradiction. Suppose we have an undiscovered vertex v for which $f(v) < g(s \rightsquigarrow r)$. Let u be a vertex lying along the shortest path from s to v. Due to admissibility, we have $f(u) \le f(v)$, and because u also must be undiscovered, $f(r) \le f(u)$. In other words, $f(r) \le f(u) \le f(v)$. Because r is the goal vertex, we have $h(r \rightsquigarrow r) = 0$ and $f(r) = g(s \rightsquigarrow r)$. From this it follows that $g(s \rightsquigarrow r) \le f(v)$, which is a contradiction. This means that there exist no undiscovered vertices that are closer to the start vertex s than the goal vertex r. ∎

Although h is sufficient to be a lower estimate on h^*, the more closely it approximates h^*, the better the search algorithm will perform. We can now compare two A* algorithms with respect to their *informedness*. Algorithm $\mathcal{A}_1$ using function h_1 is said to be more informed than algorithm $\mathcal{A}_2$ using function h_2 if

$$\forall v \in V \setminus \{r\} : h_1(v \rightsquigarrow r) \ge h_2(v \rightsquigarrow r). \tag{7.3}$$

This means that $\mathcal{A}_1$ will never expand more vertices than are expanded by $\mathcal{A}_2$. Because of informedness, there is no better approach than Algorithm A* in the sense that no other search strategy with access to *the same amount of outside knowledge* can do any less work than A* and still be sure of finding the optimal solution.

7.2.3 Algorithm A*

Algorithm 7.2 describes an implementation of Algorithm A*. As mentioned earlier, monotonicity of the evaluation function means that we need only update an open list of the candidate vertices (lines 15–20), and the algorithm can terminate when it has found the goal vertex (lines 10–12).

Algorithm 7.2 Algorithm A* for a monotonic evaluation function.

A-STAR(G, s, r)
  in: graph $G = (V, E)$; start vertex s; goal vertex r
  out: mapping $\pi : V \to V$
  local: open list S; cost function $g(u \rightsquigarrow v)$; heuristic lower bound estimate $h(u \rightsquigarrow v)$
  1: **for all** $v \in V$ **do**   ▷ Initialization.
  2:   $g(s \rightsquigarrow v) \leftarrow \infty$
  3:   $\pi(v) \leftarrow$ NIL
  4: **end for**
  5: $g(s \rightsquigarrow s) \leftarrow 0$
  6: $S \leftarrow \{s\}$
  7: precalculate $h(s \rightsquigarrow r)$
  8: **while** $S \neq \emptyset$ **do**   ▷ Search.
  9:   $v \leftarrow$ vertex $v' \in S$ that minimizes $g(s \rightsquigarrow v') + h(v' \rightsquigarrow r)$
10:   **if** $v = r$ **then**   ▷ Is the goal reached?
11:     **return** π
12:   **end if**
13:   $S \leftarrow S \setminus \{v\}$
14:   **for all** $u \in successors(v)$ **do**
15:     **if** $\pi(u) =$ NIL **or else** ($u \in S$ **and**
            $g(s \rightsquigarrow v) + weight(v, u) < g(s \rightsquigarrow u)$)) **then**   ▷ Open u.
16:     $S \leftarrow S \cup \{u\}$
17:     $g(s \rightsquigarrow u) \leftarrow g(s \rightsquigarrow v) + weight(v, u)$
18:     $\pi(u) \leftarrow v$
19:     precalculate $h(u \rightsquigarrow r)$
20:   **end if**
21: **end for**
22: **end while**
23: **error** no path from s to r exists

Figure 7.9 gives an example of how Algorithm A* works: (a) The weight of an edge describes the distance between its endpoints in the Manhattan metric. (b) First, start vertex s is selected, and its successors a and b are added to the set S (i.e. they are opened). The heuristic measure takes the maximum of the vertical and horizontal distance to the goal vertex. Because $f(b) < f(a)$, vertex b gets selected next. (c) The algorithm opens

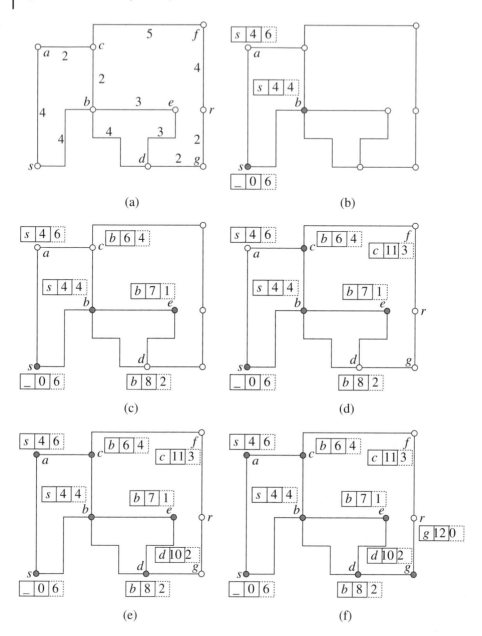

Figure 7.9 An example of Algorithm A*. The boxes next to a vertex v represent the values $\pi(v)$, $g(s \rightsquigarrow v)$, and $h(v \rightsquigarrow r)$. Filled circles indicate the selected vertices.

the successors of vertex b. Vertex e is the most promising candidate and gets selected. (d) Vertex e does not have undiscovered successors, because d has already been opened by b. The remaining candidates have the same value, so the algorithm selects c arbitrarily. Vertex f is opened. (e) Vertex a has the lowest value but has no undiscovered successors. Instead, vertex d gets selected and g is opened. (f) Of two remaining candidates, vertex

g gets selected, and goal vertex r is found. The optimum path is $s \rightarrow b \rightarrow d \rightarrow g \rightarrow r$ and its cost is 12.

Apart from optimality, there may be practical considerations when implementing Algorithm A*. First, the computational effort depends on the difficulty of computing the function h. If we use a less informed – and computationally less intensive – heuristic, we may go through more vertices but, at the same time, the total computation requirement may be smaller. Second, we may content ourselves with finding a solution reasonably close to the optimum. In such a case, we can use a function that evaluates accurately in most cases but sometimes overestimates the cost to the goal, thus yielding an inadmissible algorithm. Third, we can weight (or even change) the heuristic function when the search has proceeded far from the source vertex s. For example, we can use a more precise heuristic for the nearby vertices and approximate the magnitude for the faraway ones. For dynamic graphs (i.e. the waypoints and their relationships can change in the game world), this can be even the best approach, because it is likely that we will have to search for a new path after a while. To summarize, the choice of the function h and the resulting heuristic power of Algorithm A* depend on a compromise among these practical considerations.

If we can make assumptions on the properties of the graph, it is possible to optimize Algorithm A* further. For example, if the graph is based on a grid, we can prune the search space by using jump point search (Harabor and Grastien 2012). The basic idea is to combine open areas into a single route that covers all equivalent paths, which allows us to avoid computing paths for that area and jump over it. Another approach for optimizing the running time – at the cost of memory – it is to compute all possible paths beforehand and access this information, in a constant time, when finding a path.

7.3 Realizing the Movement

After the path has been solved in a graph, it must be realized in the game world. Although the solution may be optimal in the graph, it may be unrealistic or aesthetically displeasing in the game world (Patel 2003). For example, consider the situation illustrated in Figure 7.10, where a game character has to move from one room to

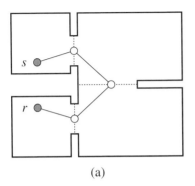 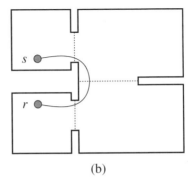

(a)   (b)

Figure 7.10 (a) The path through the waypoints may have sharp and unrealistic turns. (b) Sharp turns can be smoothed out when the movement is realized.

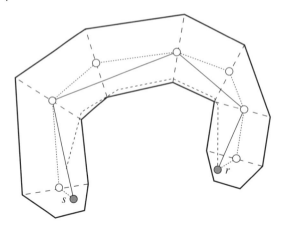

Figure 7.11 Line-of-sight testing allows the original path (dotted line) to be improved by skipping waypoints (solid line). It is not necessary to visit the waypoints, and the heading can be changed immediately whenever a farther waypoint becomes visible (dashed line).

another. Because the character goes through the waypoints, the resulting path has sharp turns instead of smooth movement. This stems from the selection of the waypoints with respect to the intended movement: The more artificial or 'virtual' the waypoint is, the more unrealistic the movement through it looks. Of course sharp turns at the wall extensions and beside the doorframes may be realistic, if the game character is under fire.

Naturally, we can use Bézier curves or B-splines (Watt 2000) instead of following the path in straight lines, but there are simpler approaches. One possibility is to use line-of-sight testing to reduce the number of waypoints the character has to visit (Snook 2000). Figure 7.11 illustrates the situation. Instead of heading to the next waypoint in the path, the character chooses the farthest waypoint it can see and heads there. This is repeated until the destination is reached. The path followed can be further reduced by changing the heading so that it is always towards the farthest visible waypoint.

To avoid (possibly dynamic) obstacles we can use the avoidance rule of the flocking algorithm (see Section 8.1) and assign obstacles a repulsion vector (Johnson 2003). Figure 7.12 illustrates a situation, where an obstacle is blocking the direct path. To avoid it the character's velocity vector combines two components, the desired direction towards the destination and the repulsion away from the obstacle, which is enough to steer the character past the obstacle. In other words, force vectors (and vector fields) are a convenient balancing mechanism between local actualizations (i.e. reactive behaviour in the continuous world) and global intentions (i.e. planning in the discretization of the world).

Because path finding can be a time-consuming task, a special care must be taken when it is accessed through a user interface. When players give orders to a game character, they expect it to respond immediately, even if the path finding required to comply with the order is not yet finished. One solution is to get the character moving in the general direction of the destination (or animate that it is preparing to move), while the full path is still being calculated (Higgins 2002). When the path finding is ready, the character, which has moved somewhat, is redirected to the path found.

Figure 7.12 Avoiding dynamic obstacles. (a) The straight path from *s* to *r* is obstructed. (b) The desired direction $\vec{d}$ towards the destination and the repulsion direction $\vec{r}$ away from the obstacle are combined to form the velocity vector $\vec{v}$.

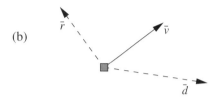

7.4   Summary

The future path for path finding is still unsolved. Many alternative methods have been proposed, but the three-stage approach presented in this chapter is still the standard approach in commercial computer games. Its main advantage is that we decompose the problem into more manageable subproblems, each of which has set readily available, reliable and reasonably fast solution methods.

Reactive agents from robotics have been proposed for solving the path-finding problem. They reduce the solution method to simple reactive rules akin to the flocking algorithm, and the emerging behaviour finds a path for the agent. At the moment the intelligence of these methods is at the level of insects, and, no matter how intelligent insects can be, designing a usable method for computer games seems a difficult task.

Analytical approaches take the opposite approach and say that more is better. They try to solve path finding straightforwardly by modelling all related factors – which may sound good in theory, but in practice some relevant details may escape precise mathematical formulation.

A third approach suggested to solve path finding is AI processors. The idea is that the usual methods for solving AI problems – including path finding – can be made into a hardware component much like graphics processing units (GPUs), which would take away many time-consuming tasks from the software (Google Brain Team 2016). Nevertheless, the method used in the AI processor has to be based on some existing software solution – possibly the one presented here.

Exercises

7-1   Imagine that you had to describe a route to a blindfolded person and describe how to get
    (a) from kitchen to living room,
    (b) from home to work/school,
    (c) from home to Rome.
    Be as accurate as necessary in your description.

7-2 A monkey is in a cage formed by grid with square-shaped cells (see Figure 7.13). He is hungry but he cannot reach the banana dangling from the ceiling. There is a box inside the cage, and the monkey can reach the banana if the box is underneath the banana. If the monkey is beside the box, he can lift it to one of his neighbouring tiles. The problem is to find a sequence of moves such that the monkey can get the banana from any given initial situation. The monkey sees the whole situation and can select the following operations: move to a tile in the grid, lift the box to a neighbouring tile, get onto the box, get down from the box, and reach for the banana.

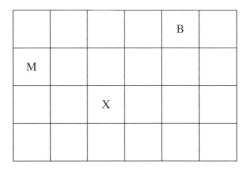

Figure 7.13 Monkey (M), box (X) and banana (B) in a cage formed by a square grid.

Express this monkey-in-a-cage problem as a path-finding problem and design an algorithm to solve it.

7-3 Waypoints can be laid down manually by the game world designer. What benefits and drawbacks does this have over the automated waypoint assigning process?

7-4 Prove that there are only three regular two-dimensional edge-sharing tessellations.

7-5 To have random-access lookup a grid should have a scheme for numbering the tiles. For example, a square grid has rows and columns which give a natural numbering for the tiles. Devise schemes for triangular and hexagonal grids. Use the numbering scheme to define a rule for determining the neighbourhood (i.e. adjacent tiles) of a given tile in the grid. For example, if we have a four-connected square grid, where the indices are i for rows and j for columns, the neighbourhood of tile $\langle i, j \rangle$ can be defined as

$$neighbourhood(\langle i, j \rangle) = \{\langle i \pm 1, j \rangle, \langle i, j \pm 1 \rangle\}.$$

7-6 A hexagonal grid is not so straightforward to represent on a screen (i.e. using square pixels). Devise an algorithm for displaying it.

7-7 Let us connect Exercise 7-5 and Exercise 7-6 and define a mapping τ from a position in a continuous game world to its corresponding tile number. For example, if we are using a square grid with edge length ℓ, we can define $\tau : \mathbb{R}^2 \to \langle \mathbb{N}, \mathbb{N} \rangle$ straightforwardly as

$$\tau : (x, y) \mapsto \langle \lfloor x/\ell \rfloor, \lfloor y/\ell \rfloor \rangle.$$

Write algorithms that calculate τ for triangular and hexagonal grids.

7-8 Triangulate the game world of Figure 7.14. Then apply the Hertel–Mehlhorn method and remove excess edges.

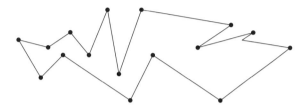

Figure 7.14   A game world as a polygon.

7-9 For what kind of search problems are breadth-first and depth-first best suited?

7-10 In the n-queens problem, n queens must be placed on an $n \times n$ chessboard so that they do not threaten each other. Figure 7.15 gives one solution to the eight-queens problem, which has in total (omitting rotations and mirror images) 12 different solutions. Formulate the n-queens problem as a search problem.

Figure 7.15   One possible solution to the eight-queens problem.

7-11 If we had an oracle function $h^*(v \rightsquigarrow r)$ which gives the exact cost of getting from v to r, how could we solve the minimum path search problem? Why is such a function so hard to form?

7-12 Although the A* algorithm works better with a more informed heuristic function, the overall computation time may be smaller with a less informed heuristic. How can that be possible?

7-13 What happens to the paths if we use an inadmissible search algorithm?

7-14 What other aesthetic considerations are there in movement realization besides smooth movements and obstacle avoidance?

7-15 Assume we have the game world of Figure 7.16. A player wants to move from the point s to the point r using only the white area (i.e. the path cannot go into the grey area). How would you solve this path-finding problem? Describe the three phases of the approach in general terms. Select a method for each phase and apply them to the given problem instance to find a path from s to r.

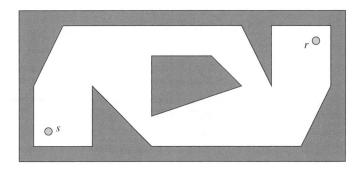

Figure 7.16 Two-dimensional game world in which the white area represents open space.

8

Group Movement

Instead of moving single entities, games often have groups of entities that have to be transported cohesively through the game world. Solving the path-finding problem for each individual entity would be a waste of effort – especially as path finding can be a computationally intensive operation. Moreover, it could lead to situations where the group does not look and behave like a group at all but a random collection of individuals. The aim of the group movement methods presented in this chapter is to solve this problem.

We can differentiate three approaches to group movement: flocks, formations and social groups (Mars and Chanut 2015). Flocks are naturally occurring phenomena where complex group behaviour emerges from individual entities. For example, the movement of a flock of birds, a school of fish or a swarm of bees has no central coordination. Conversely, formations are tightly coordinated (human) groups with a specific structure. A military troop moving in close order is a perfect example of a formation.

The third approach is to model the movement of social groups of people (Moussaïd et al. 2010; Peters and Ennis 2009). As we can readily observe, the majority of people in a public area are moving in small groups often engaged in a conversation. Depending on the density (i.e. how crowded the space is) these groups can take one of three forms (see Figure 8.1):

- When the group has enough space, people typically move abreast of each other so that they can keep up with the conversation equally.
- When the density increases, the group folds forward to form a V-shape, again minimizing the disturbance to the communication.
- When the space gets too crowded, the group reorganizes itself into a row so that navigation gets easier.

In this chapter, we focus on flocks and formations. Flocking algorithms take an entity-centred view, where force vectors model the urges affecting the game characters' decisions. Formations can be modelled using various techniques, of which we will describe behaviour-based steering, fuzzy logic control and mass–spring systems.

8.1 Flocking

Whenever we see a flock of birds flying, the whole flock seems to react as an autonomous entity rather than as a collection of separate individual birds. Still, we can be quite

Algorithms and Networking for Computer Games, Second Edition. Jouni Smed and Harri Hakonen.
© 2017 John Wiley & Sons Ltd. Published 2017 by John Wiley & Sons Ltd.

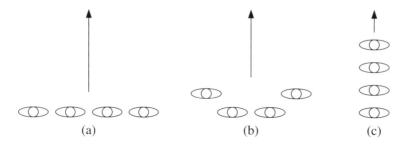

Figure 8.1 Human groups tend to move (a) side by side in low-density surroundings, (b) in a V-shape in moderate-density surroundings and (c) in a row in high-density surroundings.

sure that each bird in the flock reacts individually to the changes in the flockmates and the surroundings. The flocking algorithm, introduced by C.W. Reynolds (1987), tries to emulate this phenomenon in a computer program. The resulting behaviour resembles various natural group movements such as schools of fish, herds of sheep, swarms of bees, or – most interestingly – crowds of humans.

The core of the flocking algorithm consists of four *steering behaviour rules*, which give a group of autonomous agents (or *boids*) a realistic form of group behaviour (see Figure 8.2):

(i) *Separation.* Steer to avoid crowding local flockmates. A boid should maintain a certain distance from nearby boids to avoid collisions with them.

(ii) *Alignment.* Steer towards the average heading of local flockmates. A boid should move in the same direction as the nearby boids and match its velocity accordingly.

(iii) *Cohesion.* Steer to move towards the average position of local flockmates. A boid should stay close to the nearby flockmates.

(iv) *Avoidance.* Steer to avoid running into local obstacles or enemies. A boid should escape dangers when they occur.

As we can see, separation and alignment are complementary rules, which ensure that the boids are free to move inside the flock without collision. Separation is based on the relative position of the flockmates, ignoring their velocity. Conversely, alignment is based only on the velocity of the flockmates, ignoring their position. Alignment sustains the separation between the boids, and it can be thought of as a predictive separation: if the boid manages to match its velocity with that of its neighbours, it is unlikely that it will collide with any of them in the near future. Simply put, separation serves to establish the minimum separation distance, and alignment tends to maintain it.

Cohesion keeps a group of boids together, because it urges each boid to get to the centre of the flock. If the boids have limited perception, the centre means the centre of the nearby flockmates – but, cumulatively, this still keeps the whole flock cohesive. When a boid is inside the flock (i.e. the surrounding population density is the same in all directions), it does not have to adjust its heading or velocity due to the cohesion rule. However, when a boid is at the boundary of the flock, the centre resides on one side, forcing the boid towards the flock.

Avoidance allows the boids to avert collisions with entities not belonging to the flock. Although cohesion keeps the flock together, sometimes it has to split apart to go around

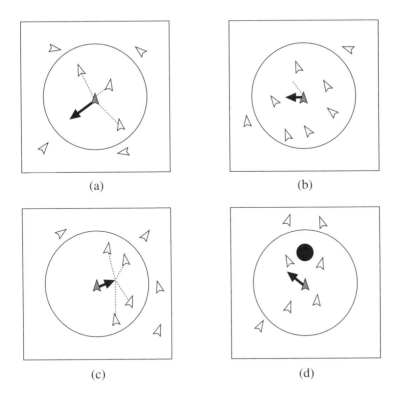

Figure 8.2 Steering behaviour rules. (a) Separation: do not crowd flockmates. (b) Alignment: move in the same direction as flockmates. (c) Cohesion: stay close to flockmates. (d) Avoidance: avoid obstacles and enemies.

an obstacle or to evade a hunter. When a flock splits, the resulting smaller flocks are drawn together again by cohesion. Later on when the obstacle has been passed or the hunter has withdrawn, the bifurcated flock can reunite.

Flocking is a stateless algorithm, because no history information needs to be maintained from update to update. Each boid re-evaluates its environment at every update cycle. There is no centralized control among the boids, but each acts individually, allowing the emergent behaviour built into the system to unfold.

Algorithm 8.1 gives an implementation for flocking. The four steering behaviour rules are described in Algorithm 8.2 using the following auxiliary function:

Unit-Vector($\vec{v}$)
   1: **if** $\vec{v} = \vec{0}$ **then return** a random unit vector
   2: **else return** $\vec{v}/\|\vec{v}\|$ **end if**

The function returns a unit vector in the direction of $\vec{v}$, or a unit vector pointing at a random direction if $\vec{v}$ is a zero vector.

This is a sequential method to update a set of boids to their next position. Another possibility is to have a concurrent method, where each boid is moved simultaneously

---

Algorithm 8.1 Flocking algorithm.

FLOCK(B, A)

    in: set B of boids in a flock; set A of avoidable elements

    out: updated set of boids R

    constant: separation weight w_s; alignment weight w_a; cohesion weight w_c; avoidance weight w_v; maximum velocity v_m

    local: set F of boids to be updated; boid f; updated boid b; acceleration vector $\vec{a}$; set $V = visible(S, x)$ of elements from S visible to x

  1: $F \leftarrow$ **copy** B

  2: $R \leftarrow \varnothing$

  3: **while** $F \neq \varnothing$ **do**   ▷ Update each boid once.

  4:   $f \leftarrow$ a boid from F

  5:   $F \leftarrow F \setminus f$

  6:   $V \leftarrow visible(F \cup R, f)$

  7:   $\vec{a} \leftarrow \vec{0}$

  8:   **if** $V = \varnothing$ **or** $leader(B) = f$ **then**

  9:     realize an individual movement

10:   **else**   ▷ There are visible flockmates.

11:     $\vec{a} \leftarrow \vec{a} + w_s \cdot$ SEPARATION(V, f)

12:     $\vec{a} \leftarrow \vec{a} + w_a \cdot$ ALIGNMENT(V, f)

13:     $\vec{a} \leftarrow \vec{a} + w_c \cdot$ COHESION(V, f)

14:   **end if**

15:   $\vec{a} \leftarrow \vec{a} + w_v \cdot$ AVOIDANCE($visible(A, f), f$)

16:   $b \leftarrow$ **copy** f ▷ The boid is updated.

17:   $velocity(b) \leftarrow velocity(b) + \vec{a}$

18:   **if** $|velocity(b)| > v_m$ **then**   ▷ Is velocity too high?

19:     $velocity(b) \leftarrow v_m \cdot$ UNIT-VECTOR($velocity(b)$)

20:   **end if**

21:   $position(b) \leftarrow position(b) + velocity(b)$

22:   $R \leftarrow R \cup \{b\}$

23: **end while**

24: **return** R

---

before the position updates are committed. Both require $O(n)$ time given that the visibility test runs in constant time, but the concurrent method consumes twice the space. However, because flocking is a reactive process, the sequential method provides sufficient results.

After release, boids that see one another begin to flock together. Due to cohesion they will stay near one another but always maintain separation from their flockmates. When the flock is forming, the boids begin to align themselves in approximately the same direction and to move approximately at the same speed with the arbitrary flock leader. Individual boids and smaller flocks join to become larger flocks, but an obstacle can split flocks into smaller ones.

Algorithm 8.2 Steering behaviour rules.

SEPARATION(M, f)

    in: set M of flockmates; boid f
    out: normalized correction vector
    constant: ideal flockmate separation distance d_s
    1: $m \leftarrow$ the flockmate in M nearest to f
    2: $\vec{v} \leftarrow position(m) - position(f)$
    3: $r \leftarrow 1 - 2 \cdot d_s/(\|\vec{v}\| + d_s)$ ▷ $\lim_{\|\vec{v}\| \to 0} r = -1$, $\lim_{\|\vec{v}\| \to \infty} r = 1$,
                                            and $r = 0$ if $\|\vec{v}\| = d_s$.
    4: **return** $r \cdot$ UNIT-VECTOR($\vec{v}$)

ALIGNMENT(M, f)

    in: set M of flockmates; boid f
    out: unit vector of the heading of the nearest flockmate
    1: $m \leftarrow$ the flockmate in M nearest to f
    2: **return** UNIT-VECTOR($velocity(m)$)

COHESION(M, f)

    in: set M of flockmates; boid f
    out: unit vector towards the centre, or zero vector if already there
    1: $\vec{v} \leftarrow \vec{0}$
    2: **for all** $m \in M$ **do**   ▷ Iterate over the flockmates.
    3:   $\vec{v} \leftarrow \vec{v} + position(m)$
    4: **end for**
    5: $\vec{v} \leftarrow \vec{v}/|M|$
    6: $\vec{v} \leftarrow position(v) - position(f)$
    7: **if** $\vec{v} \neq \vec{0}$ **then return** UNIT-VECTOR($\vec{v}$)   ▷ Not at the centre.
    8: **else return** $\vec{0}$ **end if**

AVOIDANCE(A, f)

    in: set A of objects to be avoided; boid f
    out: unit vector indicating avoidance, or zero vector if nothing to avoid
    constant: avoidance distance d_a
    1: $a \leftarrow$ the object in A nearest to f
    2: $\vec{v} \leftarrow position(f) - position(a)$
    3: **if** $\|\vec{v}\| < d_a$ **then return** UNIT-VECTOR($\vec{v}$)   ▷ Is the object close enough?
    4: **else return** $\vec{0}$ **end if**

Behavioural urges suggest which way the boid should steer. These urges can be viewed as acceleration requests, which can conflict with each other. The requests are collected, prioritized, and aggregated to form the acceleration to be realized. Prioritization can be implemented, for example, by associating the requests with weights describing their importance. For instance, avoidance can have a large weight for prey, because it represents a critical situation that must be handled promptly, whereas predators need to avoid (almost) nothing.

Since flocking is inherently reactive, the behaviour of the boids can be refined by injecting more impulses. For example, Hartman and Benes (2006) introduce a new rule, *change of leadership*, to complement the alignment: a random boid on the edge suddenly darts away from the flock, drawing the nearby boids with it. After a short while the darting boid slows down, the other rules kick in and the ordinary flocking continues until the same happens again.

8.2 Formations

Path-finding (see Chapter 7) focuses on finding a route for individual game entities. As the number of entities to move increases, computing individual paths for each of them becomes a more and more onerous task. Also, many games assume that a group of characters move in a pre-defined formation. For example, a real-time strategy game can include hundreds of units on a battlefield. Controlling the units on a higher level allows the player to control even larger groups with less effort. Operating with groups that have specific structures enriches the gameplay by increasing variability; for example, by allowing tactics such as locally strengthened or even intentionally weakened ranks. Formations can also improve the visual appeal and realism of a game, because the units seem to move in a natural-looking way rather than in unorganized groups (Mars and Chanut 2015).

We can discern three stages in coordinating formations:

1. Define a control structure for the formation.
2. Find a path for the whole formation.
3. Steer the individual entities.

The control structure gives a model to the formation and defines how to calculate the places of the entities in a formation. Figure 8.3 illustrates basic formation types, which can be realized using a control structure based, for instance, on following a leader or the average position of the neighbours.

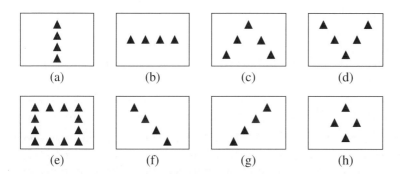

Figure 8.3 Basic formation types: (a) column, (b) line, (c) wedge, (d) vee, (e) box, (f) right flank, (g) left flank, and (h) diamond.

In path finding, we search for the shortest viable path from a start position to a goal position (Bjore 2014). When we have found a path, the formation is guided through the game world using a *steering method*, which aims to keep the entities as close to their intended place in the formation as possible. If the environment does not allow them to maintain a specified formation, it should allow the entities to deviate and later return to their designated positions.

8.2.1   Coordinating formations

There are a variety of methods for modelling and controlling formations. In this section, we first look at different approaches to model formations, which are classified according to how the point of reference of an entity in a formation is calculated. Then we study obstacle avoidance and, finally, how to maintain the correct position in a formation.

Modelling formations

Different control structures for modelling formations can be classified according to how the position of an entity in a formation is defined (see Figure 8.4):

(a) In a *leader-referenced formation*, the position of an entity is defined in relation to the position of the leader, and the movement of the formation is based on the movement of the leader (Balch and Arkin 1998). If the leader does not receive enough updates about the pace from the other entities, it can cause the formations to disperse when some entities lag behind without the leader slowing down.

(b) In a *unit-centre-referenced formation*, the position of an entity depends on the average position of the entities (Balch and Arkin 1998). This can be difficult, because purposeful movement requires that all the entities move towards the destination. One possibility would be to generate a virtual leader at the midpoint and apply the control structure of item (a).

(c) In a *neighbour-referenced formation*, the position of an entity is defined in relation to a pre-selected neighbour entity (Balch and Arkin 1998; Fredslund and Matarić 2002; Naffin and Sukhatme 2004).

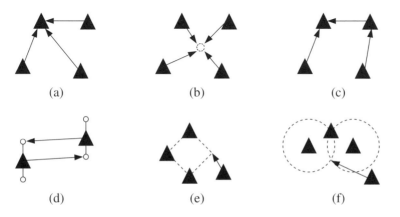

Figure 8.4 Formation models: (a) leader referenced, (b) unit-centre referenced, (c) neighbour referenced, (d) social potentials, (e) virtual structure, and (f) virtual leaders.

(d) In a formation using *social potentials*, each entity has a given number of attachment sites, which attract other entities (Balch and Hybinette 2000). We can change the shape of the formation by changing the configuration of the attachment sites. Social potentials scale up well even to larger formations, but with some attachment point configurations the shape of the resulting formation can be ambiguous. Moreover, if the formation gets divided (e.g. to avoid an obstacle) and comes back together, the shape of the formation may be different than before the division.

(e) In a *virtual structure formation*, the position of an entity is bound to a geometric form (Lewis and Tan 1997; Young et al. 2001). When this virtual structure moves, we try first to adapt the structure to the current positions of the entities, and then to move the structure towards the goal. Then all the entities are moved towards their new positions in the formation.

(f) In a *virtual leaders formation*, the entities try to maintain a given distance to one another and to one or many virtual leaders (Ögren et al. 2002). Consequently, the formation is not necessarily ambiguous but it can, for example, revolve around a virtual leader so that the formation stays together. We can add more virtual leaders to define the positions of the entities more closely.

Obstacle avoidance

We can divide the obstacles the formation encounters along the route into three groups according to their size:

- equal to or larger than the formation,
- smaller than the formation, and
- canyons.

We can omit the obstacles belonging to the first group, because it can be solved either by rerouting by path finding, or by overcoming the obstacles by reducing the route into clearly separated phases. For example, a river can be crossed via a bridge, forded in a specialized formation, or crossed by raft after some tree felling. The second group is more problematic, because it could be possible for a formation – as a whole – to travel through an area with smaller obstacles such as woods and rocks, but the individual entities have to be able to move around them. We can solve this by applying local path finding, which guarantees that an individual entity has an optimal path around an obstacle but does not ensure that the formation stays cohesive. Another possibility is obstacle avoidance, where the entities try to keep in their designated positions but move so that they do not collide with the obstacles. One way to realize this is to set repulsion which is directed away from the centre of an obstacle. If we observe that a collision is about to occur, the entity is steered away from the obstacle (Reynolds 1999), or the formation can be divided into two groups that avoid the obstacle from different sides and, having passed the obstacle, merge into one formation again (Pottinger 1999a,b).

When a formation meets a canyon or a narrow passage, it usually has to disassemble or change its size or type (e.g. into a column) to pass through (Pottinger 1999a). In the game *Force 21*, if the formation is located so that some entities would be inside an obstacle, these positions are relocated along the route from the centre of the formation so that each entity finds a free position (van Verth et al. 2000). Also, convex optimization can be used in coordinating large-scale formations in polygonal environments (Derenick and Spletzer 2007).

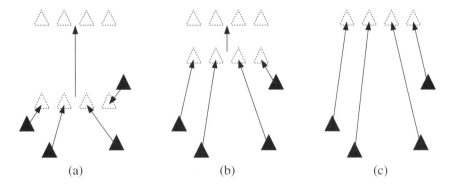

Figure 8.5 Strategies for realizing the movement into the formation: (a) entities move first into the formation and then to the destination; (b) entities move to a formation rally-point along the way to the destination and move from there to the destination; and (c) entities move into a formation at the destination.

Maintaining the formation

The complexity of assigning optimal positions for n entities in a formation is $O(n!)$. For this reason, we have to approximate, for example, by sorting the entities according to their distance to the closest available position and assigning the positions in this order (Dawson 2002). We can simplify the approximation further by using the distance to the centre of the formation as a sorting criterion – or even define sub-formations and their corresponding centres.

Once all entities have been assigned a position, they can be moved into the formation using one of the three different strategies illustrated in Figure 8.5 (Dawson 2002):

1. The formation is located in the centre of the entities, and the entities move first into the formation before they start moving towards the destination as a formation.
2. Entities move individually to a rally-point located near the destination and from there continue as a formation. It is possible that entities closer to the destination arrive at the rally-point earlier and have to stop and wait for the others.
3. Entities use path finding and move individually to the correct positions in a formation at the destination. This approach guarantees that the entities will be in a formation at the destination, but movement of the entities can appear senseless and the benefits of moving in a formation are lost.

Let us assume that the path for the formation has already been found (e.g. given by a human player or a higher-level decision-making system) and we must now steer the group using a control structure. We next present three prominent approaches to coordinate formations: a steering behaviour-based method, a fuzzy logic controller, and a mass–spring system. For a more detailed analysis of their behaviour, see Laasonen and Smed (2012).

8.2.2 Behaviour-based steering

Behaviour-based steering is based on the flocking algorithm (see Section 8.1), where the steering behaviour rules model the entity's urge to move in a certain direction (Reynolds 1987, 1999). Behaviour-based steering is a stateless algorithm that does not need to

ballistic zone

controlled zone

dead zone

Figure 8.6 Zones for the magnitude of the control vector for maintaining the formation: the control vector is maximum in the ballistic zone, zero in the dead zone, and decreases linearly in the controlled zone the closer the entity gets to the dead zone.

maintain any extra information. Moreover, there is no centralized control for the formation, but the behaviour emerges from simple individual rules. If we use the unit-centre-referenced control structure as the formation model, the behaviour-based steering can include the following rules (Laasonen and Smed 2012):

(i) *Seeking the target.* This control vector is directed to the entity's correct position in the formation.

(ii) *Maintaining the formation.* Depending on the distance to their assigned places, the entities can be in one of three zones (see Figure 8.6): in the ballistic zone the control vector has the maximal length, whereas in the controlled zone the length of the control vector changes linearly from maximum to zero, and in the dead zone the control vector has length zero. The dead zone represents the ideal area for an entity in the formation.

(iii) *Avoiding other entities.* This control vector is directed in the opposite direction from the other entities.

(iv) *Avoiding obstacles.* If there are obstacles in the current direction of the entity, we choose the closest one and set the control vector to avoid it.

(v) *Noise.* Depending solely on reactive behaviour can lead the entities to get stuck on a local maximum or minimum or to revert to a cyclic behaviour. To avoid this we can add noise by creating a control vector in a random direction. This noise remains constant for a predefined duration.

8.2.3 Fuzzy logic control

To cope with the uncertainty of the formation's actual state, we can create a rule-base using fuzzy sets (see Section 10.2). This fuzzy logic control comprises **if—then** rules using fuzzy sets as predicates in the following form (Yager and Filev 1994):

1: **if** U_1 is B_{11} **and** U_2 is B_{12} **and** ... **and** U_n is B_{1n} **then** V is D_1
2: ...
3: **if** U_1 is B_{m1} **and** U_2 is B_{m2} **and** ... **and** U_n is B_{mn} **then** V is D_m

where $U_1, \ldots, U_n$ are parameters and $B_{11}, \ldots, B_{mn}$ and $D_1, \ldots, D_m$ are fuzzy sets. The result of the output V can be computed as follows:

1. For each rule, compute the degree to which it gets fired.

2. Compute the result of the rule.
3. Aggregate the results as an output.

In order to realize a fuzzy decision, we have to defuzzify it to get a crisp result (see Section 10.2.3).

To coordinate the entities in a formation, we assign one fuzzy logic controller for steering (Laasonen and Smed 2012). In plain language, the rules for the controller are as follows:

- If the entity is far from the correct formation place and its sensors detect no obstacles, then the steering controller tries to steer towards the formation place.
- If the sensors detect no obstacles, then the steering controller steers towards the next waypoint.
- If a sensor detects an obstacle, the steering controller tries to steer in the opposite direction of the sensor.

The inputs for the fuzzy logic controller are the magnitude of the collision, C_m; the direction of the collision, C_d; the entity's magnitude, E_m; the entity's direction, E_d; the centre of the visible formation, F_c; the entity's correct location in the visible formation, F_ℓ; and the distance to the correct location in the formation, F_d. Let us also define the fuzzy sets S_d (towards the destination), S_f (towards the formation), S_a (away from the entity's direction), S_r (steep right) and S_ℓ (steep left). To approximate the distance we define the fuzzy sets Z_b (ballistic zone) and Z_c (controlled zone). We also define the quantitative fuzzy sets Q_x (very large), Q_ℓ (large) and Q_s (small). The result is steering R.

The steering controller has four types of rules:

- Seeking the target

  1: **if** F_d is Z_c **and** C_m is Q_s **and** E_m is Q_s **then** R is S_d
  2: **if** F_ℓ is Q_s **and** C_m is Q_s **then** R is S_d
  3: **if** F_c is Q_s **and** C_m is Q_s **then** R is S_d

- Staying in the formation

  1: **if** F_c is Q_ℓ **and** F_ℓ is Q_ℓ **and** F_d is Z_b **and** C_m is Q_s **and** E_m is Q_s **then** R is S_f

- Obstacle avoidance

  1: **if** C_d is S_ℓ **and** C_m is Q_x **then** R is S_r
  2: **if** C_d is S_r **and** C_m is Q_x **then** R is S_ℓ

- Avoid other entities

  1: **if** E_m is Q_ℓ **then** R is S_a

The resulting fuzzy sets can be defuzzified into crisp values to be used as direction, for example, with the mean-of-maxima method (see Section 10.2.3).

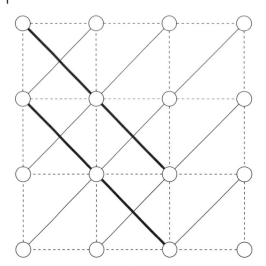

Figure 8.7 An example of a mass–spring system. The circles represent point masses, the dashed lines the structural springs, the solid lines the shear springs, and the bold lines the flexion springs.

8.2.4 Mass–spring systems

Spring models are often used in game physics to simulate soft objects, but we can also use them in coordinating formations. One can imagine that there are invisible springs between the entities that can flex but still maintain the overall structure intact. A mass–spring system comprises point masses and springs connecting them. Each spring causes the force $F = -kx$, where k is a spring coefficient and x the distance from the static state. To build a structure we need three kinds of springs as illustrated in Figure 8.7 (Wang and Devarajan 2004):

- Structural springs model the interaction between different parts of the object.
- Shear springs model the resistance against bending.
- Flexion springs model the shearing resistance.

To coordinate a formation we define first a set of springs between the n entities. If we simply create a spring between all $n(n-1)/2$ entity pairs, we can end up having excessive springs, slow update times, and possibly too rigid a formation. Therefore, it is often enough to have horizontal, vertical and diagonal springs between the neighbouring entities (Wang and Devarajan 2004). We select one of the entities as a leader of the formation, which acts as a fixed point in the formation unaffected by the spring forces. To move the formation we apply a constant force to the leader, pulling it towards the destination, while the rest of the formation follows because of the spring forces.

   To calculate the changes in a mass–spring system, let $x(t)$ be the position of an entity at a given time t and $v(t)$ its velocity. Moreover, let $F(v, x, t)$ be the force caused by the springs at a given time when the element has the given velocity and position. The task is now to calculate for each element a new position and velocity for the time step $t + \Delta t$. One of the simplest methods is explicit (or forward) Euler integration (Nealen et al. 2006):

$$x(t + \Delta t) = x(t) + \Delta t v(t),$$
$$v(t + \Delta t) = v(t) + \Delta t F(v(t), x(t), t).$$

Although explicit integration is simple to implement, it is stable only when Δt is small. To solve this we can use implicit (or backward) integration, where we have the term $t + \Delta t$ on both sides of the equation:

$$x(t + \Delta t) = x(t) + \Delta t v(t + \Delta t),$$
$$v(t + \Delta t) = v(t) + \Delta t F(v(t + \Delta t), x(t + \Delta t), t).$$

This is stable for large values Δt, but the downside is that now we have to solve an algebraic system of equations at each time step. We improve this by combining the explicit and implicit integrations into a forward–backward integration:

$$v(t + \Delta t) = v(t) + \Delta t F(v(t), x(t), t),$$
$$x(t + \Delta t) = x(t) + \Delta t v(t + \Delta t).$$

Here, we update first v using forward integration and then x using backward integration. This variant is more stable than explicit integration and, moreover, it does not incur any extra computation.

8.3 Summary

Finding a balance between individual control and conforming to group behaviour can be challenging – also in real life. Flocking algorithms emphasize the individual behaviour which gives birth to group-level phenomena, which we can then label as group behaviour. However, as with any emergent system, designing a particular group behaviour is a next to impossible task, and often the only approach available to the developer is trial and error. Emergent systems are nevertheless highly robust and well suited to dynamically changing conditions. Formations, on the other hand, are more brittle as they are often fine-tuned to specific conditions. For the developer, they offer much more control as the individual entities are subjected to the overall order.

Exercises

8-1   Observe people moving in groups, for example, in a shopping mall. Keep a record of how the groups are formed. Do your observations comply with the social groups presented on page 175?

8-2   The passageways to high-traffic exits, (e.g. in football stadiums or railway stations) are often designed to have asymmetrical structures before the actual exit. If the passageway were symmetrical, what kind of problem could it cause to the flow of exiting people (especially in an emergency situation)?

8-3   Consider what would happen if we left out one of the flocking behaviour rules? Are some rules more essential to flocking than others?

8-4   The steering behavioural urges SEPARATION and ALIGNMENT presented in Algorithm 8.2 consider only the nearest flockmate. Rewrite both routines so that the boid observes the n nearest flockmates.

8-5 What happens if a flock does not have a leader? What happens if the leader drifts to the middle of the flock?

8-6 Flocking can be used to realize the solution of a path-finding problem for a group of entities so that the leader follows the path and the other members of the group follow the leader. Are there groups which this approach does not suit?

8-7 Let us assume we have a box formation with nine entities which has to go through a canyon (see Figure 8.8). Which of the steering methods – behaviour-based, fuzzy logic control or mass–spring system – would work best in this situation and why? Which steering method would be the worst?

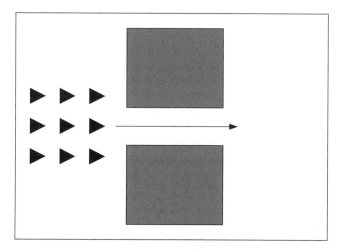

Figure 8.8 A box formation facing a canyon.

8-8 In a mass–spring system, the number of springs required depends on the formation configuration. If we create springs between all entity pairs, we keep the formation stable regardless of its type. The fewer springs we have, the less eager the entities are to keep their place in the formation. If we restrict the number of springs to include only structural and shear springs, what formation types (see Figure 8.3) can we create reliably?

8-9 Consider the following groups and decide whether they are best modelled as a flock or a formation:
- Children playing football.
- Professional athletes playing football.
- A band of guerrillas in a jungle.
- A band of gorillas in a jungle.
- The band Gorillaz in a jungle.

8-10 Is there a viable approach for designing an emergent system other than trial and error?

9

Decision-Making

The border between the game world and the entities inhabiting it is often blurred. In Chapter 1 we separated them conceptually and called the computer-controlled entities synthetic players. At the implementation level we are often forced by limited computing resources to accept some merging between the game world and the computer-generated entities inhabiting it. However, this is not necessarily a problem, since the human player is mainly interested in the other human players and the synthetic players with a recognizable identity. Moreover, the action and interaction in a computer game – as in any other form of storytelling – do not require so many participants to be compelling.

Naturally, if we are to have synthetic players in a game, they must be able to make appropriate decisions as the game progresses. Decision-making covers various topics – even path finding, game trees and tournaments, which we discussed in the previous chapters, can be seen as making a decision on what to do. In fact, almost any algorithmic method can be used in decision-making (e.g. sorting can be used when deciding on an attack against the opponent with the smallest army). For this reason, we can cover only a limited number of approaches and methods here.

We begin by taking a broader look at decision-making in computer games, which helps us to understand where different methods are best suited. This general discussion is then followed by a review of finite state machines, and we analyse their role in decision-making. Then we present influence maps which model the game world and its attributes as force fields to guide the decision-making process. Finally, we take a look at automated planning where we want to find a sequence of actions to reach a given goal.

9.1 Background

The AI system of a computer game comprises two parts: *pattern recognition* and *decision-making system* (Kaukoranta et al. 2003). In Figure 9.1, the world, which can be real or simulated, consists of primitive events and states (phenomena) that are passed to pattern recognition. The information abstracted from the current (and possibly the previous) phenomena is then forwarded to the decision-making system. The world allows a set of possible actions, and the decision-making system chooses the ones to carry out.

Because game worlds exist only virtually, computer games differ from the usual pattern recognition applications. We can omit certain problems that affect real-world pattern recognition (e.g. coping with noisy sensor data or unreliable actuators). This

Algorithms and Networking for Computer Games, Second Edition. Jouni Smed and Harri Hakonen.
© 2017 John Wiley & Sons Ltd. Published 2017 by John Wiley & Sons Ltd.

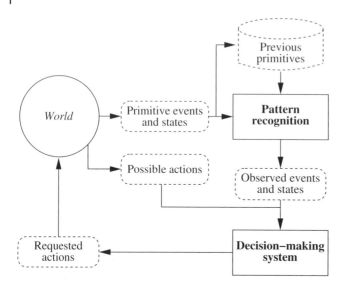

Figure 9.1 The primitive events and states originating from the world are used in pattern recognition and stored for later use. The decision-making system uses the observations made in pattern recognition to choose an appropriate action among the possibilities allowed by the world.

does not mean that the game world is wholly deterministic – if it were, we would hardly need a decision-making system. The two sources of indeterminism, as we saw in Chapter 1, are the built-in randomness and the human players' actions in the game world.

The synthetic player can act in different roles (e.g. reading the game in an ice hockey match, identifying threats during a campaign, or recognizing Proppian fairy-tale patterns in storytelling). Apart from the design considerations presented in Section 1.3, the role affects the level of decision-making, the use of the modelled knowledge, and the chosen method. These attributes set boundaries for the computational complexity and the quality required from the decision-making.

9.1.1 Levels of decision-making

Decision-making problems are classically divided into three levels: strategic, tactical, and operational. On the *strategic* level, decisions are made for a long period of time and are based on a large amount of data. The nature of the decisions is usually speculative (e.g. what-if scenarios), and the cost of a wrong decision is high. For example, a strategy for a war remains stable and should be based on all available information. Instead of considering the interactions of the soldiers in the field, the terrain is analysed to identify regions that provide an advantage (e.g. hills provide the upper hand for defence, whereas narrow passages are suitable for ambushes). This information is then used in planning the manoeuvres to minimize the risks and to maximize the effect. A poor decision at this level dooms every soldier. Clearly, some details must be left out in the process, and this quantization always includes a possibility that some vital information is lost. To avoid quantization problems, the results of pattern recognition should have as high a quality as possible. This is not an unreasonable demand, because strategic decisions are infrequent and the computing can be done offline or in the background.

The *tactical* level acts as an intermediary between strategic and operational levels. Tactical decisions usually consider a group of entities and their cooperation. For example, the decisions for a battle concentrate only on the engaging battalions and the conditions in the battleground. They weigh and predict events at the current focus points and in the dominated areas and, based on the advantages gained at the strategic level, resolve the conflicts as they occur. Ultimately, the aim of tactical decisions is to follow through the plan made at the strategic level. Although tactical decisions affect directly a limited set of entities, a poor decision can escalate to ruin the chosen strategy. Because tactical decisions are made more frequently than strategic decisions, there is less time available for decision-making. The results must be delivered in real time and their quality cannot be as high as at the strategic level.

The *operational* level is concrete and closely connected with the properties of the game world. Although the number of decision-making entities at this level is high, the decisions consists of choosing short-term actions among a given set of alternatives. For example, a soldier must decide whether to shoot, dodge, or charge. Because the computational power must be divided among numerous atomic entities, the decision-making method must be reactive and run in real time.

Let us consider football as an example of the levels of decision-making. On the strategic level, there are the choices of how to win the game (e.g. whether to play offensively or defensively). On the tactical level, the choices concern carrying out the strategy in the best possible way (e.g. whether to use man-marking defence or space-marking defence). On the operational level, the choices are simple and concrete (e.g. where should the player position himself and if he has the ball, whether to dribble it, kick it at the goal or pass it to another player). The problem is how to choose what to do (i.e. decision-making) and on what grounds (i.e. pattern recognition). It is fairly simple at the operational level – dribble if you have an opening, pass if you can do it safely – but it gets harder and harder as the level of abstraction rises.

9.1.2 Modelled knowledge

Based on the information provided by pattern recognition, the decision-making system forms a model about the world. Because models are always simplifications, they are subject to uncertainty (see Chapter 10). Nevertheless, they are useful because the modelled knowledge can be seen as a mechanism, which is used in conceptualizing and concretizing the important phenomena and in predicting events as well as producing them.

The model does not have to be confined only to the opponent and the game world but can cover the actions and reactions of the synthetic player itself. Whenever the synthetic player makes a decision, the outcome produces feedback – positive or negative, direct or indirect – which can be used in learning (Evans 2002). For example, in *Black & White* the computer-controlled pet creature learns from other entities' reactions, from feedback from the human player, or from its own experiences. Hence, the rule 'Do not eat trees' can be derived either from the villagers' disapproval for wasting resources, from a sharp slap by the owner, or from the resulting stomach ache.

The complexity of the world can be simplified with *generators*, which label the events and states with symbols. For example, the punches in a boxing game can go through a generator that produces the symbols 'jab', 'uppercut', 'cross', and 'hook'. Now, we can construct a model for the behaviour of the generator from the generated symbol sequence.

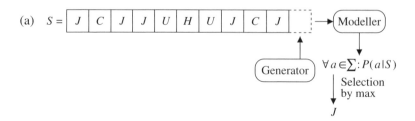

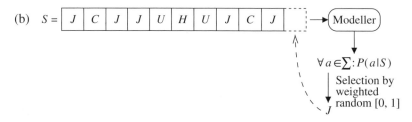

Figure 9.2 The model over a sequence S of symbols from the alphabet $\Sigma = \{J, U, C, H\}$ can be used in (a) prediction and (b) production.

Modelling recognizes the underlying dependencies between symbols, which are typically stronger between symbols that are close to each other. Often a short-term history is sufficient, but the model gets more accurate if we increase the length of the modelling context at the cost of run time.

The decision-making system can use the modelled knowledge in two ways to do temporal reasoning (see Figure 9.2): prediction and production. In *prediction*, we want to know what symbol the generator will produce next. By storing the previous primitives we can use pattern recognition to take into account not only spatial but also temporal properties. The observation passed to decision-making system can be a probability distribution of the symbols that occur rather than a single symbol. For example, if we have constructed a model of the opponent's punch series, we can compute what is the most likely punch the opponent will throw next, and use this prediction to calculate an effective counteraction.

In *production*, we use the model of a generator to produce symbols. This is no longer pattern recognition but decision-making in the form of pattern generation. For example, we can use the model to imitate the actions of a human player (Alexander 2002). Returning to our boxing example, we can model the punch series of a real-world boxer, and use the model when selecting the next punch for a computer-controlled boxer. Of course we could construct the model simply by observing the human opponent's moves and start mimicking them.

9.1.3 Methods

As computer games become ever more complex, the methods of conventional 'hard' computing are becoming less effective. Whereas hard computing is founded on precision and categorizing, *soft computing*, a term coined by L.A. Zadeh, stresses the tolerance for approximation, partial truth, imprecision, and uncertainty. It describes methodologies that try to solve problems arising from the complexity of the natural world, which include probabilistic reasoning (e.g. Bayesian networks), genetic algorithms, neural networks, and fuzzy logic. We do not strictly adhere to Zadeh's classification but discuss soft computing methods related to *optimization* and *adaptation*. One can readily see that these methods have their counterparts in the human mind: imagination does optimization and memory learns by adaptation.

Optimization

The term 'optimization' literally means the making the best of something. Mathematically speaking, optimization problems comprise three elements: an objective function which we want to minimize or maximize, a set of variables which affect the value of the objective function, and a set of constraints which limit the set of feasible variable values (see Figure 9.3). The goal is to find, among the feasible solutions, the one that gives an optimum value of the objective function.

A decision-making problem can be formed as an optimization problem provided that we have a (preferably non-complex) objective function to rank the solution candidates. Since optimization algorithms work iteratively, they are usually time-consuming and are therefore used offline or during preprocessing. For example, to balance civilizations and units in *Age of Empires II*, battles with different troop combinations were tested by using a combat comparison simulator (Street et al. 2001). Here, the attributes (such as armour, hit points, damage, and range) are the variables, which are constrained by the range of permitted values. The objective function is to minimize the difference in the number of victories in the simulator battles, and the attributes are changed to even out discrepancies.

The use of optimization techniques assumes an inherent knowledge of the problem domain. Usually we can make good use of this knowledge by implementing heuristic rules to guide the search for more promising variable values. In other words, effective heuristics attack the dominating variables. For example, if archers seem to have the upper hand in the combat simulator, a heuristic rule can increase the damage done by their counter-unit. The problem with this type of hill-climbing heuristic, which iteratively tries to find a better solution among the neighbouring solution candidates,

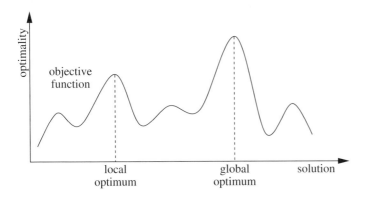

Figure 9.3 An objective function gives the optimality of a solution. The goal is to find the global optimum, but the search space is usually scattered with local optima.

is that the search can get stuck in a local optimum before finding the global optimum (see Figure 9.3). For example, instead of increasing the damage of the counter-unit, a better balance could be achieved by increasing the range of their weapons. To escape the lure of local optima a gamut of approaches have been developed with the likes of tabu search (Glover 1989) and simulated annealing (Kirkpatrick et al. 1983).

Local optima can be avoided by having multiple search traces instead of one. Genetic algorithms have a population of candidate solutions, which go through stages resembling natural selection (Goldberg 1989). The objective function is used to weed out the weak candidates, thus allowing the best ones to breed a new population. The variable values of the solution are encoded in the genes. Genetic algorithms work well when the variables are independent of each other, because the genetic operations like crossover and mutation are more likely to produce feasible solutions. In the worst case the variables have strong dependencies (e.g. they form a sequence), and most of the offspring would not represent a feasible solution.

Swarm algorithms, which are based on flocking algorithms (see Section 8.1), present another approach with multiple search traces (Kennedy et al. 2001). Whereas in genetic algorithms the solution is encoded in the population, in swarm algorithms the members of the population 'fly' in the search space. Because of avoidance they keep a minimum distance from each other and cover a larger area than a single search trace, and because they fly as a swarm, they tend to progress as a unit towards better solutions. As a way to escape local optima, the members can never slow down under a minimum velocity, which can allow them to fly past and free from a local optimum, especially if it is crowded.

The suitability of optimization methods depends mainly on the level of decision-making. When making strategic analysis, we have to scrutinize a vast amount of data. Consequently, there are many variables and (combinatorial) interdependencies between them. In their natural state, the problems are computationally hard to tackle, but if we weaken our criterion for optimality by, for example, reducing interdependencies, genetic algorithms become a viable option. Although the problem setting at the tactical level is somewhat easier – there are fewer interdependent variables and simpler combinatorial problems – the method must be more responsive. Because of the computational demands inherent in making the method more responsive, multiple search traces are not useful and we should devise heuristic search rules. The reactivity of the operational level dictates that we can only solve problems with a few variables or a simple objective function.

Adaptation

Adaptation can be defined as an ability to make appropriate responses to changed or changing circumstances. In a sense, adaptation resembles learning a skill in the real world. When we learn to ride a bike, we do not receive, for example, the physical formulae describing the motions and forces involved. Instead, we get simple – and possibly painful – feedback of success or failure. Based on this we adapt our behaviour and try again until we get it right.

Generally speaking, the difference between adaptation and optimization is that optimization searches for a solution for a given function, whereas adaptation searches for a function behind given solutions (see Figure 9.4). The assumption behind this is that the

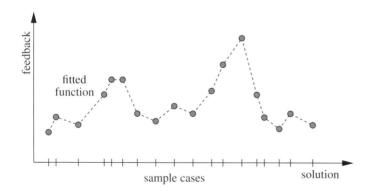

Figure 9.4 To model the underlying generator, the function is fitted to the solution samples according to the feedback.

more the function adapts to the solution domain, the better it corresponds to the originator of the modelled data. Adaptation is useful when the factors or mechanisms behind the phenomena are unknown or dynamic. The downside is that we have to sample the search space to cover it sufficiently, and the more dimensions (i.e. measured attributes) it has, the sparser our sample gets due to combinatorial explosion.

Since the task of pattern recognition is to abstract significant observations and rules from the given data, it can usually be expressed as an adaptation problem. In other words, a pattern recognition method is initially a blank slate, which then begins to adapt to the characteristics of the world. This learning process involves self-modification according to the response from the environment. For example, influence maps (see Section 9.3) are a simple and statistical way to implement adaptive pattern recognition. Based on experience we change the values in the map: if we get casualties at some point, we decrease the relevant value to avoid this in the future; otherwise, if it turns out to be safe, we increase the value.

Neural networks provide a method to adapt in situations where we do not have background knowledge of dependencies (Freeman and Skapura 1991). They work in two different operation modes: training and execution. These are separate phases in supervised learning, where a trainer provides feedback for all sample cases, and the neural network constructs an input–output mapping accordingly. In unsupervised learning, the neural network – for example, a self-organizing map (Kohonen 1995) – adapts to the structure inherent in the input without any *a priori* classification of observations. If the input is a time series, hidden Markov models (Rabiner and Juang 1986) turn out to be useful because they can adapt to recurring multidimensional structures.

We can use supervised or unsupervised learning chiefly at the strategic level because of their computational demands. The tactical level, however, is more dynamic and the results of pattern recognition are less thorough. Here, we should use methods such as hidden Markov models that yield results whose credibility can be evaluated. At the operational level, there are two possibilities: we have stochastic interpretation for input data or we use a ready-adapted neural network. One feature is common to all levels: even after we have learned a skill, we can still try to hone it to perfection.

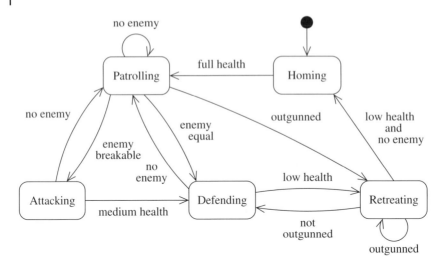

Figure 9.5 A statechart diagram for a finite state machine for a simple patrol robot. The start state is 'Homing' and there is no final state, because the robot remains operational until it is destroyed.

9.2 Finite State Machines

A finite state machine (FSM) is an algorithm described as a mechanism of a finite number of discrete *states* and directed *transitions* between them. The control flow of the FSM algorithm pauses in a state, and the outgoing transitions from this current state determine the next possible states. Each transition is labelled with an *event* name (e.g. referring to some actual event in the game world). When the event occurs, the corresponding transition from the current state is triggered and the succeeding state becomes the current state. In other words, the FSM algorithm moves from state to state in discrete steps. The set of all possible events is the input set of the FSM. Although the events can be asynchronous, the FSM handles them one at a time through a queue.

An FSM can be depicted as a statechart, which is a directed graph where vertices denote the states and edges the transitions. Furthermore, each state must be reachable from the start state by following the transitions. Figure 9.5 illustrates possible high-level states for a patrol robot. The states could flow as follows. At the beginning the robot is in the 'Homing' state, and when it is fully operational, it moves to 'Patrolling'. The robot follows its patrol route until it encounters an enemy. Depending on the resistance encountered the robot initiates an 'Attacking', 'Defending', or 'Retreating' manoeuvre. The robot's *raison d'être* is patrolling, and it can deviate from this behaviour only when it desperately needs repairing. Because we do not want to give the enemy a chance to find the route to the robot's home base, the robot heads back home only after it has shaken off any trailing enemies. If the robot is on the verge of destruction, it tries to follow a delaying engagement by swapping between 'Defending' and 'Retreating'.

An FSM is an established way to describe and implement AI for synthetic players, because it

- gives a visual overall view of the behaviour (as in Figure 9.5);

- decomposes the control flow of the FSM algorithm spatially and temporally into discrete parts;
- introduces terminology by naming the states, input events, and transitions of the FSM algorithm;
- defines what are the valid relationships between the sequential and concurrent events and possibly their corresponding actions;
- is a perspicuous and concrete model for synchronizing internal and external events (i.e. defining interaction);
- can be formulated in a different ways, which have expressive power equal to that of any other computation model;
- provides a formalism that in certain cases can be used for automatic FSM simplification, verification, or validation;
- can be used as a subpart within other methods (e.g. in decision-making);
- can be combined with other concepts (e.g. state and event stacking), probabilities, and fuzziness;
- is straightforward to implement and trace once devised; and
- has various implementation variants that allow a balance to be found between efficiency and compactness.

FSMs originate from mathematics – to be precise, from the theory of computability and complexity. The theoretical concepts behind FSMs include deterministic and non-deterministic finite automata, finite transducers, pushdown automata, pushdown transducers, extended finite state machines, and Turing machines with variants. These concepts introduce the following utility properties that an FSM can include (see Figure 9.6).

(i) An FSM can act as an *acceptor* or a recognizer that maps the input sequence to a Boolean value. In this role, the FSM has a set of final states which return true to indicate that the input sequence has the property defined by the FSM. For example, Figure 9.6(a) defines the states for an item of merchandise in an auction.

(ii) An FSM can be used as a *transducer* or an interpreter that transforms the input sequence to an output sequence (i.e. it generates a symbol response for each input event). Now, the design question is what data sequence corresponds to the input sequence. For example, the FSM in Figure 9.6(b) converts a binary input sequence to a binary sequence that indicates the starts of the bit-runs. The conversion is denoted by the transition label i/o, where i is the next input bit and o the output bit. Hence, sequence 001110000101 outputs sequence 101001000111.

(iii) A transition can include an action or procedure that is executed when the transition gets triggered. This property makes an FSM a *computator* that maps the input sequence to an action sequence (or behaviour). The computational nature of the actions allows the FSM to interact with its surroundings. The action (or sequence of actions) is appended to the event trigger of the transition label with the notation *event/action*. Figure 9.6(c) illustrates a well-known traversal strategy for closed acyclic mazes: 'Keep your right hand on the wall and you will go along every wall once and arrive back at the starting location.' To simplify the problem assume that the maze is laid out on a square grid and the walls are four-connected. Our walk

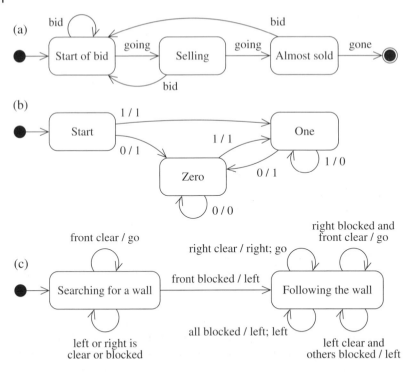

Figure 9.6 Three independent properties that an FSM can include: (a) an acceptor, (b) a transducer, and (c) a computator.

is also four-connected and we can go forward ('go') or make 90° turns (i.e. 'left' or 'right'). These actions are selected according to our sensor events: the neighbouring left, front, or right squares can be clear or blocked by a wall.

9.2.1 Computational FSM

Mathematical models for FSMs differ considerably from computational software models for FSMs. A computational FSM has numerous definitions, but perhaps the one most widely used is the FSM model of *Unified Modeling Language* (UML) notation (Object Management Group 2005). In this section, we use the following fundamental parts from UML:

Action An atomic (i.e. conceptually instantaneous) transaction that consists of computation (e.g. function calls or sending of signals). The action cannot be interrupted by an event but runs to completion.

Guard A Boolean expression that expresses a condition (enclosed in square brackets) that must be fulfilled before any action can be executed.

State An identifiable status or condition in which the FSM algorithm can pause and persist for a period of time. A state is depicted as a rectangle with rounded corners, and the state name is placed inside the state border.

The state can have an entry action (executed when the state becomes the current state) and an exit action (executed before the triggered transition is handled), which are noted with keywords 'entry' and 'exit':

entry / *action*(*arguments*)
exit / *action*(*arguments*)

In addition to actions, a state can run a non-atomic activity, which can be any kind of computation that continues until the FSM is interrupted by an event. This activity is specified by the keyword 'do':

do / *computable activity*

Current state The state where the FSM resides and waits for an event to occur. When a state becomes a current state, it is *entered* and when a transition triggers the state is *exited*. A deterministic FSM has only one current state at a time.

Initial state The default start of an FSM. Because of determinism an FSM has only one initial state, which is a pseudo-state because it can never become the current state. The initial state is denoted by a black filled circle with one outgoing triggerless transition, an *initial transition*, to the actual start state.

Start state The target of the initial transition and thus it is the default initialization for the current state indicator.

Final state A pseudo-state indicating that the FSM is terminated. An FSM can have zero or more final states, which are illustrated with a black filled circle surrounded by an unfilled circle.

Event An occurrence of phenomena that is given an identity. The event can trigger (or fire) a transition. In general, an event can be

- a signal that can be dispatched asynchronously (i.e. it does not block the control flow of the invocator),
- a method call that is invoked synchronously (i.e. it blocks the control flow of the caller),
- a time period, or
- a change in the situation.

Because signal and call events differ at the software client end only, they are illustrated similarly: the event and its content are denoted by a name and a list of arguments. The time event includes the keyword 'after' and an expression for the time period. The change event is described simply by a Boolean condition.

Transition A quaternary relationship between two states (called the source and the target), a specified event, and an action. When the source state is the current state and the event occurs, the action is executed and the target state becomes the current state. In a *self-transition* the source and target are the same, but the entry and exit actions are executed similarly to ordinary transitions. A transition is illustrated as a directed edge from the source state to the target state. The edge label can be of the form

event(*arguments*) [*guard*] / *action*(*arguments*)

where the action is executed only when the event has occurred and the supplementing guard evaluates to true.

A transition that lacks event and guard is called a *triggerless transition* (or completion transition or epsilon transition). It is fired and followed immediately after the source state becomes the current state and the possible state actions are finished. If a transition connects the initial state directly to the final state, it can include a guard and an action but not an event.

Local variable A reference to shared data structures that the FSM can use in calculation. Local variables are often used for gathering information about the input instance.

To support stepwise refinement and modularity the states of an FSM can be hierarchical, which means that a single state can contain one or more FSMs. Hierarchical structure makes it possible to hide irrelevant details and to support reuse. Typically, a state is refined to substates if its 'do' activity is complex but has discrete phases for event handling.

A state without any subparts is called a *simple state*. If a state contains concurrent sub-FSMs, it is called a *composite state* and the current state is defined as a combination of the current states of the nested FSMs. A state that is assigned to nest one FSM is called a *submachine state* and the current state is defined for each nesting level at the same time. Due to hierarchical decomposition of the states, there are *level-preserving transitions* and *level-crossing transitions*. The incoming transitions of these types to a non-simple state s poses the question what are the states of the nested FSMs when s becomes the current state. Because s defines the environment for its sub-FSMs, we can consider that any sub-FSM M is instantiated when s is entered. In this case the start state of M is indicated by its initial state.

In addition to modularity, hierarchical states provide a way to denote many-to-one communication: a transition from a non-simple state can be triggered by any of its substates. In other words, if an FSM does not have a proper transition for an event at the current state level, the event is delegated upwards to the enclosing FSM. A many-to-one transition can be an outgoing transition (i.e. the consequent state is not in the source sub-FSM) or an incoming transition (i.e. the resulting state is back in the sub-FSM). In both cases the exit and entry actions are executed.

Sometimes it is convenient to store the current states of the sub-FSMs of s, where the execution continues when s is re-entered. For this purpose, we can define two pseudostates, a shallow and deep history state. A *shallow history state* of a sub-FSM M represents the most recent current state c of M and the incoming transitions to this history state are directed to c. A *deep history state* resembles the shallow history state but is applied recursively to every nested level. The shallow history node is illustrated with a circled H and the deep history node with a circled H*.

Figure 9.7 gives an example of an FSM for a generic pull-down menu logic, in which each menu item can be attached by a help document and related to advertisement animations. The menu is constructed and its n items are indexed uniquely from 0 to $n-1$ when the FSM is instantiated. The local variable e is used to refer to the entry index of the current item; naturally the actual implementation can use other methods to access the menu item behaviour. The menu logic relies on the events 'next' and 'previous' which are guarded by the conditions on the current entry index. The current entry index wraps over from the last menu item to the first (or from the first entry to thee last) by consuming an extra 'next' (or 'previous') event without any actions.

In addition to the traversing logic, the FSM models the activation of a menu item with the state 'Execution'. When the control flow returns, the event 'done' activates the transition to the history state, which forces the menu into the same state where the execution

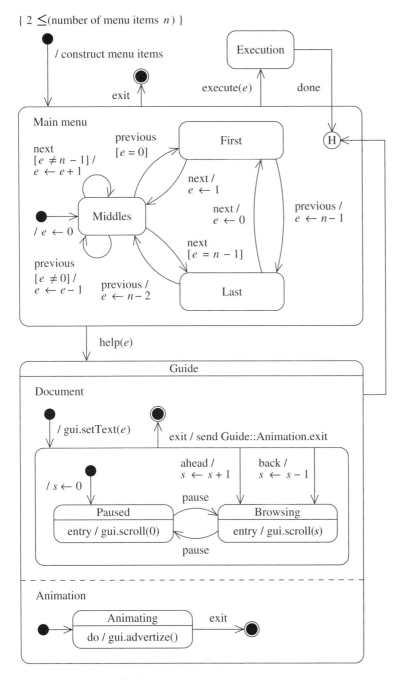

Figure 9.7 A generic FSM for a single pull-down menu with an online help logic.

was triggered. The composite state 'Guide' has concurrent substates 'Document' and 'Animation' and is instantiated for one menu item at a time by the event 'help'. When 'Guide' becomes active, both its sub-FSMs are run simultaneously. 'Guide' has a local variable 'gui' that refers to an object that can set up a help text for a given menu item, scroll the text at given speed, and run advertisement animations in the background. The scrolling text can be affected by events 'ahead' and 'back', and the cumulative scrolling speed (negative for scrolling backwards) is stored in the local variable s. It is worth noting that scrolling back the text when it is at the beginning depends solely on the object referred through 'gui' and not the FSM itself. Scrolling can be paused at any time and restored by toggling 'pause'. When the state 'Guide::Document' receives the event 'exit', it sends 'exit' signal to its co-FSM 'Guide::Animation' to finish the advertisement animation. When the sub-FSMs reach their final states, the triggerless transition (i.e. the rightmost transition in the diagram) is triggered.

The FSM presented does not describe how it should be implemented, how the menu is laid out on the screen, or how the user input is conveyed to the FSM. From the perspective of the FSM, these issues are irrelevant because it only defines the operation logic for the menu. In other words, the FSM notation – like the pseudocode used elsewhere in this book – is a convention to describe algorithmic behaviour.

9.2.2 Mealy and Moore machines

The UML description for FSMs allows an action to be attached both to a state and a transition. This approach is a mix of Mealy machine and Moore machine models. In a Mealy machine an action can be located only in a transition and thus the next action is derived from both the current state and an input event. In a Moore machine an action can only be as an entry action of a state, which means that the next action is derived solely from the target state. Figure 9.8 illustrates the difference between these two machine

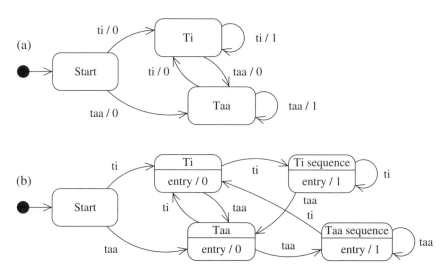

Figure 9.8 Detecting breaks in the repeating rhythm of 'ti' and 'taa' with (a) a Mealy machine, and (b) a Moore machine. The irregular beat outputs value 1.

types. Let us call a state that has an entry action a *Moore state*; otherwise we call the state a *Mealy state.*

The two machine types have equal expressive power, but in practice the Mealy formulation tends to yield a smaller number of states – which is also the reason why they are sometimes much harder to understand. If the Mealy and Moore models are equivalent, why does UML include them both? The rationale is that the models have different benefits and drawbacks with respect to the problem that is solved by the FSM. When a notation supports both models, an experienced and careful designer can determine the proper balance between the models and have a combination of the best properties. Although the structure of the FSM of mixed machine models depends strongly on the application, some guidelines should be followed in the design (see Figure 9.7):

- The Mealy and Moore machine models do not include exit actions. Both the theory and widely accepted FSM design practices indicate that the behaviour of an FSM should not be built on the exit actions. About the only acceptable use for exit actions is to end something critical such as freeing resources, cancelling timers, or finishing synchronization blocks. Otherwise, the exit action should be independent of the FSM logic.
- Triggerless transitions should be avoided, because they blur the concept of current state. The alias name of the transition – a completion transition – expresses its adequate context of use: when the task is finished, we want to end up in the completion state.
- In a Moore state, the triggering of a self-transition or a level-crossing transition also runs the exit and entry actions. If this behaviour is not desired, the state should be converted to a Mealy state. This gives us a method for testing the 'Mooreness' of a state: If some (imaginary) self-transition or level-crossing transition can cause problems with the entry and exit actions, the actions are too loosely connected to the state and should be relocated. In other words, if an action is attached to a state, the action must be an inherent property of that state without exception.
- Apart from many-to-one transitions, the level-crossing transitions should be avoided because they break the encapsulation between the FSM hierarchy levels. Also, the execution sequence for the 'entry', 'do', and 'exit' actions becomes too tedious to follow. Strict information hiding and encapsulation result in a more understandable form of modularity.
- If an application allows many alternative structures for the FSM, some transitions tend to become similar to one another and seem to emulate the role of a non-existent state. However, a transition cannot be used as a state (i.e. the FSM cannot be between states). Documenting the rationale behind the chosen FSM design (e.g. why and how the structure gives the solution) helps to keep the Mealy and Moore approaches in balance.

9.2.3 Implementation

Up to now we have described FSMs mainly from the perspective of the supplier who implements the software component. In software development, we must also take into account the client who gives the technical and intentional environment to the component by using it. This line of thinking leads to various module realization

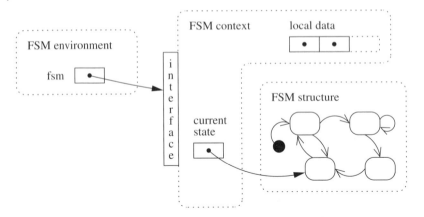

Figure 9.9 An FSM as a software object has a static structure, dynamic context, a fixed interface, and a use environment.

techniques – such as design by contract principle (Meyer 1997) – that bring these two conceptual participants together. This discussion is a part of a larger philosophy of software development which – regrettably! – falls outside the scope of this book. Nevertheless, let us discern the main software components of an FSM:

- a set of relationships between the states, transitions, events, and actions;
- control logic that handles the instantiation and termination, implements the event dispatching mechanisms, keeps track of state changes, and invokes the action executions;
- local data structures that can be accessed by the actions and activities of a state, by the guards and actions of a transition, and by the possible sub-FSMs;
- software client interface that describes the responsibilities of the FSM and how it is connected to the use environment (e.g. the application).

Figure 9.9 illustrates how these elements can be grouped according to their role. The *structure* objects describe the FSM as static data, the *context* objects manage the dynamics of the FSM, and the *environment* models a software client that uses the FSM through a designed interface. Discerning the three roles makes it easier to transfer an FSM to a pseudocode algorithm (and back). Moreover, it guides the direct implementation of an FSM (especially hierarchical states). For instance, we can deduce that if a state can have a sub-FSM, the interface part of Figure 9.9 must inherit the same properties as the states have. Why? Because in this case the state also fulfils the environment role for its sub-FSM.

The context role is important when we are defining an FSM. The context realizes the interface for the software clients (and possibly for other users through middleware interfaces) and describes how the dynamic memory is used to control the FSM implementation. This means that the FSM context gives us some freedom for designing FSMs in an object-oriented software system. In particular, local variables make it possible to transfer responsibilities from the FSM to the data object structures. In other words, we can simplify, for example, FSM communication by using object sharing and collapse combinatorial FSM substructures to member functions. We have already used member

(a)

(b)

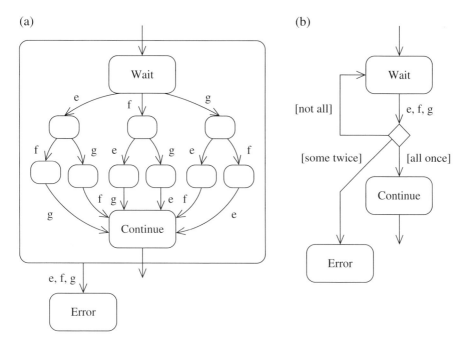

Figure 9.10 A combinatorial FSM that waits for signals 'e', 'f', and 'g' before proceeding. (a) Many-to-one signalling for detecting all erroneous situations is managed by a composite state. (b) The same FSM is collapsed by using a choice point and three Boolean guards.

functions in Figure 9.7, where the properties of 'gui' are defined to support the FSM logic of the menu.

To sum up, there are two kinds of freedom for managing complexity in an FSM: nested states and local variables. Let us take an example and assume that we have to wait for three different signals 'e', 'f' and 'g' (in any order) before we can proceed in the transition sequence. Figure 9.10(a) models this behaviour between the states 'Wait' and 'Continue'. The 'Error' state and nesting are used to collect invalid signalling. As we can see, the FSM has repetitive substructures, which usually indicate that with proper indirection constructs we could have designed a simpler solution. If we introduce three Boolean variables for the signals, we can check that each of them has occurred exactly once. Figure 9.10(b) illustrates the resulting FSM. The diamond represents a multiselection choice point of the disjointly guarded branches. Because Boolean flags and other mode variables rapidly ruin understandability, a better alternative is to introduce an object with two member routines that hide the accounting logic. Now, we use a procedure to keep a record of the encountered signals, and call a three-valued query function in the choice point to select the suitable transition branch.

9.2.4 Discussion

Computer games often use FSMs to control the behaviour of synthetic players. In other words, the FSM describes the 'main loop' of a synthetic player and the necessary activities are hooked into the states and transitions as actions (e.g. Figure 9.6(c) gives a complete decision-making logic for a friendly minotaur). However, this kind of approach suits only for synthetic players whose behaviour can be defined and described directly in discrete terms. When considering FSM as an implementation, one must heed the following principles:

- The structure of an FSM is essentially static and defies modifications to its config-uration. The purpose of an FSM is to define sequential and parallel relationships to achieve the intended behaviour for every possible input sequence. Since it gets harder to preserve the integrity of a complex FSM for all input instances, automatic modifi-cations become troublesome to implement. In other words, the behaviour of an FSM is not very parametric at the FSM structure level.
- An FSM introduces a sequential control memory of reactive behaviours, which are triggered by an event. The current state is a memoryless representation of every pos-sible transition chain leaving from the start state. Because the set of succeeding actions is determined solely by the current state, responding to (possibly numerous) excep-tional situations that have not been taken into account beforehand is an onerous task.
- The states of an FSM are mutually exclusive at the same hierarchy level, and each deterministic FSM is exactly in one certain state. Since there is no 'between states' condition, a normal FSM is not well suited to situations where states should be con-tinuous or have degrees of variation. Although states can describe proposition logic, operations more suitable for predicate logic (e.g. comparing game situations) are dif-ficult to model with FSMs.
- If one state machine is used for modelling independent properties, it can easily cause a combinatorial explosion in the number of states or transitions. For example, if we model a ranger in a role-playing game so that she can wander in the wilderness, eat when hungry, and illuminate her surroundings with a torch, the all-in-one FSM solu-tion resembles that given in Figure 9.11. By using this approach the number of states and transitions multiply for each new property the ranger has. This seems to imply that the independent features should be modelled with separate FSMs, and they must be managed by some higher-level context, which controls what FSMs are informed when an event occurs. Alternatively, all the separated FSMs can be constructed to discard unknown events as in Figure 9.12.

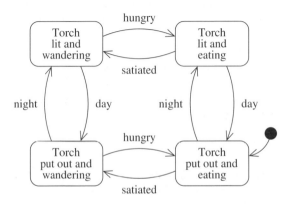

Figure 9.11 An FSM that joins two independent properties together.

Figure 9.12 Two concurrent FSMs where the properties are disjoint. The FSMs discard every unknown event by the transition labelled as <<any>>.

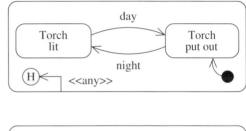

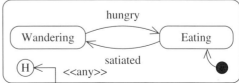

- FSMs tend to raise the risk of 'total rewriting' in the iterative software development processes. This problem stems from the fact that the software gets built up gradually: it is possible that the required set of states is not known when the first FSMs are sketched and their dominant structures are fixed. Because the FSMs are often highly cohesive, they are rarely patchable and, instead, they should be restructured – with enthusiastic effort.

Based on these observations it looks quite obvious that FSMs are not at their best in controlling the synthetic player directly but in keeping up the state of the entity. If we take a closer look at the decision-making component of a synthetic player (see Figure 9.1), the synthetic player's decision-making is based on a sense of self, others, the world, and the causality of the actions and events. When the decision-making system compares the appropriate actions, it tries to manage time-related issues as follows: the history repository models the past, the present is upheld by defining what the current state means, and the future is understood through the dynamic models of information and rules. FSMs have properties that are needed when we are implementing any of these supportive tasks. First, a state in an FSM represents all possible transition walks from the initial state (i.e. a state is a compressed image of the past). Second, the FSM maintains the current state that is recursively defined according to its nesting structure. Third, the outgoing transitions from the current state determine the set of possible actions in the future. On the other hand, FSMs lack many capabilities that are useful in realizing intelligent behaviour.

By limiting the scope of FSMs to supporting components for decision-making (e.g. pattern recognition) rather than decision-making itself, the purpose of FSMs becomes clearer and their implementation more manageable. For each specific sequential or concurrent task, we can design an FSM of our own that is relatively independent of other FSMs. This leads to better software modularity because it adheres the principle of 'low coupling and high cohesion'. Due to modularity the decision-making subsystem becomes more adaptable. As AI programmers know, this property is essential because general decision-making methods must be adjusted, tuned, and made robust until they become practical in the application.

9.3 Influence Maps

An influence map is a discrete representation of the synthetic player's knowledge of the world. In a sense, grids and navigation meshes, which are discussed in Section 7.1, are influence maps representing the cost of travelling. However, an influence map can also provide the decision-making system with other kinds of strategic and tactical information. The idea of using influence maps (or spheres of influence) in the game of Go was introduced by A.L. Zobrist (1969). Because of its simplicity, the method is widely used especially in real-time strategy games such as *Age of Empires II* (Pottinger 2000).

Each influence map collects information about a certain type of effect in the game world (e.g. strengths and positions of military troops or deposits of natural resources). Influence is a twofold function, because it can indicate *repulsiveness* or *alluringness*: enemy troops should be avoided (i.e. their influence is repulsive), and untapped resources should be capitalized upon (i.e. their influence is alluring). Influence maps also allow inferences to be made about the characteristics of different locations in the game world (e.g. finding strategic control points and pointing out weaknesses in the enemy's defence). For a discussion of different strategic and tactical dispositions for outmanoeuvring the opponent, see Woodcock (2002) and Mark (2015).

Although an influence map overlays the game world, it does not have to follow its geography. However, for the sake of argument, we assume that the map is divided into tiles with a regular grid. As in path finding, the granularity of the grid is a trade-off between accuracy and computational demands. Each tile in the grid holds numeric information on the corresponding area of the game world. The tile can represent alluringness with positive values and repulsiveness with negative values.

Influence maps are constructed in two phases (see Figure 9.13). Initially, the tiles where the given influence exists are assigned a corresponding value. Then the influence is propagated over the map by spreading the influence already allocated to the tiles to the neighbouring tiles. The influence has a fall-off that diminishes (usually linearly or exponentially) its effect when it is spread. Moreover, if the influence map includes floating point values, there should be some cut-off point so that minuscule influence values, which have little if no effect at all, do not get spread all over the map.

Influence maps based on terrain or other static features of the game world can be created beforehand. Unfortunately, most of the influences are dynamic in nature and the maps need to be updated periodically. As a remedy, we can categorize the maps based on the rate of changes so that the more animate ones are updated more frequently. Also, lazy evaluation, where the values are updated only when the influence map is accessed, may improve the overall performance.

It is possible to generalize influence maps to graphs. For example, consider the game *Hunt the Wumpus* (Yob 1975), which has become a classic in AI research. Although the game world is usually simplified into a grid, G. Yob, the game creator, was bored with grid-based games, and the squashed dodecahedron depicted in Figure 9.14 was his original design for the game world. The subsequent versions of the game included a diverse set of game worlds based on, for example, torus surfaces and Möbius strips. Fundamentally, the game world comprises a graph, where the vertices represent the rooms and the edges are the tunnels between two rooms (see Figure 9.14). The somewhat simplified rules of the game are as follows. A hunter roams inside this world, equipped with a

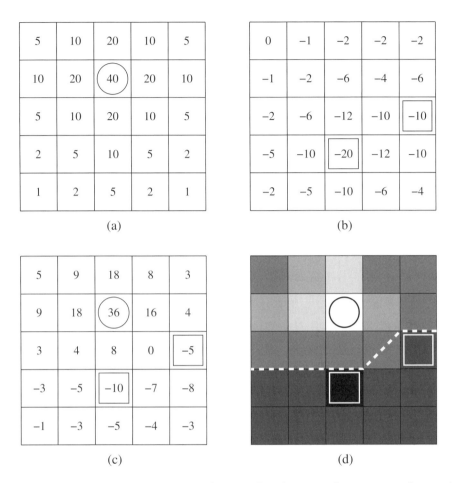

5	10	20	10	5
10	20	(40)	20	10
5	10	20	10	5
2	5	10	5	2
1	2	5	2	1

(a)

0	−1	−2	−2	−2
−1	−2	−6	−4	−6
−2	−6	−12	−10	[−10]
−5	−10	[−20]	−12	−10
−2	−5	−10	−6	−4

(b)

5	9	18	8	3
9	18	(36)	16	4
3	4	8	0	[−5]
−3	−5	[−10]	−7	−8
−1	−3	−5	−4	−3

(c)

(d)

Figure 9.13 Let the circled tile represent the strength and position of own troops and squared tiles enemy's troops. (a) After the initial influence values have been assigned, their effect is propagated over the map. The fall-off halves the influence in the neighbouring tiles. (b) The same is done to the influence map based on the enemy's troops. (c) By aggregating the two influence maps, we get a new influence map which combines the troop information. (d) The resulting map demarcates, for example, the frontier between the players.

limited supply of arrows, in search of a wumpus. At each turn, the hunter must decide between two actions: move through a tunnel into a new room, or shoot an arrow through the tunnel to a neighbouring room. If the hunter moves to the same room as the wumpus, it eats him and the game is lost; if the hunter shoots an arrow to the room where the wumpus is lurking, he kills it and wins the game. There are also other hazards hidden in the game world: if the hunter encounters bats, they will carry him into a randomly selected room. If there is a pit in the room, the hunter will fall into it and the game is over. Luckily, the hunter can sense if there is danger in any of the neighbouring rooms (although he does not know in which one): he can smell the wumpus, hear the noise of the bats, and feel the draft from the pit.

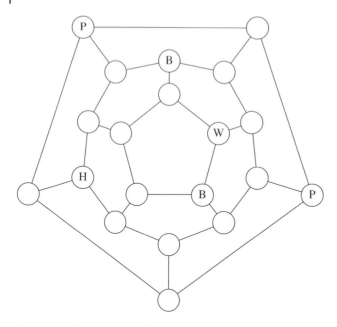

Figure 9.14 The game world of *Hunt the Wumpus* is a graph, where the vertices are the rooms and the edges the tunnels connecting them. The hunter (H) moves from room to room avoiding bats (B) and pits (P), and is ready to shoot the wumpus (W).

Algorithm 9.1 describes a simple decision-making system for the hunter, which is based on influence maps. The hunter maintains four influence maps – bats, pit, wumpus, and visited rooms – which are updated based on sense data and discoveries. Here, a large value means repulsion. All maps are initialized to the value 1. When the hunter enters a room and nothing happens, we know that there are no bats, pit, nor wumpus there, and the associated map positions are set to the value 0. The visited map, which encourages the hunter to choose undiscovered rooms, is updated so that the value of the current room is doubled. If the hunter perceives any sensory information about the neighbourhood, all neighbouring rooms are updated by doubling the current values in the relevant influence map. The hunter makes a decision based on two rules: if any of the neighbouring rooms exceeds a given threshold value in the wumpus map, the hunter will shoot an arrow into that room. Otherwise, he will move to the room for which the sum of influence map values is the smallest. Hence, the hunter tries to avoid possible dangers and already visited rooms.

9.4 Automated Planning

Automated planning is about devising actions to achieve a given objective. Formally speaking, a planning problem assumes that the world has a unique initial state, a goal state, a set of available operations and a set of constraints limiting the planning. The aim is to create a sequence of operations changing the world from the initial state to the goal state while observing the constraints. Usually we can assume that the world is

Algorithm 9.1 Decision-making for a wumpus hunter using influence maps.

WUMPUS-HUNTER-REACT(v)

    in: current room $v \in V$

    out: action $\langle a \in \{\text{SHOOT}, \text{MOVE}\}, u \in neighbourhood(v) \rangle$

    constant: threshold t_s for shooting an arrow

    local: influence maps *bats*, *pit*, *wumpus*, and *visited* (initially

                 $\forall u \in V : bats(u) = pit(u) = wumpus(u) = visited(u) = 1$)

1: $bats(v) \leftarrow pit(v) \leftarrow wumpus(v) \leftarrow 0$
2: $visited(v) \leftarrow 2 \cdot visited(v)$
3: **for all** $u \in neighbourhood(v)$ **do**
4:   **if** $noise(v)$ **then**
5:     $bats(u) \leftarrow 2 \cdot bats(u)$
6:   **else**
7:     $bats(u) \leftarrow 0$
8:   **end if**
9:   **if** $draft(v)$ **then**
10:   $pit(u) \leftarrow 2 \cdot pit(u)$
11: **else**
12:   $pit(u) \leftarrow 0$
13: **end if**
14: **if** $smell(v)$ **then**
15:   $wumpus(u) \leftarrow 2 \cdot wumpus(u)$
16: **else**
17:   $wumpus(u) \leftarrow 0$
18: **end if**
19: **end for**
20: $w \leftarrow$ vertex $w' \in neighbourhood(v)$ that maximizes $wumpus(w')$
21: **if** $wumpus(w) \geq t_s$ **and** arrows left **then**
22: $wumpus(w) \leftarrow 0$
23: **return** $\langle \text{SHOOT}, w \rangle$
24: **end if**
25: $u \leftarrow u' \in neighbourhood(v)$ which minimizes $bats(u') + pit(u') + wumpus(u')$
      $+ visited(u')$
26: **return** $\langle \text{MOVE}, u \rangle$

---

limited, finite, deterministic, static (i.e. there are no outside events changing the world) and completely observable (i.e. we can find out the truth value of any condition related to the world).

Planning systems based on logic were created already in the 1950s for specific application areas, but the most influential system, Stanford Research Institute Problem Solver (STRIPS), was developed to solve general planning problems and its notation forms the basis for modern planning systems (Fikes and Nilsson 1971). To improve the efficiency and usability later systems introduced abstraction, where the less important details are hidden at the beginning, allowing the planning system to focus on the difficult parts of the problem (Sacerdoti 1974). Then the planning opens the abstractions and solves the details. This approach allowed different levels of abstraction to be created, leading to conceptual hierarchies. We humans tend to use the same approach when solving complex planning problems by abstracting and dividing them into smaller parts. This allows us to focus first on the essentials. Once we know the solution at a higher level, it is easier to work out the details. Often we divide the problem into subproblems, which we solve apart from the other subproblems – like the approach to path finding presented in Chapter 7.

Here, we focus on hierarchical task networks (HTNs), which have been widely used in many games for a range of purposes, from modelling synthetic player behaviour (Humphreys 2015; Wallace 2003) to generating interactive narrative (Cavazza et al. 2001; Riemer 2015). Another common approach for automated planning in games is goal-oriented action planning, which is an improvement on STRIPS allowing emergent behaviour to be generated in real time (Orkin 2003).

In HTNs, tasks are divided into primitive tasks that can be carried out directly and compound (i.e. non-primitive or abstracted) tasks that the planning system has to figure out how to perform. The planning system comprises (Erol et al. 1994a):

- a task network that represents the problem to be solved;
- a set of operations that indicates the action corresponding to each primitive task;
- a set of methods that tells how to perform the compound tasks.

Figure 9.15 illustrates a simple HTN for a guard, who is patrolling an area equipped with a bow and sword. The highest-level compound task is 'Guard', which has three methods 'Attack', 'Heal' and 'Patrol'. Each method has a precondition: 'Attack' requires that the guard has seen an enemy, 'Heal' requires that the guard is wounded, and for 'Patrol' the precondition is true, which means that it is always applicable. When selecting a method, we are basically selecting a search strategy (e.g. depth-first or breadth-first). For simplicity's sake, let us assume that we have prioritized the methods so that 'Attack' is evaluated first, followed by 'Heal' and 'Patrol' (top-down order in the figure). If the world state satisfies the precondition, we select the method; otherwise, we continue to the next method. 'Patrol' is the final choice if no other method is selected.

If we look next at the compound state 'Attack', we can see that it has two methods leading to either 'Ranged attack' or 'Melee attack'. If the guard has neither bow and arrow nor sword, neither of these plans is selected and the selection rolls back to 'Guard' and ultimately leads to 'Patrol'. 'Ranged attack' has a higher priority and it has three primitive subtasks that are connected to the operations in the game world. Hence, the resulting sequence of operations would be 'Move to shooting distance', 'Prepare the bow' and 'Shoot an arrow'.

To solve the planning problem Algorithm 9.2 presents a simplified version of an HTN; for a more general approach, see Erol et al. (1994b). The algorithm starts from the initial task, which in our example would be 'Guard'. The tasks to be processed are stored in a stack, where we pop out one task for each iteration. If the task is a compound task, we go through its methods and select one for which the precondition is true. All the subtasks – both primitive and compound – of that method are pushed to the stack and we save the current situation for a possible rollback. If no suitable method is found, we roll back to

Algorithm 9.2 Simple hierarchical task network algorithm.

SIMPLE-HTN(i)

in: initial task i

out: sequence of operations O

local: sequence R used as a stack for backtracking; sequence T used as a stack for task to be processed

1: $O \leftarrow \langle\ \rangle; R \leftarrow \langle\ \rangle; T \leftarrow \langle\ \rangle$ ▷ Empty sequences.
2: STACK-PUSH(T, i)
3: **repeat**
4:   $t \leftarrow$ STACK-POP(T)
5:   **if** $compound(t)$ **then**
6:     $M \leftarrow methods(t)$
7:     select $m \in M$ so that $precondition(m) = $ TRUE
8:     **if** $m \neq$ NIL **then**
9:       **for all** $s \in subtasks(m)$ **do**
10:         STACK-PUSH(T, s)
11:       **end for**
12:       STACK-PUSH($R, \langle t, T, O \rangle$)   ▷ Save for rollback.
13:     **else**   ▷ No suitable method found.
14:       **if** $R \neq \varnothing$ **then**
15:         $\langle t, T, O \rangle \leftarrow$ STACK-POP(R)   ▷ Roll back.
16:       **else**
17:         **error** no plan exists
18:       **end if**
19:     **end if**
20:   **else**   ▷ Primitive task.
21:     **if** $precondition(t) = $ TRUE **then**
22:       $O \leftarrow O \parallel \langle operation(t) \rangle$
23:     **else**
24:       **if** $R \neq \varnothing$ **then**
25:         $\langle t, T, O \rangle \leftarrow$ STACK-POP(R)
26:       **else**
27:         **error** no plan exists
28:       **end if**
29:     **end if**
30:   **end if**
31: **until** $T = \varnothing$
32: **return** O

the previous saved situation – unless there is nothing to roll back, in which case there is no viable plan. For a primitive task, the algorithm first ensures that its precondition holds and then adds the associated operation to the resulting sequence of operations. If the precondition is false, then we roll back to the previous situation and continue from there. Again, if the rollback is not possible, the planning fails.

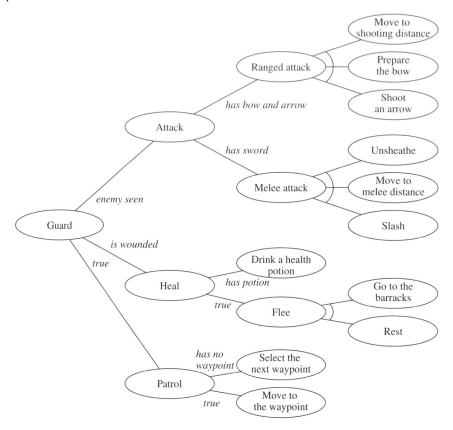

Figure 9.15 Guard's decision-making represented as a hierarchical task network using the and–or tree notation.

9.5 Summary

The technical requirements and expectations on synthetic players are constantly increasing. Whereas in the traditional turn-based games the computer opponent can think (almost) as long as it takes, nowadays games mostly require real-time response. This puts considerable computational strain on the synthetic player, because it can no longer take too long to find an optimal strategy but must react promptly. Response is the keyword – even to such an extent that game developers tend to think that it is better to have hordes of mindless cannon-fodder than to grant synthetic players a shred of intelligence. In the past the main reason for this was that the decision-making was not given a fair share of the overall processing resources. Surprisingly, even today AI in commercial computer games can require a significant amount of the available processor capacity.

Distribution of processing has become more important now that games using networking are more common. This may present one solution to the dilemma of achieving both real-time response and intelligence: instead of running the synthetic players on one machine, they can be distributed so that the cumulative computational power of the networked nodes is utilized. For example, *Homeworld* uses this technique and distributes the computer-controlled opponents among the participating computers.

Distribution naturally begs the question as to how autonomous the synthetic players should be. As long as we can rely on the network there is no problem, but if nodes can drop out and join at any time, distributed synthetic players must display autonomy. This means two things. First, the synthetic player must be persistent, because it can be migrated to or re-created at another node if the one where it is currently run gets cut off. Second, the synthetic player must be self-sufficient, because it cannot rely on outside processes but should be able to operate on its own. This is not necessarily a drawback, because autonomy can lead to smaller and better design, and complex behaviour can emerge from seemingly simple autonomous agents.

A corollary of autonomy is that the synthetic players must have a way to communicate explicitly with each other. Because there is no central intelligence controlling them, they have to inform others on their decisions, indicate their plans, and negotiate with each other – just like we humans do in the real world. Of course these communication skills may come in handy also when interacting with the human players.

Exercises

9-1 Consider the process of doing the groceries. What strategic, tactical and operational decisions are involved in it?

9-2 Humans are predictable players. Verify this claim by implementing a modeller for rock–paper–scissors, which analyses the sequence of human opponent's choices and predicts the next move. Analysis could be based on statistical data (i.e. it is likely that the human player favours a certain choice), or sequential data (i.e. it is likely that the human player repeats a certain sequence of choices).

9-3 Consider the following problems. Which of the them should be solved with optimization and which with adaptation?
  (a) Deciding which building to construct next in a real-time strategy game.
  (b) Driving a jeep in a convoy.
  (c) Selecting the contents of a backpack in a role-playing game.
  (d) Casting a spell against a known enemy.
  (e) Casting a spell against an unknown enemy.

9-4 Execute the FSM illustrated in Figure 9.6(c) for the maze given in Figure 9.16. The starting location is at (5, f) and the heading is north.

9-5 Let us analyse the maze circulator of Exercise 9-4. Assume that a maze does not include unnecessary wall tiles. Given a $m \times n$ maze with w wall tiles, what is the maximum number of events keeping us in the state 'Searching for a wall'? How about remaining in the state 'Following the wall' for one walk cycle around the maze? Give at least two reasons why this kind of knowledge about an FSM is useful.

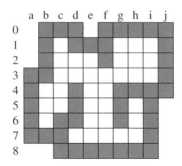

Figure 9.16 A closed acyclic maze on a square grid. The maze has walls (dark tiles) and an interior (white tiles), which are four-connected.

9-6 The right-hand rule modelled in the FSM of Figure 9.6(c) benefits left-handers (including the authors). Is it possible to define an equivalent rule for right-handers?

9-7 Figure 9.6(c) describes the FSM with natural language, which is typical in the high-level design phase of a software development process. Refine the FSM so that it is closer to the implementation by incorporating more formal handling of the sensory events $sensor(l, f, r)$. Boolean variables l, f, and r indicate whether there is a wall on the neighbouring left, front, or right tile. Also introduce a simple local variable interface for executing actions 'go forward', 'turn left 90°', and 'turn right 90°'.

9-8 Inspired and amazed by the mazes you decide to implement a stealth-based game called 'Metal Hear Oil', in which the player secretly dwells in a maze-like world populated by hostile but nearsighted robots. Fortunately, each robot gives visual feedback about its internal state through a row of lights etched on its occiput. By observing the robot the player can learn how it reacts to the surroundings according to the sensory stimuli. You can even intensify the mood by including movable façade walls.

   The robot's control logic is based on an FSM similar to the one in Exercise 9-7. Modify this FSM and its local variable interface so that the robot recognizes the following game world situations and flashes its backlights accordingly: 'in a convex corner', 'in a concave corner', 'in a corridor', 'in a dead end', 'beside the player', and 'facing the player'. In the last two cases the robot also gives an intruder alert.

9-9 Assume that the game world is an infinite square grid. Figure 9.17 defines an acceptor FSM for events 'north', 'east', 'south', and 'west' that model unit steps towards the principal compass points. What is the general condition when the FSM terminates? Also give more descriptive names to the states.

9-10 At first glance the menu FSM given in Figure 9.7 seems to serve only the user interface subsystem and have little – if anything – to do with decision-making. To counter this let us put aside the menu logic and just focus on the events, states and transactions. Consider a bartender in a small and cosy bar serving drinks to

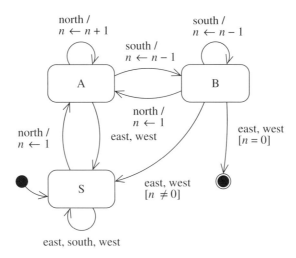

Figure 9.17 An acceptor FSM on a square grid.

customers, entertaining them with stories, managing the bar bookkeeping, and occasionally doing some maintenance work. Use the skeleton of the menu FSM to define a control logic for this simple but busy synthetic bartender.

You can use this alternative view in Exercises 9-11 to 9-14.

9-11 Implement the 'Guide::Document' state of Figure 9.7 using the pseudocode notation and the **case–of** control structure.

9-12 The 'Main menu' state in Figure 9.7 is a Mealy machine. Redesign it as a Moore machine.

9-13 The 'Guide::Document' state in Figure 9.7 has one anonymous state that contains a sub-FSM with 'Paused' and 'Browsing' states. This sub-FSM is a combination of Mealy and Moore machine models. Change it to a pure Mealy model that does not have any incoming transitions from the superstate.

9-14 Figure 9.7 describes an FSM for a simple but generic pull-down menu. Supplement it with the following features:
  (a) In the original FSM, the help documentation of a menu item is accessed through the main menu. Change the FSM so that it is possible to go through all item documentations without leaving the 'Guide' state.
  (b) The original FSM is designed to handle only one pull-down menu. Or is it? How would you proceed if your application required multiple disjoint submenus with various nesting levels?

9-15 Figure 9.8 defines a Mealy machine and a Moore machine for detecting the rhythm breaks 'ti'–'ti' and 'taa'–'taa'. Device a Mealy machine and a Moore machine for detecting the subsequences of the form 'ti'–'taa'–'taa'–'ti' from any given input.

9-16 Study Figure 9.9 and give a condition for when it is possible to share an FSM substructure among multiple FSM structures. The condition should be necessary and sufficient. Give at least two reasons why shared sub-FSMs are beneficial.

9-17 Model a simple pocket calculator with an FSM that uses floating point values and operators '+', '−', '*', and '/'. To avoid parentheses the expressions are given using *reverse Polish notation* and evaluated using a stack as a data structure. For example, $(3+1)/4$ can be given to the FSM as the input events '3', '1', '+', '4', '/', 'print'. The event 'print' outputs the topmost value of the stack without other side-effects. Is the FSM notation suited to this kind of problem? Would an algorithmic pseudocode be easier to understand? Can you generalize your observation by considering only the FSM structure? If you can, what consequences does it have concerning decision-making methods?

9-18 The structure of the FSM of Exercise 9-9 can also be interpreted as a model for a specific walking pattern in a square grid. Supplement it by introducing suitable frequency counters so that it can be used for predicting the player's movements. What kind of software client interface should the FSM have? How can it be used for producing randomized square grid walks with respect to the model?

9-19 Table 9.1 defines the states for a player on the move as a combination of step and heading directions. How can you model this matrix with an FSM? Is it worth the effort?

Table 9.1 The states of a player on the move in terms of a step direction and a heading direction. The directions are absolute in the game world (i.e. they are not relative to the player). The 'Forward step' state is denoted by 'F', 'Backward step' by 'B', 'Left sidestep' by 'L', and 'Right sidestep' by 'R'.

	Heading towards			
Step towards	*north*	*east*	*south*	*west*
north	F	L	B	R
east	R	F	L	B
south	B	R	F	L
west	L	B	R	F

9-20 In Section 9.2 we do not describe how the FSM context of Figure 9.9 actually receives the events. There are two opposite approaches for conveying signals, routine calls, time delays, and condition changes to an FSM. In a *pull approach* the FSM actively polls the events that can affect it. In a *push approach* the FSM is passive until it is given an indication about the events. Of course each event type can have its own delivering logic, and the approaches can be combined. What object-oriented design patterns – for example, from the catalogue by Gamma et al. (1995) – can be used when implementing these pull and push approaches?

9-21 Let us continue Exercise 9-20. What object-oriented design patterns would you use when implementing the hierarchical FSMs? Note that the *State* design pattern of Gamma et al. (1995) is not necessarily the best way to implement an FSM state.

9-22 Influence maps – like any discretization – can lead to quantization problems, where relevant details get lost because of the coarseness of the model. How can this problem be tackled?

9-23 Influence maps are often closely connected to path finding. Explain why and how.

9-24 Influence maps are often used in path finding. In the game of Goldrush (see Figure 9.18) the game world is formed by a square grid, where each tile has a height. Piles of gold have been scattered randomly in the world, and a gold-digger, starting from home, must find a path through all the piles and ending up back home. The game world also includes towers, which can shoot arrows to the north, south, east and west. The accuracy of a tower depends on the distance d to the gold-digger, and the probability of a hit is $1/2^d$. Going uphill or being shot reduces the gold-digger's vitality. Design a method that helps the gold-digger to find a path that conserves his vitality as much as possible.

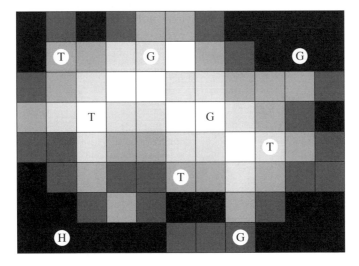

Figure 9.18 Game world for Goldrush. The gold-digger starts from home (H) and must visit all gold piles (G) and return home. The towers (T) shoot arrows to the four principal compass points. The colour of a tile illustrates the height of the terrain (i.e. the lighter the colour, the higher the ground). To conserve his vitality the gold-digger should avoid travelling uphill and getting too close to the towers.

9-25 Trace the wumpus hunter's decisions using Algorithm 9.1 in the game world of Figure 9.14. What happens if you change the multiplier of the influence map *visited*($\bullet$) from 2 to $1\frac{1}{2}$ or $2\frac{1}{2}$?

9-26 Algorithm 9.1 does not always lead the hunter to the wumpus. Design a game world where the hunter can get stuck. Update the algorithm so that the hunter can escape these situations.

9-27 If the game world of *Hunt the Wumpus* were a Möbius strip, what would that mean for the hunter's decision-making?

9-28 The bats and the wumpus in *Hunt the Wumpus* do not move. If they could wander around in the cave (as in the original game), what would that mean for the hunter's decision-making?

9-29 Let us add two new features to the guard's behaviour modelled as an HTN in Figure 9.15:
- If there is more than one enemy, the guard sounds an alarm and waits for backup troops before attacking.
- If the guard observes a wounded companion in arms and has a healing potion, he uses the potion to heal the companion's wounds.

Restructure the HTN and prioritize the new features. Devise the necessary subtasks.

9-30 Line 7 of Algorithm 9.2, where the method is selected, is the key to searching the HTN. Instead of prioritizing the methods, what other possibilities could we use? How would they affect the behaviour of the algorithm?

10

Modelling Uncertainty

Because decision-making is based on a model of the world, it is often subject to uncertainties. The dictionary gives us two meanings for the word 'uncertainty': something that is uncertain, or the state of being uncertain. In the first case we usually talk about probability (like the outcome of casting a die), whereas in the latter case the uncertainty concerns our own abilities or possibility to classify objects. If you draw a circle freehand, there is uncertainty about whether it is a circle. However, that uncertainty has nothing to do with probability. This *possibilistic* uncertainty brings forth problems of classification, and we face them everyday. In their purest form, they present themselves as *sorites* paradoxes: when does a heap of sand cease to be a heap if we remove one grain of sand at a time from it?

In this chapter we look at both probabilistic and possibilistic uncertainty. Statistical reasoning models beliefs based on the probability of events, whereas fuzzy sets help us model the possibility of events by allowing partial membership in a set. Fuzziness can be embedded in 'classical' solution methods, and, as an example, we present how constraint satisfaction problems can be fuzzified.

10.1 Statistical Reasoning

Sometimes we do not have enough evidence for full certainty, and we have to make decisions based on beliefs. This situation can occur when we are facing random events (e.g. throwing dice or drawing cards from a shuffled deck) or when we have only statistical knowledge on the chain of events. In the latter case, the belief in the likelihood of an event can be based on statistical data. In this section we go through some techniques for modelling probabilistic or statistical knowledge.

10.1.1 Bayes' theorem

Bayes' theorem, introduced by T. Bayes in the eighteenth century, provides a method to calculate conditional probabilities. Suppose that we have a hypothesis H and evidence E, and we know *a priori* the probabilities of the hypothesis $P(H)$, the evidence $P(E)$, and the evidence assuming the hypothesis is true $P(E|H)$. Bayes' theorem gives us the probability of the hypothesis based on the evidence:

$$P(H|E) = \frac{P(H \cap E)}{P(E)}, \tag{10.1}$$

Algorithms and Networking for Computer Games, Second Edition. Jouni Smed and Harri Hakonen.
© 2017 John Wiley & Sons Ltd. Published 2017 by John Wiley & Sons Ltd.

which we can rewrite as

$$P(H|E) = \frac{P(E|H) \cdot P(H)}{P(E)}. \tag{10.2}$$

More generally, if we have a set of n hypotheses $\{H_0, H_1, \ldots, H_{n-1}\}$, Bayes' theorem can be restated as

$$P(H_i|E) = \frac{P(E|H_i) \cdot P(H_i)}{\sum_{j=0}^{n-1}(P(E|H_j) \cdot P(H_j))} \tag{10.3}$$

provided that the whole event space equals $\bigcup_{i=0}^{n-1} H_i$, $H_i \cap H_j = \emptyset$ when $i \neq j$, and $P(E) > 0$.

Bayes' theorem has assumptions which restrict its usability. First, all the statistical data regarding the evidence with the various hypotheses are assumed to be known. Because Bayesian reasoning requires complete and up-to-date probabilities, we have to adjust them whenever we find a new connection between a hypothesis and the evidence. Second, the terms $P(E|H_i)$ must be independent of one another (i.e. the hypotheses are alternative explanations for the evidence). Both of these assumptions can be quite problematic to establish in the real world.

Let us take a simple (but instructive) example of Bayes' theorem. Suppose there is a 10% probability that an alpha-tested computer game has a bug in it. From past experience we have observed that the likelihood of a detected bug resulting from an actual bug in the program is 90%. The likelihood of detecting a bug when it is not present (e.g. it is caused by the test arrangement) is 10%. Now, the components are:

- H – there is a bug in the code;
- E – a bug is detected in the test;
- $E|H$ – a bug is detected in the test given that there is a bug in the code;
- $H|E$ – there is a bug in the code given that a bug is detected in the test.

The known probabilities are:

$$P(H) = 0.10,$$
$$P(E|H) = 0.90,$$
$$P(E|\neg H) = 0.10.$$

By using the law of total probability we can calculate for partitions H and $\neg H$,

$$P(E) = P(E|H) \cdot P(H) + P(E|\neg H) \cdot P(\neg H) = 0.18.$$

To get the probability of detecting an actual bug in the code, we apply Equation (10.2) and get

$$P(H|E) = 0.5.$$

To conclude, even if we can detect actual bugs 90% of the time, there is a fifty–fifty chance that a detected bug is not in the actual code – which is not a reassuring result for a programmer.

Figure 10.1 A Bayesian network as a directed acyclic graph.

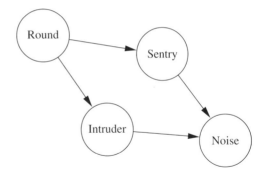

10.1.2   Bayesian networks

Bayesian networks try to solve the independence problem by modelling the knowledge in a modular fashion. Generally, propositions can affect each other in two alternative ways:

(i) observing a cause changes the probabilities of its effects, or
(ii) observing an effect changes the probabilities of its causes.

The idea of a Bayesian network is to make a clear distinction between these two cases by describing the cause-and-effect relationships with a directed acyclic graph. The vertices represent a proposition or variable. The edges represent the dependencies as probabilities, and the probability of a vertex is affected by the probabilities of its successors and predecessors.

Let us take an example, where a guard is observing his surroundings. If he hears a noise, its cause is either a sentry making the rounds or an intruder, who is likely to avoid the time when the sentry is doing the rounds. The situation can be expressed as a graph, illustrated in Figure 10.1. If we know the probabilities for the dependencies between the vertices, we assign them to the edges or list them as in Table 10.1.

We still need a mechanism to compute the propagation between the vertices. Suppose the guard hears a noise, what does it say about the probability of an intruder? The propagation methods are based on the idea that the vertices have local effects. Instead of trying to manage the complete graph, we can reduce the problem by focusing on one

Table 10.1 Probabilities for a Bayesian network.

$H \mid E$	$P(H \mid E)$
Noise | Sentry $\wedge$ Intruder	0.95
Noise | Sentry $\wedge$ ¬Intruder	0.9
Noise | ¬Sentry $\wedge$ Intruder	0.8
Noise | ¬Sentry $\wedge$ ¬Intruder	0.1
Sentry | Round	1.0
Sentry | ¬Round	0.0
Intruder | Round	0.1
Intruder | ¬Round	0.9
Round	0.3

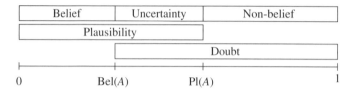

Figure 10.2 Belief and plausibility.

subgraph at a time; for details, see Pearl (1986). Still, the problems of Bayesian reasoning – establishing the probabilities and updating them – remain, and Bayesian networks are usually too static for practical use.

10.1.3 Dempster–Shafer theory

To address the problems of Bayesian reasoning, Dempster–Shafer theory (Shafer 1990) allows beliefs about propositions to be represented as intervals

$$[\text{belief}, \text{plausibility}] \subseteq [0, 1].$$

Belief (Bel) gives the amount of belief that directly supports the proposition. Plausibility (Pl), which is defined

$$\text{Pl}(A) = 1 - \text{Bel}(\neg A),$$

describes how much the belief supporting the contradicting proposition $\neg A$ reduces the possibility of proposition A (i.e. $\text{Bel}(A) \leq \text{Pl}(A)$). In particular, if $\text{Bel}(\neg A) = 1$ (i.e. the contradicting proposition is certain), then $\text{Pl}(A) = 0$ (i.e. A is not plausible) and the only possible belief value is $\text{Bel}(A) = 0$ (i.e. A is not believable).

The belief–plausibility interval indicates how much information we have about the propositions (see Figure 10.2). For example, suppose that the proposition 'there is an intruder' has a belief of 0.3 and a plausibility of 0.8. This means that we have evidence in supporting of the proposition being true with probability 0.3. The evidence contrary to the hypothesis (i.e. 'there is no intruder') has probability 0.2, which means that the hypothesis is possible up to the probability 0.8, since the remaining probability mass of 0.5 is essentially 'indeterminate'. Additional evidence can reduce the interval – increase the belief or decrease the plausibility – unlike in the Bayesian approach, where the probabilities of the hypotheses are assigned beforehand. For instance, at the beginning when we have no information about hypothesis A, we let $\text{Bel}(A) = 0$ and $\text{Pl}(A) = 1$. Now, any evidence that supports A increases $\text{Bel}(A)$ and any evidence that supports the contradicting hypothesis decreases $\text{Pl}(A)$.

Let us take an example and see how we use the belief function with a set of alternative hypotheses. Suppose that we have four hypotheses, 'weather', 'animal', 'trap' and 'enemy' which form the set $\Theta = \{W, A, T, E\}$. Our task is to assign a belief value to each element of Θ. The evidence can affect one or more of the hypotheses. For example, evidence 'noise' supports hypotheses W, A and E.

Whereas Bayesian reasoning requires that we assign a conditional probability to each combination of propositions, Dempster–Shafer theory operates with sets of hypotheses. A *mass function* (or basic probability assignment) $m(H)$, which is defined for all $H \in \wp(\Theta) \setminus \emptyset$, indicates the current belief in the set H of hypotheses. Although the number of subsets is exponential and the sum of their probabilities should be 1, most of the subsets will be ignored and their probability is zero.

Let us continue with our example. At the beginning we have no information at all, and we let $m(\Theta) = 1$ and all the subsets have the value 0. In other words, all hypotheses are plausible and we have no evidence supporting any of them. Next, we observe a noise and know this evidence points to the subset $\{W, A, E\}$ (i.e. we believe that the noise is caused by the weather, an animal or an enemy) with probability 0.6. The corresponding mass function m_n is

$$m_n(\{W, A, E\}) = 0.6, \quad m_n(\Theta) = 0.4.$$

Note that the 'excess' probability 0.4 is not assigned to the complement of the subset but to the set of all hypotheses.

We can now define belief for a set X of hypotheses with respect to $m(\bullet)$ as

$$\mathrm{Bel}(X) = \sum_{Y \subseteq X} m(Y) \tag{10.4}$$

and its plausibility as

$$\mathrm{Pl}(X) = \sum_{Y \cap X \neq \varnothing} m(Y). \tag{10.5}$$

To combine beliefs we can use Dempster's rule. Let m_1 and m_2 be the mass functions and X and Y subsets of Θ for which m_1 and m_2 have non-zero values. The combined mass function m_3 is

$$m_3(Z) = \frac{\sum_{X \cap Y = Z} m_1(X) \cdot m_2(Y)}{1 - \sum_{X \cap Y = \varnothing} m_1(X) \cdot m_2(Y)}. \tag{10.6}$$

An implementation of this is given in Algorithm 10.1. Dempster's rule can be used in both chaining (e.g. $A \rightarrow B$ and $B \rightarrow C$) and conjoining (e.g. $A \rightarrow C$, $B \rightarrow C$) multiple propositions.

In our example, evidence 'footprints' (supporting the hypotheses 'animal', 'trap' and 'enemy') has the mass function m_f, which is defined

$$m_f(\{A, T, E\}) = 0.8, \quad m_f(\Theta) = 0.2.$$

Assuming that the intersections $X \cap Y$ are non-empty, we get the combination m_{nf} for the two pieces of evidence directly from the numerator of Equation (10.6):

$$m_{nf}(\{A, E\}) = 0.48, \qquad m_{nf}(\{A, T, E\}) = 0.32,$$
$$m_{nf}(\{W, A, E\}) = 0.12, \qquad m_{nf}(\Theta) = 0.08.$$

It is possible to get the same intersection set Z more than once, but in that case we just add the mass functions together.

The situation gets a bit more complicated if the intersection of subsets is empty. The numerator in Equation (10.6) ensures that the sum of different probabilities is 1 (provided that this also holds for m_1 and m_2). If some intersections are empty, the amount given to the empty sets must be distributed to all non-empty sets, which is handled by the denominator of Equation (10.6).

Algorithm 10.1 Combining two mass functions.

COMBINED-MASS-FUNCTION(m_1, m_2)
    in: mapping $m_1 : \wp(\Theta) \setminus \emptyset \to [0, 1]$ (the domain elements with non-zero
                range value is denoted by $\mathcal{M}_1 \subseteq \wp(\Theta) \setminus \emptyset$); mapping m_2 is defined sim-
                ilarly as m_1
    out: combined mapping m_3
    constant: set of hypothesis Θ

1: **for all** $M \in (\wp(\Theta) \setminus \{\emptyset, \Theta\})$ **do**
2:   $m_3(M) \leftarrow 0$
3: **end for**
4: $m_3(\Theta) \leftarrow 1$
5: $\mathcal{M}_3 \leftarrow \Theta$
6: $e \leftarrow 0$
7: **for all** $M_1 \in \mathcal{M}_1$ **do**   ▷ For pairs of members between $\mathcal{M}_1$ and $\mathcal{M}_2$.
8:   **for all** $M_2 \in \mathcal{M}_2$ **do**
9:     $M_3 \leftarrow M_1 \cap M_2$
10:     $p \leftarrow m_1(M_1) \cdot m_2(M_2)$
11:     $m_3(\Theta) \leftarrow m_3(\Theta) - p$
12:     **if** $M_3 = \emptyset$ **then**   ▷ Excess for imaginary $m_3(\emptyset)$.
13:       $e \leftarrow e + p$
14:     **else**   ▷ M_3 contributes to $\mathcal{M}_3$.
15:       $m_3(M_3) \leftarrow m_3(M_3) + p$
16:       **if** $M_3 \notin \mathcal{M}_3$ **then**
17:         $\mathcal{M}_3 \leftarrow \mathcal{M}_3 \cup \{M_3\}$
18:       **end if**
19:     **end if**
20:   **end for**
21: **end for**
22: **if** $0 < e < 1$ **then**   ▷ Normalization.
23:   **for all** $M \in \mathcal{M}_3$ **do**
24:     $m_3(M) \leftarrow m_3(M)/(1 - e)$
25:   **end for**
26: **end if**
27: **return** m_3

Let us add m_c to the mass functions, which describes the evidence 'candy wrapper':

$$m_c(\{E\}) = 0.6, \qquad\qquad m_c(\{T\}) = 0.3,$$
$$m_c(\Theta) = 0.1.$$

By combining functions m_{nf} and m_c we get the following result from the numerator:

$$m_{nfc'}(\{E\}) = 0.6, \qquad\qquad m_{nfc'}(\{T\}) = 0.12,$$
$$m_{nfc'}(\{A, E\}) = 0.048, \qquad\qquad m_{nfc'}(\{A, T, E\}) = 0.032,$$
$$m_{nfc'}(\{W, A, E\}) = 0.012, \qquad\qquad m_{nfc'}(\Theta) = 0.008,$$
$$m_{nfc'}(\emptyset) = 0.18.$$

The denominator is $1 - m_{nfc'}(\varnothing) = 0.82$, and we use it to scale to get m_{nfc} (rounded to two decimal places):

$$m_{nfc}(\{E\}) = 0.73, \qquad m_{nfc}(\{T\}) = 0.15,$$
$$m_{nfc}(\{A, E\}) = 0.06, \qquad m_{nfc}(\{A, T, E\}) = 0.04,$$
$$m_{nfc}(\{W, A, E\}) = 0.01, \qquad m_{nfc}(\Theta) = 0.01.$$

From this it follows that if we have evidence 'noise', 'footprints' and 'candy wrapper', Equation (10.4) gives belief in the hypothesis 'enemy' $\mathrm{Bel}(E) = 0.73$, and Equation (10.5) gives its plausibility $\mathrm{Pl}(E) = 0.85$. In comparison, the combined hypothesis 'trap or enemy' has belief $\mathrm{Bel}(\{T, E\}) = 0.88$ and plausibility $\mathrm{Pl}(\{T, E\}) = 1$, which means that a human threat is a more likely explanation for the evidence than a natural phenomenon.

10.2 Fuzzy Sets

Fuzzy sets acknowledge uncertainty by allowing elements to have a partial membership in a set. In contrast to classical sets with Boolean memberships, fuzzy sets admit that some information is better than no information. Although multivalued logic was developed in the 1920s by J. Łukasiewicz, the term 'fuzziness' was coined forty years later. In a seminal paper L.A. Zadeh (1965) applied Łukasiewicz's multivalued logic to sets: instead of belonging or not belonging to a set, in a fuzzy set an element belongs to a set to a certain degree.

One should always bear in mind that fuzzy sets depend on the context: there can be no universal agreement on a membership function, for example, on small (cars, humans, nebulae), and, subjectively speaking, a small car may be something completely different for a basketball player than for a racehorse jockey. Furthermore, fuzziness is not a solution method in itself but we can use it in modelling to cope with uncertainty. For example, we can describe the objective function using an aggregation of fuzzy sets (see Figure 10.3). In effect, fuzziness allows us to do more fine-grained evaluations.

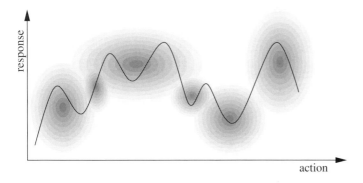

Figure 10.3 Uncertain or complex dependencies can be modelled with fuzzy sets that cover the solution space.

10.2.1 Membership function

In classical (or 'crisp') set theory the elements of a set S are defined using a two-valued characteristic function

$$\chi_S(x) = \begin{cases} 1, & \Longleftrightarrow x \in S, \\ 0, & \Longleftrightarrow x \notin S. \end{cases}$$

In other words, all the elements x in the universe U either belong to S or not (and there is nothing in between).

Fuzzy set theory extends the characteristic function by allowing an element to have a degree to which it belongs to a set. This degree is called a *membership* in a set, and a fuzzy set is a class where every element has a membership value.

Theorem 10.2.1 *Let U be a set (universe) and $\mathcal{L}$ a lattice, $\mathcal{L} = \langle L, \vee, \wedge, 1, 0 \rangle$. A fuzzy set A in the universe U is defined by a* membership function μ_A,

$$\mu_A : U \to L. \tag{10.7}$$

Each element $x \in U$ has an associated membership function value $\mu_A(x) \in L$, which is the membership value of the element x. If $\mu_A(x) = 0$, x does not belong to the set A. If $\mu_A(x) = 1$, x belongs to the set A. Otherwise, (i.e. if $\mu_A(x) \neq 0, 1$) x belongs partly to the set A.

This general definition of a fuzzy set is usually used in a limited form, where we let the lattice $\mathcal{L}$ be $L = [0, 1] \subset \mathbb{R}$, $\mathbf{0} = 0$ and $\mathbf{1} = 1$. In other words, the membership function is defined on a real number range $[0, 1]$, and the fuzzy set A in universe U is defined by the membership function

$$\mu_A : U \to [0, 1],$$

which assigns to each element $x \in U$ a membership value $\mu_A(x)$ in the fuzzy set A. Another way to interpret the membership value is to think of it as the truth value of the statement 'x is an element of the set A'. For example, Figure 10.4 illustrates different fuzzy sets for a continuous U. Here the universe is distance d in metres, and the sets describe the accuracy of different weapons with respect to the distance to the target.

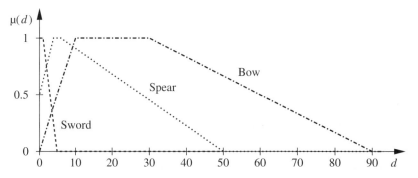

Figure 10.4 Membership functions μ_{sword}, μ_{spear} and μ_{bow} for the attribute 'accuracy' of weapons with respect to the distance (in metres) to the target.

When defining fuzzy sets we inevitably face the question how one should assign the membership functions. Suggested methods include:

- *Real-world data.* Sometimes we can apply physical measurements, and we can assign the membership function values to correspond to the real-world data. Also, if we have statistical data on the modelled attribute, they be can used for defining the membership functions.
- *Subjective evaluation.* Because fuzzy sets often model human cognitive knowledge, the definition of a membership function can be guided by human experts. They can draw or select among predefined membership functions the one corresponding to their knowledge. Even questionnaires or psychological tests can be used when defining more complex functions.
- *Adaptation.* The membership functions can be dynamic and evolve over time, using the feedback from the input data. This kind of a hybrid system can use, for example, neural networks or genetic algorithms for adaptation as the nature of the attribute modelled becomes clear.

The beauty (and agony) of fuzzy sets is that there are an infinite number of possible different membership functions for the same attribute. Although by tweaking the membership function we can get a more accurate response, in practice even simple functions work surprisingly well as long as the general trend of the function reflects the information modelled. For example, if we are modelling the attribute 'young', it is sufficient that the membership value decreases as the age increases.

10.2.2 Fuzzy operations

The logical fuzzy operations $\vee$ (i.e. disjunction) and $\wedge$ (i.e. conjunction) are often defined using $\max\{\mu_A(\bullet), \mu_B(\bullet)\}$ and $\min\{\mu_A(\bullet), \mu_B(\bullet)\}$, although they can be defined in various alternative ways using t-norms and t-conorms (Yager and Filev 1994). Also, negation can be defined in many ways, but the usual choice is $1 - \mu_A(\bullet)$. All classical set operations have fuzzy counterparts.

Theorem 10.2.2 *Let A, B and C be fuzzy sets in the universe U. Further, assume that all operations have the value range $[0, 1]$. We can now define, for each element $x \in U$,*

Union	$C = A \cup B$	$\Longleftrightarrow$	$\mu_C(x) = \max\{\mu_A(x), \mu_B(x)\},$	(10.8)
Intersection	$C = A \cap B$	$\Longleftrightarrow$	$\mu_C(x) = \min\{\mu_A(x), \mu_B(x)\},$	(10.9)
Complement	$C = A^C$	$\Longleftrightarrow$	$\mu_C(x) = 1 - \mu_A(x).$	(10.10)

Figure 10.5 illustrates the use of fuzzy set operations for a discrete U. The universe consists of three elements (swordsman, spearman, and archer) and they have three attributes (mobility, strength, and expensiveness). The union of mobility and strength describes the set of mobile or strong soldiers, whereas the intersection describes the set of mobile and strong soldiers. The intersection of the complement of expensiveness and strength gives the set of inexpensive and strong soldiers.

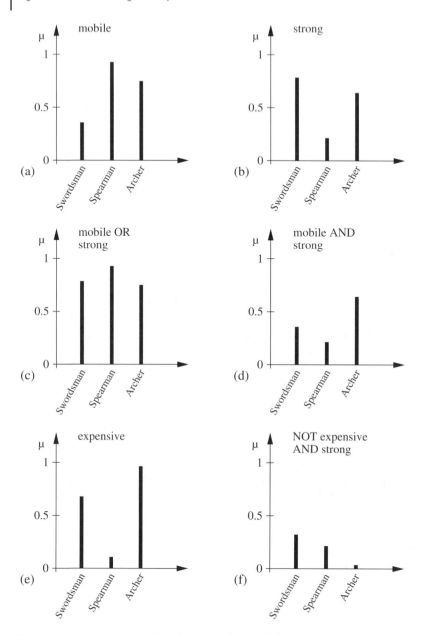

Figure 10.5 Fuzzy operations for different attributes. (a) The membership function for mobility. (b) The membership function for strength. (c) The membership function for the union of mobility and strength. (d) The membership function for the intersection of mobility and strength. (e) The membership function for expensiveness. (f) The membership function for the intersection of the complement of expensiveness and strength.

10.2.3 Defuzzification

Occasionally it is necessary to form, or defuzzify, a crisp value from a fuzzy set. If Y is a fuzzy set, let us denote y^* the defuzzified value of the fuzzy set Y. We can use different methods in defuzzification (Yager and Filev 1994):

- *Maximum grade.* Select an element $y \in Y$ with the greatest membership value $\mu_Y(y)$.
- *Centre of area.* Calculate the centre of the area indicated by the membership function:

$$y^* = \frac{\int_Y y\mu_Y(y)\,dy}{\int_Y \mu_Y(y)\,dy}. \tag{10.11}$$

- *Mean of maxima.* Select the elements that have the greatest membership value and calculate their mean,

$$y^* = \frac{1}{|J^*|} \sum_{y \in J^*} y, \tag{10.12}$$

  where J^* is the set of all the members in Y that have greatest degree of membership $\mu_Y(y)$.

- *Random generation.* Transform the fuzzy set into a probability distribution and choose a crisp value randomly using this probability distribution. A straightforward way to do this is to normalize Y, and then the probability of an element y is

$$P(y) = \frac{\mu_Y(y)}{\sum_{i=1}^{|Y|} \mu_Y(y_i)}. \tag{10.13}$$

When we have converted the fuzzy set into a probability distribution, we divide the unit interval into n sections so that each member y_i in the set Y corresponds to one section $R_i = [a_i, b_i]$, where $a_1 = 0$, $b_1 = P_1$, $a_i = b_{i-1}$ and $b_i = a_i + P_i$ for all $i > 1$. Then we randomly select a number r from the range $[0, 1]$. If $r \in R_i$, then $y^* = y_i$.

10.3 Fuzzy Constraint Satisfaction Problem

Fuzzy optimization originates from ideas proposed by Bellman and Zadeh (1970), who introduced the concepts of fuzzy constraints, fuzzy objective and fuzzy decision. Fuzzy decision-making in general is concerned with deciding on future actions based on vague or uncertain knowledge (Fullér and Carlsson 1996; Herrera and Verdegay 1997). The problem in making decisions under uncertainty is that the bulk of the information we have about the possible outcomes, the value of new information, and the dynamically changing conditions are typically vague, ambiguous or otherwise unclear. In this section we focus on multiple-criteria decision-making, which refers to making decisions in the presence of multiple and possibly conflicting criteria.

In a constraint satisfaction problem (CSP) one must find states or objects in a system that satisfy a number of constraints or criteria. A CSP consists of

- a set of n variables X,
- a domain D_i (i.e. a finite set of possible values) for each variable x_i in X, and
- a set of constraints restricting the feasibility of the tuples $(x_0, x_1, \ldots, x_{n-1}) \in D_0 \times \cdots \times D_{n-1}$.

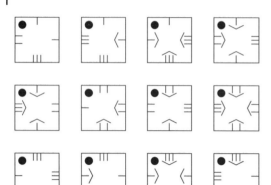

Figure 10.6 A monkey puzzle of 3 × 4 tiles. The monkey is depicted as an arrow with separated tail and head ends. The solution is an arrangement of the tiles so that tiles are not rotated (i.e. the black circle stays in the upper left corner of each tile) and all the tails and heads match (i.e. form a one-directed arrow) inside the 3 × 4 rectangle.

A solution is an assignment of a value in D_i to each variable x_i such that every constraint is satisfied. Because a CSP lacks an objective function, it is not an optimization problem. As an example of a CSP, Figure 10.6 illustrates a monkey puzzle problem (Harel 1987, pp. 153–155). The $3 \cdot 4 = 12$ tile positions identify the variables, the tiles define the domain set, and the requirement that all the monkey halves must match defines $(3 - 1) \cdot 4 + 3 \cdot (4 - 1) = 17$ constraints.

Unfortunately, the problems modelled are not always as discrete and easy to form. Fuzzy sets have also been proposed for extending CSPs so that partial satisfaction of the constraints is possible. The constraints can be more or less relaxable or subject to preferences. These flexible constraints are either soft constraints, which express preferences among solutions, or prioritized constraints that can be violated if they conflict with constraints with a higher priority (Dubois et al. 1996).

In the *fuzzy constraint satisfaction problem* (FCSP) both types of flexible constraints are regarded as local criteria that give (possibly partial) rank orderings to instantiations and can be represented by means of fuzzy relations (Guesgen 1994; Slany 1995). A fuzzy constraint represents the constraints as well as the criteria by the fuzzy subsets C_i of the set S of possible decisions. If C_i is a fuzzy constraint and the corresponding membership function μ_{C_i} for some decision $s \in S$ yields $\mu_{C_i}(s) = 1$, then decision s totally satisfies the constraint C_i, while $\mu_{C_i}(s) = 0$ means that it totally violates C_i (i.e. s is infeasible). If $0 < \mu_{C_i}(s) < 1$, s satisfies C_i only partially. Hence, a fuzzy constraint gives a rank ordering for the feasible decisions much like an objective function.

More formally, the FCSP is a five-tuple

$$P = \langle V, C_\mu, W, T, U \rangle$$

which comprises the following elements:

- a set of variables V;
- a set U of universes (domains) for each variable in V;
- a set C_μ of constraints where each constraint is a membership function μ from the value assignments to the range $[0, 1]$ and has an associated weight w_c representing its importance or priority;
- a weighting scheme W (i.e. a function that combines a constraint satisfaction degree $\mu(c)$ with w to yield the weighted constraint satisfaction degree $\mu^w(c)$);
- an aggregation function T that produces a single partial order on value assignments.

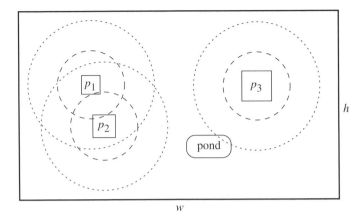

Figure 10.7 The set-up of Dog Eat Dog for three players. Player p_1 has the enemy p_2 and the prey p_3, player p_2 has the enemy p_3 and the prey p_1, and player p_3 has the enemy p_1 and the prey p_2. The dashed circles represent the limit of the players' visual range and dotted circles their olfactory range. Players p_1 and p_2 can see one another but cannot smell the pond. Player p_3 does not see the other players but can smell the pond. The game world is a rectangle of size $w \times h$.

Let us go through the FCSP stages using the game Dog Eat Dog as an example (see Figure 10.7). Players move inside a closed two-dimensional playfield. Each player has one prey, which is to be hunted, and one enemy, which is to be avoided. The playfield also includes a pond, which restores the player's health. Initially, the players and the pond are placed at random positions in the playfield. The players have two senses: they can see other players or smell the pond. However, the senses have limitations: the farther away an object is, the noisier the player's sensory data become, until beyond a cut-off distance the player receives no sensory input from the object. The players have no control over their velocities, but they get set randomly for each turn. Instead, the player's only decision at every turn is to choose a direction in which to move.

10.3.1 Modelling the criteria as fuzzy sets

Each criterion associated with the problem can be fuzzified by defining a membership function which corresponds to the intuitive 'rule' behind the criterion. In our example, we need membership functions to describe different attributes. Intuitively, the rules are simple:

- If the visual observation of the enemy is reliable, then avoid the enemy.
- If the visual observation of the prey is reliable, then chase the prey.
- If the olfactory observation of the pond is reliable, then go to the pond.
- If the visual observation of the enemy is reliable, then stay in the centre of the playfield.

Although we have given the rules as if–then statements, the first (i.e. if) part defines the importance given to the second (i.e. then) part. For example, the first rule could be rewritten 'The more reliable the visual observation of the enemy is, the more important it is to avoid the enemy'. We return to this when we are discussing weighting.

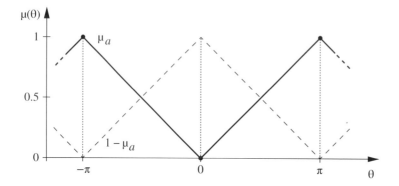

Figure 10.8 Membership function $\mu_a(\theta)$ for the attraction of the direction θ. The complement $1 - \mu_a(\theta)$ gives a membership value for avoidance.

First, let us define a membership function $\mu_a(\theta)$ for the 'attraction' of direction θ given in radians (see Figure 10.8). If $n \in \mathbb{Z}$, direction $\theta = 2n\pi - \pi$ is towards the target, for which $\mu_a(\theta) = 1$; direction $\theta = 2n\pi$ is away from the target, for which $\mu_a(\theta) = 0$. The rest of the function is defined linearly between these points. For 'avoidance' we do not have to define a new membership function, but we can use the complement of attraction, $1 - \mu_a(\theta)$.

Since the players' senses are unreliable, we can model them conveniently with fuzzy sets. Figure 10.9 gives simple linear membership function $\mu_s(d)$ for reliability of visual input at distance d. The membership value starts at 1 and decreases as the distance increases, until beyond the visual cut-off distance s the membership value is 0. The membership function $\mu_o(d)$ for reliability of olfactory input is defined in similar fashion.

Getting trapped in the side or corner of the playfield is a bad move, especially when the enemy is chasing. The closer the player is to the centre of the playfield, the better it can manoeuvre away from the enemy. Figure 10.10 illustrates a two-parameter membership function $\mu_c(x, y)$ for the centralness of the position (x, y) in the playfield.

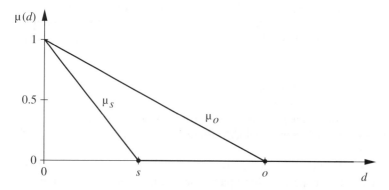

Figure 10.9 Membership functions for the reliability of sensory inputs: $\mu_s(d)$ for the reliability of visual input at the distance d, and $\mu_o(d)$ for the reliability of olfactory input at the distance d.

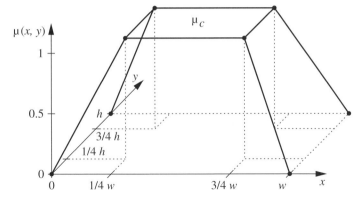

Figure 10.10 Membership function $\mu_c(x, y)$ for the centralness of position (x, y).

10.3.2 Weighting the importance of criteria

Our set of rules includes importance, which can be realized by weighting the corresponding fuzzy sets. Weights ensure that the important criteria have a greater effect on the decision than the less important ones. In our example, we want to weight the avoidance of the enemy and attraction of prey with the reliability of the visual observation. Similarly, the attraction of the pond is weighted with the reliability of the olfactory observation, and the attraction of the centre with the reliability of the visual observation of the enemy.

Weighting can be based on an interpretation of the fuzzy implication as a boundary which guarantees that a criterion has at least a certain fulfilment value. If a fuzzy criterion C_i has a weight $w_i \in [0, 1]$, where a greater value w_i corresponds to a greater importance, the weighted value of a criterion is obtained from the implication $w_i \to C_i$. The weighting operation can be defined classically (i.e. $A \to B \iff \neg A \vee B$), which gives us the rule $\max\{(1 - w_i), C_i\}$.

We can also use the weighting scheme defined by Yager (1981), where the weighted membership value $\mu_C^w(x)$ of a criterion C is defined as:

$$\mu_C^w(x) = \begin{cases} 1, & \text{if } \mu_C(x) = 0 \text{ and } w = 0, \\ (\mu_C(x))^w, & \text{otherwise.} \end{cases}$$

In the case $w = 0$ the criterion is 'turned off' because the corresponding weighted membership value always equals 1 (i.e. it does not affect the overall aggregated result).

10.3.3 Aggregating the criteria

To make the decision the different criteria must be aggregated together. Although we can use any fuzzy conjunction operator, it is usually preferable that the aggregator has compensatory properties, because then the effect of one poorly satisfied criterion is not so drastic on the overall result. Mean-based operators have this property, and the *ordered weighted averaging* (OWA) operator, proposed by Yager (1988), is particularly useful, because the amount of compensation can be freely adjusted.

An OWA operator of dimension n is a mapping $F : \mathbb{R}^n \to \mathbb{R}$, which has an associated weight sequence $W = \langle w_0, w_1, \dots, w_{n-1} \rangle$ where each weight $w_i \in [0, 1]$, $0 \le i \le (n - 1)$, and $\sum_{i=0}^{n-1} w_i = 1$. Furthermore, $F(a_0, \ldots, a_{n-1}) = \sum_{j=0}^{n-1} w_j b_j$ where b_j is the $(j+1)$th largest element of the sequence $A = \langle a_0, \ldots, a_{n-1} \rangle$. A fundamental aspect of this operator is the reordering step. An aggregate a_i is not associated with a particular weight w_i, but rather a weight is associated with a particular ordered position of the aggregate. Algorithm 10.2 gives an implementation of the OWA operator.

Algorithm 10.2 Ordered weighted aggregation.

OWA(M, W)
   in: sequence of membership values M; sequence of weights W
   out: aggregated result
  1: $V \leftarrow$ **copy** M
  2: sort V into non-increasing order
  3: $r \leftarrow 0$
  4: **for** $i \leftarrow 0 \ldots (|V| - 1)$ **do**
  5:   $r \leftarrow r + W_i \cdot V_i$
  6: **end for**
  7: **return** r

By setting the weight sequence W we can get different aggregation operators ranging from conjunction $W = \langle 0, 0, \ldots, 1 \rangle = \min\{A\}$ to disjunction $W = \langle 1, 0, 0, \ldots, 0 \rangle = \max\{A\}$ and average $W = \langle 1/n, 1/n, \ldots, 1/n \rangle$. One possibility is to use the 'soft-and' operator (Slany 1994), where the weight sequence is

$$w_i = \frac{2(i+1)}{n(n+1)}.$$

This weight distribution yields a fair compensation, which in our Dog Eat Dog example is better than imposing strict rules on the evaluation of the optimality of the direction.

10.3.4 Making a decision

We are now ready for the actual decision-making (see Algorithm 10.3). The player decides on the direction by first evaluating possible choices one by one, and then choosing the best one. The evaluation follows the phases laid out in this section (and the routines WEIGHT-CRITERION and SOFT-AND-WEIGHTS are defined accordingly). First, we calculate the distances and directions to the enemy, prey and pond. That information is used for weighting the four criteria – avoid the enemy, chase the prey, go to the pond, and stay in the centre – which are finally aggregated together to form evaluation value for the desirability of the given direction.

Surprisingly, even a small number of direction choices leads to good results – of course as long as they allow the player to move within the two-dimensional playfield. Also, if we increase the level of noise in the observations, the players can cope with it quite well without any modification of their decision-making. Naturally, if the environment gets too noisy (i.e. the observations get too random), it becomes almost impossible to form a coherent picture of what is going on.

Algorithm 10.3 Fuzzy decision-making for Dog Eat Dog.

DECIDE-DIRECTION()

out: best direction θ_b
local: best evaluation e_b; direction candidate θ; evaluation e of the direction
constant: number of directions s

1: $\theta_b \leftarrow 0$; $e_b \leftarrow 0$
2: $\theta \leftarrow -\pi$
3: **for** $i \leftarrow 1 \ldots s$ **do**   ▷ Check each direction.
4:   $e \leftarrow$ EVALUATE-DIRECTION(θ)
5:   **if** $e > e_b$ **then**
6:     $\theta_b \leftarrow \theta$
7:     $e_b \leftarrow e$
8:   **end if**
9:   $\theta \leftarrow \theta + 2\pi/s$
10: **end for**
11: **return** θ_b

EVALUATE-DIRECTION(θ)

in: direction candidate θ
out: evaluation of the direction
constant: enemy position E; prey position P; pond position W; own position O; at-
              traction membership function μ_a; reliability of sight membership func-
              tion μ_s; reliability of smell membership function μ_o; centralness mem-
              bership function μ_c

1: $d_x \leftarrow E_x - O_x$; $d_y \leftarrow E_y - O_y$
2: $\delta_e \leftarrow \sqrt{d_x^2 + d_y^2}$ ▷ Distance to the enemy.
3: $d_e \leftarrow \mathrm{sgn}(d_y) \cdot \arccos(d_x/\delta_e)$ ▷ Direction to the enemy.
4: $d_x \leftarrow P_x - O_x$; $d_y \leftarrow P_y - O_y$
5: $\delta_p \leftarrow \sqrt{d_x^2 + d_y^2}$ ▷ Distance to the prey.
6: $d_p \leftarrow \mathrm{sgn}(d_y) \cdot \arccos(d_x/\delta_p)$ ▷ Direction to the prey.
7: $d_x \leftarrow W_x - O_x$; $d_y \leftarrow W_y - O_y$
8: $\delta_w \leftarrow \sqrt{d_x^2 + d_y^2}$ ▷ Distance to the pond.
9: $d_w \leftarrow \mathrm{sgn}(d_y) \cdot \arccos(d_x/\delta_w)$ ▷ Direction to the pond.
10: $m_e \leftarrow$ WEIGHT-CRITERION($1 - \mu_a(d_e - \theta)$, $\mu_s(\delta_e)$)
11: $m_p \leftarrow$ WEIGHT-CRITERION($\mu_a(d_p - \theta)$, $\mu_s(\delta_p)$)
12: $m_w \leftarrow$ WEIGHT-CRITERION($\mu_a(d_w - \theta)$, $\mu_o(\delta_w)$)
13: $m_c \leftarrow$ WEIGHT-CRITERION($\mu_c(O_x + \cos(\theta), O_y + \sin(\theta))$, $\mu_s(\delta_e)$)
14: **return** OWA($\langle m_e, m_p, m_w, m_c \rangle$, SOFT-AND-WEIGHTS(4))

10.4 Summary

As the complexity of the game world increases, it becomes more difficult to model it accurately. In fact, adhering to precision tends to make the model less usable, because modelling is not about collecting detailed information but abstracting (from Latin *abstrahere*, 'to drag away') knowledge from the details. Therefore, the model should tolerate uncertainties – both probabilistic and possibilistic – rather than single them out.

The key to knowledge is conciseness: having some information – albeit not perfect and complete – is better than having no information or having too much information. If we humans were to follow perfect and complete information all the time, we would hardly be able to make any decisions at all. Instead, we are able and willing to base our actions on beliefs, conjectures, rules of thumb, hunches, and even sheer guesswork.

Exercises

10-1 Whenever we discretize an attribute, we get exposed to sorites paradoxes (deriving from the Greek word *soros*, 'heap'). Consider the case where you first see a lone enemy soldier wandering towards your area. Is that an invasion? What if another does the same, then another, and so forth? When does the invasion begin, and – more importantly – when should you make the decision and start ringing the alarm bells?

10-2 For the following questions, is the uncertainty probabilistic or possibilistic?
(a) Is the vase broken?
(b) Was the vase broken by a burglar?
(c) Is there a burglar in the closet?
(d) Is the burglar in the closet a man?
(e) Is the man in the closet a burglar?

10-3 We can improve the software development practices of the example given on page 222 by investing in either the implementation or testing phase. Which improvement yields a better result: the probability of catching an actual bug increases from 90% to 95%, or the probability of bugs being caused by the test arrangement decreases from 10% to 5%?

10-4 Let us extend the Bayesian network of Figure 10.1. The noise could be caused by a dog who is likely to bark if a sentry or an intruder is on the move. Assume that the probability of barking because of a sentry is 0.3 and because of an intruder is 0.6 (and sometimes the dog barks just because he is lonely). Add this information to the Bayesian network and recalculate the values in Table 10.1.

10-5 Explain (intuitively) how the terms 'plausibility' and 'doubt' presented in Figure 10.2 relate to one another.

10-6 Model the situation of Exercise 10-4 using Dempster–Shafer theory.

10-7 Why is the empty set excluded from the mass function?

10-8 Let us add to the example given on page 225 the new evidence 'eaten leaves' with mass function m_e:

$$m_e(\{A\}) = 0.85, \qquad m_e(\{E\}) = 0.1,$$
$$m_e(\Theta) = 0.05.$$

Replace the evidence 'candy wrapper' with this new evidence and determine a new combined mass function m_{nfe}. What are the belief and plausibility of the hypotheses 'enemy' and 'animal'?

   What are the beliefs and plausibilities, if we observe all four pieces of evidence 'noise', 'footprints', 'candy wrapper' and 'eaten leaves'?

10-9 Figure 10.4 gives fuzzy sets for the accuracy of weapons and Figure 10.5 the attributes of infantry. Given that we know the distance to the enemy and the current economic situation, how can this information be combined for making the decision on what kind of troops to train.

10-10 Model the criteria affecting the decision-making of a race driver as fuzzy sets.

10-11 Formulate the n-queens problem of Exercise 7-10 as a constraint satisfaction problem.

10-12 Write an algorithm that solves the monkey puzzle of Figure 10.6. How many solutions does it have? What is the time complexity of the program?

10-13 A monkey puzzle tile has four monkey halves that can be labelled north (N), east (E), south (S), and west (W). In addition to the shape of the border rectangle, these halves determine what edges can be placed next to one other. There is also another way to define how the tiles can be placed: each tile corner (i.e. compass directions NE, SE, SW, and NW) has a monkey quarter. If we abstract this quarter, for example, with a letter, only the tiles with the same letter in their touching corners can be adjacent. Figure 10.11 illustrates one valid solution for this

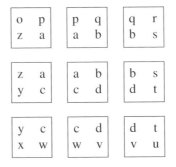

Figure 10.11 Monkey puzzle variant where the tiles can be adjacent only when their corner letters match.

quarter monkey puzzle. Are the two monkey puzzle representations equivalent in the sense that if we have a pile of 'half monkey' tiles H, it is possible to define a pile of 'quarter monkey' tiles Q that gives exactly the same set of solutions for the puzzle (and vice versa)?

10-14 Is is possible to formulate the monkey puzzle problems of Exercises 10-12 and 10-13 as a fuzzy constraint satisfaction problems?

10-15 Let us denote the quarter monkeys of Exercise 10-13 by numbers. To evaluate the solution we observe the difference in the corner numbers: the closer the numbers, the better the solution. Formulate this generalization of the monkey puzzle as a fuzzy constraint satisfaction problem.

10-16 Formulate the gold-digger's decision-making in Goldrush (see Exercise 9-24) as a fuzzy constraint satisfaction problem.

Part II

Networking

11

Communication Layers

When multiple participants take part in the same activity such as a game, they interact through some *shared-space technology*. Figure 11.1 illustrates a broad classification of shared-space technologies by Benford et al. (1998). The transportation axis indicates the level to which the participants leave behind their local space (i.e. whether they remain in the physical world or leave their body behind), and the artificiality axis represents the level to which a space is computer generated or from the real world. The model also includes a third dimension, spatiality, but as it is not as strongly portrayed together with the other two dimensions it is often omitted (Suovuo et al. 2015). By using the dimensions of transportation and artificiality, we can discern four main categories:

- Physical reality resides in the local, physical world where things are tangible and the participants are corporeal (e.g. children playing football in the yard).
- Telepresence allows the participants to be present at a real-world location but remote from their physical location (e.g. remote-controlled drones with sensory feedback).
- Augmented reality overlays synthetic objects on the local environment (e.g. using the camera of a mobile device and adding illustrative graphical elements to the video feed displayed on the screen).
- Virtual reality allows the participants to be immersed in a remote, synthetic world (e.g. adults playing football in a computer game).

Apart from physical reality, where interaction is immediate, other shared-space technologies require a distributed system – namely, computers and networks – so that the participants can interact with each other.

Networked computer games mainly belong to the virtual reality category, although location-based games (e.g. *Ingress*), which use wireless networking and mobile platforms, have more in common with augmented reality. Nevertheless, what is universal to all networked computer games is that they must be able to manage network resources, cope with data loss and network failures, and maintain concurrency. In addition, networked games differ from many other distributed applications (e.g. databases) in that they are *interactive real-time applications*, where the players should experience and share the same game world as if it exists locally in their computers.

To clarify conceptually how networked games work we can discern three communication layers:

(i) The physical platform induces resource limitations (e.g. bandwidth and latency) that reflect the underlying infrastructure (e.g. cabling and hardware).

Algorithms and Networking for Computer Games, Second Edition. Jouni Smed and Harri Hakonen.
© 2017 John Wiley & Sons Ltd. Published 2017 by John Wiley & Sons Ltd.

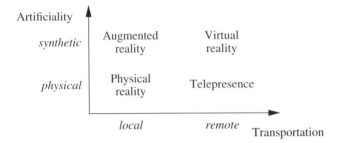

Figure 11.1 Classification of shared-space technologies by transportation and artificiality.

(ii) The logical platform builds upon the physical platform and provides architectures for communication, data, and control (e.g. mutually exclusive data locks and communication rerouting mechanisms).

(iii) The networked application adds context interpretation to the data (e.g. an integer value represents a position) and orchestrates separate control flows together (e.g. by managing synchronization and resolving deadlocks).

Operations on data – storing, processing, and transferring – have related concepts at each level, which are illustrated in Table 11.1. Normally, there is not much we can do to change the physical platform – except perhaps invest in new hardware. The logical platform is intended for system designers, since it provides programming language level abstractions like data entities and communication channels. The networked application is built upon the logical platform and is related to the end-users. Let us now go through each of these levels in more detail.

11.1 Physical Platform

Networking is subject to resource limitations (e.g. physical, technical and computational), which set boundaries on what is possible to do. Once we have established a network of connections between a set of *nodes* (i.e. the computers in the network), we need a technique for transmitting the data from one node to another. The content and delivery of information are expressed using a protocol, which defines the form of the data transmission so that the nodes can understand it.

Table 11.1 Layers of networking with respect to data.

Level	Operation on data		
	Storing	*Processing*	*Transferring*
Physical platform	Memory	Processor	Network
Logical platform	Data entity	Control process	Communication channel
Networked application	State	Integrity control	Multisource support

11.1.1 Resource limitations

Networked applications face three resource limitations (Singhal 1996):

- network bandwidth,
- network latency, and
- the nodes' processing power for handling the network traffic.

These resources refer to the technical attributes of the underlying network and impose physical restrictions, which the networked application cannot overcome and which must be considered in its design.

Bandwidth refers to the transmission capacity of a communication line such as a network. Simply put, bandwidth is the proportion of the amount of data transmitted or received per time unit, measured as bits per second. The bandwidth can range from tens of megabits per second (Mbps) in wireless local area networks (WLANs) up to 100 gigabits per second in wide area networks (WANs) using optical cables. In addition to how often and how large messages are sent, bandwidth requirements depend on the amount and distribution of users and the transmission technique, as we will see in Section 11.1.2.

Networking *latency* indicates the length of time (or delay) that incurs when a message gets from one designated node to another. The variance of latency over time (i.e. jitter) is another feature that affects networked applications. Latency cannot be totally eliminated. For example, speed-of-light propagation delays and the slowdown of electrical signal in a cable alone yield a latency of 25–30 ms for crossing the Atlantic. Moreover, routing, queuing and packet handling delays add tens of milliseconds to the overall latency – which is partly due to nodes processing the traffic. It should be noted that latency and bandwidth are not necessarily related: we can have a high-bandwidth network that has a low latency and vice versa.

Claypool and Claypool (2006) recognize two effects of latency for the players:

- the precision required to complete the action (e.g. sniping needs higher precision than using a machine gun); and
- the deadline by which it has to be completed (e.g. casting a spell has a tighter deadline than moving).

For interactive real-time systems such as computer games, the rule of thumb is that latency between 0.1 and 1.0 seconds is acceptable. For instance, the Distributed Interactive Simulation (DIS) standard used in military simulations specifies that the network latency should be less than 100 ms (Neyland 1997). Latency affects the user's performance nonlinearly: Continuous and fluid control is possible when the latency does not exceed 200 ms, after which the interaction becomes more observational and cognizant. Consequently, the threshold when latency becomes inconvenient for the player depends on the type of the game. The thresholds for different game genres – illustrated in Figure 11.2 – can be listed as follows (Bettner and Terrano 2001; Chang et al. 2010; Claypool and Claypool 2006; Fritsch et al. 2005; Ida et al. 2010):

- first-person games (e.g. first-person shooters), 100 ms;
- third-person games (e.g. role-playing and sport games), 500 ms;
- omnipresent games (e.g. real-time strategy games), 1000 ms.

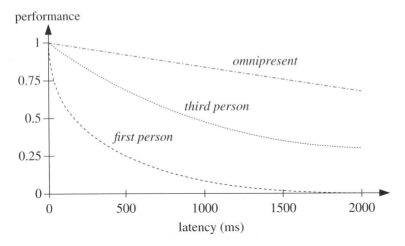

Figure 11.2 The effect of latency on the performance in different game types (Claypool and Claypool 2006). The players' threshold for latency is around the performance level 0.75.

The higher the latency is, the more important it is that it remains constant, which means that jitter should be low. Interestingly, experiments on collaborative virtual environments have yielded similar results (Chen et al. 2005; Park and Kenyon 1999; Shirmohammadi and Georganas 2001).

11.1.2 Transmission techniques and protocols

Transmission techniques can be divided into three types (see Figure 11.3):

- Unicasting is communication between a single sender and a single receiver, which allows the traffic to be controlled and directed from point to point. If the same message is intended for multiple receivers, unicasting wastes bandwidth by sending redundant messages.

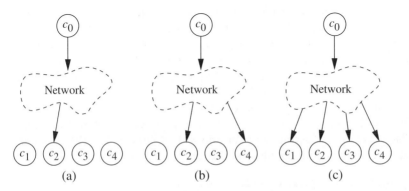

Figure 11.3 Transmission techniques. (a) In unicasting, the message is sent to a single receiver. (b) In multicasting, the message is sent to one or more receivers that have joined a multicast group. (c) In broadcasting, the message is sent to all nodes in the network.

- Multicasting is communication between a single sender and multiple receivers, which allows receivers to subscribe to groups that interest them. The sender does not need to know all the subscribers but sends only one message, which is received by multiple receivers belonging to the group. Because no duplicate messages are sent down the same distribution path, multicasting provides an efficient way to transmit information among a large number of nodes.
- Broadcasting is communication between a single sender and all recipients, which means that every node has to receive and process every broadcast message. Obviously, this leads to problems as the number of participants grows, which is why broadcast transmissions are not guaranteed on WANs.

A *protocol* is a set of rules that two applications can follow in order to communicate with each other. In networking, the protocol includes definitions on the message format (i.e. understanding what the other endpoint is transmitting), message semantics (i.e. what the node can assume and deduce when it receives a packet), and error behaviour (i.e. what the node can do if something goes wrong). For example, the Internet Protocol (IP) comprises low-level protocols that guide the messages from source to destination node, hiding the actual transmission path (Defense Advanced Research Projects Agency 1981). Networked applications rarely use the IP directly but the protocols that are written on top of the IP. The most common among them are the Transmission Control Protocol (TCP/IP) and the User Datagram Protocol (UDP/IP):

- TCP/IP provides a reliable point-to-point connection by dividing the data into network packets. To extract the data the receiver sorts the packets in the correct order, discards duplicates, and asks the sender to retransmit lost or corrupted packets. Naturally, this reliability results in processing time and larger packets. Also, because the transmission is sequential, it is hard to have random access to the data.
- UDP/IP provides a connectionless best-effort delivery, which means that transmission and receiving are immediate. Because it does not guarantee that data are in order (or received at all) or that data are not corrupted, the transmission is unreliable. However, the packets contain minimal header information, are easy to process, and can be sent to multiple hosts, which means UDP/IP can be used also in broadcasting and multicasting.

11.2 Logical Platform

Whereas the physical platform sees the network as nodes that are connected together physically, the logical platform defines how the messages flow in this network. The logical platform defines architectures for *communication*, *data*, and *control*.

11.2.1 Communication architecture

The communication architecture can be chosen from different models, which can be arranged as communication graphs according to their *degree of deployment* (see Figure 11.4). In a communication graph, the nodes represent the processes running on remote computers and the edges denote that the nodes can exchange messages. The simplest configuration has only a *single node* (i.e. one computer and no network). For

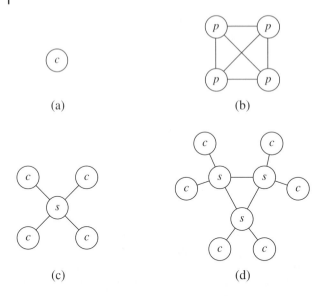

Figure 11.4 Communication architectures as degrees of deployment: (a) a single node; (b) a peer-to-peer architecture; (c) a client–server architecture; and (d) a server-network architecture.

example, two or more players can participate in the same game, if the screen is split so that they each have their own view.

In a *peer-to-peer* architecture, we have a set of equal nodes connected by a network. Since no node is more special than the others, they must be connected to each other (at least latently). There is no intermediary and each node can transmit its messages to every node in the network. Peer-to-peer was widely used in the first networked computer games, because it is quite straightforward to realize and to expand from a single-player game. However, it does not scale up easily due to the lack of hierarchical structure. It is useful when the number participants is small or they communicate in a LAN.

In a *client–server* architecture, one node is promoted to the role of server. Now all communication is handled through this server node, while the other nodes remain in the role of client. Each client sends packets to the other clients through the server. Although the server slows down the message delivery, we get benefits because we can control the packet flow: we do not have to send all packets to all players (see Section 12.6), and we can aggregate multiple packets into a single packet and smooth out the packet flow (see Section 12.2). Moreover, the client–server architecture allows administration features to be implemented, because the server has a special message routing position.

In a *server-network* (or server pool) architecture, there are several interconnected servers. Here, the communication graph can be thought of as a peer-to-peer network of servers over a set of client–server subnetworks. A client is connected to a local server, which is connected to the remote servers and, through them, to the remote clients. Of course we can extend the server network hierarchically so that servers themselves act as clients to higher-level servers. The server network reduces the capacity requirements imposed on a server. In consequence, this provides better scalability but increases the complexity of handling the network traffic.

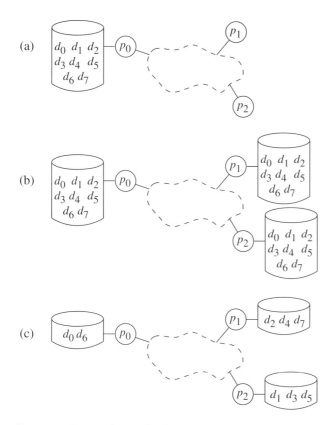

Figure 11.5 Data and control architectures. (a) In a centralized data architecture, one (data server) node stores all the data. (b) In a replicated architecture, each node manages a replica of all the data. (c) In a distributed architecture, the data are partitioned among the nodes.

11.2.2   Data and control architecture

Two attributes define the models for data and control architecture: *consistency* and *responsiveness* (see Section 12.1.1). To achieve high consistency, the architecture must guarantee that processes running on remote nodes are tightly coupled. This usually requires high bandwidth, low latency, and a small number of remote nodes. To achieve high responsiveness (or timeliness), the queries made to the data must be responded to quickly, which leads to loosely coupled nodes. In this case, the nodes include more computation to reduce the bandwidth and latency requirements. In reality, an architecture cannot achieve both high consistency and high responsiveness at the same time, and the choice of architecture is a trade-off between these two attributes.

Figure 11.5 illustrates three fundamental data and control architectures:

- In a centralized architecture, only one node holds all the data.
- In a replicated architecture, a copy of the same data exists in all nodes.
- In a distributed architecture, each node holds a subset of the data.

A centralized architecture can be seen as a shared database that keeps the system consistent at all times. Obviously, it is likely to lack responsiveness, which is elemental for real-time networked applications like computer games. Distributed and replicated architectures are more suitable, because they allow higher responsiveness. The distinction between these architectures is that a distributed architecture adapts more easily, for instance, to player-controlled entities, whose behaviour is unpredictable and for whom there can be only one source of commands (Chang 1996; Verna et al. 2000). Conversely, synthetic players are usually predictable and need not send frequent control messages, and a replicated architecture provides a better alternative (see Section 12.5). In short, indeterminism leads to distribution and determinism to replication.

11.3 Networked Application

A networked application is built on a logical platform. Real-time, interactive networked applications have been researched in the fields of military simulations, virtual environments, and computer games (Smed et al. 2002, 2003b). The key technical issues in their design are:

- scalability (i.e. the ability to adapt to resource changes);
- persistence (i.e. leaving and entering the game world);
- collaboration between players (i.e. upholding integrity when sharing an object).

Scalability concerns how to construct an online application that dynamically adapts to varying numbers of players and how to allocate the computation of synthetic players among the nodes. This can be achieved only if we can utilize the network of nodes (i.e. hardware parallelism) for implementing asynchronous computation (i.e. software concurrency) of the networked application (see Section 12.1.2). Scaling up a networked application brings forth two complementary views: each new participant naturally burdens the communication resources but, at the same time, also offers additional computational power to the whole application.

Persistence concerns how a remote node can coexist with an application. Initially, the application has a state and the attaching node must be configured to conform to this state (e.g. when players join an online server, they receive the object data corresponding to the current situation). Throughout the gameplay the node and application live in symbiosis, which is supported by the underlying logical platform. For example, when a node leaves the application, the application must have a mechanism to uphold the game state by forwarding the node's responsibilities. On the other hand, if a node is abruptly disconnected, the networked application loses the objects maintained by the node. To sum up, persistence must account, among other things, for configuration management, error detection and recovery, and administration on both the application and node.

Collaboration usually means that there are team members that act together to achieve a shared goal (e.g. eliminate the other team or overcome some common obstacles). To support collaboration the networked application has to provide a player with rich and accurate information about the other participants (Benford et al. 2001; Shirmohammadi and Georganas 2001). Technically, collaboration requires that the communication between players is prioritized: The closer two entities are in the game world, the more they communicate with each other. However, the distance between team members does not have to be defined in spatial terms (e.g. they can have implicit knowledge about each other's status or they can share a dedicated communication channel). Clearly, a team is an application-level concept. Because the concept of collaboration distance can be complex, cooperation consumes more resources than confrontation.

11.4 Summary

We have presented the communication as three layers – physical, logical, and application. This follows from the idea that some parts can be implemented as a software engine (e.g. graphics engines). Here, the logical layer acts as an engine, which provides the basic concepts and mechanisms for advanced distributed computing. We can think of the logical layer as a toolbox (derived from research and standards), which combines the networked application with the physical layer. In practice, to achieve this we have to select and possibly hybridize the basic approaches.

Figure 11.6 gives an example of the three communication layers. It illustrates a networked application from the perspective of login management. The control of the access permissions and session log maintenance are centralized by using a server network (i.e. nodes s_0, s_1, and s_2), to which the clients (i.e. nodes c_0, c_1 and c_2) subscribe. The servers s_1 and s_2 provide the application state which is replicated in the other satellite servers over the Internet. For example, s_0 serves the clients in the local LAN

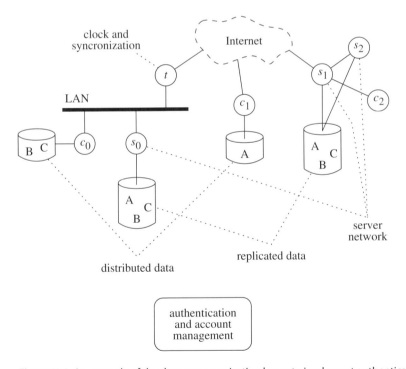

Figure 11.6 An example of the three communication layers to implement authentication and account management features. The physical platform consists of nodes (circles), data stores (cylinders), and cabling (lines). The logical platform includes a server-network (i.e. a communication architecture), distributed and replicated data (i.e. a data architecture), and timing functionality (i.e. a control architecture).

(e.g. c_0) and possibly other geographically near clients (e.g. c_1). To supervise the game the console clients (e.g. c_2) can connect directly to the server. The state data are distributed to the clients so that the clients are more responsive. Consequently, the networked application becomes more reliable, because we can tolerate a single point of server failure while having an unreliable or high-latency connection to a server. Finally, the workload of the networked application is balanced by dedicating the node t for timing purposes only (e.g. sending clock signals and providing dispatching services).

To summarize, the physical layer, stemming from the underlaying hardware, tells us what we can do. The networked application layer, derived from the design specification of the game, tells us what we should to do. Most of the important decisions concerning resource utilization are then made on the logical layer. However, the compensatory techniques of the next chapter provide us with additional margin in the design and implementation.

Exercises

11-1 Consider the children's game of tag. How would you implement it in different shared-space technologies?

11-2 Latency cannot be completely eliminated. What does this mean for the design of a networked application?

11-3 The two effects of latency – precision and deadline – manifest themselves in different ways. Consider the following actions and how much they depend on precision and deadline:
(a) driving a race car;
(b) driving a tank;
(c) fighting with a bow and arrow;
(d) fighting with a sword;
(e) constructing a building;
(f) upgrading a building.

11-4 Multicasting and broadcasting can be simulated using unicasting. How can this be done? What problems arise in doing it?

11-5 In positive acknowledgement scheme, the receiver sends an acknowledgement message every time it receives a message, whereas in negative acknowledgement scheme an acknowledgment message is sent, if the receiver has not received the message. What problems are included in these schemes? How would you solve them?

11-6 Internet Protocol version 4 (IPv4) was deployed on 1 January 1983. The address format in IPv4 is a 32-bit numeric value often expressed with four octets from the interval [0, 255] separated by periods. At the time of writing, Internet Protocol version 6 (IPv6), with addresses 128 bits wide, is still in the process of slowly replacing IPv4. In theory, how many IP addresses can be assigned in IPv4 and IPv6?

11-7 Which protocol, TCP/IP or UDP/IP, is better suited to the following situations:
   (a) Updating the player's current position.
   (b) Informing that the player changed his weapon.
   (c) Indicating that the player fired a weapon.
   (d) Informing that the player got hit.
   (e) Informing that a new player joined the game.
   (f) Chatting with other players.

11-8 Compare the communication architectures (i.e. peer-to-peer, client–server, and server-network), and data and control architectures (i.e. centralized, distributed and replicated). Analyse their usability together and explain in what kind of situations they are useful.

11-9 In *Amaze* (Berglund and Cheriton 1985) multiple players roam in a *Pac-Man*-like maze and try to shoot one another. You are updating this idea to meet the current twenty-first-century standard by designing an online *Amaze* game to be run over the Internet. The game would be ongoing and the players can form teams and participate from all over the world. Devise a design for this game and list the possible problems stemming from the physical and logical platform.

11-10 Suppose that a networked application distributes autonomous synthetic players to the participating nodes to balance the workload. In other words, a synthetic player b resides only in one node c and participates in the game similarly to the human players. If node c is abruptly cut off from the game, not only does the human player disappear from the game world but also the synthetic players assigned to that node. What are the problems when we are implementing a single point (i.e. node) of failure capability for distributed synthetic players?

11-11 The game $2n$-Gong, where $2 \leq n$, takes place in a regular polygon of $2n$ sides (see Figure 11.7). The game consists of $2n$ players who each have one side as a dedicated goal to defend. Each player controls a paddle by moving it parallel to his own goal. The goal of the game is to score points by bouncing the ball into the other players' goals. All collisions are elastic and the ball follows its trajectory continuously (i.e. there is no kickoff after a goal). If a player scores an own goal, his score is reduced.

   Design and describe how $2n$-Gong operates on the three communication layers. You can assume that the game runs on a LAN and the human players' nodes are connected using peer-to-peer. By default each paddle is controlled by a synthetic player. When a human player joins the game, she replaces a randomly selected synthetic player. When a human player leaves the game, a synthetic player takes over the control again. If there are no synthetic players left to be replaced, the joining player becomes an observer of the game until some other human player leaves the game.

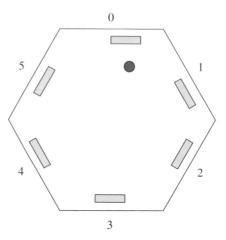

Figure 11.7 The game 2*n*-Gong with $n = 3$ has six players indicated by numbers [0, 5]. Each player controls a paddle (rectangle) that can be used to bounce the ball (circle).

11-12 Physical platforms can be organized in different ways. For example, we can have an Ethernet LAN that has a single coaxial cable shared by all nodes, or a hub connecting the nodes with twisted pair cables into a star-like network. Moreover, the number of nodes and their capabilities can also vary from LAN to LAN. If we want to run a massive networked application over a diverse set of physical platforms, we have to implement a workload balancing mechanism for the logical platform to make it more dynamic.

How can we make communication and data and control architectures more dynamic in the following cases? Approach the problem from the point of view of roles, responsibilities and functionalities and consider how they are interconnected.

(a) Dynamic communication: If we have a server network on a LAN, how can we increase and decrease the number of servers on the fly without informing clients of this change?

(b) Dynamic data: Suppose the data are distributed among the nodes on a WAN and we want to keep the overall delay of the data updates low. How can we realize handing over the data ownership (and its location site) to the node that is geographically nearest to the source of the update messages?

(c) Dynamic control: Suppose we have peer-to-peer nodes on a LAN. The most time-consuming features of the networked application are implemented as autonomous components, which are runnable entities that implement some functionality with a fixed use interface. How can we transfer a component from a node with a high workload to a more idle one?

You can refer to the terminology of patterns presented by Buschmann et al. (1996), and enthusiastic readers might even want to acquaint themselves with Schmidt et al. (2000).

12

Compensating Resource Limitations

Because a networked application has limited resources at its disposal, we have to find ways to utilize them effectively. The amount of resources required in a networked application is directly related to how much information has to be sent and received by each participating computer and how quickly it has to be delivered by the network. Singhal and Zyda (1999) formulate this rule as the *information principle equation*

$$\text{Resources} = M \times H \times B \times T \times P \tag{12.1}$$

where M is the number of messages transmitted, H is the average number of destination nodes for each message, B is the average amount of network bandwidth required for a message to each destination, T is the timeliness with which the network must deliver messages to each destination (large values of T imply a need for a small delay and vice versa), and P is the number of processor cycles required to receive and process each message. These measures can be illustrated as a radar diagram as shown in Figure 12.1.

If the resource requirements are fixed, we have a certain level of qualities (e.g. responsiveness or scalability) in the application. In this case Equation (12.1) has many possible solutions for given 'resources' and a system designer can use it as a tool to balance implementation requirements and restrictions. When we intensify the expenditure of one resource, we have to compensate it in some way. This means that another variable in the equation decreases or the quality of experience of the gameplay becomes weaker (e.g. movements become jerkier). The choice of which variables are increased and which variables are used for compensating depends naturally on the application's requirements and resource bottlenecks. For example, if the number of players increases, the bandwidth (B) requirement also increases, because each additional player must receive the initial game state and the updates that other users are already receiving. Each new player introduces new interactions with the existing players and requires additional processing power from the existing players, which means that H and P increase. Also, if we want to keep Equation (12.1) in balance, we have to send fewer messages (M) or allow more delay (T) in our communication.

In this chapter we present different compensation methods which try to reduce resource requirements, usually by increasing processing. Processing power can be used, for example, to compress the outgoing messages or to filter out the recipients who are interested in receiving them. But before reviewing the compensation methods we must look at two aspects affecting the choice of method: the balance between consistency and responsiveness, and achieving scalability in computation and communication.

Algorithms and Networking for Computer Games, Second Edition. Jouni Smed and Harri Hakonen.
© 2017 John Wiley & Sons Ltd. Published 2017 by John Wiley & Sons Ltd.

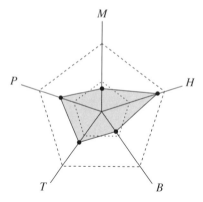

Figure 12.1 The information principle equation as a radar diagram.

12.1 Aspects of Compensation

If we look at the terms in Equation (12.1), we can recognize two questions that resource compensation must address: how to achieve a balance between consistency and responsiveness (i.e. how to reduce T) and how to scale up to include more players in the game (i.e. how to reduce H). Since these two aspects form the basis for resource compensation, let us study both of them more closely.

12.1.1 Consistency and responsiveness

Consistency refers to the similarity of the nodes' view to the data in the other nodes belonging to a network. Absolute consistency means that each node has uniform information, and to guarantee this we have to wait until everybody has received the information update before we can proceed. *Responsiveness* refers to the time it takes for an update event to be registered conceptually by the nodes, and to have high responsiveness we may have to proceed before everybody has physically received the information update. Consistency and responsiveness are not independent of each other. Traditionally, responsiveness has always been subject to consistency requirements in database research. However, because of real-time interaction, responsiveness becomes a more important element in networked computer games and we may have to compromise consistency. Consistency and responsiveness can have different requirements within the same game (Savery 2014, pp. 14–16). For example, life-and-death decisions usually require both high consistency and responsiveness, whereas trading in-game resources requires high consistency but can tolerate low responsiveness. Conversely, tracking an avatar's movements requires high responsiveness but can tolerate lower consistency.

To achieve high consistency a data and control architecture must guarantee that processes running on remote nodes are tightly coupled. This usually requires high bandwidth, low latency, and a small number of remote nodes. To achieve high responsiveness the queries made to the data must be responded to quickly, which requires loosely coupled nodes. In this case, the nodes must include more computation to reduce the bandwidth and latency requirements. In reality, a network architecture cannot achieve both high consistency and high responsiveness at the same time, and the choice of architecture is essentially a trade-off between these two attributes (Singhal and Zyda 1999).

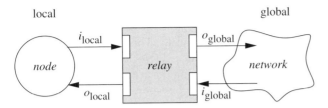

local   global

Figure 12.2 A data and control architecture defines how messages are relayed between local and remote nodes in a communication architecture.

At the extremes, the game world is either consistent, where all nodes maintain identical information, or dynamic, where information changes rapidly.

To clarify, we can discern three parts in data and control architectures: the local node, the network, and the relay connecting them (Smed et al. 2002). Figure 12.2 illustrates the situation in which a networked application running in a local node sends control messages to a relay and receives data messages from it. In turn, the relay communicates with the relays of other nodes through a network. Here, a relay is a logical concept which illustrates how the control affects the data.

The relay acts as an intermediary between the local node and the network, and its structure defines how consistent and how responsive the architecture can be. Obviously, the messages flow from i_{local} to o_{global}, and a stream from i_{global} to o_{local} must also exist. Let f and g be operations that the relay does on the messages upon sending and receiving (e.g. compression and decompression or encryption and decryption). This gives us the minimum form, a *two-way relay* (see Figure 12.3a), where $o_{global} = f(i_{local})$ and $o_{local} = g(i_{global})$. The two-way relay is the model used, for instance, in distributed databases and centralized systems. All new local messages are relayed to the network, and they do not appear in the local node until a message from the network is received. For example, a dumb terminal sends the characters typed on the keyboard to a mainframe, which sends back the characters to be displayed on the monitor. The two-way relay allows us to achieve high consistency, because all messages have to go through the network, where a centralized server or a group of peers can confirm and establish a consistent set of data. However, the two-way relay cannot guarantee high responsiveness, because it depends on the available networking resources.

To overcome this limitation we can bridge the two flows with an operation h, which forms a *short-circuit relay* (see Figure 12.3b), where $o_{global} = f(i_{local})$ as before, but

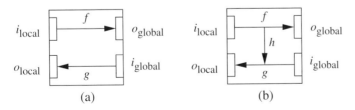

(a)   (b)

Figure 12.3 A relay has two basic alternatives for its structure: (a) A two-way relay sends the local control messages to the network, which sends back data messages to the node. (b) A short-circuit relay sends the local control messages to the network and passes them locally back to the node.

$o_{local} = g(i_{global}) \times h(i_{local})$. The locally originated messages are now passed back into the local output inside the relay. We do not have to wait for the messages to pass the network and return to us, but we short-circuit them back locally. This short-circuiting can be realized with immediate feedback as in the DIS standard (Neyland 1997), acknowledgements (Frécon and Stenius 1998), or buckets delaying the arrival of local messages (Diot and Gautier 1999). Clearly, we can now achieve high responsiveness, but it comes at a price: the local data can become inconsistent with the other nodes. This means that some kind of rollback or negotiation mechanism is required to solve the inconsistencies when they become a problem.

It is important to differentiate these two structures. A high-consistency architecture requires a two-way relay, because all updates require confirmation from the other nodes. On the other hand, high responsiveness entails a short-circuit relay, because the local control messages must appear promptly in the local data. With this in mind, we can now look at the three data and control architectures: centralized, distributed, and replicated. In a centralized architecture, the relay mostly conveys local control to the network and receives data from it, which is reversed in a distributed architecture. In a replicated architecture, the local input and output are a mixture of control and data messages. Each architecture also has characteristic problems: in a centralized architecture, access to the data may take time; in a distributed architecture, the allocation of the data fragments between the nodes must be handled properly; in a replicated architecture, updating the data in each replica can be tricky.

A networked application often has a hybrid architecture, where the system functionalities have their own implementation logic. For example, login authentication relies mostly on the client–server approach but configurations that affect the GUI representation are convenient to distribute to each node. By assigning designated relay types to each functionality we can identify and manage this variety of architecture choices in one application. From this perspective the relays can be seen as a part of the logical communication layer (see Section 11.2) and they define dedicated points for architecture realization and modification (e.g. in a form of interfaces). For example, the relays can be implemented so that they not only forward messages but also serve as a backbone for monitoring and administrating features of the whole networked application.

12.1.2 Scalability

Scalability is the ability to adapt to *resource changes*. In computer games this concerns, for example, how to construct an online server that dynamically adapts to varying numbers of players, or how to allocate the computation of synthetic players among the nodes. To achieve this kind of scalability there must be physical (i.e. hardware-based) parallelism that enables logical (i.e. software) concurrency of computation.

Serial and parallel execution

The potential speedup obtained by applying multiple nodes is bounded by the system's inherently sequential computations. Pipelining is a typical way to optimize such consecutive operations. Now the operations are chunked and allocated to a chain of nodes, and the data flow to a node gets processed and then forwarded to the next node. Because each node runs simultaneously, the theoretical speedup is no more than the number of nodes. In practice, pipelining requires that data are transmitted quickly between nodes and are available when needed, which means that it does not go well with interaction or remote nodes. Thus, the time required by the serially executed parts of a networked application cannot be reduced by parallel computation.

The theoretical speedup S is achieved by non-centralized control and can be measured by

$$S(n) = \frac{T(1)}{T(n)} \leq \frac{T(1)}{T(1)/n} = n \tag{12.2}$$

where $T(1)$ is the execution time with one node and $T(n)$ with n nodes. The execution time can be divided into a serial part T_s and parallel part T_p. Let $T_s + T_p = 1$ and $\alpha = T_s/(T_s + T_p)$. If the system is parallelized optimally, Equation (12.2) can be rewritten as

$$S(n) = \frac{T_s + T_p}{T_s + T_p/n} = \frac{1}{\alpha + (1 - \alpha)/n} \leq \frac{1}{\alpha}. \tag{12.3}$$

This is called *Amdahl's law* for a fixed problem setting (Gustafson 1988). For example, if 5% of the program must be executed serially (i.e. $\alpha = 0.05$), the maximum speedup obtainable is 20.

Ideally, the serial part should be non-existent so that everything can be computed in parallel. However, in that case there cannot exist any coordination between the nodes. The only example of such multiplayer computer games is where each player is playing their own game regardless of the others. The other extreme is that there is no parallel part with respect to the game state, which is the case in a round robin or a turn-based game. Between these extremes are the games which provide real-time interaction and which, consequently, comprise both parallel and serial computation (see Figure 12.4).

For the serial parts, the nodes must agree on the sequence of events. The simplest way to realize this is to utilize a client–server architecture, where the server can control the communication by forwarding, filtering and modifying the messages. It should be noted that even in a peer-to-peer architecture the network acts like a server (i.e. the peers share the same serializing communication channel), unless the nodes are connected to each other by a direct physical cable or they communicate by multicasting.

To concretize, let us calculate the communication capacity in a client–server architecture using unicast. Suppose that each client sends 5 packets per second using the IPv6 communication protocol in a 10 Mbps Ethernet. Each packet takes at least a frame of size $68 \cdot 8 + 26 \cdot 8 = 752$ bits (or 94 bytes). Let d equal the number of bits in a message, f the transmission frequency, n the number of unicast connections, and C the maximum capacity of the communication channel. Obviously, the condition

$$d \cdot f \cdot n \leq C$$

must hold. By using values $d = 752 + 32$ (i.e. the payload comprises one 32-bit integer value), $f = 5$ and $C = 10^7$, we can solve the upper bound for the number of clients. Thus, if we are using a client–server architecture, one server can provide serializability for at most 2551 clients. In reality the update frequency is higher and the payload much larger and, consequently, the estimate on the number of clients is highly optimistic. Moreover, client communication requires computation power from the server.

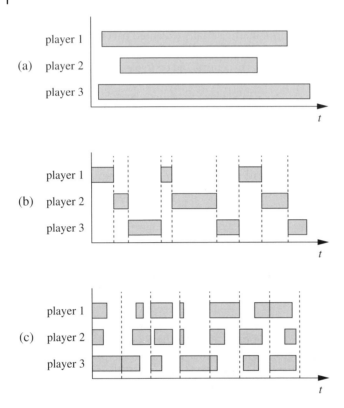

Figure 12.4 Serial and parallel execution in computer games. (a) Separate real-time games can run in parallel but without interaction. (b) A turn-based game is serialized and interactive but not real-time, unless the turns are very short. (c) An interactive real-time game runs both in serial and in parallel.

Communication capacity

Because the coordination of serialized parts requires communication, scalability is limited by the communication capacity requirements of the chosen deployment. Let us assume that clients are allowed to send messages freely at any moment (i.e. asynchronous messaging). In the worst case, all nodes try to communicate at the same time and the network architecture must handle this traffic without saturation.

Table 12.1 collects the magnitudes of communication capacity requirements for different deployment architectures (see Figure 11.4). Obviously, a single node needs no networking. In peer-to-peer, when all n nodes have direct connections to the other

Table 12.1 Communication capacity requirements for different deployment architectures when the network has n nodes and m servers.

Deployment architecture	Capacity requirement
Single node	0
Peer-to-peer	$O(n) \ldots O(n^2)$
Client–server	$O(n)$
Peer-to-peer server-network	$O(n/m + m) \ldots O(n/m + m^2)$
Hierarchical server-network	$O(n)$

nodes or the communication is handled by multicasting, the magnitude of the communication capacity is $O(n)$; otherwise, the peers use unicasting, which yields $O(n^2)$. In a client–server architecture, the server end requires a capacity of $O(n)$, because each client has a dedicated connection to it. In a server-network architecture, the server pool has m servers, and n clients are divided evenly among them. If the servers are connected as peer-to-peer, the server communication requires $O(m) \ldots O(m^2)$ in addition to $O(n/m)$ capacity for client communication. If the servers are connected hierarchically (e.g. as a tree), the server at the root is the bottleneck requiring a capacity of $O(n)$.

In an earlier example we calculated that a server can support up to 2551 clients. This demonstrates that, in practice, linear capacity requirement is too large. Therefore, the heart of scalability is to achieve *sublinear communication*. In effect, this means that a client cannot be aware of all the other clients all the time.

To guarantee sublinear communication in a hierarchical server-network we must limit the communication between the servers. Suppose that the hierarchy is a k-ary tree. If we can now guarantee that a server sends to its parent a fraction $1/k$ of its children's messages, we have a logarithmic capacity requirement (i.e. communication in the root is $O(\log n)$). Now the problem is how to realize this reduction. This is where the compensatory techniques provide an answer. Children's messages can be compressed and aggregated if we can guarantee that the size reduction is $1/k$ on each server level – which is quite unlikely. A more usable solution is, at each step, to apply first interest management (e.g. refrain from passing messages whose potential receivers are already inside the subtree; see Section 12.6), and then select one of the outgoing messages for the server to pass on. For each suppressed message, the nodes can approximate the information (e.g. by using dead reckoning; see Section 12.3).

Parallelizing the game world

When the game has to support massively multiple players, the game world is often parallelized. The two most common approaches are *zoning* and *instancing* (see Figure 12.5).

In zoning, the game world is divided into independent, disjoint zones which are processed in parallel on dedicated servers. Usually the zones follow the game world geography (e.g. valleys, islands or planets). When the player enters a zone, the client is connected to the respective zone server. The server handles the communication between the clients residing in the same zone but there is no communication from the client to the other servers and their clients. The only exception is when the player moves from one zone to another and the servers exchange the responsibility for the client.

Zoning scales up well – provided that the game world is easy to subdivide – and it is used in many massively multiplayer online games. For example, in *Eve Online* each star system is a zone with its own server (dedicated servers for high-load star systems, shared ones for low-load star systems). In addition, the servers are connected to a main database to maintain overall consistency.

In instancing, certain areas of the game world are maintained by multiple, independent servers (or shards) each holding its own copy of the area. These areas are usually highly populated by the players (e.g. dungeons or market places), which is why they need to scale up. Because the players in different, parallel instances (i.e. servers) cannot communicate with one another and the interaction is limited, a group of players playing together is usually allocated to the same instance. For example, *World of Warcraft* uses instancing to service the players.

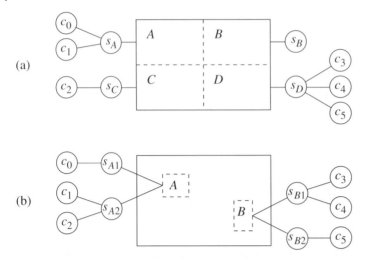

Figure 12.5 Game world parallelization where the clients c_i are connected to the servers s_j managing regions *A–D*: (a) By dividing the game world into zones we can assign a separate server for each zone. (b) Certain regions of the game world can be copied into parallel servers which run independently of one another.

12.2 Protocol Optimization

Since every message sent to the network incurs a processing penalty, we can improve the resource usage by reducing the size of each message or the number of messages.

12.2.1 Message compression

The networked application can save bandwidth at the cost of computational power by compressing the messages. Since the purpose of compression is to reduce the number of bits needed to represent particular information, it provides us with an intuitive approach to minimize network traffic. With respect to Equation (12.1), we are reducing the average packet size (B) but due to encoding and decoding processes the computational work (P) increases.

Compression techniques can be classified according to their ability to preserve the information content (see Table 12.2). Lossless techniques preserve all information, and

Table 12.2 Compression technique categories.

Compression	*Lossless*	*Lossy*
Internal	Encode the message in a more efficient format and eliminate redundancy within it.	Filter irrelevant information or reduce the detail of the transmitted information.
External	Avoid retransmitting information that is identical to that sent in the previous messages.	Avoid retransmitting information that is similar to that sent in the previous messages.

the reconstructed data are exactly the same as the data before compression. To achieve a higher compression ratio we can employ lossy compression techniques, where the idea is to leave out less relevant information so that the distortion in the reconstructed data remains unnoticeable. For further information on compression methods, see Witten et al. (1999).

Based on how compression operates on data in a sequence of messages, we can divide the techniques into internal and external. Internal compression concentrates on the information content of one message without references to other, previously transmitted messages, which is why it is suitable for unreliable network transmission protocols (e.g. UDP). On the other hand, external compression can utilize information that has been already transmitted and can be assumed to be available to the receivers. For example, we can transmit delta (i.e. the amount of change) or transition information, which is likely to require fewer bits than the absolute information, or give reference pointers to a previously transmitted message if the same message occurs again. External compression can consider a large amount of data at a time and thus can better observe redundancy in the information flow and allow better compression ratios than internal compression. However, because of the references to the previous packets, external compression requires a reliable transmission protocol (e.g. TCP).

12.2.2 Message aggregation

Message aggregation reduces transmission frequency by merging information from multiple messages. Bundling up messages saves bandwidth because there is less header information but requires extra computation and weakens the responsiveness. In the terms of Equation (12.1), the number of messages (M) and timeliness (T) decrease, the average message size (B) increases, and the overall bandwidth consumption is reduced at slight processing cost (P).

Message aggregation needs a criterion that indicates when we have collected enough messages to be sent as a one merged message. In the *timeout-based approach*, all messages that are initiated before a fixed time period are merged. This approach guarantees an upper bound on the delay caused by aggregation. Now bandwidth savings depend on the message initiation rate, and in the worst case no savings are made because no messages (or only one) are initiated during the period. In the *quorum-based approach*, a fixed number of messages are always merged. Because the transmission of the merged message is delayed until enough messages have been initiated, there is no guarantee for the transmission delay. Although bandwidth savings are predictable, long transmission delays can hinder the gameplay. The limitations of both approaches can be compensated by combining them. In this hybrid approach, merging occurs whenever one of the conditions is fulfilled: either the time period expires or there are enough messages to merge.

12.3 Dead Reckoning

Dead reckoning dates back to navigational techniques used to estimate a ship's current position based on a known start position, travelling velocity and elapsed time. In networked applications, dead reckoning is used to reduce bandwidth consumption by

Figure 12.6 Dead reckoning is used to calculate positions between the update messages. The actual movement (indicated by the grey arrow) differs from the movement predicted by dead reckoning (black arrows). The dotted lines indicate a position change caused by the update message which has to be corrected using a convergence method.

sending update messages less frequently and estimating the state information between the updates (see Figure 12.6). Apart from extrapolating the current state from past states, the state update can include additional information for predicting how the state will change in the future.

Dead reckoning is normally used to reduce positional information, and dead reckoning algorithms mainly focus on predicting the entity's movement. In terms of network traffic, this suits many games very well; for example, in a first-person shooter game over a half of the network traffic may be updates related to movement (Savery 2014, p. 15).

With respect to Equation (12.1), dead reckoning transmits update messages less frequently, which reduces M and T, but the nodes have to compensate this by computing predictions, which increases P. When the next update message arrives, the predicted value can differ from the actual value, which can cause disruptive visual effects. To minimize this the difference can be corrected by converging it, over time, closer to the true value.

12.3.1 Prediction

The most common prediction technique is to use derivative polynomials. If the state information represents a position p, the first two derivatives have natural interpretations as velocity v and acceleration a. State updates using zero-order derivative polynomials comprise only position information and no prediction information. In the case of first-order derivative polynomials, we transmit the velocity of an entity in addition to its position:

$$p(t) = p(0) + v(0)t. \tag{12.4}$$

To improve the accuracy of the prediction we can add acceleration to the transmitted information:

$$p(t) = p(0) + v(0)t + \frac{1}{2}a(0)t^2. \tag{12.5}$$

This second-order polynomial (see Algorithm 12.1) models moving vehicles quite accurately, but the first-order polynomial is more suitable for less predictably moving entities such as human characters. The reason for this is that high-order polynomials are sensitive to errors, because the derivative information must be accurate. The prediction is more sensitive for high-order terms, and a small inaccuracy in them can result in significant deviations that might make the prediction worse. In other words, we must have a better model for high-order terms – but higher-order derivatives must be often estimated or tracked over time, because it is hard to get accurate instantaneous information. For example, although acceleration models how a car responds to the throttle, a third-order polynomial (i.e. jerk) would require some insight into the mind of the driver (i.e. his decision-making process). Also, with higher-order polynomials, more information has to be transmitted, which means that the computational complexity increases (i.e. each additional term requires a few extra operations) and each additional term consumes the bandwidth resources.

Algorithm 12.1 Second order prediction of a position.

PREDICTION-SECOND-ORDER(S, t)
  in: state information S; time stamp t
  out: predicted state value
  1: $d \leftarrow t - time(S)$
  2: $v \leftarrow velocity(prediction(S))$
  3: $a \leftarrow acceleration(prediction(S))$
  4: **return** $state(S) + vd + ad^2/2$

We can omit the derivative polynomials altogether and use the known history to extrapolate the data. The position history-based dead reckoning protocol transmits only the absolute positions, and the entity's instantaneous velocity and acceleration are approximated by using the update history (Singhal 1996). The method evaluates the motion over the three most recent position updates and chooses dynamically between first-order and second-order polynomials: if acceleration is small or substantial, we use a first-order polynomial; otherwise, we use a second-order polynomial. The rationale behind this is to reduce the inaccuracies caused by the acceleration term. For example, if the entity's acceleration changes often, an incorrect value is likely to be applied to the prediction at some point and it might be safer to be content with first-order prediction at that time.

Naturally, prediction can be specialized to suit the entity in question. Derivative polynomials do not take into account what the entity is currently doing, what the entity is capable of doing, or who is controlling the entity. For instance, cars and aeroplanes – albeit obeying the same laws of physics – could have different prediction algorithms based on their overall behaviour. By including entity-specific information in the dead reckoning technique we can achieve more accurate and natural movement (Krumm-Heller and Taylor 2000). However, this can be time-consuming and maintaining several different algorithms requires a special care.

The transmission frequency for updates need not be constant but the messages can be sent only when dead reckoning exceeds some error threshold (see Algorithm 12.2). By taking advantage of the knowledge about the computations at remote nodes, the source node can reduce the required state update rate. Because the source can use the same prediction algorithm as the remote nodes, it is enough to transmit updates only when the actual position and the predicted position differ significantly. This reduces the update rate if the prediction algorithm is reasonably accurate. The source node can even dynamically balance its network transmission resources so that when bandwidth is limited, it increases the error threshold according to the distance between the objects (Aggarwal et al. 2004; Cai et al. 1999; Duncan and Gračanin 2003; Hakiri et al. 2010; Lee et al. 2000; Shim and Kim 2001; Zhang et al. 2004) or the update interval (Hanawa and Yonekura 2006; Yu and Choy 2001). In the case of high latency, the error can be estimated using three-way interpolated simulation (de Carpentier and Bidarra 2005) and dead reckoning can be used to improve the behaviour of computer-controlled players (Bai et al. 2009).

Algorithm 12.2 Constructing dead reckoning messages.

DEAD-RECKONING-MESSAGE(s, t, P, Q)
   in: state value s; time stamp t; prediction information P; previously sent state Q
   out: new update message U or NIL if not necessary
   constant: difference threshold ℓ
  1: **if** $|s - \text{PREDICTION}(Q, t)| < \ell$ **then**
  2:   **return** NIL   ▷ Difference below the threshold.
  3: **end if**
  4: $state(U) \leftarrow s$
  5: $time(U) \leftarrow t$
  6: $prediction(U) \leftarrow P$
  7: **return** U

12.3.2 Convergence

When a node using a dead reckoning technique receives an update message, the predicted state of the entity is likely to differ from the state based on the information just arrived. In this case, the entity has to be updated to this new state using a convergence technique. The simplest technique is zero-order convergence (or snap), where the entity is changed immediately to a new state without any smoothing adjustments (e.g. visual corrections). However, this can cause annoyingly jerky or even impossible (e.g. through a wall) changes, which are known in many networked games as 'warping'.

A good convergence technique corrects errors quickly and as unnoticeably as possible. To achieve this we must select a convergence period within which we want to correct the error. If the state represents a position of an entity, we can pick a convergence point along the new predicted path so that after the convergence period the displayed position coincides with the prediction. After that, we render the entity as if it travels between its current displayed position and the convergence point. When the entity has reached the convergence point, it begins to follow the new predicted path – until a new update is received and the convergence procedure is repeated (see Algorithm 12.3).

Algorithm 12.3 Using dead reckoning messages.

DEAD-RECKONING-VALUE(S, t)
    in: state information S; time stamp t
    out: state value
    constant: convergence period c
    1: $t' \leftarrow time(current(S))$
    2: $t'' \leftarrow t' + c$
    3: **if** $t > t''$ **then**
    4:    **return** PREDICTION($state(current(S))$, t)
    5: **else**
    6:    $s' \leftarrow$ PREDICTION($state(previous(S))$, t')
    7:    $s'' \leftarrow$ PREDICTION($state(current(S))$, t'')
    8:    **return** CONVERGENCE(s', t', s'', t'', t)
    9: **end if**

In linear convergence, the entity is moved along a direct path from the current position s' to the convergence point s''. The velocity is determined by fixing the start time t' when the entity is at s' and the target time t'' for arriving at s''. In terms of Algorithm 3.3, on time stamp t ($t' \leq t \leq t''$) the entity is converged at position (see Figure 12.7)

$$\text{UNIT-LERP}(s', s'', \text{UNIT-RESCALE}(t', t'', t)) = \text{RESCALE}(s', s'', t', t'', t).$$

Although linear convergence is clearly better than zero-order convergence, it can still make unnatural turns when leaving the previously predicted path and entering the new predicted path. To smooth out these problems, more sophisticated curve-fitting

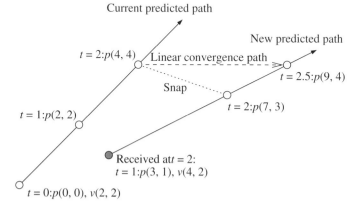

Figure 12.7 Dead reckoning comprises prediction and convergence. Open circles represent predicted information about the entity's position p at given time t. The closed circle represents the entity's received position p and velocity v at given time t when the communication delay is 1 s. In zero-order convergence (or snap), the position is corrected immediately at $t = 2$ to the new predicted path. In linear convergence, the change is made smoothly along a linear convergence path during a convergence period of 0.5 s.

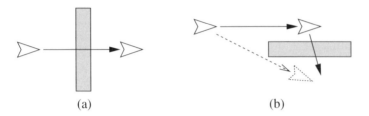

Figure 12.8 Locational problems caused by dead reckoning. (a) If prediction is not used with collision detection, the ship following its predicted path can pass through a wall. (b) If the predicted path has led the ship to the wrong side of a wall, convergence has to correct the situation, possibly letting the ship pass through the wall.

techniques can be applied. The idea is to select, in addition to the current position and convergence point, a number of points along the previously predicted path and the new predicted path. The curve is fitted to go through all the selected points, and it is used as a path to shift the entity to its new predicted path. For example, in the case of a third-order curve (cubic spline), we pick one additional point on the previously predicted path before the current position and another additional point along the new predicted path after the convergence point. High-order curves provide smooth transition from the old path to the new path, but they can computationally intensive for some applications.

Although convergence helps to make errors less noticeable, there are situations where dead reckoning causes locational problems that cannot be solved otherwise than by letting visual disruptions occur. These problems can stem both from prediction and convergence, as illustrated in Figure 12.8. When repairing inconsistencies Savery (2014, pp. 101–109) observes that the further the correction is from the player's locus of attention, the less noticeable it is. Furthermore, experimental data indicate that smooth corrections using convergence are superior to warping, unless the corrections become very large.

12.4 Local Perception Filters

Local perception filters (LPFs) hide communication delays by exploiting human perceptual limitations (Ryan and Sharkey 1999; Sharkey et al. 1998). Whereas in dead reckoning we try to maintain a consistent view by predicting the state, LPFs allow temporal distortions in the view and entities can be rendered at slightly out-of-date locations based on the underlying communication delays. *Half-Life* is the earliest example of a similar idea where remote state information is shown delayed while the local player is presented in the real timeframe (Bernier 2001). Naturally, we want to make these temporal distortions of the game world as unnoticeable as possible. Although we describe LPFs in visualization terms, the underlaying idea is more general, because the application's control logic and proto-view (see Section 1.1) can also perceive the out-of-date state instance.

The entities of a game world can be separated into two classes:

(i) *Players* are indeterministic entities (e.g. controlled by human players), whose behaviour cannot be predicted. Based on the communication delay, we divide the players to local players (e.g. sharing the same computer) and remote players (e.g. players connected by a network).

(ii) *Passive entities* are deterministic entities whose behaviour follows, for example, the laws of physics (e.g. projectiles) or which are otherwise predictable (e.g. buildings).

Interaction means, theoretically speaking, that the interacting entities must communicate with each other to resolve the outcome. If the communication delay between entities is negligible (e.g. they reside in the same computer), the interaction seems credible. On the other hand, networking incurs communication delays which can hinder the interaction between remote players.

LPFs address the problem of delays by discerning the actual situation from the rendered situation. The rendered situation, which is perceived by the player, need not coincide with the current actual situation, but it can comprise some out-of-date information. The amount of this temporal distortion is easy to determine for players: local players are rendered using up-to-date state information, while a remote player with a communication delay of d seconds is rendered using the known, d-seconds-old state information.

To preserve the causality the temporal distortion of the passive entities changes dynamically. The nearer a passive entity is to a local player, the closer it has to be rendered to its current state, because it is possible that the player will interact with it. Conversely, a passive entity nearing a remote player must be rendered closer to that remote player's time, because if there is an interaction between the remote player and the passive entity, the outcome is rendered after the communication delay. In other words, the rendered remote interactions, albeit occurring in real time, have happened in the past, and only when the local player itself participates in the interaction must it happen in the present time.

Figure 12.9 gives an example in which the player controlling the white ship shoots a bullet (i.e. a passive entity) towards the grey ship controlled by a remote player. The players' views are not entirely consistent with each other. At the beginning the white ship renders the bullet in the actual position but as it closes on the grey ship it begins to lag behind the actual position. Conversely, when the grey ship first learns about the bullet, it has already travelled some distance. For example, let us assume that the communication delay between the ships is 0.5 seconds and the bullet travels in 2.0 seconds from the white ship to the grey ship. When the white ship fires, it sees the bullet immediately, but then the rendered bullet starts to drag behind the actual position. After 2.0 seconds the bullet has arrived at the grey ship, but it is rendered as though it has travelled only 1.5 seconds. It takes 0.5 seconds for the grey ship's reaction to be conveyed to the white ship, and once that message arrives, after 2.5 seconds, the bullet is rendered near the grey ship and reaction occurs at an appropriate moment. From the grey ship's perspective the chain of events is different. When it learns about the bullet, it has already travelled 0.5 seconds, but it is rendered coming from the white ship. The rendered bullet must now catch up with the actual bullet so that at 2.0 seconds both the rendered and actual bullet arrive at the grey ship, which can then react and send its reaction to the white ship.

Each player has its own perception of the game world, where all entities, in addition to spatial coordinates (x, y, z), are associated with a time delay (t), thus forming a $3\frac{1}{2}$-dimensional coordinate system. The local player is at the current time $t = 0$, and remote players are assigned t values according to their communication delays. Once we have assigned these values, we can define a *temporal contour* (or causal surface) over the game

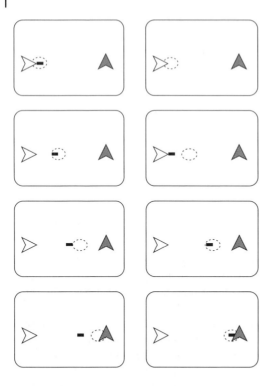

Figure 12.9 An example of local perception filters with two stationary players (white and grey ship) and one moving passive entity (a bullet shot by the white ship). On the left, from top to bottom, are the rendered views from the white ship's perspective; on the right are the corresponding views from the grey ship's perspective. Dashed ovals indicate the actual position of the bullet and black rectangles its rendered position. As the bullet closes on the grey ship, the white ship perceives it to slow down, while the grey ship perceives it to gain speed.

world for each player. The temporal contour defines suitable t values for each spatial point. Figure 12.10 illustrates one possible temporal contour for the white ship of the previous example. When the bullet leaves the white ship, $t = 0$, but the t value increases as the bullet closes on the grey ship, until they both have the same t value.

The changes in the movement of a passive entity caused by the temporal contour should be minimal and smooth. Moreover, all interactions between players and passive entities should appear to be realistic and consistent (e.g. preserve causality of events). The requirements for temporal contours can be summarized into three rules:

(i) Player should be able to interact in real time with nearby entities.
(ii) Player should be able to view remote interactions in real time, although they can be out of date.
(iii) Temporal distortions in the player's perception should be as unnoticeable as possible.

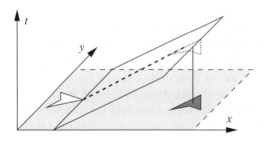

Figure 12.10 The $2\frac{1}{2}$-dimensional temporal contour from the white ship's perspective. The bullet travels 'uphill' until it reaches the t value of the grey ship.

The most important limitation of LPFs, which follows from the first rule, is that a player cannot interact *directly* with a remote player. The players can engage in an exchange of passive entities (e.g. bullets, arrows, missiles or insults) but they cannot get into a mêlée with each other. In fact, the closer the players get to each other the more noticeable the temporal distortion becomes, until they reach a critical proximity, when even interaction using passive entities becomes impossible.

The underlying assumption behind LPFs is that we know the exact communication delays between the players. In reality, latency and the amount of traffic in a network tend to vary over time, which means that the height of the peaks of the temporal contour must reflect these changes. If this jitter becomes too high, the passive entities begin to bounce back and forth in time instead of making smooth temporal transitions. Also, because remote players define the temporal contour, any sudden changes in their position or existence can cause drastic effects in the rendered view. For example, if a nearby remote player leaves the game world, it no longer affects the temporal contour and some passive entities may suddenly jump forward in time to match the updated temporal contour.

In the following subsections we study first how to define linear temporal contours in the case of two players, and then extend the discussion to cover multiple players. Then we present how LPFs can be used to realize the bullet time effect in a multiplayer computer game.

12.4.1   Linear temporal contour

Let us first look at a case where we have only two players, p and r, and one passive entity e. The players and the passive entity have a spatial location, and the players are associated with a communication delay, which is due to the network latency and cannot be reduced. If i and j are players or entities, let $\delta(i,j)$ denote the spatial distance between them and $d(i,j)$ the delay from the perspective of i. The communication delay between players does not have to be the same in both directions but we can allow $d(i,j) \neq d(j,i)$.

In the case of two players, the delay function d for the entity e must have the properties

$$d(p,e) = \begin{cases} 0, & \text{if } \delta(p,e) = 0, \\ d(p,r), & \text{if } \delta(r,e) = 0. \end{cases} \qquad (12.6)$$

Simply put, if e and p are at the same position, the delay to p is zero, and if e and r are at the same position, the delay from p is the same as the communication delay from p to r.

The rest of the function can be defined, for example, linearly as

$$d(p,e) = d(p,r) \cdot \max\left\{ 1 - \frac{\delta(r,e)}{\delta(p,r)}, 0 \right\}, \qquad (12.7)$$

which is illustrated in Figure 12.11. The delay function now defines a symmetrical temporal contour around r, which the entities must follow when they are rendered. This is not the only possibility, and the delay function can even be asymmetric (i.e. the slope does not have to be the same in all directions).

Let us take an example, which is illustrated in Figure 12.12, where player p shoots a bullet e towards player r. If we look at the situation from the perspective of player p, initially the distance to the bullet $\delta(p,e) = 0$ and the delay $d(p,e) = 0$. The delay increases as the bullet closes on r, until $d(p,e) = d(p,r)$ when $\delta(r,e) = 0$. Once the bullet has passed r,

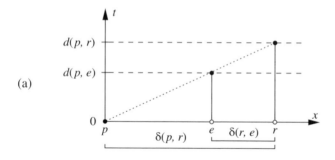

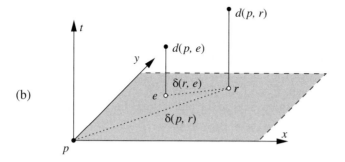

Figure 12.11 Examples of the linear delay function of Equation (12.7) defining the temporal contour in (a) a one-dimensional game world and (b) a two-dimensional game world.

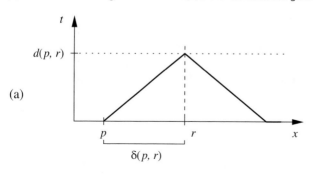

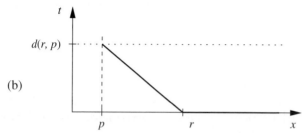

Figure 12.12 Player p shoots at player r in a one-dimensional world. (a) The temporal contour from the perspective of player p. The corresponding values on the t-axis illustrate the delay (i.e. the temporal difference) between the actual and rendered position at each actual spatial point on the x-axis. (b) The temporal contour from the perspective of player r.

the delay falls back to zero. Player p perceives the temporal contour so that the bullet moves more slowly when it is climbing 'uphill' and faster when it is going 'downhill'. From the perspective of player r, the bullet initially has delay $d(r, e) = d(r, p)$, which reduces to $d(r, e) = 0$ when $\delta(r, e) = 0$. In other words, player r perceives the bullet as moving faster than its actual speed until it has passed the player.

If we define the temporal contour observing the constraints of Equation (12.6), we may notice a slight visual flaw in the rendered outcome. Assume player p shoots a bullet e towards remote player r. The bullet slows down, and when $\delta(r, e) = 0$, the delay function has reached its maximum and $d(p, e) = d(p, r)$. However, when the actual bullet reaches r, the rendered bullet of p is still short of reaching r (see the bottom left frame of Figure 12.9). Because the temporal contour is already at its peak value, the bullet begins to speed up before it is rendered at r. This can look disruptive, because the change happens before the bullet is rendered to interact with the remote player. Intuitively, acceleration should occur only after the bullet has passed the remote player. From the perspective of player r, the rendering has a similar problem. Once r learns about the bullet, its rendered position is not next to p but some way forward along the trajectory. Simply put, the problem is that the delay function is defined using actual positions, whereas it should also observe the movement of the entity during the communication delay. This means that each individual entity requires a slight refinement of the temporal contour to reduce these perceptual disruptions.

To solve the problem, let us first introduce the function $\delta_e(t)$, which represents the distance that the entity e travels in the time t. Obviously, the function is based on the velocity and acceleration information, but the given generalization suffices for our current use. Let us now define a *shadow r'* of player r that has the property

$$\delta(r, r') = \delta_e(d(p, r)). \tag{12.8}$$

The shadow r' represents the position where the entity e actually resides when player p is rendering it at the position of remote player r. Now we can rewrite Equation (12.6) as

$$d(p, e) = \begin{cases} 0, & \text{if } \delta(p, e) = 0, \\ d(p, r), & \text{if } \delta(r', e) = 0. \end{cases} \tag{12.9}$$

Simply put, this means that we push the peak of the temporal contour forward a distance $\delta_e(d(p, r))$ to r', which is illustrated in Figure 12.13. The reason why we want to use the actual spatial positions is that they, unlike the rendered positions, are consistent among all players.

When we have multiple remote players, they each have their own delay functions, and to get the temporal contour we must aggregate them. To realize the aggregation we can use the following approaches (see Figure 12.14):

- Try to minimize the number of entities that are not in the local time (i.e. whose delay is not zero). This means that once an entity has passed a remote player, its delay returns to zero. The aim of this approach is to maintain the situation as close to the actual situation as possible, and it is best suited when there is a lot of interaction between the entities. The drawback is that an entity may bounce back and forth between local and remote time, which can make its movements look jerky.

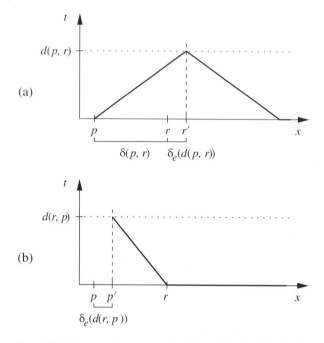

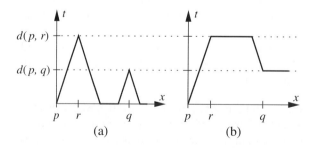

Figure 12.13 Temporal contours are adjusted by the distance the entity travels in the communication delay. (a) The corrected temporal contour of player p, where the peak is pushed forward to r'. (b) The corrected temporal contour of player r, where the peak is pushed forward to p'.

- Try to minimize the number of delay changes. Once an entity has reached some delay level, it remains unchanged unless it begins to approach a new remote player. This helps to reduce bouncing between different times, which is common especially if there are several remote players along the path of the entity. The drawback is that the rendered view, in its entirety, does not remain as close to the actual situation as in the first approach.

Once we have formed the temporal contour, it is used similarly as in the case of two players.

Figure 12.14 Two approaches to aggregate the temporal contour of player p, when there are two remote players r and q. (a) Minimize the number of entities that are not in local time. (b) Minimize the number of delay changes.

12.4.2   Adding bullet time to the delays

In the bullet time effect, a player can get more reaction time by slowing down the surrounding game world. Whereas the bullet time effect is quite easy to implement in a single-player game (e.g. *Max Payne*), simply by slowing down the rendering, in multiplayer games the bullet time effect – if used at all – is implemented by speeding up the player rather than slowing down the environment. For instance, force speed in *Jedi Knight II* implements the bullet time effect differently in the single-player mode than in the multiplayer mode. The reason for this is obvious: if one player could slow down the time of its surroundings, it would be awkward for the other players within the influence area because, rather than enhancing the gameplay of the player using the bullet time, it would only hinder the gameplay of the other human players.

Since the player using bullet time has more time to react to the events of the surrounding game world, the delay between the bullet-timed player and the other players increases. This is quite straightforward to include in LPFs (Smed et al. 2005): in addition to real-world communication delays, we have artificial, player-initiated delays – the bullet time – which are then used to form the temporal contours. The outcome is that entities approaching a bullet-timed player slow down and entities coming from a bullet-timed player speed up. Obviously, the game design should prevent the players from overusing bullet time by making it a limited resource which can be used only for a short period. Also, incorporating the temporal distortions as an integral part of the game could lead to new and intriguing game designs.

Let us denote by $b(p)$ the bullet time of player p. As in the previous section, assume we have two players, p and r, and a bullet e shot by player p. Figure 12.15 illustrates

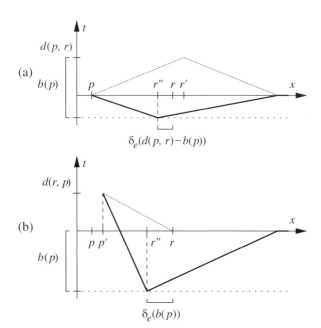

Figure 12.15 Player p shoots player r, and player p is using bullet time. (a) The temporal contour of player p. (b) The temporal contour of player r.

the players' temporal contours when player p is using bullet time. From the perspective of player p, when the bullet reaches r the delay is $d(p, r) - b(p)$. As before, the delay function represents the temporal difference between the actual entity and the rendered entity. However, whereas normally the delay values are positive (i.e. the actual position is ahead of the rendered position), bullet time can lead to negative delay values (i.e. the rendered position is ahead of the actual position). This becomes more obvious when we consider the same situation from the perspective of player r. When the bullet reaches player r, the delay is $-b(p)$ because the bullet time, in effect, takes away time from player r. Naturally, collision detection and other reactions must be based on this rendered entity rather than the actual entity, which is still on the way to the target.

Like normal temporal contours, bullet-timed temporal contours also require refining to avoid visual disruptions. The *bullet time shadow r''* of player r corrects the temporal contour based on the movement of e: for player p, r'' must have the property

$$\delta(r, r'') = \delta_e(d(p, r) - b(p)),\tag{12.10}$$

and for player r, r'' must have the property

$$\delta(r, r'') = \delta_e(b(p)).\tag{12.11}$$

In Figure 12.16 player r is using bullet time while being shot by player p. In this case, the bullet time $b(r)$ is added to the normal communication delay in the temporal contour of player p, which means that the delay is $d(p, r) + b(r)$ when the bullet reaches r. Conversely, player r has the delay $b(r)$ when the bullet reaches it. Again, to refine the

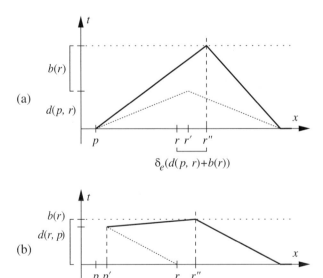

Figure 12.16 Player p shoots player r, and player r is using bullet time. (a) The temporal contour of player p. (b) The temporal contour of player r.

temporal contours, we must calculate the bullet time shadow r''. For player p, r'' must have the property

$$\delta(r, r'') = \delta_e(d(p, r) + b(p)), \tag{12.12}$$

and for player r, r'' must have the property

$$\delta(r, r'') = \delta_e(b(r)). \tag{12.13}$$

Bullet-timed temporal contours can be generalized to include multiple players in the same way as normal temporal contours.

12.5   Synchronized Simulation

In synchronized (or simultaneous) simulation we have a replicated architecture with absolute consistency, where all players have their own copy of the game world and these replicas are always identical (i.e. synchronized) to one another. For example, *Age of Empires II* uses communication turns (see Figure 12.17) and synchronized simulation to support up to eight players and 1600 controllable entities (Bettner and Terrano 2001). A similar kind of a bucket synchronization is also proposed by Zhao et al. (2009).

To reduce the number of messages sent among the nodes we try to keep the game states as synchronized as possible. The events in the game world can be divided to

 (i) deterministic (events generated by the simulation) and
(ii) indeterministic (commands issued by a synthetic or human player).

Because each simulation run can generate the same deterministic information, only non-deterministic commands must be distributed among the participants. We reduce the communication even further if each node runs the same synthetic players. The only unpredictable events are then generated by the human players; they are the only ones that need to be transmitted over the network.

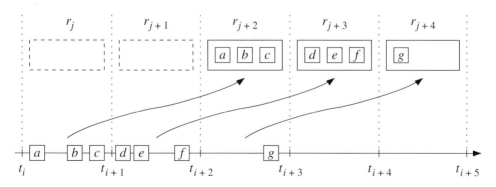

Figure 12.17 Communication turns in synchronized simulation delay the execution of both local and remote commands so that they occur at the same time in all nodes. The rounds have an equal duration. The commands from round r_j (a, b and c) are executed two rounds later in round r_{j+2}.

To achieve indeterminism in the synthetic player's decision-making we can use pseudo-random numbers. Now the computer-issued commands – albeit deterministic – appear to be arbitrary enough. Ideally, the simultaneously run simulations agree on the seed value at the beginning, and then pass on only the commands issued by the human players. Of course a real-world implementation also requires consistency checks and recovery mechanisms in case some input gets lost.

Consider a simple game, Guess a Number. At the beginning each player chooses one number within a given interval. Next, a randomly selected player from the remaining players guesses a number and all the other players that have chosen that number drop out of the game. This is repeated until only one player, the winner, remains. Algorithm 12.4 describes an implementation of this game, where the players can be controlled by either humans or the computer. Moreover, the algorithm can be run in a network, and the execution will be synchronized. The only information that must be distributed among the computers is the human players' input.

Algorithm 12.4 Synchronized simulation for Guess a Number.

GUESS-NUMBER(H, C)

    in: set of human participants H; set of computer participants C
    out: winner w
    constant: minimum number n_{min}; maximum number n_{max}
    local: guessed number g

1: agree on the seed value v with the participating nodes
2: SET-SEED(v)
3: **for all** $h \in H$ **do**
4:    $number(h) \leftarrow$ the chosen number of the human participant h
5: **end for**
6: **for all** $c \in C$ **do**
7:    $number(c) \leftarrow$ RANDOM-INTEGER($n_{min}, n_{max} + 1$)
8: **end for**
9: $P \leftarrow$ **copy** $H \cup C$
10: **repeat**
11:   select $p \in P$ randomly
12:   **if** $p \in H$ **then** $\triangleright$ Human guesses.
13:     $g \leftarrow$ guess from the human participant p
14:   **else** $\triangleright$ Computer guesses.
15:     $g \leftarrow$ RANDOM-INTEGER($n_{min}, n_{max} + 1$)
16:   **end if**
17:   **for all** $q \in P \setminus \{p\}$ **do**
18:    **if** $number(q) = g$ **then**
19:      $P \leftarrow P \setminus \{q\}$
20:    **end if**
21:   **end for**
22: **until** $|P| = 1$
23: $w \leftarrow$ the single value in P
24: **return** w

12.6 Interest Management

The entities usually produce update packets that are relevant only to a minority of the nodes. Therefore, an obvious way to save bandwidth is to disseminate update packets only to those nodes that are interested in them. This *interest management* (IM) includes techniques that allow the nodes to express interest in a subset of relevant information (Benford et al. 2001; Morse et al. 2000). Liu and Theodoropoulos (2014) observe that an IM technique must provide

- filtering precision (i.e. find a minimal set of relevant data),
- runtime efficiency (i.e. minimize the computational overhead), and
- event-capturing ability (i.e. capture and report all the relevant events to ensure consistency).

The approaches to IM can be based on auras (i.e. the entity's spatiality), zones (i.e. the tessellation of the game world into disjoint areas), visibility (i.e. the spatial structures of the game world), or class (i.e. other than spatial attributes of the entity) (Heger 2013; Liu and Theodoropoulos 2014). Boulanger et al. (2006) provide results from a comparison of different IM schemes. With respect to Equation (12.1), IM techniques aim to reduce the average number of messages (M) and bandwidth use (B) per message. This requires more organizing between the nodes, and, consequently, more processing (P).

12.6.1 Aura-based interest management

An aura is an expression of data interest, which usually correlates with the sensing capabilities of the entity being modelled. Simply put, an aura is a subspace where interaction occurs; see Figure 12.18(a). Thus, when two players' auras intersect, they can be mutually aware of each other's actions and should receive update messages from each other. Awareness can be based on senses like seeing or hearing and we can have separate auras for different media (e.g. visual and aural awareness). To simplify computation we can add extents that approximate the actual aura such as bounding boxes.

Figure 12.18 Aura-based interest management. (a) When two entities' auras intersect, they are aware of each other and receive update messages. (b) With focus (dashed areas) and nimbus (grey areas) the awareness need not be symmetric. The grey ship's focus intersects the white ship's nimbus, which means that the grey ship receives update messages from the white ship. Because the white ship's focus does not intersect the grey ship's nimbus, it does not receive update messages from the grey ship.

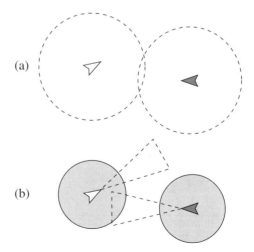

Filtering update messages with auras is always symmetric, but an aura can be divided further into a *focus* and a *nimbus*, where focus represents an observing entity's interest and nimbus an observed entity's wish to be seen in a given medium (Benford et al. 1994; Greenhalgh 1998). Thus, the player's focus must intersect with another player's nimbus in order to be aware of him; see Figure 12.18(b). For example, in hide-and-seek the nimbus of the hiding person could be smaller than that of the seeker, and the seeker cannot interact with the hider. At the same time, the hider can observe the seeker if the seeker's nimbus is larger and intersects the hider's focus.

12.6.2 Zone-based interest management

Zone-based (also called cell-based, grid-based or region-based) interest management tessellates the game world into disjoint zones. This tessellation can be static (i.e. done beforehand and remaining constant) or dynamic (i.e. changing according to the game state). Moreover, the tessellation does not have to be regular, but the zones can follow the topology of the game world (Quax 2007). The players are assigned to the zones, for example, based on their position, so that the zones represent their area of interest (see Figure 12.19). Now, the zones define how messages are propagated in such a way that the players receive only updates related to the zones of interest to them. In other words, zones present an approximation of the player's interest – and, in this way, the aura-based approach can be combined with zones so that an entity is interested in the zones inside its aura (Han et al. 2008).

A natural implementation for zones is to assign each zone to a multicast group of its own. Now, all entities within the zone transmit updates to the corresponding multicast address. Typically entities subscribe to groups corresponding to their own zone and the neighbouring zone. This kind of extrinsic filtering is computationally less intensive, because the receivers of a message are determined merely based on its network attributes (e.g. address). In contrast, the aura-based approach represents intrinsic filtering, which uses the application-specific data content of an update message to determine which nodes need to receive it. This filtering provides fine-grained information delivery, but message processing may require a considerable amount of time.

12.6.3 Visibility-based interest management

Aura- and zone-based interest management can turn out to be excessively crude models, especially for indoor environments with small, confined spaces limiting visibility

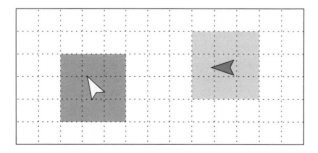

Figure 12.19 In zone-based interest management the entities express interest in their nearby zones.

and, consequently, the need for direct communication. Potentially visible sets provide an approach to analyse the environment and determine cells (e.g. rooms) within it (Airey et al. 1990; Teller and Séquin 1991). All the cells that are visible from a given cell, for example, through openings and portals, form its potentially visible set. An obvious approach now would be to limit the interest of an entity to those entities residing in its corresponding potentially visible set.

The frontier set approach utilizes a similar idea but oppositely to potentially visible sets (Steed and Angus 2005; Steed and Zhu 2008). A frontier defines regions that are guaranteed to be hidden from each other. Let the set C consist of all the cells of interest. For a subset $B \subseteq C$, function $s(B)$ gives a set of cells that can be seen from any of the cells in B:

$$s(B) = \{c \mid c \in C \land (c \text{ can be seen from some cell in } B)\}.$$

Suppose we are interested in the relationship of cells $a \in C$ and $b \in C$. A frontier of these two cells is a pair of sets $F_{a \to b} \subseteq C$ and $F_{b \to a} \subseteq C$ which mutually have the following property:

$$\begin{cases} F_{a \to b} \cap s(F_{b \to a}) = \varnothing \\ s(F_{a \to b}) \cap F_{b \to a} = \varnothing. \end{cases}$$

That is, for any cell $d \in F_{a \to b}$, that particular d cannot be seen from any of the cells in $F_{b \to a}$ and for any cell $e \in F_{b \to a}$, that e cannot be seen from any of the cells in $F_{a \to b}$. Clearly, the sets $F_{a \to b}$ and $F_{b \to a}$ are disjoint. Also, if the cells a and b have a line of sight, the frontier sets are empty. This means that as long as entity e_1 resides in $F_{a \to b}$ and entity e_2 resides in $F_{b \to a}$, they cannot see one another and need not exchange any updates (see Figure 12.20). The frontier sets can be created beforehand as they usually stay static throughout the game – unless it is possible to create new openings in the game world.

12.6.4 Class-based interest management

Whereas the previous approaches emphasize spatiality, interest management can also be based on other characteristics of the entities. For example, we can utilize the visual limitations of the players to reduce the set of interesting entities. As humans can only focus on a small number of objects at once, we can try to detect where the player's attention is focused and only send updates from those entities. The downside is that the player's interest changes often, which means that this set of entities of interest must also change frequently. For the entities outside the focus, it is enough to send rudimentary information and their state can be extrapolated.

For example, Bharambe et al. (2008) limit the size of the interest set to five entities. To rank the entities of interest they measure proximity (i.e. players are more likely to pay attention to nearby entities), aim (i.e. players are more likely to pay attention to entities they are aiming at) and recency of interaction (i.e. players are more likely to pay attention to entities that they have recently interacted with). When combining these metrics it is important to also consider the player's state to set the corresponding weights. For instance, a player with a mêlée weapon typically focuses more on nearby entities, whereas the attention of a player with a ranged weapon is on more distant entities.

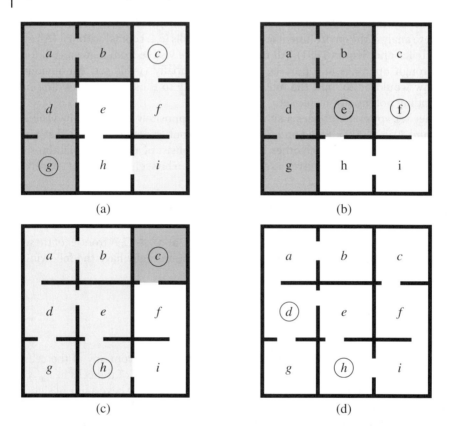

Figure 12.20 Examples of frontier sets. (a) The players are in cells c and g and the frontier sets are $F_{c \to g} = \{c, f, i\}$ and $F_{g \to c} = \{a, b, d, g\}$. The cells e and h do not belong to the frontier: if $e \in F_{g \to c}$ it could be seen from $i \in F_{c \to g}$, and similarly for the case $h \in F_{c \to g}$. (b) The players are in cells e and f and the frontier sets are $F_{e \to f} = \{a, b, d, e, g\}$ and $F_{f \to e} = \{c, f\}$. (c) The players are in cells c and h and the frontier sets are $F_{c \to h} = \{c\}$ and $F_{h \to c} = \{a, b, d, e, g, h\}$. (d) The players are in cells d and h and can possibly see one another; the frontier sets are $F_{d \to h} = \varnothing$ and $F_{h \to d} = \varnothing$.

12.7 Compensation by Game Design

Achieving real-time responses is a major hurdle, for example, for mobile platforms, because of their limited processing power, memory capacity, display capabilities, and communication channels. In particular, the resources for handling the network communication impose restrictions on real-time communication, which the application cannot overcome and which must be considered in the game design. Although we can wait and hope for improvements in the underlying technology, we can take a more proactive view and use game design as a way of reducing communication requirements (Smed and Hakonen 2006).

Real-time communication is not the only method to allow multiple players to participate in a game simultaneously. For example, the oldest form of non-real-time multiplaying, dating back from the 1970s, is a high-score list which provides an after-game place for the players to meet and compete by comparing their results. It is still a viable form of interaction, and the competition can be distributed so that the participants provide their results which are then compiled to form the final standings.

Let us look the three game design concepts, which are based on different levels of decision-making: operational, tactical and strategic (see Section 9.1.1, p. 190). These correspond to the time span and abstractness of the decisions: operational decisions are concrete and frequently issued commands, tactical decisions comprise instructions aimed at a given situation, and strategic decisions focus on long-term planning. For each concept, we outline how light-weight communication can be used so that the game still remains enjoyable for everyone to play.

12.7.1   Short active turns

The simplest way to achieve interaction is to serialize the game events so that each player has a turn when it comes to making decisions. Thus, in a turn-based game the players have active turns followed by passive turns where they are observing the game progress. If the player's decisions are carried out immediately, this active turn cannot be too long so that all the players have an equal chance to interact and the waiting times remain reasonable. Whereas the active turns matter most to the player, we should smooth out their difference with respect to the passive ones. This means that the game design should make the players also find the compulsory passive turns interesting and captivating.

Figure 12.21 illustrates how the gameplay works. Each turn has a predefined length. When the active player is taking a turn, the passive players can view statistics, prepare for their turn, or customize the presentation of the game content (e.g. the type of filler material shown). When the active player has completed her turn, she can watch a replay or post-turn animation or get comments from the coach. Meanwhile, the relevant data are transferred to the other players, who can then render it. There is no need for a server, but the communication can be based on a peer-to-peer architecture. However, joining requires a way to handle the participation management so that the players can connect with one another.

The main requirement for such a game design is that the player's operational decisions are made within short time intervals (i.e. active turns). Natural candidates for this kind of a game are certain fast-paced and turn-taking-based sports events such as javelin, long jump, ski jumping, and darts. Such games also retain the excitement in the passive turns, because it is interesting to watch and anticipate other players' turns. Moreover, this makes it easy to generate relevant filler material (e.g. statistics or slow motion replays) to be shown during the passive turns.

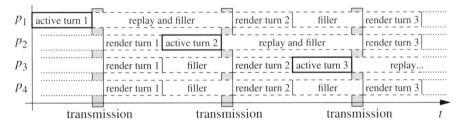

Figure 12.21 Each player has a short active turn followed by passive turns in which the other players take their turn.

Figure 12.22 Players p_1, p_2 and p_3 issue tactical instructions to the corresponding avatars a_1, a_2 and a_3.

12.7.2 Semi-autonomous avatars

Instead of operational commands, we can raise the abstraction level to tactical commands, which means that they are not so time-sensitive. This demonstrates the idea of compensating communication with computation. Let us elaborate by using a simple shooter as an example. Rather than giving commands like 'move forward', 'turn left' or 'shoot', which require prompt communication, the avatars can be semi-autonomous, with the players giving them tactical instructions such as 'attack', 'flee' or 'guard' (see Figure 12.22). The avatars then carry out these tactics the best they can. However, their response is not immediate and the outcome can be something other than the player expected. This resembles the characters of *The Sims*, which have limited free will to carry out the player's commands.

Semi-autonomous avatars provide a way to realize light-weight communication in a client–server architecture. The players (i.e. clients) send tactical commands to the server, which updates the situation and returns the game events. High latency can be compensated by slowing down the pace of the game or by gathering the commands of a certain period and issuing them simultaneously like the SMS television games (Seppänen 2003). Because the computational burden now lies in the server, we can even allow the players to code the operational level logic themselves as in *Core War* (Dewdney 1984) or *AIsHockey* (Smed et al. 2003a).

To summarize, this concept requires the game design to have a clear separation between the tactical and operational level. In order to have intelligent avatars the game world should be non-complex (e.g. a limited arena) or the set of actions in the tactical level should be limited. For example, team sports games provide natural command interfaces that accept tactical commands like 'attack on the right side', 'defence go forward', or 'increase pressure'.

12.7.3 Interaction via proxies

The gameplay at the strategic level does not require the participating players to be present at the same time. The players can set proxies that later on interact with other players on their behalf, and, conversely, they encounter proxies set by other players. For example, the bone files of *NetHack* allow the player to interact with the ghost of another player, who has died earlier at that level. The ghost then acts as a proxy for the deceased player, but that player himself does not interact with the active player. In addition to fully autonomous avatars, the proxies can be game entities (e.g. mechanistic objects or gizmos) and can even include programmable parts.

As an example, let us introduce a novel game called Entrappers (see Figure 12.23). The game comprises levels generated and stored in a server. When a player enters a level, she gets either a computer-generated or previously stored level. A stored level can contain traps set by previous players (i.e. the traps act as their proxies). The player is alone in the

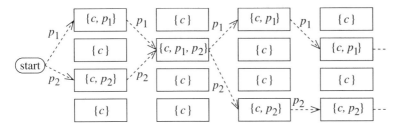

Figure 12.23 A level layout for the game Entrappers. The columns represent level alternatives for a player. The arrows indicate the routes already taken by players p_1 and p_2. Inside each level are traps set by the computer (c) or the players.

level and only when she exits is the level – containing the possible modifications and new traps she has set – stored back in the server. The player is credited immediately with clearing the level and indirectly over time when somebody else falls into a trap set by her.

This concept requires the game design to allow unrestricted play time for the players (i.e. they can join and leave whenever they want and the rewards are collected over time). Moreover, the gameplay lacks immediate human interaction, which also restricts the game design. However, from these restrictions it follows that we can implement a form of light-weight communication that allows games to be organized with massively multiple players.

12.8   Summary

The basic idea of compensation techniques is to replace communication with computation. If we want to reduce network traffic, we can do so at the cost of processing power: in dead reckoning we compute predictions and correct them, in synchronized simulation we re-create the deterministic events, and in interest management we select to whom to send the updates.

The compensation techniques address two aspects: the consistency–responsiveness dichotomy and scalability. To balance consistency and responsiveness we must choose which is more important to us, because one can be achieved only by sacrificing the other. In computer games, unlike many other networked applications, we may have to give up the consistency requirement to get better responsiveness. Scalability is about dividing the resources among multiple participants, whether they are human or synthetic players. It begs the questions which parts of the program can be run in serial or parallel and what is the communication capacity of the chosen communication architecture.

Dead reckoning and local perception filters provide more responsiveness by sacrificing consistency, whereas synchronized simulation retains consistency at the cost of responsiveness and scalability. Interest management aims to provide scalability, but managing the entities' interests reduces the responsiveness as well as introducing inconsistencies among the nodes. Despite all these compensation methods, the fact remains that whatever we do we cannot completely hide the resource limitations – but if we are lucky, we can select the places where they occur so that the nuisance they cause is tolerable.

Savery (2014) presents experimental results for different compensation methods. The consistency metrics used include

- state divergence (i.e. how consistent the players' views are),
- propagation delay (i.e. the time from one player performing an action to the other player perceiving it),
- corrections (i.e. the number and magnitude of modifications required to repair incorrect state information),
- response time (i.e. the time from performing an action to seeing it), and
- animation delay (i.e. the rate of on-screen updates).

The test results indicate that dead reckoning has the best overall balance between the metrics and works well if modest divergence and occasional corrections are allowed. The worst case for dead reckoning is if the avatar can have erratic movements that are hard to predict (which is quite typical in first-person shooter games). Synchronized simulation is a good choice if the game has low state divergence, which requires few corrections (e.g. real-time strategy games where the player's control is indirect). The biggest downside is in the growing response time which starts hindering the playing experience. The LPF performs poorly on state divergence but really well on corrections. It is recommended if the game requires fast response and players seeing the same things (although displaced in time).

Although we cannot escape technical limitations, we can change the resource requirements by altering the game design cleverly. By considering the different decision-making levels we can steer the game design so that it is possible to combine the need for multiplayer support with light-weight communication.

Exercises

12-1 If we decide to send update messages less often and include several updates to each message, what does this mean in the light of Equation (12.1)? What if we send the messages to only those who are really interested in receiving them?

12-2 Why is processing power included in the network resource limitations?

12-3 Suppose you have 12 computers with equal processing and networking capabilities. You can freely arrange and cable them in a peer-to-peer, client–server or server-network (e.g. three servers connected peer-to-peer with three clients each) architecture. With respect to Equation (12.1), compare the resource requirements of these communication architectures. Then consider how realizable are they on the Internet.

12-4 To achieve consistency the players have to reach an agreement on the game state. However, this opens the door to distributed consensus problems. Let us look at one of them, called the two-generals problem. Two generals have to agree whether to attack a target. They have couriers carrying messages to and fro, but the message delivery is unreliable. Is it possible for them to be sure that they have an agreement on what do? For a further discussion on consensus problems, see Lamport and Lynch (1990).

12-5 Why is it that we can have sublinear communication? What are the results of using it?

12-6 The game world can be parallelized by zoning (i.e. dividing it into zones and assigning a server to each zone) or instancing (i.e. creating copies of certain areas which run in parallel in separate servers). Observe massive multiplayer online games and determine which approach they are using. Is the game genre or the game design reflected in the approach chosen?

12-7 Assume that we are sending update messages about the three-dimensional position (x, y, z) to other players. The coordinates are expressed using 32 bits, but the actual changes are of magnitude $[-10, +10]$. To have more bandwidth, how would you compress this network traffic?

12-8 Assume that we have a centralized architecture, where all players report their coordinates to a server. Explain how timeout-based and quorum-based message aggregations work in such an environment. Assume we have 12 players, and their update interval ranges from 0.1 to 3 seconds. Which approach would be recommended?

12-9 Consider the following entities. How easy or difficult is it to predict their future position in 1 second, in 5 seconds, and in 1 minute?
(a) A rabbit
(b) A human being
(c) A sports car
(d) A jeep
(e) An aeroplane.

12-10 Why does a first-order polynomial (e.g. velocity) give better predictions, if the second-order derivative (e.g. acceleration) is small or substantial?

12-11 If we do not use a convergence technique, the game character can 'warp', for example, through a wall. Does a convergence technique remove visually impossible moves?

12-12 Compare dead reckoning and local perception filters by considering their visual and temporal fidelities.

12-13 What other possibilities are there to define the temporal contour? What would be a theoretically ideal temporal contour?

12-14 In *Pong* two players at opposite ends try to hit with a paddle a ball bouncing between them. How can we use local perception filters to hide communication delays between the players?

12-15 One way to hide technical limitations is to incorporate them as a part of the game design. Instead of hiding communication delays, local perception filters could be used to include temporal distortions. Devise a game design that does so.

12-16 In local perception filters, a critical proximity is the distance between players when interaction using entities becomes impossible. Assume that we are using linear temporal contours. Define the critical proximity using the terms of Section 12.4.

12-17 The bullet time effect opens the door to temporal cheating. Consider the situation in which players s, n and t stand in line. Player s shoots at t, who cannot use bullet time. What happens if player n, who is between s and t, uses the bullet time effect?

12-18 Assume we have a game that uses synchronized simulation. If we want to extend the game by including new players, which will become the limiting factor first: the number of human players or the number of synthetic players?

12-19 Interest management reduces update messages between entities that are not aware of one another. Can this lead to problems with consistency?

12-20 In order to use auras, foci and nimbi a entity has to be at least aware of the existence of other entities. How can you implement this? (Hint: First select a suitable communication architecture.)

12-21 Devise an algorithm for assigning frontier sets (see Figure 12.20).

12-22 Take an operational-level game (e.g. a first-person shooter) and redesign it to use semi-autonomous avatars. What tactical commands would the player issue? Would the game be still playable? What would be the effect on network communication?

12-23 Implement the game Entrappers (see p. 284 and Figure 12.23).

13

Cheating Prevention

There are many reasons why a player might feel motivated to cheat and, as in real life, any player can turn into a cheat if the rewards are large enough and the risk of getting caught is small. Common motivations for cheating are (Consalvo 2007)

- lack of skill or time (i.e. the player cheats to overcome a part of the game which is too difficult or time-consuming),
- money (i.e. the player cheats to win prize money or to create virtual assets to trade with real-world money),
- boredom (i.e. the player wants to skip uninteresting content),
- fun (i.e. the player gets entertainment from cheating),
- causing havoc (i.e. the player cheats to ruin the other players' game experience),
- experimentation and exploration (i.e. the player wants to find out all the content and secret areas),
- extending the life span of the game (i.e. the player wants to continue to play after the original content is finished),
- creativity (i.e. the player cheats to create new experiences such as mods or total conversions),
- non-conformity (i.e. the player seeks to do forbidden things or rebel against authority), and
- fame (i.e. the player seeks recognition and prestige by cheating to win the game or from inventing a way to cheat).

Sometimes even the concept of cheating can have different definitions from player to player: for some players even using hints constitutes cheating, whereas for others anything goes.

As online gaming has grown into a lucrative business, greed has become a driving force behind cheating. Cheating occurs because of the financial gain from selling virtual assets (e.g. special items or ready-made game characters). Naturally, potential financial losses, caused directly or indirectly by cheats, are a major concern among online gaming sites and the main motivation to implement countermeasures against cheating. On the other hand, game sites can sometimes even postpone fixing detected cheating problems, because the possibility of cheating can attract players to participate in the game.

For many games, the end user licence agreement and terms of service often contain clauses that prohibit cheating. Moreover, to make enforcement possible they may also include invasive clauses whereby the player agrees to be monitored (e.g. with the help of spyware). For example, *World of Warcraft* searches the process list of the host computer

Algorithms and Networking for Computer Games, Second Edition. Jouni Smed and Harri Hakonen.
© 2017 John Wiley & Sons Ltd. Published 2017 by John Wiley & Sons Ltd.

for known ways of cheating and sends the data back to Blizzard. Game companies' stance on cheating varies, but the usual punishment involves blocking or banning the cheating client. Legal action is the final form of cheat prevention. However, legislation is often intended to prevent piracy and is ill-suited to cheating prevention.

Cheating prevention has three distinct goals (Smed et al. 2002; Yan and Choi 2002):

- to protect sensitive information,
- to provide a level playing field, and
- to uphold a sense of justice inside the game world.

Each of these goals can be viewed from a technical or social perspective. Sensitive information (e.g. players' accounts) can be accessed, for instance, by cracking passwords or by pretending to be an administrator and asking players to give their passwords (Watte 2008). A level playing field can be compromised, for instance, by tampering with the network traffic or by colluding with other players. The sense of justice can be violated, for instance, by abusing inexperienced and ill-equipped players or by ganging up and controlling parts of the game world.

In this chapter we look at different ways to cheat in online multiplayer games and review some algorithmic countermeasures that aim to prevent them.

13.1 Technical Exploitations

In a networked multiplayer game, a cheat can attack the clients, the servers, or the network connecting them. Figure 13.1 illustrates typical types of attack (Hoglund and McCraw 2007; Kirmse and Kirmse 1997). On the client side, the attack can take place over the client (e.g. using macros or triggering keyboard events for control and reading pixel values from the user interface), under the client (e.g. hacking a driver to access the video memory or tampering with the network traffic), or in the client (e.g. altering the code in the client's memory). Game servers are vulnerable to network attacks as well as physical attacks such as theft or vandalism. Third-party attacks on clients or servers include IP spoofing (e.g. intercepting packets and replacing them with forged ones) and denial-of-service attacks (e.g. blocking networking of some player so that he gets

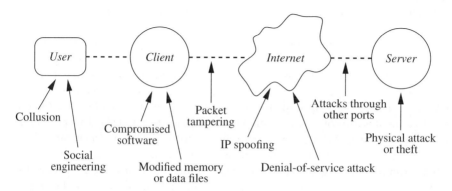

Figure 13.1 Typical attacks in a networked multiplayer game.

dropped from the game). In the following we review common technical exploitations used in online cheating – but it is worth remembering that sometimes the player can be the weakest link against attacks such as collusion (see Section 13.2) or social engineering.

13.1.1   Packet tampering

In first-person shooter games, a usual way to cheat is to enhance the player's reactions with *reflex augmentation* (Kirmse 2000). For example, an aiming proxy can monitor the network traffic and keep a record of the opponents' positions. When the cheat fires, the proxy uses this information and sends additional rotation and movement control packets before the fire command, thus improving the aim. Alternatively, in *packet inter-ception* the proxy prevents certain packets from reaching the cheat. For example, if the packets containing damage information are suppressed, the cheat becomes invulnera-ble. In a *packet replay* attack, the same packet is sent repeatedly. For example, if a weapon can be fired only once per second, the cheat might send the fire command packet a hun-dred times a second to boost its firing rate.

A common method for breaking the control protocol is to change bytes in a packet and observe the effects. A straightforward way to prevent this is to use checksums. For this purpose, we can use message-digest algorithms, which are one-way functions that transform a message of any length into a constant length message digest (or fingerprint). These algorithms are used to guarantee the integrity of the data as follows. A sender cre-ates a message and computes its message digest. The message digest (possibly encrypted with the sender's private key or receiver's public key) is attached to the message, and the whole message is sent to a receiver. The receiver extracts the message digest (possibly decrypting it), computes the message digest for the remaining message, and compares both message digests.

Preferably, no one should be able – or at least it should be computationally infeasible – to produce two messages having the same message digest or to produce the original message from a given message digest. However, a digest algorithm has the weakness that if two messages A and B have the same message digest, it cannot authenticate which is the original message. If a cheat can find two messages that produce the same message digest, she could use a collision attack. For example, in algorithm MD5 developed by R.L. Rivest (1992), producing digests of length 128 bits, it is possible even to append the same payload P to both messages M and N ($M \neq N$) so that the message digests remain the same (i.e. MD5($M \parallel P$) = MD5($N \parallel P$)). For this reason, MD5 can be used to detect accidental corruptions but not intentional ones (Wang and Yu 2005).

There are two weaknesses that cannot be prevented with checksums alone: a cheat can reverse-engineer the checksum algorithm or can mount an attack with packet replay. If the command packets are encrypted, the cheat has less chance of recording and forging information. However, preventing a packet replay attack requires that the packets carry some state information so that even packets with a similar payload appear to be different. Instead of serial numbering, pseudo-random numbers, discussed in Section 2.1, provide a better alternative. Random numbers can also be used to modify the packets so that even identical packets do not appear the same. Dissimilarity can be further induced by adding a variable amount of junk data to the packets, which eliminates the possibility of analysing their contents by size.

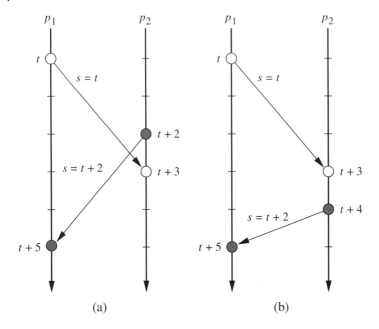

(a)   (b)

Figure 13.2 Assume the senders must time-stamp (i.e. include the value s in) their outgoing messages, and the latency between the players is 3 time units. (a) If both players are fair, p_1 can be sure that the message from p_2, which has the time-stamp $t + 2$, was sent before the message issued at t has arrived. (b) If p_2 has a latency of 1 time unit but pretends that it is 3, look-ahead cheating using forged time-stamps allows p_2 to base decisions on information that it should not have.

13.1.2   Look-ahead cheating

In peer-to-peer architecture, all nodes uphold the game state, and the players' time-stamped actions must be conveyed to all nodes. This opens up the possibility of look-ahead cheating, where the cheat gains an unfair advantage by delaying his actions – as if he had a high latency – to see what the other players do before choosing his action. The cheat then forges the time-stamped packets so that they seem to be issued before they actually were (see Figure 13.2). To prevent this we review two methods: the lockstep protocol and active objects.

Lockstep protocol

The lockstep protocol tackles the problem by requiring that each player first announces a commitment to an action; when everyone has received the commitments, the players reveal their actions, which can then be checked against the original commitments (Baughman and Levine 2001). The commitment must meet two requirements: it cannot be used to infer the action, but it should be easy to compare whether an action corresponds to a commitment. An obvious choice for constructing the commitments is to calculate a hash value for the action.

Algorithm 13.1 describes an implementation of the lockstep protocol, which uses the auxiliary functions introduced in Algorithm 13.2. The details of the function HASH are omitted, but hints for its implementation can be found in Knuth (1998c, Section 6.4).

Algorithm 13.1 Lockstep protocol.

LOCKSTEP(ℓ, a, P)
   in: local player ℓ; action a; set of remote players P
   out: set of players' actions R
   local: commitment C; action A; set of commitments S
   1: $C \leftarrow \langle \ell, \text{HASH}(a) \rangle$
   2: SEND-ALL(C, P)   ▷ Announce commitment.
   3: $S \leftarrow \{C\}$
   4: $S \leftarrow S \cup \text{RECEIVE-ALL}(P)$ ▷ Get other players' commitments.
   5: SYNCHRONIZE(P)   ▷ Wait until everyone is ready.
   6: $A \leftarrow \langle \ell, a \rangle$
   7: SEND-ALL(A, P)   ▷ Announce action.
   8: $R \leftarrow \{A\}$
   9: $R \leftarrow R \cup \text{RECEIVE-ALL}(P)$ ▷ Get other players' actions.
  10: **for all** $A \in R$ **do**
  11:   $C \leftarrow$ the commitment $C' \in S$ for which $C'_0 = A_0$
  12:   **if** $C_1 \neq \text{HASH}(A_1)$ **then**   ▷ Are commitment and action different?
  13:     **error** player A_0 cheats
  14:   **end if**
  15: **end for**
  16: **return** R

It is evident that the game progresses at the pace of the slowest player because of the synchronization. This may be suitable for a turn-based game, which is not time-critical, but if we want to use the lockstep protocol in a real-time game, the turns have to be short or there has to be a time limit within which a player must announce the action or pass that turn altogether.

To overcome this drawback, we can use an *asynchronous lockstep protocol*, where each player advances in time asynchronously from the other players but enters into a lockstep mode whenever interaction is required. The mode is defined by a sphere of influence surrounding each player, which outlines the game world that can possibly be affected by a player at the next turn (or subsequent turns). If two players' spheres of influence do not intersect, they cannot affect each other at the next turn, and hence their decisions will not affect each other when the next game state is computed and they can proceed asynchronously.

In the *pipelined lockstep protocol*, synchronization is loosened by having a buffer of size p in which the incoming commitments are stored (Lee et al. 2002); in basic lockstep, $p = 1$. Instead of synchronizing at each turn, the players can send several commitments, which are pipelined, before the corresponding opponents' commitments are received. In other words, when player i has received the commitments C_n^j of all other players j for time frame n, she announces her action A_n^i (see Figure 13.3). The pipeline may include commitments for the frames $n, \ldots, (n + p - 1)$, when player i can announce commitments $C_n^i, \ldots, C_{n+p-1}^i$ before having to announce action A_n^i. However, this opens up the possibility of reintroducing look-ahead cheating. If a player announces her action

---

Algorithm 13.2 Auxiliary methods for the lockstep protocol.

SEND-ALL(m, R)
  in: message m; set of recipients R
  1: **for all** $r \in R$ **do**
  2:   send m to r
  3: **end for**

RECEIVE-ALL(S)
  in: set of senders S
  out: set of messages M
  1: $M \leftarrow \varnothing$
  2: **for all** $s \in S$ **do**
  3:   $received(s) \leftarrow$ FALSE
  4: **end for**
  5: **repeat**
  6:   receive message m from $s \in S$
  7:   $received(s) \leftarrow$ TRUE
  8:   $M \leftarrow M \cup \{m\}$
  9: **until** $\forall s \in S : received(s)$
 10: **return** M

SYNCHRONIZE(H)
  in: set of remote hosts H
  1: SEND-ALL($\varnothing$, H)
  2: RECEIVE-ALL(H)

---

earlier than required by the protocol, the other players can change both their commitments and actions based on that knowledge. This can be counteracted with an *adaptive pipeline protocol*, where the idea is to measure the actual latencies between the players and to grow or shrink the pipeline size accordingly (Cronin et al. 2003).

Active objects

The lockstep protocol requires the players to send two transmissions – one for the commitment and one for the action – at each turn. Let us now address the question whether we can use only one transmission and still detect look-ahead cheating. A single transmission means that the action must be included in the outgoing message, but the receiver is allowed to view it only after he has replied with his own action. But this leaves open the question how a player can make sure that the exchange of messages in another player's computer has not been compromised. It is possible that he is a cheat who intercepts and alters the outgoing messages or has hacked the communication system.

We can use active objects to secure the exchange of messages which happens in a possibly 'hostile' environment (Smed and Hakonen 2005a). Now the player (or the originator) provides an active object, a *delegate*, which includes program code to be run by

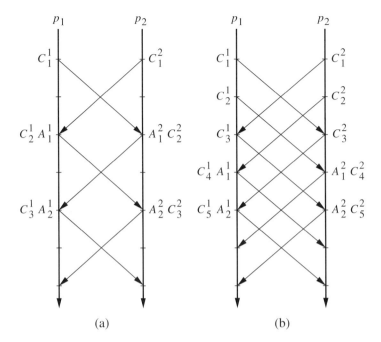

Figure 13.3 Lockstep and pipeline lockstep protocols. (a) The lockstep protocol synchronizes after each turn and waits until everybody has received all commitments. (b) The pipelined lockstep protocol has a fixed size buffer (here the size is 3), which holds several commitments.

the other player (or the host). The delegate then acts as a trusted party for the originator by guaranteeing the message exchange in the host's system.

Let us illustrate the idea using the game rock–paper–scissors as an example. Player p goes through the following stages:

(i) Player p decides on the action 'paper', puts this message inside a box and locks it. The key to the box can be generated by the delegate of player p at player r's end, since p's delegate has been sent beforehand to player r.

(ii) Player p gives the box to the delegate of player r, which closes it inside another box before sending it to player r. Thus, when the message is sent out from the delegate, player p cannot tamper with its contents.

(iii) Once the double-boxed message has been sent, the delegate of player r generates a key and gives it to player p. This key will open the box enclosing the incoming message from player r.

(iv) When player p receives a double-boxed message originating from player r, he can open the outer box, closed by his own delegate, and the inner box using the key he received from the delegate of player r.

(v) Player p can now view the action of player r.

At the same time, player r goes through the following stages:

(i) Player r receives a box from player p. She can open the outer box, closed by her own delegate, but not the inner box.

   (ii) To get the key to the inner box, player r must inform the delegate of player p of her action. Player r chooses 'rock', puts it in a box and passes it to the delegate.

  (iii) When the message has been sent, player r receives the key to the inner box from the delegate of player p.

  (iv) Player r can now view the action of player p.

Although we can trust, at least to some extent, our delegates, there still remain two problems to be solved. First, the delegate must ensure that it really has a connection to its originator, which seems to incur extra talk-back communication. Second, although we have secured one-to-one exchange of messages, there is no guarantee that the player does not alter its action when it sends a message to a third player.

Let us tackle first the problem of ensuring the communication channel. Ideally, the delegate, once started, should contact the originator and convey a unique identification of itself. This identification should be a combination of dynamic information (e.g. the memory address where the delegate is located or the system time when the delegate was created) and static information (e.g. a built-in identification number or the Internet address of the node where the delegate is being run). Dynamic information is needed to prevent a cheating host from creating a copy of the delegate and using that as a surrogate to work out how it operates. Static information helps ensure that the delegate has not been moved somewhere else or replaced after the communication check.

If we could trust the run environment where the delegate resides, there would be no need to do any check-ups at all. On the other hand, in a completely hostile environment we would have to ensure the communication channel every time, and there would be no improvement over the lockstep protocol. To reduce the number of check-up messages the delegate can initiate them randomly with some parameterized probability. In practice, this probability can be relatively low – especially if the number of turns in the game is high. Rather than detecting attempts to cheat, this incurs a threat of being detected: although a player can get away with cheating, in the long run attempts to cheat are likely to be noticed. Moreover, as the number of participating players increases, so also does the possibility of getting caught.

A similar approach helps us to solve the problem of preventing a player from sending differing actions to the other players. Rather than detecting an inconsistent action in the current turn, the players can 'gossip' among themselves about the actions taken in the previous turns. The information exchanged can then be compared with the recorded actions from the previous turns, and any discrepancy indicates that somebody has cheated. Although the gossip can comprise all earlier actions, it is enough to include only a small, randomly chosen subset of them – especially if the number of participants is high. This gossiping does not require any extra transmissions because it can be piggy-backed in the ordinary messages. Naturally, a cheat can send a false gossip about other players, which means that if the action and the gossip differ, the veridicality of the gossip has to be confirmed (e.g. by asking randomly selected players).

Other approaches

Mogaki et al. (2007) present a cheating-prevention protocol, which uses time-stamp servers, that would minimize the latency to the actual delay between the players. Each player sends the action to the other players and a hash of the action to the time-stamp server, which returns the hash signed with a time-stamp and serial number. These hashes and signatures are then used to verify the actions after the game is over. The proposed protocol, however, makes two strong assumptions: there must be time-stamp servers near every player, and there cannot be any communication breakdowns.

Ferretti (2008) proposes a method for detecting look-ahead cheating, where we have one trusted player p_ℓ amongst the participants. This trusted player can check whether player p_i is cheating by artificially increasing the delay of the outgoing messages from p_ℓ to p_i and observing the delays from p_i to p_ℓ. If player p_i is not cheating, the delays should not change, whereas if p_i is using look-ahead cheating, the response delays will increase as the artificial delay increases.

13.1.3 Cracking and other attacks

Networking is not the only target for attacks, but the cheat can affect the game through the software or even through the hardware (Pritchard 2000). Cracked client software may allow the cheat to gain access to the replicated, hidden game data (e.g. the status of other players). On the surface, this kind of passive cheating does not tamper with the network traffic, but the cheat can base her decisions on more accurate knowledge than she is supposed to have. For example, typical exposed data in real-time strategy games are the variables controlling the visible area on the screen (i.e. the fog of war). This problem is also common in first-person shooters where, for instance, a compromised graphics rendering driver may allow the player to see through walls.

Strictly speaking, these information exposure problems stem from the software and cannot be prevented with networking alone. Clearly, the sensitive data should be encoded and its location in the memory should be hard to detect. Nevertheless, it is always susceptible to ingenious hackers and, therefore, requires some additional countermeasures. In a centralized architecture, an obvious solution is to utilize the server, which can check whether a client issuing a command is actually aware of the object with which it is operating. For example, if a player has not seen the opponent's base, he cannot give an order to attack it – unless he is cheating. When the server detects cheating, it can drop the cheating client. A democratized version of the same method can be applied in a replicated architecture: every node checks the validity of every other node's commands (e.g. by using gossiping as in Section 13.1.2), and if some discrepancy is detected, the nodes vote on whether its source should be debarred from participating in the game. In addition, hardware-based methods (Feng et al. 2008) or behaviour analysis (Laurens et al. 2007) can be used in ensuring that a client is not comprised.

Network traffic and software are not the only vulnerable places in a computer game, but design defects can create loopholes, which cheats are apt to exploit. For example, if the clients are designed to trust each other, the game is unshielded from *client authority abuse*. In that case, a compromised client can exaggerate the damage caused by a cheat, and the rest accept this information as such. Although this problem can be tackled by using checksums to ensure that each client has the same binaries, it is more advisable to alter the design so that the clients can issue command requests, which the server puts into operation. Naturally, this schema can be hybridized or randomized so that only some operations are centralized using some control exchange protocol.

In addition to poor design, distribution – especially the heterogeneity of network environments – can be the source of unexpected behaviour. For instance, there may be features that emerge only when the latency is extremely high or when the server is under a denial-of-service attack (i.e. an attacker sends it a large number of spurious requests).

13.2 Collusion

Many games assume that the players are rivals and, therefore, the rules forbid collusion, where two or more opposing players cooperate covertly towards a common goal. Imperfect information games, where each player has access only to a limited amount of information, especially forbid collusion by sharing information. For example, in poker the judgements are based on the player's ability to infer information from the bets, thus outwitting the opponents. If the players are physically present, it is easier to detect any attempts at collusion (e.g. coughs, hand signals, or coded language). For example, in bridge all attempts to collude are monitored by the other players as well as the judges. However, the anonymity of multiplayer online games makes collusion detection a difficult problem.

The colluders can share knowledge or resources among themselves, which means that collusion can take many forms. Cooperating players can engage in soft play and refrain from attacking one another. A gang of players can ambush and rob other players in a role-playing game. A novice chess player can resort to an expert – human or computer program – to make better moves. Participants in a tournament can pre-arrange the outcome of their matches to eliminate other players. Players belonging to the same clan can send numerous and apparently independent complaints to the administrator to get an innocent player banned. A friend participating as a spectator in a first-person shooter game can scout the arena and reveal the location of the enemy.

The terms and rules of an online poker site usually stipulate that anyone attempting to collude will be permanently prohibited from using the services provided by the site and their account will be terminated immediately. Collusion detection is mainly based on investigating complaints from other players, although some sites use methods for analysing the game data to find play patterns typical of collusion. Poker players can collude in two ways. In active collusion, colluding players play more aggressively than they normally would (e.g. outbet non-colluding players). In passive collusion, colluding players play more cautiously than they normally would (e.g. only the one with the strongest hand continues while the others fold). Active collusion can be detected afterwards by analysing the game data, but it is next to impossible to discern passive collusion from cautious normal play (Johansson et al. 2003).

Collusion also applies to other types of games, because a gang of cooperating players can share information that they normally would not have or they can ambush and rob other players. It is also possible in tournaments, and the type of tournament dictates how effective it can be (Murdoch and Zieliński 2004). For example, in a scoring tournament colluding players play normally against other players and agree who is going to win the match where they face one another and score more points (see Table 13.1). In a

	p	c_0	c_1
p	—	draw	draw
c_0	draw	—	c_0
c_1	draw	c_0	—

Table 13.1 Winners in a scoring tournament, where all players have equal strength and play optimally. If players c_0 and c_1 collude so that c_0 always wins, player c_0 scores more points than a non-colluding player.

hill-climbing tournament, colluding players can gain benefit by affecting the result of initial matches (see Figure 13.4).

Collusion in games has been studied mainly in card games (Johansson et al. 2003; Mazrooei et al. 2013; Vallvè-Guionnet 2005; Yampolskiy 2007, 2008; Yan 2010), bridge (Yan 2003), first-person shooters (Laasonen and Smed 2015; Laasonen et al. 2011; VanderKnyff et al. 2009), soft play (Islam et al. 2009; Palshikar and Apte 2008), and anti-communities (Chen et al. 2013, 2014; Yu and Chen 2013). Outside the field of computer games collusion has been addressed in multiple choice examinations (Ercole et al. 2002), covert communication channels (Zander et al. 2008), stock market trading (Palshikar and Apte 2008), grid computing (Staab and Engel 2009), social moderation (Lou et al. 2009) and spectrum auctions (Zhou and Zheng 2010).

13.2.1 Classification

Let us look at the types of collusion in which the cheating players can engage. Cheating players use collusion to encourage the non-colluding players to misjudge a game situation and even overreact in it. Typically, there are two styles of play: in active style the colluders play aggressively and in passive style they are more cautious than normally. These styles can change during the game flow and also swapped between the colluders. The colluders gain the advantage by recognizing who should play in what style and when.

When players decide to collude, they make an agreement on the terms of collusion (Smed et al. 2006). This agreement has four components:

Consent How do the players agree on collusion?
- *Express collusion.* The colluders make an explicit hidden agreement on cooperation before or during the game.
- *Tacit collusion.* The colluders have made no agreement but act towards a mutually beneficial goal (e.g. try to force the weakest player out of the game).

Scope What areas of the game will the collusion affect?
- *Total collusion.* The colluders cooperate in all areas of the game.
- *Partial collusion.* The colluders cooperate only in certain areas and compete in others (e.g. sharing resource pools but competing elsewhere).

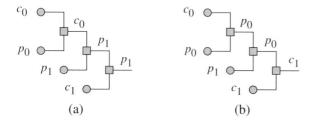

Figure 13.4 Collusion in a hill-climbing tournament, where c_0 and c_1 can win against p_0, p_0 can win against p_1, and p_1 can win against c_0 and c_1. (a) If everyone plays normally, p_1 wins the tournament. (b) If players c_0 and c_1 collude, c_0 can deliberately lose his match so that c_1 will get an easier opponent later in the tournament.

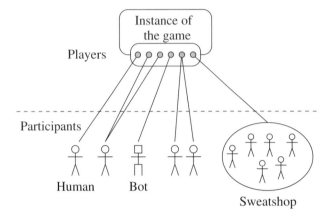

Players

Participants

Human   Bot

Sweatshop

Figure 13.5 Players and participants are the partakers of a game. The relationship is usually assumed to be one-to-one, but one human participant can control two or more players, a player can be controlled by a computer program (i.e. a bot), or two or more participants (e.g. a sweatshop).

Duration When does the collusion begin and end?
- *Enduring.* The collusion agreement lasts for the duration of the game.
- *Opportunistic.* Collusion agreements are formed, disbanded, and altered continuously.

Content What is being exchanged, traded, or donated in the collusion?
- *Knowledge.* The colluders share expertise (e.g. inside information on the game mechanics), in-game information (e.g. the colluders inform one another of the whereabouts of the non-colluding players) or stance (e.g. the colluders agree on soft play against one another).
- *Resources.* The colluders share in-game resources (e.g. donating digital assets to one another) or extra-game resources (e.g. a sweatshop is playing a character which will be sold later for real-world money).

This classification is not sufficient for online computer games, because we must also discern the roles of the partakers – players and participants – of the game (Smed et al. 2007). A player in a game can be controlled by one or more participants, and a participant can control one or more players in a game (see Figure 13.5). This means that there are two types of collusion: collusion among the *players*, which happens *inside* the game; and collusion among the *participants*, which happens *outside* the game. To detect player collusion, we have to analyse whether the players' behaviour diverges from what is reasonably expected. To detect participant collusion, we have to analyse the participants behind the players to detect whether they are colluding.

This gives a fine-grained classification of collusion types:

Participant identity collusion How is a single player perceived to participate in a game?
- *Player controller collusion.* Many participants are controlling one player (e.g. two participants controlling the same character alternatively).
- *Self-collusion.* One participant is controlling many players (e.g. one participant controls many players at a poker table).

Inter-player collusion How are the participants affecting the game?
- *Spectator collusion.* Co-colluder provides a different type of information (e.g. ghost scouting, post-game information).
- *Assistant collusion.* Co-colluder plays (possibly sacrificially) to assist the other to win (e.g. as a sidekick, passive scout, or spy).
- *Association collusion.* Colluders achieve individual goals by engaging in cooperation.

Game instance collusion How do factors outside the game instance affect the game?
- *Multigame collusion.* Players of different game instances collude (e.g. finding a suitable server, studying the game properties or fixing tournament match results).
- *Insider collusion.* The co-colluder is a game administrator or game developer that reveals or modifies the workings of the game instance.

Because collusion prevention requires that collusion is first detected, let us next take a closer look at what is required from collusion detection.

13.2.2 Collusion detection

Only the organizer of an online game, who has full information on the game, can take countermeasures against collusion. These countermeasures fall into two categories: *tracking* (i.e. determining who the players actually are) and *styling* (i.e. analysing how the players play the game). Unfortunately, there are no pre-emptive or real-time countermeasures against collusion. Although tracking can be done in real time, it alone is not sufficient. Physical identity does not reflect who is actually playing the game, and a cheat can always avoid network location tracking with rerouting techniques. Styling allows one to find out if there are players who participate often in the same games and, over a long period, profit more than they should. For example, online poker sites usually do styling by analysing the betting patterns and investigating the cases where the overall win percentage is higher than expected. However, this analysis requires a sufficient amount of game data, and collusion can be detected only afterwards.

The general approach to detect collusion works as follows (Smed et al. 2007):

1. Generate game data with different numbers of players, colluders, game types, and collusion strategies.
2. Devise detection methods.
3. Run the detection method against the data to get results.
4. Compare accuracy: how many (if any) of the colluders were detected?
5. Compare swiftness: how quickly were the colluders detected?

When comparing collusion detection methods, we should observe the following two properties:

 (i) *Accuracy.* How justified is the suspicion raised by the detection method?
(ii) *Swiftness.* How early is the suspicion raised?

Naturally, accuracy is important so that normal behaviour does not set off an alarm and cause uncalled-for inspection or unjust punishment. Swiftness is usually related to accuracy so that the less accurate the detection is, the more swiftly the suspicion is raised.

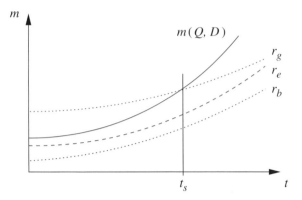

Figure 13.6 Collusion is detected when the observed results using a measure m deviate significantly from the expected results r_e. Suspicion arises at the moment t_s when the results are getting either too 'good' and cross the threshold r_g or too 'bad' and cross the threshold r_b.

Let us try to interpret these properties in a somewhat more formal – but simple – manner (see Figure 13.6). Suppose that our detection is based on applying some numeric function m to the participants P of the game and some game data D. Let $Q \subseteq P$ and let r_g be some chosen threshold value for the best possible play. If $m(Q, D) > r_g$, we decide that the players in the set Q are colluding. In this framework the questions to be asked are:

(i) How is the value of m related to the probability that Q really contains colluders?
(ii) How much data D is needed before r_g is exceeded?

Ideally, we would like to have a measure that indicates as early as possible when players are colluding or when their behaviour is showing suspicious traits. Should the detection happen before collusion actually gives any notable gain for the colluders, we have managed to prevent it altogether. How then to find such methods? From an intuitive point of view, any abnormal behaviour in a game should raise suspicion. This is the case especially when the results of some of the players get too good (i.e. exceeding the threshold r_g) or too bad (i.e. going under the threshold r_b) in comparison to their playing skills (the latter would indicate a case of assistant collusion). The function m could then indicate the (absolute) difference between the expected behaviour (e.g. wins in a card game) and the observed behaviour.

How, then, is Q selected? Instead of inspecting all $|\wp(P)| - |P|$ different colluder sets, we can limit $|Q|$ to a certain range, depending on the collusion pay-off of the game. Figure 13.7 illustrates the pay-off of collusion with respect to the number of colluders. As the number of colluders increases, the total amount of pay-off also increases. However, when the pay-off is divided among the colluders, there exists an optimum where the pay-off per colluder is greatest. For example, robbery is more effective when there are many robbers in a gang, but a big gang of robbers has to focus on big heists to provide everyone with a large amount of loot. When we are detecting colluders, $|Q|$ can be limited near to this optimum. For the game design this means that it is possible to discourage large-scale collusion by pushing down the peak of the curve. For example, if robbery is allowed in the game but a part of the loot is damaged (or otherwise loses its value), the optimum size of a gang of robbers is reduced.

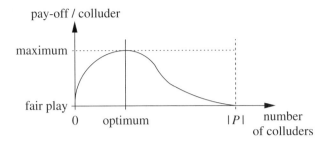

Figure 13.7 The pay-off of collusion per colluder increases until the optimum number of colluders is reached, after which it asymptotically approaches the fair play pay-off.

Preventing collusion in multiplayer online games is possible – either by making it difficult to engage in collusion in the first place or by increasing the risk of getting caught afterwards. Consequently, the countermeasures are based on either prevention or detection. The benefits are immediate: the players in multiplayer online games can be sure that there are no illicit alliances, gangs, clans or cooperation among rivals and everybody has a level playing field, which is one of the main goals of cheating prevention.

There is a need for a third-party organization that grants and manages player licenses, and, for example, Zetterström (2005) calls for an anti-cheating organization for online multiplayer games equivalent to the anti-doping organization WADA in sports. Such an organization could provide authentication of players and monitor their progress (e.g. maintain player rankings) but it would also provide a way to weed out players who systematically break the rules. Nevertheless, an institution of this kind cannot exist without gaining the members' trust on privacy and security issues.

13.3 Rule Violations

The definition of a game states that the players agree to follow the rules of the game (see Chapter 1). We can then say that all players not adhering to the rules are cheats. For example, collusion where two or more opposing players play towards a common goal is explicitly forbidden in many games. However, the situation is not always so black and white, because the rules can leave certain questions unanswered. The makers of the rules are fallible and can fail to foresee all possible situations that a complex system like a computer game can generate. If a player then exploits these loopholes, it can be hard to judge whether it is just creative gameplay or cheating. Ultimately, the question of upholding justice in a game world boils down to the question what is the ethical code that the players agree and can be expected to follow.

Although players may act in accordance with the rules of a game, they can cheat by acting against the spirit of the game. For example, in online role-playing games, killing and stealing from other players are common problems that need to be solved (Sanderson 1999). The players committing these 'crimes' are not necessarily cheating, because they can operate well within the rules of the game. For example, in the online version of *Terminus* different gangs have ended up owning different parts of the game world, where they assault all trespassers. Nonetheless, we may consider an ambush by a more experienced and better-equipped player on a beginner cheating, because it is neither fair nor justified. Moreover, it can make the challenge of the game impossible or harder than the game designer originally intended.

There are different approaches to handle this problem. *Ultima Online* originally left the policing of the game to the players, but eventually this led to gangs of player killers who terrorized the whole game. This was counteracted with a rating system, where everybody is initially innocent, but any misconduct against other players (including the synthetic ones) brands the player as a criminal. Each crime increases the bounty on their head, ultimately preventing them from entering shops. The only way to clear one's name is not to commit crimes for a given time. *EverQuest* uses a different approach, where the players can mark themselves able to attack and be attacked by other players, or completely unable to engage in such activities. This approach has become more and more the norm for online games today.

Killing and stealing are not the only ways to harm another player. There are other, non-violent ways to offend such as blocking exits, interfering with fights, and verbal abuse. The main methods used against these kinds of attacks are filtering (e.g. banning messages from annoying players), or reporting them to the administrator of the game – which of course opens up the possibility of collusion, where players belonging to the same clan send numerous and apparently independent complaints about a player. One can of course ask whether this kind of behaviour is cheating but a feature of the game, and then concede that everything allowed by the game rules is acceptable and cannot be considered as cheating (Kimppa and Bissett 2005).

13.4 Summary

Multiplayer computer games thrive on fair play. Nothing can be more off-putting than an unfair game world, where beginners are robbed as soon as they start, where some players have superhuman reflexes, or where an unsuspecting player is cheated out of his money. Cheating prevention is then crucial to guarantee the longevity and enjoyment of the computer game.

Networked computer games present unique security problems because of the real-time interactivity. Since the data need to be secure for a relatively short period of time, the methods do not have to be as tightly secure as in other contexts. At the same time, the methods should be fast to compute, since all extra computation slows down the communication between the players.

It is impossible to prevent all cheating. Some forms are so subtle that they are hard to observe and judge using technical methods alone – they might even escape the human moral compass. For good or bad, computer games always reflect the real world behind them.

Exercises

13-1 Is it possible to catch reflex augmentation cheating by monitoring the network traffic and events in the game world alone? Can this lead to problematic situations?

13-2 What data and control architecture is the most susceptible to packet interception? How it can be improved to prevent this kind of cheating?

13-3   The easiest way to prevent packet replay cheating is to include some state information in each packet. Why should this information not be a linearly increasing serial number but a pseudo-random number?

13-4   Describe how the lockstep protocol works when we have three or more players.

13-5   When using active objects, even a small amount of gossiping can help to catch a cheat. Suppose that a cheat who forges 10% of his messages participates in a game. What is the probability of his getting caught, if the other players gossip about the choices made in one previous turn and if there are
(a) 10 players, 60 turns and 1% gossip
(b) 10 players, 60 turns and 10% gossip
(c) 100 players, 60 turns and 1% gossip
(d) 10 players, 360 turns and 1% gossip.

13-6   What countermeasures do we have against using illicit information (e.g. removing the fog of war or using a compromised graphics rendering device) in centralized, distributed and replicated architectures?

13-7   Is it possible to collude in a perfect information game?

13-8   Active collusion means that cheats take more risks than they normally would, because they have knowledge that the risk is not as high as it appears to be (e.g. the colluding players raise the stake by outbetting one another). In passive collusion, cheats take fewer risks than they normally would, because they have knowledge that the risk is higher than it appears to be (e.g. colluding players fold when a co-colluder has a better hand). State why active collusion can be recognized whereas passive collusion is difficult to discern from normal play.

13-9   In the game of Fortress Circle each player places their own fortress somewhere in a circular playground (see Figure 13.8). The players proceed in random order.

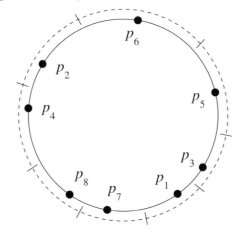

Figure 13.8 An example of the situation after the first round of Fortress Circle with eight players. Each player's fortress dominates the area around it.

A fortress dominates the area around it, which extends up to the area of the two neighbouring fortresses (i.e. the borderline is the midpoint between the two fortresses). The player who dominates the largest area at the end wins.

Assume that m players are playing Fortress Circle and there are n colluding players ($n < m$). If the colluders want to maximize the area they dominate, what kind of a strategy should they use? In this case, what would be the pay-off for each individual colluder?

What if instead of maximizing their own gain, the colluders aim to maximize the losses of the non-colluding players? What would be the pay-offs for the whole group and the individual colluders?

13-10 Consider the following approaches to upholding justice in a game world. What are their good sides? How difficult are they to implement technically? Can a cheat abuse them?

(a) Human players handle the policing themselves (e.g. forming a militia).

(b) The game system records misconduct and brands offenders as criminals.

(c) Players themselves decide whether they can offend and be offended against.

13-11 Is it possible to devise an algorithmic method to catch a player acting against the spirit of the game?

14

Online Metrics

Nowadays metrics form an integral part of game design and development. Anything the player does in an online game can be collected and analysed to enhance the design of the game and to improve its revenue. This reflects the change brought about by digital distribution, whereby games are no longer seen as products (i.e. something ready-made that the user buys) but as a *service* (i.e. the user pays a fee in exchange for content).

This also affects how online games are developed. Whereas traditionally the aim of game development was to prepare the product to meet the release date, online games are constantly developed – even after they have been launched – and, for this reason, they require a broad set of data collected continuously from the players. The development embraces the 'fail fast' ideology, where games are often launched having only the main features implemented so as to establish quickly whether the concept works (based on user data). After the launch, the development continues as an iterative process through three phases (Seufert 2014):

- implementing the features that were designed before the launch but were de-prioritized over some other features;
- fixing bugs found after the launch;
- designing and implementing new features to increase the lifetime value and playability of the game.

To carry out these tasks the developers need analysed data from the players' behaviour and progress, which form the basis for the decisions on where the development should focus next. Based on the data the development team can ensure that the game development is going in the right direction, and if it is not, then they can analyse the situation and take corrective measures to affect the outcome.

Traditionally, the main monetization model for games has been retail sale (i.e. *premium* games). Before the advent of digital distribution, this would have meant paying upfront for a hard copy of the game. This premium model has also been transported to digital distribution (e.g. even successfully as in the case of *Badland*), but online games mainly employ other monetization models:

- *Pay-to-play* (P2P) games require the player to pay periodically (typically once a month) for access to the game. A well-known example of this kind of subscription model is *World of Warcraft*.

Algorithms and Networking for Computer Games, Second Edition. Jouni Smed and Harri Hakonen.
© 2017 John Wiley & Sons Ltd. Published 2017 by John Wiley & Sons Ltd.

- *Free-to-play* (F2P) or *freemium* games are provided free for the player. However, there are many different business models for the sources of revenue. The most obvious ones are advertising and in-application purchases, which can ease the player's progression in the game. Revenue can also be generated by selling cosmetic enhancements to the players (usually without affecting the gameplay) or giving specialized account services. One successful example of this model is *Path of Exile*.
- *Pay-to-win* (P2W) is an extreme variant of F2P, where the game content is available to the player at the beginning, but at some point the player will hit a 'pay wall'. A pay wall is a challenge in the game that cannot be solved (or is very laborious) by playing alone and requires the player to pay a certain amount. In some sense, P2W can turn into P2P if these pay walls are encountered evenly during the gameplay.

The ease of progression is usually realized by offering the player a chance to avoid 'grinding' (i.e. repetition of the same tasks for a long period of time). Consequently, game balancing has become the main challenge, because if players can speed up their progression by investing more money, it can spoil the game for the non-paying players (Koskenvoima and Mäntymäki 2015). Greedy and unethical incidents in F2P business have led to a situation where F2P is viewed negatively by some games companies. To ensure revenue, maintaining the players' trust is vital – which, in turn, leads towards more ethical game design (Alha et al. 2014; Kimppa et al. 2015).

Figure 14.1 contrasts the demand curves for a premium game and a freemium game (Heijari 2014). In premium games, the biggest challenge is setting the price p at an appropriate level so that the revenue (the shaded area in the figure) is maximized. The higher the price, the fewer potential customers there are; setting the price lower can increase the customer base but reduce the overall revenue. Ideally, the freemium model allows the players to pay what they want, and the potential revenue (the shaded area) is larger than in the premium model. This means that the game can have a large number of players who are not paying, whereas a minority of the players are ready to invest higher sums in the game (Lescop and Lescop 2014). The top-tier players, comprising less than 10% of the user base, often spend twenty times more money on the game than an average player (Fields 2013).

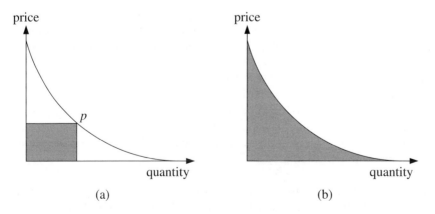

Figure 14.1 Demand curves of the purchase price and quantity (i.e. products sold) for (a) a premium game and (b) a freemium game.

Among the paying players there is a small but important minority who are willing to put considerable sums of money into the game. These 'whales' – a name originating from casinos for a gambler who wagers large amounts of money – are often the most important players as far as income is concerned. They are also much sought after and the games often compete for the interest of the same whales (Shi et al. 2015). This can sometimes lead to situation where the non-paying players are omitted in favour of whales, which, in turn, can lead to the majority of players leaving the game altogether.

In many cases, the portion of non-paying players can be as high as 95% (Seufert 2014). At first sight, non-paying players might not seem an important resource. However, having a large player base is essential in generating awareness, popularity and community around the game. The non-paying players can also provide free marketing if they spread the word about the game, and they can serve also as content for the game by acting as enemies to other paying and non-paying players alike. Business finds its way more easily in cohesive crowds.

Liew (2008) provides a comprehensive list of business models for games, including the following monetization methods for online games:

- *Advertising* relies on a large player base and frequent sessions. This requires a balance in quantity so that the advertisements (banners or transition ads) do not interfere with the player too much. Typically, the advertisements are provided by a third-party supplier who acts as a broker between games company and advertisers. Offer walls, where the player has to watch an advertising video in exchange for in-game resources, are another way to increase the advertising revenue (Luton 2013).
- *In-application purchases* allow the players to transform real-world currency into in-game resources. By making in-application purchases the players can make their progress easier or customize their assets. The items can be classified into the following groups (Weidemann 2014):
  - permanent (e.g. armour), which the player owns until the end of the game unless there is a trading system; or
  - consumable (e.g. health kit), which has a one-time effect and needs to be replenished regularly.

  In addition, to increase variation in a game the players can be encouraged to explore the content, different game mechanics, and playstyles by receiving samples of or renting the in-game equipment or other assets: the items can be used only temporarily, but long enough for the player to try out their various features.

  Buying can be direct, if the players get exactly what they want, or indirect, if the players have a virtual vending machine (e.g. *gacha*) which provides a random item (possibly a rare and valuable one). The aim of all this effort is to lower the bar for spending money on in-application purchases, because the earlier the players spend money, the more likely they are to continue to do so in the future (Hanner and Zarnekow 2015).
- In *merchandising* the intellectual property of the game is used or licensed to produce real-world items which are sold for profit.

Typically, these methods are not all used together; the selection depends on the game and strategy of the company.

Next, we will look into four types of metrics related to player behaviour, monetization, player acquisition and game sessions. These are the most important aspects when considering improving the game design or monetization.

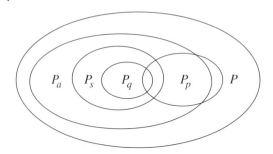

Figure 14.2 Player groups: P all players, P_a active players, P_p paying players, P_s players who have started, and P_q acquired players.

14.1 Players

In online game analytics, it is essential to recognize and differentiate players and how and when they are playing the game. In the following, let us assume that $P(t)$ is the set of all players, $P_a(t)$ the set of active players, and $P_s(t) \subseteq P_a(t)$ the set of players starting during the interval t (see Figure 14.2). The interval t can typically vary from one day (d) to one month (m).

Daily active users (DAU)   This is a basic metric tracking how many unique players have played the game during a given day:

$$\text{DAU} = |P_a(d)|. \tag{14.1}$$

It is important to notice that this does not measure game sessions, but if the same player has played the game four times during the day, it counts as one. Typically, DAU is calculated as an average over seven days.

Monthly active users (MAU)   This metric observes the long-term activity by summing the numbers of unique players over a month:

$$\text{MAU} = |P_a(m)|. \tag{14.2}$$

Stickiness   To measure how well the game retains the players we can calculate the number of daily active users as a proportion of the monthly active ones:

$$s = \frac{\text{DAU}}{\text{MAU}}. \tag{14.3}$$

The larger the value of s, the stickier the game (i.e. players keep returning to the game regularly).

Peak concurrent users (PCU)   There are often big variations in how many simultaneous users the game has. The number at the busiest times might become a critical question, especially if the game is run on dedicated servers with a limited computational and networking capacity.

Retention rate   This metric indicates how well the game is able to keep the players playing the game. For example, 10% monthly retention means that 10% of the players who started to play the game a month ago are still playing today. More generally, to calculate

x-day retention we calculate the proportion of players who started x days ago and are still active:

$$r_x = \frac{|P_s(d-x)|}{|P_a(d)|}.$$

(14.4)

In estimating the game's success, retention is often the most important indicator, because the players investing a lot of time in the game are also more likely to invest money in it. Retention typically follows the so-called 40–20–10 rule, which means that retention is 40% daily, 20% weekly, and 10% monthly (Ketola 2014).

Churn rate   This metric is the dual of retention, because it indicates the proportion of players who have left over a period of x days:

$$c_x = 1 - r_x.$$

(14.5)

The vast majority of the players are 'churners', who play the game until they lose interest in it. Normally, a player is considered churned (i.e. lost) after a week's absence (Luton 2013).

14.2 Monetization

To analyse the monetization we need to know how much the players are spending on the game. Here, we assume that $P_p(t)$ is the set of paying players and $P_n(t) = P(t) \setminus P_p(t)$ the set of non-paying players during the interval t (see Figure 14.2). Also, let $v(t)$ be the total revenue during the interval t.

Average revenue per daily active user (ARPDAU)   This metric tracks how much players are spending on average in a day:

$$\mathrm{ARPDAU} = \frac{v(d)}{\mathrm{DAU}}.$$

(14.6)

The game's success is often measured based on this value. Furthermore, it is used to make monetary decisions for the future.

Average revenue per user (ARPU)   This metric is typically measured on a monthly basis:

$$\mathrm{ARPU} = \frac{v(m)}{\mathrm{MAU}}.$$

(14.7)

This value can be understood as the lifetime value (LTV) normalized to 30 days (Ketola 2014).

Average revenue per paying user (ARPPU)   This metric follows how much the paying players spend on the game on average:

$$\mathrm{ARPPU} = \frac{v(m)}{|P_p(m)|}.$$

(14.8)

For subscription-based games, ARPU and ARPPU are practically equal as the active players have to pay subscription fees.

Lifetime value (LTV)   To measure how much a single player spends in total, we divide the overall revenue by the number of players:

$$\text{LTV} = \frac{v}{|P|}. \tag{14.9}$$

An alternative way to define LTV is to multiply ARPU by the average playtime of the players. For a premium game, LTV then equals the purchase price multiplied by the number of customers.

LTV is often used in calculating the budget for player acquisition (Ketola 2014). Hanner and Zarnekow (2015) provide a detailed analysis on game customer lifetime value.

Lifetime network value (LTNV)   This counts in – or at least estimates – all the non-monetary values that a user can bring (e.g. increased virality, nurturing of new players or assisting to get a higher chart position).

Conversion rate (CVR)   This metric tracks the proportion of non-paying players who have become paying players (sometimes calculated over a week or month instead of a day):

$$\text{CVR} = \frac{|P_p(d) \cap P_n(d-1)|}{|P(d)|}. \tag{14.10}$$

For successful games, CVR is usually greater than 2% (Pulkkanen and Seppänen 2012).

14.3 Acquisition

When a game gets new players, we can discern two groups:

- organic users who have come to the game with no direct involvement (e.g. because of word-of-mouth recommendation, a feature story in the digital marketplace or a high position in the charts);
- paid users who are directly acquired by investing money (e.g. via a third-party service provider).

Let us denote by $P_q(t) \subset P_s$ the set of acquired users during the interval t (see Figure 14.2) and by $q(t)$ the related investment in user acquisition.

Cost per acquisition (CPA)   This metric measures how much it costs to attract a new user:

$$\text{CPA} = \frac{q(t)}{|P_q(t)|}. \tag{14.11}$$

This is only straightforward for paid users. The cost of acquisition decreases the more users the game already has (i.e. earlier users are more costly to acquire than later users).

Effective cost per acquisition (ECPA)   This metric also considers the organic users:

$$\text{ECPA} = \frac{q(t)}{|P_s(t)|}. \tag{14.12}$$

Obviously, ECPA is smaller than CPA.

k-factor   This metric – borrowed from epidemiology – measures the viral growth rate of the user base. Let i be the number of invitations that each user sends to friends outside P and c the conversion rate (i.e. how many of the invitations lead to action). Then

$$k = ic. \tag{14.13}$$

If $k = 1$, the user base is in a steady state. If $k > 1$, the user base is growing exponentially, and if $k < 1$, the user base is declining exponentially.

14.4   Game Session

We can also observe what happens when the user is playing the game.

Entry event distribution (EED)   This focuses on the first action the user performs when launching the game. This can help the designers to understand what the players want from the game or what their motivation is.

Exit event distribution (XED)   We can also observe the last action the user performs before leaving the game. This can help to understand why players are quitting the game.

Session length   When we measure how long the player remains in the game, we can compare it to how the designers envision the game (i.e. we can expect a casual game to have short sessions, whereas a strategy game with complex and immersive campaigns tends to have longer sessions). This also allows us to observe what happens after the introduction of new features or a new localization into the game (Ekberg 2016).

Progression through game   The observation can focus on how the players are progressing through the game and its levels. This helps to discern, for instance, whether there are levels that are too difficult and require much grinding. Data on the players' progress is also important when analysing the effect of the in-application purchases.

14.5   Summary

Digital distribution and online games have turned around the old model of the game-as-a-product into the game-as-a-service. Consequently, games are becoming ever more metrics-driven as their revenue is generated gradually over their lifetime. The most successful freemium games such as *Clash of Clans* and *Candy Crush Saga* thrive – apart from their design and implementation values – on their focus on analysing the metrics and paying heed to what the players are doing.

Games are no longer developed in isolation, but the design process is becoming more iterative as the players can affect the fundamental features in the game. This means that the developers have to be adaptable and open to new possibilities. Balancing this with the vision of the game can turn out to be a big challenge – but conquering it will take the game to the next level.

Exercises

14-1 Review the games you are currently playing the most. How did you learn about them (e.g. via a feature article, the charts, or a recommendation)? What other factors affected your choice to (a) try the game out and (b) continue playing it?

14-2 Look at the lists of top downloaded and top crossing games at a digital marketplace. Categorize them based on whether they follow the premium or freemium model. Which are the majority and why?

14-3 Avoid doing what you would do normally when looking for a new game and check out games outside the normal charts (e.g. by random selection or starting from the bottom of the list). How do these games reflect to the most popular ones? Why are they not so popular?

14-4 What reasons could there be to publish a game as premium on a digital marketplace? What qualities must it have in comparison to freemium games?

14-5 Assume that a game has 100,000 players. The DAU is 20,000 and MAU is 35,000. How sticky is the game? What does this mean in more concrete terms?

14-6 What are the benefits of the P2P model for the player? How does it affect the game design?

14-7 A typical game design for a freemium game follows the action–wait–reward–upgrade loop. For example, in *FarmVille* the action is planting and harvesting crops, the waiting means waiting for the crops to grow, the reward happens when the player harvests the crops, and the upgrade is selling the crops for money and buying a better tractor so as to make the harvesting easier.

   Choose a freemium game and analyse how it utilizes this design. Why is it beneficial for retention?

14-8 What kind of indicators would we like to observe on the player's progression in an endless runner game?

14-9 Consider the effect of releasing a new product build of a game. What kind of impact could one expect to see on the metrics? Which would be the critical signs to watch out for and which would be the positive ones?

14-10 If we see games as a service, what does that entail for the way they are being developed? How does it affect the players?

14-11 Archiving games is becoming ever more difficult. This is also true for other digital media; for instance, the web of the 1990s has been mainly studied from old instructional videos and news clips. Can we still say that there is a definite state (or artefact) that is the game? How can we archive online games for posterity so that people can experience the game as it was originally played?

Appendices

A

Pseudocode Conventions

We describe the algorithms using a pseudocode format, which, for the most part, closely follows the guidelines set by Cormen et al. (2001). The conventions are based on common data abstractions (e.g. sets, sequences, and graphs), and the control structures resemble the Pascal programming language (Jensen et al. 1985). Since our aim is to reveal the algorithmic ideas behind the implementations, we present the algorithms using pseudocode instead of an existing programming language. This choice is backed up by the following arguments:

- Although common programming languages (e.g. C, C++, Java, and scripting languages) share similar control structures, their elementary data structures differ significantly in terms of both interface level and language philosophy. For example, if an algorithm uses a data structure from STL of C++, a Java programmer has three alternatives: reformulate the code to use Java's collection library, write a custom-made data structure to serve the algorithm, or acquire a suitable third-party library. Apart from the last option, programming effort is unavoidable, and by giving a general algorithmic description we do not limit the choices on how to proceed with the implementation.
- Software development should account for change management issues. For instance, sometimes the understandability of a code segment is more important than its efficiency. Because of these underlying factors affecting the software development, we content ourselves with conveying the idea as clearly as possible and leaving the implementation selections to the reader.
- The efficiency of a program depends on the properties of its input. Often code optimizations favouring certain kind of inputs lead to 'pessimization' which disfavours other kinds of inputs. In addition, optimizing a code that is not the bottleneck of the whole system wastes development time, because the number of code lines has increased and they also more difficult to test. These two observations lead us to give only a general description of a method that can be moulded so that it suits the reader's situation best.
- The implementation of an algorithm is connected to its software context not only through data representation but also through control flow. For example, time-consuming code segments are often responsible for reporting their status to a monitoring subsystem. This means that algorithms should be modifiable and easy to augment to respond to software integration forces, which tend to become more tedious when we are closer to the actual implementation language.

Algorithms and Networking for Computer Games, Second Edition. Jouni Smed and Harri Hakonen.
© 2017 John Wiley & Sons Ltd. Published 2017 by John Wiley & Sons Ltd.

- Presenting the algorithms in pseudocode has also a pedagogic rationale. There are two opposing views as to how a new algorithm should be taught. First, the teacher describes the overall behaviour of the algorithm (i.e. its substructures and their relations), which often requires explanations in a natural language. Second, to provide guidance on how to proceed with the implementation, the teacher describes the important details of the algorithm, which calls for a light formalism that can easily be converted into programming code. The teacher's task is to find a balance between these two approaches. To support both approaches the pseudocode formalism with simple data and control abstractions allows the teacher to explain the topics in natural language when necessary.

The pseudocode notation tries to obey modern programming guidelines (e.g. avoiding global side-effects). To indicate clearly what kind of effect the algorithm has in the system we have adopted, liberally, the functional programming paradigm, where an algorithm is described as a function that does not mutate its actual parameters, and side-effects are allowed only in the local structures within a function. For this reason, the algorithms are designed so that they are easy to understand – which sometimes means compromising on efficiency that could be achieved using the imperative programming paradigm (i.e. procedural programming with side-effects). Nevertheless, immutability does not mean inefficiency, but sometimes it is the key to managing object aliasing (Hakonen et al. 2000) or efficient concurrency (Hudak 1989). Immutability does not cause extra effort in the implementation phase, because a functional description can be converted into a procedural one just by leaving out copy operations. The reader has the final choice on how to implement algorithms efficiently using the programming language of his or her choice.

Let us take an example of the pseudocode notation. Assume that we are interested in changing a value so that some fraction α of the previous change also contributes to the outcome. In other words, we want to introduce an inertia-like property to the change in the value of a variable. This can be implemented as linear momentum: if a change c affects a value v_t at time t, the outcome v_{t+1} is calculated as

$$v_{t+1} = v_t + c + \alpha(v_t - v_{t-1}) \iff \Delta v_{t+1} = c + \alpha \Delta v_t. \tag{A.1}$$

The $\alpha \in [0, 1]$ is called a momentum coefficient and $\alpha \Delta v_t$ a momentum term. To keep a record of the value generated, the history can be stored as a tail-growing sequence ⟨first value, second value,..., most recent value⟩. Algorithm A.1 describes this method as a function in the pseudocode format.

If the use context of Algorithm A.1 assigns the returned sequence back to the argument variable, for example,

1: $V \leftarrow$ LINEAR-MOMENTUM(V, c, α)

the copying in line 1 can be omitted by allowing a side-effect on the sequence V.

Let us take a closer look at the pseudocode notation. As in any other formal programming language, we can combine primitive constants and operators to build up expressions, control the execution flow with statements, and define a module as a routine. To do this the pseudocode notation uses the reserved words listed in Table A.1.

Table A.2 lists the notational conventions used in the algorithm descriptions. The constants FALSE and TRUE denote the truth values, and value NIL is a placeholder for

Algorithm A.1 Updating a value with a change value and a momentum term.

LINEAR-MOMENTUM(V, c, α)

   in: sequence of n values $V = \langle V_0, V_1, \ldots, V_{n-1} \rangle$ $(2 \le n)$; change c; momentum
        coefficient α $(0 \le \alpha \le 1)$

  out: sequence of $n + 1$ values W where the first n values are identical to V and the
        last value is $W_n = W_{n-1} + c + \alpha(W_{n-1} - W_{n-2})$

  1: $W \leftarrow$ **copy** V ▷ Make a local copy from V.

  2: $W \leftarrow W \; || \; \langle W_{n-1} + c + \alpha(W_{n-1} - W_{n-2}) \rangle$ ▷ Append a new value.

  3: **return** W ▷ Publish W as immutable.

Table A.1 Reserved words for algorithms.

all	div	error	not	repeat	while
and	do	for	of	return	xor
case	else	if	or	then	
copy	end	mod	others	until	

an entity that is not yet known. The assignment operator $\leftarrow$ defines a statement that updates the structure on the left-hand side to a value evaluated on the right-hand side. Equality can compared using operator $=$. To protect an object from side-effects, it can be copied (or cloned) by the prefix operator **copy**. In a formal sense, the trinity of assignment, equality and copy can be applied to the identity, shallow structure, or deep structure of an object. Furthermore, a mixture of these structure levels is possible. Because the algorithms presented in this book do not have relationships across their software interfaces (e.g. classes in object-oriented languages), we use these operations informally, and if there is a possibility of confusion, we elaborate on it in a comment.

At first sight, the difference between primitive routines and algorithmic functions can appear one of happenstance, but a primitive routine can be likened to an attribute of an object or a trivial operation. For example, when operating with linearly orderable entities, we can define *predecessor*(e) and *successor*(e) for the predecessor and successor of e. The *successor*(•) – where • denotes a dummy variable – can be seen just as a function

Table A.2 Algorithmic conventions.

Notation	Meaning
FALSE, TRUE	Boolean constants
NIL	unique reference to non-existent object
$x \leftarrow y$	assignment
$x = y$	comparison of equality
$x \leftarrow$ **copy** y	copying of object
▷ Read me.	comment
primitive(x)	primitive routine for object x
HELLO-WORLD(x)	algorithmic function call with parameter x
mathematical(x)	mathematical function with parameter x

Table A.3 Mathematical functions.

Notation	Meaning
$\lfloor x \rfloor$	the largest integer n such that $n \leq x$
$\lceil x \rceil$	the smallest integer n such that $x \leq n$
$\log_b x$	logarithm to base b
$\ln x$	natural logarithm ($b = e \approx 2.71828$)
$\lg x$	binary logarithm ($b = 2$)
$\max C$	maximum of a collection; similarly $\min C$
$\tan x$	trigonometric tangent; similarly $\sin x$ and $\cos x$
$\arctan \alpha$	inverse of tangent; similarly $\arcsin \alpha$ and $\arccos \alpha$

that extracts its result from the given argument. A primitive routine that indicates a status can also be seen as an attribute that changes – and can be changed – during the execution of an algorithm. For this reason, we can assign a value to a primitive routine. For example, to mark a town t visited we can define a primitive routine *visited*(•) to characterize this status, and then assign

1: *visited*(t) ← TRUE

If towns are modelled as software objects, the primitive routine *visited*(•) can be implemented as a member variable with appropriate get and set functions.

Sometimes the algorithms include functions originating from elementary mathematics. For example, we denote the sign of x by $\mathrm{sgn}(x)$, defined as

$$\mathrm{sgn}(x) = \begin{cases} -1, & \text{if } x < 0, \\ 0, & \text{if } x = 0, \\ 1, & \text{if } 0 < x. \end{cases} \tag{A.2}$$

Table A.3 lists the mathematical functions used throughout this book.

A.1 Changing the Flow of Control

The algorithms presented in this book run inside one control flow or thread. The complete control command of the pseudocode is a *statement*, which is built from other simpler statements or subparts called *expressions*. When a statement is evaluated, it does not yield a value but affects the current state of the system. In contrast, the evaluation of an expression produces a value but does not change the visible state of the system.

A.1.1 Expressions

Anything that yields a value after it is evaluated can be seen as an expression. The fundamental expressions are constants, variables, and primitive routines. An algorithm also represents an expression, because it returns a value.

Table A.4 Arithmetic operators.

Notation	Meaning
$x + y$	addition
$x - y$	subtraction
x/y	division $(y \neq 0)$
$x \cdot y$	multiplication, also as xy
n **div** m	integer division
n **mod** m	integer modulo

To change, aggregate and compare values we need operators (see Table A.4) which can be used to build up more descriptive expressions. Although the pseudocode operators originate mainly from mathematics, some of them are more related to computer calculations. For example, if we have two integers x and y, the expression x **div** y is equal to the integer part of x/y so that the outcome is truncated towards $-\infty$. The operator mod produces the remainder of this division, which means that the Boolean expression $x = (x \, \textbf{div} \, y) \cdot y + (x \, \textbf{mod} \, y)$ is always true. It should be noted that some mathematical conventions are context sensitive. For example, for a value x, the operator $|x|$ denotes its absolute value, but for a set S, the operator $|S|$ means its cardinality (i.e. the number of its members). If the meaning of our notation is ambiguous, we clarify it with a comment.

The value of an arithmetic expression is stored in a variable or compared to another value as a Boolean expression. To construct expressions from truth values we resort to mathematical logic. We use the logical operators listed in Table A.5 in the main text, and their algorithmic counterparts listed in Table A.6 in pseudocode. The conditional logical operators **and then** and **or else** differ in that that their evaluation, proceeding from left to right, is terminated immediately when the result can be inferred. There are no reserved words for logical implication or equivalence, but, if necessary, they can be formed as $x \Rightarrow y \equiv \neg x \lor y$ and $x \Leftrightarrow y \equiv \neg(x \oplus y)$.

Table A.5 Logical operators in the text.

Notation	Meaning
$\neg x$	logical negation
$x \land y$	logical and
$x \lor y$	logical or
$x \oplus y$	logical exclusive-or
$x \Rightarrow y$	logical implication
$x \Leftrightarrow y$	logical equivalence

Table A.6 Logical operators in algorithms.

Notation	Meaning
not x	logical negation
x **and** y	logical and
x **or** y	logical or
x **xor** y	logical exclusive-or
x **and then** y	conditional logical and
x **or else** y	conditional logical or

Table A.7 Bitwise operations in algorithms.

Notation	Meaning
$\sim x$	bitwise negation
$x \sqcap y$	bitwise and
$x \sqcup y$	bitwise or
$x \boxplus y$	bitwise exclusive-or
$x \ll s$	arithmetical left-shift
$x \gg s$	arithmetical right-shift
$x \ggg s$	logical right-shift

Table A.7 lists the bitwise operations used in the algorithmic descriptions. Arithmetic shift operations preserve the sign of the operand, whereas logical right-shift can be used only when operating with unsigned values.

A.1.2 Control structures

Pseudocode notation follows the widely accepted idea of structured programming, where the control flow is described using sequence, selection, and repetition structures (Dahl et al. 1972; Dijkstra 1968). However, we allow this rule of 'single entry and single exit points of control' to be broken with an explicit return statement.

Sequence

A sequence of statements is indicated by writing the statements one after the other. If there is more than one statement in the line, they are separated by a semicolon (;). For example, swapping the values of variables x and y using a temporary variable t can be written

1: $t \leftarrow x; x \leftarrow y; y \leftarrow t$

The line numbers are used only for reference purposes, and they do not imply any algorithmic structure.

Many programming languages include a compound structure that combines multiple statements into one. Because we do not scope the variables (e.g. define their lifetimes), this construct is expressed only implicitly: Any statement can be replaced with a sequence of statements without stating it explicitly.

Selection

To describe a branch in the control flow we have two selection structures. The first, the **if–then–else** structure, proceeds according to the value of a Boolean expression: if the value is **true**, the control flows to the **then** statement; otherwise, the control flows to the **else** statement. The **else** branch is optional.

1: **if** *Boolean expression* **then**
2:   *statement$_0$*   ▷ Executed only for true case.
3: **else**
4:   *statement$_1$*   ▷ Executed only for false case.
5: **end if**

The **case–of** construct defines a multi-selection that is based on the value of an arithmetic expression. To indicate clearly which control branch is executed we require that they are labelled with disjoint, constant-like values. Unlike in some programming languages, the control does not flow from one branch to another. The label **others** can be used to indicate the branch 'any other value not mentioned'. If the selection expression returns a truth value, we prefer the **if–then–else** structure.

1: **case** *expression* **of**
2:    *constant$_0$*: *statement$_0$*   ▷ Control branch for value *constant$_0$*.
3:    *constant$_1$*: *statement$_1$*
4:    ⋮
5:    **others**: *default statement*
6: **end case**

If none of the branching labels match with the expression, the control moves directly to the next statement following the **case–of** structure.

Repetition

To iterate statements we introduce one definite loop structure and two indefinite loop structures. The definite loop is called the **for–do** structure and it is used when the number of iteration cycles can be calculated before entering the loop body.

1: **for** *iteration statement* **do**
2:    *statement*
3: **end for**

The iteration statement has two variants. First, it can represent an enumeration by introducing a loop variable v that gets values sequentially from a given range $[f, t]$: $v \leftarrow f...t$ (i.e. the initial value of v is f and the final value is t). Second, the iteration statement can represent a sequential member selection over a collection C: **all** $v \in C$. This loop variant bounds v once to each member of C in an unspecified order. To preserve clarity, C cannot be changed until the loop is finished.

As an example of the difference between these two **for** loops, let us find the maximum value from a sequence S of n values. We denote the ith member of S by S_i, for $i \in [0, n - 1]$. The most concrete algorithm for the problem is to define the order in which the sequence S is traversed:

1: $c \leftarrow S_0$
2: **for** $i \leftarrow 1 ... (n - 1)$ **do**
3:    **if** $c < S_i$ **then** $c \leftarrow S_i$ **end if**
4: **end for**
5: ▷ Value in c is the maximum of S.

If there is no need to restrict the way the algorithm can traverse S, the iteration statement of the loop can be formed as a member selection:

1: $c \leftarrow$ some member in S
2: $S' \leftarrow S \setminus \{c\}$
3: **for all** $m \in S'$ **do**
4:   **if** $c < m$ **then** $c \leftarrow m$ **end if**
5: **end for**
6: ▷ Value in c is the maximum of S.

Of course, finding a maximum from a linear structure is so trivial that we can express it using the mathematical convention $c \leftarrow \max S$.

To find the position of a maximum value we can use the primitive function $indices(S)$ that returns the set $\{0, 1, \dots, |S| - 1\}$ of valid indices in S. The index set can be used for iteration coordination:

1: $I \leftarrow indices(S)$
2: $c \leftarrow$ some member in I
3: $I' \leftarrow I \setminus \{c\}$
4: **for all** $i \in I'$ **do**
5:   **if** $S_c < S_i$ **then** $c \leftarrow i$ **end if**
6: **end for**
7: ▷ Value S_c is some maximum of S.

We can express the same thing in mathematical notation as $c \leftarrow \arg \max S$.

If we cannot determine a close-form equation for the number of loop cycles, it is preferable to use an indefinite loop structure instead. If it is possible that the loop body is not visited at all, we use the **while–do** structure. The loop exits when the control flow evaluates the Boolean expression as FALSE.

1: **while** *Boolean expression* **do**
2:   *statement*
3: **end while**

If the loop body is executed at least once, we use the **repeat–until** structure. The loop exits when the control flow evaluates the Boolean expression as TRUE.

1: **repeat**
2:   *statement*
3: **until** *Boolean expression*

Control shortcuts
As a general rule, control structures with single entry and single exit points are easier to maintain than structures that use control shortcuts. For this reason, we use only two

statement-level mechanisms for breaking the control flow in the middle of an algorithm. Normally, an algorithm ends with a **return** statement that forwards the control back to the invoker of the algorithm, possibly including a return value:

> 1: **return** *expression*

We allow multiple **return** statements to be placed on any pseudocode line. When the control flow reaches a **return** statement, it exits the algorithm and forwards the evaluated value of the given expression immediately.

Another way to exit the algorithm is when an error has occurred and control flow cannot proceed normally:

> 1: **error** *description*

Because the algorithm cannot fulfil its operative contract with the invoker, the situation resembles exception handling, as is the way with many programming languages. The invoker can catch errors using a **case–of** structure:

> 1: $v \leftarrow$ AVERAGE(S)
> 2: **case** v **of**
> 3:   **error** empty: $v \leftarrow$ UNDEFINED   ▷ Unexpected situation: $|S| = 0$.
> 4: **end case**

A.2 Data Structures

The generality of the description of an algorithm follows from proper abstractions, which is why we have abstracted data structures to fundamental data collections such as sets, mappings and graphs. For accessing data from these data collections, we use primitive routines and indexing abstractions.

A.2.1 Values and entities

The simplest datum is a value. Apart from the constants FALSE, TRUE and NIL, we can define other literals for special purposes. A value is the result of an expression and can be stored in a variable. The values in the pseudocode notation do not imply any particular implementation. For example, NIL can be realized using a null pointer, integer value -1 or a sentinel object.

Values can be aggregated so that they form the attributes of an entity. These attributes can be accessed through primitive routines. For example, to define an entity e with physical attributes we can attach primitive routines *location*(e), *size*(e) and *weight*(e) to it. Because an attribute concerns only the entity given as an argument, the attribute can also be assigned. For example, to make e weightless we can assign *weight*(e) $\leftarrow 0$. If an entity is implemented as a software record or object, the attributes

Notation	Meaning
$e \in S$	Boolean assertion: e is a member of S
$|S|$	cardinality (i.e. the number of elements)
$\emptyset$	empty set
$\{x\}$	singleton set
$R \cup S$	union set
$R \cap S$	intersection set
$R \setminus S$	difference set
$R \subset S$	Boolean assertion: R is a proper subset of S
$R \times S$	Cartesian product
S^d	set $S \times S \times \cdots \times S$ of d-tuples
$\wp(S)$	power set of S

Table A.8 Set notation used in the text and in pseudocode.

are natural candidates for member variables and the respective get and set member functions.

A.2.2 Data collections

A collection imposes relationships between its entities. Instead of listing all commonly used data structures, we take a minimalist approach and use only a few general collections. A collection has characteristic attributes and provides query operations. Moreover, it can be modified if it is a local structure in an algorithm. The elements of a data structure must be initialized, and an element that has not been given a value cannot be evaluated.

Sets

The simplest collection of entities (or values) is a set. The members of a set are unique (i.e. they have different values) and they are not ordered in any way. Table A.8 lists the usual set operations.

The set of natural numbers is $\mathbb{N} = \{0, 1, 2, \ldots\}$, the set of integer numbers is $\mathbb{Z} = \{\ldots, -2, -1, 0, 1, 2, \ldots\}$, and the set of real numbers is $\mathbb{R}$. In a similar fashion, we can define the set $\mathbb{B} = \{0, 1\}$ for referring to binary numbers. We can now express, for example, a 32-bit word by denoting $w \in \mathbb{B}^{32}$, and refer to its ith bit as w_i.

We can define a set also by using interval notation. For example, if it is clear from the context that a set contains integers, the interval $[0, 9]$ means the set $\{0, 1, \ldots, 9\}$. To indicate that the interval notation refers to real numbers we can write $[0, 9] \subset \mathbb{R}$. The ends of the interval can be closed, marked with a bracket [or], or open, marked with a parenthesis (or).

The cardinality of a set is its attribute. If the final size of a (locally defined) set is known beforehand, we can emphasize it by stating

1: $|S| \leftarrow n$ ▷ Reserve space for n values.

This idiom does not have any effect in the algorithm; it is merely a hint for implementation.

Table A.9 Sequence notation used in the text and in pseudocode.

Notation	Meaning
$e \in S$	Boolean assertion: e is a member of S
$|S|$	length
$indices(S)$	set $\{0, 1, \ldots, |S| - 1\}$ of valid indices
S_i	the ith element; $i \in indices(S)$
$\langle \, \rangle$	empty sequence
$R \parallel S$	catenation sequence
$sub(S, i, n)$	subsequence $\langle S_i, S_{i+1}, \ldots, S_{i+n-1} \rangle$; $0 \le n \le |S| - i$

Sequences

To impose a linear ordering on a collection of n elements we define a sequence as $S = \langle e_0, e_1, \ldots, e_{n-1} \rangle$. Unlike a set, a sequence differentiates its elements with an index, and, thus, it can contain multiple identical elements. We refer to the elements with subscripts. For example, the ith element of S is denoted S_i. The indexing begins at 0 – and not at 1 – and the last valid index is $|S| - 1$. The cardinality of a sequence is equal to its length (i.e. the number of elements in it). In addition to the notation presented in Table A.9, we have a primitive routine *enumeration(C)*, which gives some order to its argument collection C in the form of a sequence. In other words, *enumeration(C)* returns a sequence S that is initialized by the following pseudocode:

```
1: |S| ← |C|        ▷ Reserve space for |C| elements.
2: i ← 0
3: for all e ∈ C do
4:   S_i ← e
5:   i ← i + 1
6: end for
7: ▷ Sequence S is initialized.
```

We can declare the length of a sequence S before it is initialized using a pseudocode idiom but – unlike with sets – the assignment affects the algorithm by defining a valid index range for S:

```
1: |S| ← n        ▷ Reserve space for n values.
```

The context of use can impose restrictions on the sequence structure. A sequence S of n elements can play many roles:

- If S contains only unique elements, it can be seen as an *ordered set*.
- If the utilization of S does not depend on the element order, S can represent a *multiset* (or bag). A multiset consists possibly multiple identical elements and does not give any order to them.

- If the length of S is constant (e.g. it is not changed by a catenation), S stands for an *n-tuple*. This point of view is emphasized if the elements are of the same 'type' or the tuple is part of a definition of some relation set.
- If S includes sequences, it defines a *hierarchy*. For example, a nesting of sequences $S = \langle a, \langle b, \langle c, \langle d, \langle \rangle \rangle \rangle \rangle \rangle$ defines a list structure as recursive pairs $\langle \text{datum}, \text{sublist} \rangle$. The element d can be accessed with the expression $(((S_1)_1)_1)_0$.
- If a sequence is not stored in a variable but we use it on the left of the assignment operator, the sequence becomes a *nameless record*. This can be interpreted as a multi-assignment operator with pattern matching. For example, to swap two values in variables x and y we can write

> 1: $\langle x, y \rangle \leftarrow \langle y, x \rangle$

This *unification* mechanism originates from the declarative programming paradigm. However, this kind of use of sequences is discouraged, because it can lead to infinite structures and illegible algorithms. Perhaps the only viable use for this kind of interpretation is for receiving multiple values from a function:

> 1: $\langle r, \alpha \rangle \leftarrow$ AS-POLAR(x, y)
> 2:   ▷ Variables r and α are assigned and can be used separately.

This saves introducing an extra receiver variable and referring to its elements.

Although a sequence is one-dimensional structure, it can be extended to implement tables or multidimensional arrays. For example, a hierarchical sequence $T = \langle \langle a, 0 \rangle, \langle b, 1 \rangle, \langle c, 2 \rangle \rangle$ represents a table of three rows and two columns. An element can be accessed through a proper selection of subsequences (e.g. the element c is at $(T_2)_0$). However, this row major notation is tedious and it is cumbersome to refer a whole column. Instead of raising one dimension over another, we can make them equally important by generalizing the one-dimensional indexing mechanism of the ordinary sequences.

Arrays

An array allows an element to be indexed in two or more dimensions. An element in a two-dimensional array A is referred to as $A_{i,j}$, where $i \in \{0, \dots, rows(A) - 1\}$ and $j \in \{0, \dots, columns(A) - 1\}$. A single row can be obtained with $row(A, i)$ and a column with $column(A, j)$. These row and column projections are ordinary sequences. For convenience' sake, we let $A_{\langle i,j \rangle} = A_{i,j}$, which allows us to refer to an element using a sequence.

For a t-dimensional array $A_{i_0, i_1, \dots, i_{t-1}}$, the size of the array in dimension d ($0 \le d \le t - 1$) is defined as $domain(A, d)$. Hence, for a two-dimensional array A we have $rows(A) = domain(A, 0)$ and $columns(A) = domain(A, 1)$. An array $A_{i_0, i_1, \dots, i_{t-1}}$ is always rectangular: if we take any dimension d of A, the value $domain(A, d)$ does not change for any valid indices $i_0, i_1, \dots, i_{d-1}, i_{d+1}, \dots, i_{t-2}, i_{t-1}$.

Mappings

A mapping is a data structure that behaves like a function (i.e. it associates a single result entity to a given argument entity). To distinguish mappings from primitive functions, algorithms, and mathematical functions they are named with Greek letters.

The definition also includes the domain and codomain of the mapping. For example, $\tau : [0,7] \times [0,3] \to \mathbb{B} \cup \{$ FALSE, TRUE $\}$ defines a two-dimensional function that can contain a mix of bits and truth values (e.g. $\tau(6,0) = 1$ and $\tau(4,2) =$ FALSE). It is worth noting that a sequence S that has elements from the set R can be seen as a mapping $S : [0, |S| - 1] \to R$. In other words, we denote $S : i \mapsto r$ simply with the access notation $S_i = r$. Similarly, arrays can be seen as multiargument functions. However, the difference between $\tau(\bullet, \bullet)$ and an array with eight rows and four columns is that the function does not have to be rectangular.

Because a mapping is a data structure, it can be accessed and modified. A mapping $\mu(k) = v$ can be seen as an associative memory, where μ binds a search key k to the resulting value v. This association can be changed by assigning a new value to the key. This leads us to define the following three categories of functions. A function $\mu : K \to V$ is *undefined* if it does not have any associations, which means that it cannot be used. When μ is a local structure of an algorithm and its associations are under change, μ is *incomplete*. A function is *complete* after it is returned from an algorithm where it was incomplete.

To define *partial functions* we assume that NIL can act as a placeholder for any entity but cannot be declared into the codomain set explicitly. If mapping $\mu : K \to V$ is undefined, it can be made 'algorithmically' partial:

1: **for all** $k \in K$ **do**
2:   $\mu(k) \leftarrow$ NIL
3: **end for**

Now, each search key is bound to NIL but not to any entity in the codomain V. The separation of undefined and partial functions allows us to have explicit control over incomplete functions: accessing an unbound search key means a fault in the algorithm, but we can refer to the members of the set $\{ k \mid k \in K \wedge \mu(k) =$ NIL $\}$.

Mappings are useful when describing self-recursive structures. For example, if we have $V = \{a, b, c, d\}$, a cycle can be defined with a successor mapping $\sigma : V \to V$ so that $\sigma(a) = b$, $\sigma(b) = c$, $\sigma(c) = d$, and $\sigma(d) = a$.

Graphs

To describe discrete elements and their relationships we use graphs. Graphs provide us with a rich terminology that can be used to clarify a vocabulary for problem and solution descriptions. Informally put, an *undirected graph* $G = (V, E)$ (or a graph for short) comprises a finite set of vertices V and a set of edges $E \subseteq V \times V$. A vertex is illustrated with a circle and an edge with a line segment. An edge $e = (u, v) \in E$ is undirected and is considered identical to (v, u). An edge (v, v) is called a *loop*. The ends of an edge $e = (u, v) \in E$ are returned by the primitive routine $ends(e) = \{u, v\}$. If a vertex u is connected to another vertex v ($u \neq v$) by an edge, u is said to be *adjacent* to v. The set of adjacent vertices of a vertex v is called a *neighbourhood*, and it is returned by the routine *neighbourhood*(v). A sequence $W = \langle e_0, e_1, \ldots, e_{n-1} \rangle$ is called a *walk* of length n, if $e_i = (v_i, v_{i+1}) \in E$ for $i \in [0, n-1]$. If we are not interested in the intermediate edges of a walk but only in its starting vertex and ending vertex, we denote $v_0 \rightsquigarrow v_n$. If $v_0 = v_n$, the walk W is *closed*. The walk W is called a *path* if all of its vertices differ (i.e. $v_i \neq v_j$ when

$i \neq j$) and it does not contain loops. A closed walk that is a path, except for $v_0 = v_n$, is a *cycle*. A graph without cycles is *acyclic*.

A *directed graph* (or digraph) changes the definition of the edge. An edge has a direction, which means that $(u, v) \neq (v, u)$ when $u \neq v$. In this case, an edge $e = (u, v)$ is illustrated with an arrow from u to v. The vertex v is the *head* and u the *tail* of the edge, and we have routines *head(e)* and *tail(e)* to retrieve them. Naturally, $ends(e) = \{head(e)\} \cup \{tail(e)\}$. In a directed graph, the successors of the vertex v are in a set returned by the routine $successors(v)$, and if v has no successors, then $successors(v) = \emptyset$. Similarly, the predecessors of the vertex v are given by $predecessors(v)$. The neighbourhood is the union of adjacent vertices: $neighbourhood(v) = successors(v) \cup predecessor(v)$. Because we allow loops, a vertex can be in its own neighbour. The definitions of the concepts *directed walk, directed path*, and *directed cycle* are similar to their respective definitions for undirected graphs.

In a *weighted graph*, derived from an undirected or directed graph, each edge has an associated weight given by a weight function $weight : E \rightarrow \mathbb{R}_+$. We let *weight(e)* and *weight(u, v)* denote the weight of the edge $e = (u, v) \in E$.

A *tree* is an undirected graph where each possible vertex pair u and v is connected with a unique path. In other words, the tree is acyclic and $|E| = |V| - 1$. A *forest* is a disjoint collection of trees. We are often interested in a *rooted tree*, where one vertex is called a *root*. We can call a vertex of a rooted tree a *node*. The root can be used as a base for traversing the other nodes, and the furthermost nodes from the root are *leaves*. The non-leaf nodes, the root included, are called *internal nodes*. The adjacent nodes of node n away from the root are called the *children* of node n, denoted by *children(n)*. The unique node in *neighbourhood(n)* \ *children(n)* is called the *parent* of node n. If *parent(n)* $= \emptyset$, n is the root node.

A.3 Format of Algorithms

Algorithm A.2 gives an example of an algorithm written using pseudocode. The algorithm iteratively solves Towers of Hanoi, and the solution can be generated with the following procedure:

> TOWERS-OF-HANOI(n)
> **in:** number of discs n $(0 \leq n)$
> **out:** sequence S of states from the initial state to final state
> 1: $S \leftarrow \langle \text{INITIAL-STATE}(n) \rangle$
> 2: **while** $turn(S) \neq 2^n - 1$ **do**
> 3: $S \leftarrow S \parallel \langle \text{NEXT-MOVE}(S_{|S| - 1}) \rangle$
> 4: **end while**
> 5: **return** S

The details of how this algorithm works are left as an exercise for the interested reader. However, we encourage the casual reader to study the notation used and to identify conventions described in this appendix.

Algorithm A.2 Iterative solution to Towers of Hanoi.

INITIAL-STATE(n)

  in: number of discs n $(0 \leq n)$
  out: triplet $S = \langle s_0, s_1, s_2 \rangle$ representing the initial state

1: $s_0 \leftarrow \langle n, n-1, \ldots, 1 \rangle; s_1 \leftarrow s_2 \leftarrow \langle\,\rangle$
2: $S \leftarrow \langle s_0, s_1, s_2 \rangle$ ▷ Start s_0, goal s_1, aid s_2.
3: $turn(S) \leftarrow 0$
4: $direction(S) \leftarrow 1$ ▷ Clockwise rotation.
5: **if** n is even **then**   ▷ Counterclockwise rotation.
6:   $direction(S) \leftarrow -1$
7: **end if**
8: **return** S

NEXT-MOVE(S)

  in: triplet $S = \langle s_0, s_1, s_2 \rangle$ representing the current game state
  out: triplet $R = \langle r_0, r_1, r_2 \rangle$ representing the new game state
  local: pole indices $a, b, z \in \{0, 1, 2\}$; disc numbers $g, h \in [2, n]$; $last(Q) = Q_{|Q|-1}$, if
        $1 \leq |Q|$, otherwise, $last(Q) = +\infty$

1: $R \leftarrow$ **copy** S ▷ Now $r_i = s_i$, $0 \leq i \leq 2$.
2: $direction(R) \leftarrow direction(S)$
3: $a \leftarrow$ the index of the pole where $1 \in r_a$
4: $b \leftarrow (3 + a + direction(R))$ **mod** 3
5: $z \leftarrow (3 + a - direction(R))$ **mod** 3
6: **if** $turn(R)$ is even **then**   ▷ Move the smallest disc.
7:   $r_b \leftarrow r_b \,\|\, \langle 1 \rangle$
8:   $r_a \leftarrow sub(r_a, 0, |r_a| - 1)$
9: **else**   ▷ Move the non-smallest disc.
10:   $g \leftarrow last(r_b)$ ▷ $+\infty$, if $|r_b| = 0$.
11:   $h \leftarrow last(r_z)$ ▷ $+\infty$, if $|r_z| = 0$.
12:   **if** $g < h$ **then**
13:     $r_z \leftarrow r_z \,\|\, \langle g \rangle$
14:     $r_b \leftarrow sub(r_b, 0, |r_b| - 1)$
15:   **else if** $h < g$ **then**
16:     $r_b \leftarrow r_b \,\|\, \langle h \rangle$
17:     $r_z \leftarrow sub(r_z, 0, |r_z| - 1)$
18:   **else**
19:     **error** already in the final state
20:   **end if**
21: **end if**
22: $turn(R) \leftarrow turn(S) + 1$
23: **return** R

The *signature* of an algorithm includes the name of the algorithm and the arguments passed to it. It is followed by a *preamble* which may include the following descriptions:

in: This section describes the call-by-value arguments passed to the algorithm. The most important preconditions concerning an argument are given in parentheses. Because an algorithm behaves as a function from the caller's perspective, there is no need for preconditions on the state of the system. If the algorithm has multiple arguments, their descriptions are separated by semicolons.

out: This section outlines the result passed to the caller of the algorithm. In most cases it is sufficient to give the postcondition in natural language. Because the algorithms are functions, each algorithm must include a description of its return values.

constant: If an algorithm refers to constant values or structures through a symbolic name, they are described in this section. The constraints are given in parentheses, and multiple constants are separated by semicolons. The difference between an argument and a constant of an algorithm depends on the point of view, and the constants do not necessary have to be implemented using programming language constants.

local: Changes are allowed only to the entities created within the local scope of the algorithm. This section describes the most important local variables and structures.

The preamble of an algorithm is followed by enumerated lines of pseudocode. The line numbering serves only for reference purposes and does not impose any structure on the pseudocode. For example, we can elaborate that line 3 of NEXT-MOVE in Algorithm A.2 can be implemented in $O(1)$ time by introducing an extra variable.

A.4 Conversion to Existing Programming Languages

To concretize how an algorithm written in pseudocode can be implemented with an existing programming language, let us consider the problem of converting a given arabic number to the equivalent modern roman number. Modern roman numerals are the letters M (for the value 1000), D (500), C (100), L (50), X (10), V (5), and I (1). For example, $1989 = 1000 + (1000 - 100) + 50 + 3 \cdot 10 + (10 - 1)$ is written as MCMLXXXIX. Algorithm A.3 solves the conversion problem by returning a sequence R of multipliers of 'primitive' numbers in $P = \langle 1000, 900, 500, 400, 100, 90, 50, 40, 10, 9, 5, 4, 1 \rangle$. In our example, 1989 becomes $R = \langle 1, 1, 0, 0, 0, 0, 1, 0, 3, 1, 0, 0, 0 \rangle$.

A Java programmer could implement Algorithm A.3 by modelling first the primitive numbers with the enumeration type `RomanNumeral`. Each **enum** constant (I, IV,..., M) is declared with its decimal value which can be accessed with the function `getValue()`:

```java
public enum RomanNumeral {
    I(    1),
    IV(   4), V(    5), IX(   9), X(   10),
    XL( 40), L(   50), XC( 90), C( 100),
    CD(400), D( 500), CM(900), M(1000);

    private int value;
    private RomanNumber(int v) { value = v; }

    public int getValue() { return value; }
}
```

Algorithm A.3 Conversion from an Arabic number to a modern Roman number.

ARABIC-TO-ROMAN(n)

   in: decimal number n $(0 \leq n)$

   out: sequence $R = \langle s_0, s_1, \ldots, s_{12} \rangle$ representing the structure of the roman
                number ($R_i = $ number of primitives V_i in n for $i \in [0, 12]$)

   constant: sequence $P = \langle 1000, 900, 500, 400, 100, 90, 50, 40, 10, 9, 5, 4, 1 \rangle$ of primit-
                ive roman numbers

   local: remainder x to be converted $(0 \leq x \leq n)$; coefficient c for a primitive
                roman numbers (for other than P_0, $0 \leq c \leq 3$)

  1: $|R| \leftarrow |P|$ $\triangleright$ Reserve space for $|P| = 13$ values.

  2: $x \leftarrow n$

  3: **for** $i \leftarrow 0 \ldots (|P| - 1)$ **do**

  4:    $c \leftarrow x$ **div** P_i $\triangleright$ Number of multiplicands P_i in x.

  5:    $R_i \leftarrow c$

  6:    $x \leftarrow x - c \cdot P_i$

  7: **end for**

  8: **return** R

The actual conversion is implemented as a static function `toRoman(int)` in the class `ArabicToRomanNumber`. Note that the original algorithm has been modified as follows:

- The conversion returns a string instead of a sequence of integers. Because a roman number does not include zeros, the **for** loop at lines 3–7 is replaced by two nested **while** loops. The inner loop takes care of possible repetitions of the same primitive number.
- The precondition is strengthened to $1 \leq n$.
- To emphasize that the values $4000 \leq n$ are cumbersome to express in roman numerals, the postcondition gives an estimate of how long the result string will be.

The actual Java code looks like this:

```java
public class ArabicToRomanNumber {
    /** Convert an arabic number to a modern roman number.
     *   @.pre   1 <= n
     *   @.post result.length() <= (n div 1000) + (3 * 4)
     */
    public static String toRoman(int n) {
        RomanNumeral[] primitives = {
            RomanNumeral.M,   RomanNumeral.CM,  RomanNumeral.D,
            RomanNumeral.CD,  RomanNumeral.C,   RomanNumeral.XC,
            RomanNumeral.L,   RomanNumeral.XL,  RomanNumeral.X,
            RomanNumeral.IX,  RomanNumeral.V,   RomanNumeral.IV,
            RomanNumeral.I
        };
        int remainder = n;
```

```
        StringBuffer result = new StringBuffer();
        int i = 0;
        while ( remainder != 0 ) {
            while ( primitives[i].getValue() <= remainder ) {
                result.append(primitives[i]);
                remainder -= primitives[i].getValue();
            }
            ++i;
        }
        String res = result.toString();
        return res;
    }
}
```

A programmer more accustomed to the quirks of the C programming language could implement Algorithm A.3 by following the original form more closely. However, the primitive sequence P has a regular structure and can be compressed to four values by introducing a scaling variable. To include the possibility of memory allocation optimizations, the caller must provide the storage buffer for the roman number.

```
#include <string.h>

/* Convert an arabic number to a modern roman number.
 * Pre:   (the length of buffer is at least 13) and (0 <= n).
 * Post:  (result == buffer) and (result[0..12] represents
 *        roman number).
 */
int* arabicToRoman(int* buffer, int n) {
    memset(buffer, 0, 13 * sizeof(int));
    /* Here: For all i: buffer[i] == 0. */
    int conversions[] = { 1000, 900, 500, 400 };
    int divider = 1;
    int i = 0;
    int value;
    while ( n != 0 ) {
        value = conversions[i % 4] / divider;
        buffer[i] = n / value;
        n -= buffer[i] * value;
        ++i;
        if ( i % 4 == 0 ) divider *= 10;
    }
    return buffer;
}
```

The rise of the modern dynamic programming languages has made it possible to experiment easily with various approaches and solutions without investing much time or meticulous effort. For example, built-in data structures, higher-order routines and runtime mechanisms for reflection keep the codebase compact and modifiable. And sometimes there is not even a need for further optimization because only the outcome counts, or the actual bottleneck of the system is somewhere else.

A typical Ruby language implementation of Algorithm A.3 would be based on refining the integer numbers to support the conversion function directly. The refinement is activated locally by the caller, preventing the *monkey-patching* from affecting the other parts of the program. The actual conversion is about accumulating the result in steps, and for this Ruby already has suitable operations.

```ruby
module RomanFixnum
  refine Fixnum do
    def to_roman
      i = self
      { 'M' => 1000, 'CM' => 900, 'D' => 500, 'CD' => 400,
        'C' =>  100, 'XC' =>  90, 'L' =>  50, 'XL' =>  40,
        'X' =>   10, 'IX' =>   9, 'V' =>   5, 'IV' =>   4,
        'I' =>    1
      }.reduce('') { |memo, (s, v)|
        n, i = i.divmod(v)
        memo << s * n
      }
    end
  end
end


# Usage example:
using RomanFixnum
puts 2016.to_roman    # Outputs string "MMXVI".
(0...16).each { |i| puts i.to_roman }
```

As we can see the Java, C and Ruby implementations include numerous language-specific details that can be omitted from the pseudocode representation. When the syntax and semantics of Ruby, C, C++, and Java seem as peculiar as Algol68, Cobol, and Fortran do today, descriptions resembling Algorithm A.3 are likely to remain understandable in the future and can be reimplemented using the favourite programming language of the time.

B

Practical Vectors and Matrices

One of the most practical mathematical applications – together with geometry and trigonometry – is modelling and calculating with points, vectors and matrices. An algorithm-inclined game developer will encounter them from low-level graphics processing to high-level decision-making. Each of these three areas has a long and rich history of research, because they reveal answers to questions involving spatiality.

The amount of material on these topics is voluminous and solid, but, at the same time, to become proficient with these tools requires dedication. To reduce this burden, our aim here is to present the fundamentals of vectors and matrices in a practical manner. We will not delve into their mathematical properties – however interesting they are in their own right – but gather together and summarize the essentials. We introduce the key concepts step by step and develop the ideas behind them. We begin with points and vectors to see how and why they relate to each other. Then we take a peek at matrices and clarify why it is worth the effort to study them.

A concrete example

The concept of a vector is simple but expressive, making it easy to grasp and to apply to numerous problems. Sometimes it is impressive how a cunning plan with vectors sidesteps the need for detailed derivations of equations or calculations. To demonstrate the usefulness of vectors, let us consider a problem called *the closest distance of approach*. If two vessels follow their own fixed line trajectory with their own steady velocity, what is their closest possible distance?

To model the problem we use an arrow to point in the direction a vessel is heading. Also, to represent the velocity of the vessel we encode it as the length of the arrow – the scale could be such that a length of 1 cm corresponds to a velocity of 1 km/h. Given an instance of the problem (e.g. you and a friend *en route*) we replace the vessels at their specific positions, denoted •, with arrows as defined. For example, the situation in Figure B.1(a) shows the short-term trajectories visualized with grey line segments.

However, because the vessels can have different velocities, the point where the trajectory lines possibly cross is not the closest point in general. In addition to the directions, we have to consider also the lengths of the arrows. To do this we observe that there is a third partaker in the situation – the *map*. Since the map does not move, we can think of it as a space that is fixed and then define a point of reference in it to serve as the origin of that space, denoted ○. Now it is time for a trick from the bag of vectors: a change of reference point. We copy the arrow of 'you' and turn it around; it is intuitively clear that

Algorithms and Networking for Computer Games, Second Edition. Jouni Smed and Harri Hakonen.
© 2017 John Wiley & Sons Ltd. Published 2017 by John Wiley & Sons Ltd.

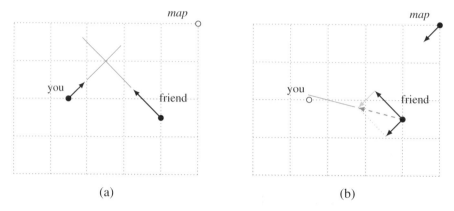

Figure B.1 The problem of the closest distance of approach. (a) The reference point of the world is on 'map'. (b) The reference point is on 'you'.

the net effect to the vessel is zero (i.e. it does not move). To keep the arrangement consistent with the earlier set-up, the turned arrow must be copied also to the other partakers, resulting in Figure B.1(b). Vessel 'you' has become the origin and, hence, 'map' must be on the move. The net effect of a set of arrows for 'friend' can be resolved by setting them into a chain but keeping their directions. One of the arrows is set at the vessel's position and the rest are placed so that the nock of an arrow always matches the head of another arrow. Then the chain of arrows can be replaced by a single arrow that goes from the vessel's position to the head of the last arrow in the chain. The dashed arrow in B.1(b) depicts this all-in-one arrow. Now the situation has become static, and the problem is about determining the distance from a point to a line, which is much easier to solve. Actually, this simplification has some magnitude since we presented the problem on a plane but the argumentation we made did not assume that. In other words, the method works regardless of the dimensionality of the problem.

As a corollary, we can see from Figure B.1(b) that this development also proves why the old sailor's wisdom 'constant bearing, decreasing range' (i.e. a friend will collide when it is getting closer but keeps its relative bearing) holds water: the dashed arrow then simply points towards the observer.

B.1 Points and Vectors

When we want to refer to a *position* in a space, we need to fix a reference *origin*, an ordered set of reference *axes* and a *unit length*. These three measures define all the positions in the space uniquely.[1] For example, positions in Euclidean space can be referred to with the familiar Cartesian coordinates that define the real-number axes x, y, and z. We can also use other coordinate systems such as spherical coordinates, but we will focus here on Cartesian coordinates.

---

1 Provided the axes are independent (i.e. none of the axes is defined in terms of the others) and the number of axes equals the degrees of freedom in the space. We incorporate these requirements into the concept of 'axis' implicitly.

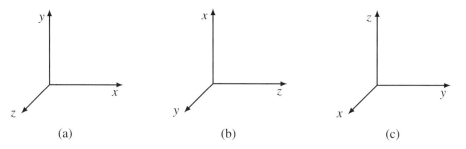

Figure B.2 The same right-handed frame of the real-number axes *x*, *y*, and *z* from three viewing angles. Arrows indicate positive directions. The axis pointing outwards, towards the rear left of the reader, from this page is the (a) *z*-axis, (b) *y*-axis, and (c) *x*-axis.

The origin, the axes, and the unit length together form a frame of reference, or a *frame* for short. To give a precise definition of a frame in *n* dimensions, we first have to state the origin point and then state *n* other reference points at unit distance from the origin along each intended axis. The order in which the reference points are stated is significant. For example, in three dimensions the axes can be oriented two ways. In a *right-handed frame*, the positive directions of the real-number axes are defined so that the *x*-axis points to the right, the *y*-axis upwards, and the *z*-axis towards the reader as illustrated in Figure B.2(a). In other words, if we orient ourselves along the positive *x*- and *y*-axes, we will be looking in the direction of the negative *z*-axis. In the *left-handed frame*, the *z*-axis is reversed, and we would be then looking along the positive *z*-axis. For remainder of this chapter, we will use the right-handed frame since it is the standard frame in mathematics and physics. Nevertheless, the left-handed system is frequently utilized in some specific problem domains such as computer graphics.

A position is uniquely specified by its *coordinates*, which are an ordered tuple of real numbers measuring the signed distances along the axes from the origin. This means that on a plane the origin has coordinates $(0, 0)$ and in a three-dimensional space $(0, 0, 0)$. The position (c_1, c_2, c_3) can be located, with respect to the origin, by travelling first a distance c_1 along the first axis, then c_2 along a line parallel to the second axis, and c_3 along a line parallel to the third axis.

To sum up so far, we fix a right-handed frame somewhere in the space to define the concrete and unique coordinates for all the positions in that space. This is the setting we then use to operate with points and vectors. However, it is important to understand that both a point and a vector *exist* without being placed in any position, but they can both be *represented* by positions.

This dissociation from coordinates emphasizes the relative nature of points and vectors, because they are entities that can be operated without imposing, for instance, a concept of dimension from the outside. Actually, dimensionality can be derived from the world of vectors. To understand this we can think in the following manner. A *point* is an entity that does not have any dimensional measurements such as width or volume but can have other attributes (e.g. an identifying name *p*). It is useful to define a *vector* as an entity that has a signed direction and a finite non-negative size (i.e. a magnitude). To identify a vector *v* we use the notation $\vec{v}$. We can operate with vectors even in this general form; for example, it is intuitive to expect the vector $-\vec{v}$ to have the same size as

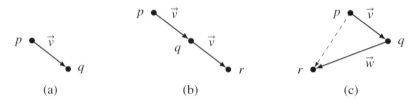

Figure B.3 Examples of applying a vector to a point. (a) $\vec{v}$ applied to point p fixes point q. (b) Visualizing $\vec{v} + \vec{v}$ using q as the midpoint. (c) The dashed arrow demonstrates the vector $\vec{v} + \vec{w}$ applied to p.

$\vec{v}$ but the opposite direction, whereas the vector $\vec{v} + \vec{v} = 2\vec{v}$ has the same direction but twice the size.

We can apply the vector $\vec{v}$ to the point p, and this binding fixes two points: the *initial* point p with respect to $\vec{v}$ and the *terminal* point q with respect to $\vec{v}$. The point q is at a distance equal to the size of $\vec{v}$ in the direction of $\vec{v}$ from p. To declare compactly the application of $\vec{v}$ to p we can use the notation $\vec{v} = \vec{pq}$, where we can interpret the equality '=' as name aliasing. Importantly, the vector $\vec{pq}$ is *not at* the point p, it is just applied there – and it can be applied also to other points.

By using points we can present a vector as a directed line segment from the initial point to the terminal point, which leads to more intuitive and fine-grained demonstrations as illustrated in Figure B.3(a). Furthermore, adding this kind of a structure to the vectors does not contradict the mathematics developed for vectors that do not refer to points. Continuing the previous example, if $\vec{v} = \vec{pq}$, then we can describe $-\vec{v} = \vec{qp}$. Also, if $\vec{v} = \vec{qr}$, then we can express $\vec{v} + \vec{v} = \vec{pq} + \vec{qr} = \vec{pr} = 2\vec{v}$ as illustrated in Figure B.3(b). In this case, it is convenient to choose q as the intermediate point to illustrate that $2\vec{v}$ has to have double the size of $\vec{v}$.

Exercising the freedom to choose the points to exemplify the properties of vectors, let us observe the vector $\vec{v} + \vec{w}$ in general. Imitating the previous example, let $\vec{v} = \vec{pq}$ and $\vec{w} = \vec{qr}$; see Figure B.3(c). To be consistent with $\vec{v} + \vec{v} = 2\vec{v}$, in this case also the point q must be considered as an intermediate point only, which gives us the result $\vec{v} + \vec{w} = \vec{pr}$. The size and direction of the vector $\vec{pr}$ are described in the terms of $\vec{v}$ and $\vec{w}$, and p is used as an application point. It is worth noting that if $\vec{pr}$ is applied to q and $\vec{v}$ is applied also to r, we have a parallelogram, or slanted rectangle, that demonstrates $\vec{w} + \vec{v} = \vec{pr}$. In other words, two vectors can be added in any order. The sum operation generalizes similarly to multiple vectors.

Assuming that we have arbitrary vectors $\vec{v}$ and $\vec{w}$, what can be said about their sum? If $\vec{w}$ is actually equal to $-\vec{v}$, the initial and terminal points of the vector describing $\vec{v} + \vec{w} = \vec{v} + (-\vec{v})$ must be the same (i.e. $\vec{pq} + \vec{qp} = \vec{pp}$), which we can observe considering the situation in Figure B.3(c). The resulting vector $\vec{pp}$ is a vector applied to the point p. To wriggle out of this space oddity where a vector returns back to its ground, we need to define a unique vector $\vec{0}$, which has neither size nor direction. Conversely, the sum vector is longest when the summand vectors have the same direction.

The subtraction of two arbitrary vectors can be realized using summation and reversion: If $\vec{v} + \vec{w} = \vec{pr}$, then by adding $-\vec{v}$ to both sides and simplifying $\vec{0}$ away, we get $\vec{w} = \vec{pr} + (-\vec{v}) = \vec{pr} - \vec{v}$. The last equality can be seen as a definition for the difference between two vectors. As a mnemonic, the terminal point r of vector $\vec{pr} - \vec{pq}$ is pointed by the minuend and the initial point q by the subtrahend.

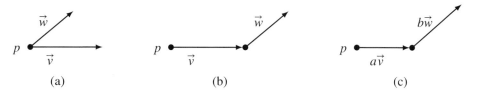

Figure B.4 Vectors applied to point p. (a) Vectors $\vec{v}$ and $\vec{w}$. (b) Vector $\vec{v} + \vec{w}$. (c) Linear combination vector $a\vec{v} + b\vec{w}$ of vectors $\vec{v}$ and $\vec{w}$ with scalers $a, b \in \mathbb{R}$.

Scaling and adding vectors together can be seen as mechanisms that yield new vectors from the already existing ones. For example, suppose we are given the vectors $\vec{v}$ and $\vec{w}$. Their *linear combination* with scalers[2] $a, b \in \mathbb{R}$ is a vector $\vec{u} = a\vec{v} + b\vec{w}$ as illustrated in Figure B.4(c). If we consider illustrations (a) and (b) in Figure B.4, they have the same proportions, and the scaler instances depicted in (c) can be estimated as $0 < a < 1$ and $1 < b$. A linear combination is like a chain of vectors, where the vectors telescope in, out and in reverse according to the scalers without changing their direction lines.

What can be said about $\vec{u} = a\vec{v} + b\vec{w}$? If $a, b = 0$, then clearly $\vec{u} = \vec{0}$. Is it possible to have $\vec{u} = \vec{0}$ also when $a \neq 0$ or $b \neq 0$? Yes it is. For example, assuming $a \neq 0$ and $\vec{w} = c\vec{v}$ ($c \neq 0$), we can select $b = -a/c \neq 0$, leading to $\vec{u} = a\vec{v} + b\vec{w} = a\vec{v} + (-a/c)c\vec{v} = \vec{0}$. In other words, if one of the given vectors is a linear combination of the other, there are at least two ways to end up with $\vec{0}$. This observation can be generalized to define linear independence: the vectors in a finite set $\{\vec{v}_1, \vec{v}_2, \ldots, \vec{v}_n\}$ are *linearly independent* only when the equation

$$a_1\vec{v}_1 + a_2\vec{v}_2 + \ldots + a_n\vec{v}_n = \vec{0}$$

has the unique solution

$$a_1 = a_2 = \ldots = a_n = 0$$

for $a_i \in \mathbb{R}$ ($i = 1, \ldots, n$).

Linearly independent vectors $\vec{v}$ and $\vec{w}$ are called a *basis* for all the vectors expressed in the form $a\vec{v} + b\vec{w}$, and all those vectors can be referred to simply by stating their unique *components* a and b, given $\vec{v}$ and $\vec{w}$. Let us consider a possibly infinite set of vectors V. The *dimension* of V is the size of a maximal (finite) set $L \subseteq V$ that is linearly independent. L is not necessarily unique for V but its dimension is, and the vectors of L can be used as a basis of V. The space we are arrowing to begins to show marks.

Up to this point, we have established the scaling of vectors by any real number ($a\vec{v}$, $a \in \mathbb{R}$), the concept of a zero vector ($\vec{0}$), and the addition and subtraction of vectors. However, these notions are limited if we want to compare vectors (i.e. measure how their sizes or directions relate). Naturally, there are constructions where intuitive measuring is possible, but it becomes vague in general. For example, suppose we have three non-zero vectors $\vec{pq}$, $\vec{qr}$, and $\vec{rp}$ of equal size. Since they form an equilateral triangle, it is natural to expect that the internal angles are also equal, but *is* the measurement of the angle actually $60° = \pi/3$ rad or something else? When vectors $3\vec{v}$, $4\vec{v}$, and $5\vec{v}$ are chained

---

2 Not to be confused with 'scalars', which are real numbers defining a vector: if $\vec{v} = (x, y)$ then x and y are the scalars of $\vec{v}$.

into a cycle, we expect the angle opposite to $5\vec{v}$ to be a right angle ($90° = \pi/2$ rad). How do we *define* such a property in general, independently of the scalers 3, 4, and 5?

The concepts of size and angle can be clarified not only by giving them more structure but also by making them dependent. Sizes and angles can be defined independently and in many ways, but since we want to utilize them together, only the sensible combinations are of interest to us. For example, in practically useful definitions the summation of angles behaves as $angle(\vec{u}, \vec{v}) + angle(\vec{v}, \vec{w}) = angle(\vec{u}, \vec{w})$, the angles are independent of the sizes of the vectors $angle(\vec{u}, \vec{v}) = angle(a\vec{v}, b\vec{w})$ ($0 < a, b$), and the angles have continuously unique values over the range $[0, \pi]$ rad.

Without delving into the mathematical details,[3] it can be proven that when 'size' and 'angle' play nicely together, there also exists a concept called the *inner product* of two vectors that becomes uniquely defined by this binding of nicety. Or, in the other direction, the size and angle depend on how an inner product is chosen. Since we are focusing on Euclidean space, we do not define the requirements, or axioms, of a general inner product here. Instead, we can confine ourselves to its Euclidean specialization called the *dot product*, and this choice fixes the unique definition for it. Let us next lay down the geometrical foundations by describing these central concepts and what kind of dependencies we actually want.

The size of a vector $\vec{v}$ is a non-negative real number denoted by $\|\vec{v}\|$, which is called the *norm* of $\vec{v}$. A vector is called a *unit vector* when $\|\vec{v}\| = 1$. Since unit vectors are frequently referred to, for instance, when specifying a direction, they can be declared with the shorthand notation $\hat{v}$. The hat $\hat{}$ can also be seen as a function that maps the vector $\vec{v}$ to another vector $\vec{v}/\|\vec{v}\|$. This means that the vector $\vec{v}$ heads $\|\vec{v}\|$ units in the direction $\hat{v}$. Note that $\|-\vec{v}\| = \|\vec{v}\|$, and only the zero vector $\vec{0}$ has norm equal to 0.

The dot product is a function that maps a pair of vectors to a real number, $\bullet : (\vec{v}, \vec{w}) \mapsto \alpha \in \mathbb{R}$, and we can use α to derive the measurement for the angle between $\vec{v}$ and $\vec{w}$. Following from the (unstated) axioms defining the inner product, and hence also the dot product, the quotient $(\vec{v} \bullet \vec{w})/(\|\vec{v}\| \|\vec{w}\|)$ lies in $[-1, 1] \subset \mathbb{R}$. Observing that the cosine function has the convenient property $\cos \theta : [0, \pi] \to [-1, 1]$, the angle θ between non-zero vectors $\vec{v}$ and $\vec{w}$ can be defined as

$$\cos \theta = \frac{\vec{v} \bullet \vec{w}}{\|\vec{v}\| \|\vec{w}\|}. \tag{B.1}$$

Actually, θ is a function $\theta(\vec{v}, \vec{w})$, but since the vectors are clear from the context, we can use the simpler notation.

Equation (B.1) has the following consequences:

- $\vec{v} \bullet \vec{w} = \vec{w} \bullet \vec{v}$, since $\cos(\theta) = \cos(-\theta)$.
- For unit vectors, $\cos \theta = \hat{v} \bullet \hat{w}$.
- When $\vec{v} \bullet \vec{w} = 0$, the vectors are perpendicular: $\theta = \frac{1}{2}\pi$ (i.e. 90°) or $\frac{3}{2}\pi$ (i.e. 270°).
- Codirectional vectors have $\theta = 0$, giving $\vec{v} \bullet \vec{w} = \|\vec{v}\| \|\vec{w}\|$.

---

3 These are fascinating, and we warmly encourage the reader to seek out things like inner product space, normed vector space, parallelogram identity and polarization identity and to see how neatly they fit together.

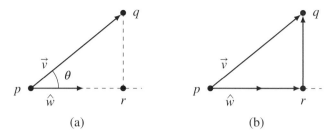

Figure B.5 Vector components. (a) The vector $\vec{v}$ is projected in the direction $\hat{w}$ so that the angle $\angle prq$ is a right angle. The projection is vector $\vec{pr} = (\vec{v} \bullet \hat{w})\hat{w}$. (b) The vector components of $\vec{v}$ in the direction $\hat{w}$ are $\vec{v}_{\parallel \hat{w}} = \vec{pr}$ and $\vec{v}_{\perp \hat{w}} = \vec{rq} = \vec{v} - \vec{pr} = \vec{v} - \vec{v}_{\parallel \hat{w}}$.

- Equal vectors imply $\vec{v} \bullet \vec{v} = \|\vec{v}\|\, \|\vec{v}\| = \|\vec{v}\|^2$, which means that, in the terms of the dot product, the norm is

$$\|\vec{v}\| = \sqrt{\vec{v} \bullet \vec{v}}. \tag{B.2}$$

Reversing the dependencies, if the measurements 'angle' and 'norm' are given, Equation (B.1) can be used to define the dot product. It can even be proven that a 'norm' alone is sufficient to express $\vec{v} \bullet \vec{w}$. However, by introducing more structure into our geometry it is possible to state $\vec{v} \bullet \vec{w}$ without referring directly to the sizes of and angle between $\vec{v}$ and $\vec{w}$.

To appreciate Equation (B.1), let us assume that $\vec{w}$ is actually a unit vector $\hat{w}$ used just for specifying a direction, giving $\cos\theta = (\vec{v} \bullet \hat{w})/\|\vec{v}\|$. Because the cosine of an angle in a right-angled triangle is the ratio of the adjacent side length to the hypotenuse side length, a vector $(\vec{v} \bullet \hat{w})\hat{w}$ of size $\vec{v} \bullet \hat{w} = \|\vec{v}\|\,\cos\theta$ can be interpreted as the perpendicular *projection* of $\vec{v}$ to the direction parallel to $\hat{w}$, which is visualized in Figure B.5(a). Since $\|\vec{v}\| \in \mathbb{R}_{\geq 0}$, the projected vector is in the same direction as or opposite direction to $\hat{w}$, or it is a zero vector $\vec{0}$. The projected vector is highly convenient and deserves its own notation $\vec{v}_{\parallel \hat{w}}$, where the symbol $\parallel$ refers to the parallel property. As it takes two to make the perpendiculars, the other one is the share of $\vec{v}$ *rejected* from the projection, denoted by $\vec{v}_{\perp \hat{w}}$, where the symbol $\perp$ portrays the perpendicular property. Figure B.5(b) summarizes the implication of this: given a direction $\hat{w}$, any vector $\vec{v}$ can be decomposed into the vector components that are parallel and perpendicular to $\hat{w}$:

$$\vec{v} = \vec{v}_{\parallel \hat{w}} + \vec{v}_{\perp \hat{w}}. \tag{B.3}$$

Because the hat notation $\hat{}$ can be seen just as a function, the decomposition applies to any vectors $\vec{v}$ and $\vec{w}\ (\neq \vec{0})$ giving $\vec{v}_{\parallel \hat{w}} = \vec{v}_{\parallel \vec{w}}$ due to

$$\vec{v}_{\parallel \hat{w}} = (\vec{v} \bullet \hat{w})\hat{w} = \left(\vec{v} \bullet \frac{\vec{w}}{\|\vec{w}\|}\right)\frac{\vec{w}}{\|\vec{w}\|} \overset{\text{Eq(B.2)}}{=} \left(\frac{\vec{v} \bullet \vec{w}}{\vec{w} \bullet \vec{w}}\right)\vec{w} = \vec{v}_{\parallel \vec{w}},$$

from which $\vec{v}_{\perp \vec{w}}$ also follows. Furthermore, the equalities $\vec{v} \bullet \vec{w} = \vec{v}_{\parallel \hat{w}}\,\|\vec{w}\| = \vec{w}_{\parallel \hat{v}}\,\|\vec{v}\|$ hold.

As a sidenote, projection helps us to justify the fact that the dot product over the addition of vectors is distributive: $(\vec{v} + \vec{w}) \bullet \vec{u} = \vec{v} \bullet \vec{u} + \vec{w} \bullet \vec{u} = \vec{u} \bullet (\vec{v} + \vec{w})$; see Figure B.6 for a visual proof.

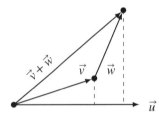

Figure B.6 The sizes of the projection vectors onto $\vec{u}$ are additive, implying distributivity $(\vec{v} + \vec{w}) \bullet \vec{u} = \vec{v} \bullet \vec{u} + \vec{w} \bullet \vec{u}$.

If a set of linearly independent vectors $\{\vec{v}, \vec{w}\}$ is the basis of some possibly infinite set of vectors V, then, apparently, $\{\vec{v}_{\parallel \vec{w}}, \vec{v}_{\perp \vec{w}}\}$ is also the basis of V. Is there some elemental difference between these bases? Since the dot product is fundamental in our discussion, let us connect it with the linear independence to see how the details interact. Suppose $\vec{n} = a_1\vec{v} + b_1\vec{w}$ and $\vec{m} = a_2\vec{v} + b_2\vec{w}$ are in V. Then

$$\vec{n} \bullet \vec{m} = (a_1\vec{v} + b_1\vec{w}) \bullet \vec{m}$$

$$\stackrel{*}{=} (a_1\vec{v}) \bullet \vec{m} + (b_1\vec{w}) \bullet \vec{m}$$

$$= (a_1\vec{v}) \bullet (a_2\vec{v} + b_2\vec{w}) + (b_1\vec{w}) \bullet (a_2\vec{v} + b_2\vec{w})$$

$$\stackrel{*}{=} (a_1\vec{v}) \bullet (a_2\vec{v}) + (a_1\vec{v}) \bullet (b_2\vec{w}) + (b_1\vec{w}) \bullet (a_2\vec{v}) + (b_1\vec{w}) \bullet (b_2\vec{w})$$

$$= a_1 a_2 (\vec{v} \bullet \vec{v}) + a_1 b_2 (\vec{v} \bullet \vec{w}) + a_2 b_1 (\vec{w} \bullet \vec{v}) + b_1 b_2 (\vec{w} \bullet \vec{w}),$$

where the steps marked with $*$ follow from the distributivity and the last step from the general equality $(a\vec{v}) \bullet w = \|a\vec{v}\| \, \|\vec{w}\| \, \cos(\theta(a\vec{v}, \vec{w})) = a \|\vec{v}\| \, \|\vec{w}\| \, \cos(\theta(\vec{v}, \vec{w})) = a(\vec{v} \bullet \vec{w})$, where $a\vec{v}$ and $\vec{v}$ stay in the same direction.

Although the basis vectors $\{\vec{v}, \vec{w}\}$ are linearly independent, their 'shares' in the linearly combined vectors of V 'overlap' when $\vec{v} \bullet \vec{w} \neq 0$. However, when $\vec{v} \bullet \vec{w} = 0$, meaning $\vec{v}$ and $\vec{w}$ are perpendicular, the dot product simplifies to

$$\vec{n} \bullet \vec{m} = a_1 a_2 (\vec{v} \bullet \vec{v}) + b_1 b_2 (\vec{w} \bullet \vec{w}).$$

Furthermore, remembering that $\vec{v} \bullet \vec{v} = \|\vec{v}\| \, \|\vec{v}\| = \|\vec{v}\|^2$ and setting $\|\hat{v}\| = 1$, we end up with basis vectors that are perpendicular unit vectors, and the dot product is simply

$$\vec{n} \bullet \vec{m} = a_1 a_2 + b_1 b_2 \tag{B.4}$$

which also rephrases Equation (B.2) into the radical expression

$$\|\vec{n}\| = \sqrt{\vec{n} \bullet \vec{n}} = \sqrt{a_1^2 + b_1^2}.$$

What makes Equation (B.4) intriguing is that it does not include the basis vectors or the angle of $\vec{n}$ and $\vec{w}$. In other words, the same equation applies to any basis that consists of mutually perpendicular unit vectors, and it generalizes straightforwardly to any number of basis vectors (i.e. all dimensions). This is the basis of the many benefits that we get from using points and vectors.

In three-dimensional worlds, we can denote the mutually perpendicular unit vectors as $\hat{e}_x, \hat{e}_y$, and $\hat{e}_z$, which correspond to the right-handed frame coordinates discussed earlier. Now we can *represent* the vector $\vec{v} = a\hat{e}_x + b\hat{e}_y + c\hat{e}_z$ as coordinates (a, b, c). Obviously, these coordinates do not refer to a position or a point but encode the vector $\vec{v}$ in a coordinate form. To avoid confusion between points and vectors – and to conform later with matrices – we identify the vectors over $\hat{e}_x$, $\hat{e}_y$ and $\hat{e}_z$ with a *column* notation where the components are written vertically. For example,

$$\vec{v} = \begin{bmatrix} a \\ b \\ c \end{bmatrix}, \quad \vec{0} = \begin{bmatrix} 0 \\ 0 \\ 0 \end{bmatrix}, \quad \hat{e}_x = \begin{bmatrix} 1 \\ 0 \\ 0 \end{bmatrix}, \quad \hat{e}_y = \begin{bmatrix} 0 \\ 1 \\ 0 \end{bmatrix}, \quad \hat{e}_z = \begin{bmatrix} 0 \\ 0 \\ 1 \end{bmatrix}.$$

We can represent a column vector $\vec{v}$ compactly in line form as $[\,a \ \ b \ \ c\,]^{\mathsf{T}}$ where the symbol ^{T} reminds us that the components must actually be interpreted as written vertically.

All our preceding observations, operations and calculations also have representations using column vectors. For example, given $\vec{v} = [\,v_1 \ \ v_2 \ \ v_3\,]^{\mathsf{T}}$ and $\vec{w} = [\,w_1 \ \ w_2 \ \ w_3\,]^{\mathsf{T}}$,

$$\vec{v} \pm \vec{w} = [\,v_1 \pm w_1 \quad v_2 \pm w_2 \quad v_3 \pm w_3\,]^{\mathsf{T}},$$

$$a\vec{v} = [\,av_1 \quad av_2 \quad av_3\,]^{\mathsf{T}},$$

$$\hat{e}_x + \hat{e}_y + \hat{e}_z = \vec{1} = [\,1 \quad 1 \quad 1\,]^{\mathsf{T}}.$$

It is worth remembering that when we select a representation for the vectors, the vectors are not applied to points or positions. For example, $\vec{0} = [\,0 \ \ 0 \ \ 0\,]^{\mathsf{T}}$ is not at the origin or at the position $(0, 0, 0)$. However, the component values in a column vector can be interpreted as displacements, and when the column vector is applied to a point the displacements uniquely define the terminal point. For this reason it is natural that the points are placed into positions, represented, for example, as coordinates. But in essence the worlds of the displacements and the positions are separate, and mixing those realms invites bewilderment.

A displacement measures the shortest distance from the initial point p to the terminal point q (i.e. it demonstrates both size and direction), making the unification of displacements and vectors sensible. The displacements can be combined and split to components as vectors. The component values of a vector are equal to the differences of the corresponding coordinates where the points reside. For example, if point p is at the position (p_1, p_2) and point q at (q_1, q_2), the displacement from p to q can be represented as a vector $\vec{s} = [\,q_1 - p_1 \ \ q_2 - p_2\,]^{\mathsf{T}}$ for which $\|\vec{s}\| = \sqrt{(q_1 - p_1)^2 + (q_2 - p_2)^2}$.

Moving back and forth between the positions and displacements is tedious, but we can get rid of the commuting by fixing a coordinate system and then introducing a *position vector*. Its initial point is always at the origin of the space and its terminal point is at the position we want to refer to. Now, instead of dealing with the positions, we substitute them with the position vectors and operate only with them. In other words, the position vectors represent the displacements from the origin and they are compatible with the other displacement vectors discussed earlier.

This is a subtle but important realization, because when the positions are actually represented as vectors, all vector operations apply to them. For example, the 'difference' between positions actually means the difference between their position vectors, yielding a displacement. Also, applying a vector to a point is just the ordinary addition of the position vector with the displacement vector, resulting in a position vector. The benefit of this is uniformity, as we are dealing with vectors only. One of the drawbacks is the same uniformity: since both 'positions' and displacements are vectors, we have to bookkeep which is which. Another drawback is that the position vectors depend on the chosen coordinate system, whereas the displacement vectors do not.

The position vectors are valuable when dealing with time. For example, a three-dimensional position $r(t)$ as a function of time t can be modelled as $r(t) = x(t)\hat{e}_x + y(t)\hat{e}_y + z(t)\hat{e}_z$ where functions $x(t)$, $y(t)$, and $z(t)$ define the separate components of the change.

There is still one more curiosity with vectors in three-dimensional space, the *cross product* of two vectors. Without going into a theoretical discussion, the definition of the cross product turns out to have a similar form to the dot product in Equation (B.1):

$$\sin \theta = \frac{\vec{v} \times \vec{w}}{\hat{n} \, \|\vec{v}\| \, \|\vec{w}\|}. \tag{B.5}$$

However, the interpretation of Equation (B.5) is more detailed. Assume that we are given the vectors $\vec{v}$ and $\vec{w}$ and the angle between them is θ. Then $\vec{v} \times \vec{w}$ is the vector which has the direction $\hat{n}$ and size $\|\vec{v} \times \vec{w}\| = \|\vec{v}\| \, \|\vec{w}\| \sin \theta$. The direction of the unit vector $\hat{n}$ is perpendicular to the plane defined by the linear combinations of $\vec{v}$ and $\vec{w}$. If the vectors do not define the plane then the cross product is $\vec{0}$. Because there are two perpendiculars to a plane, the direction of $\hat{n}$ is defined by the right-handed rule *from $\vec{v}$ to $\vec{w}$*:

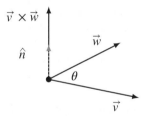

This means that the cross product is *not* associative, but $\vec{w} \times \vec{v} = -\vec{v} \times \vec{w}$. This change of sign is understandable because the two perpendiculars to a plane must be in opposite directions.

The fact that the cross product yields a perpendicular vector is often useful. Let us consider an example in three-dimensional space where we have a camera at a position vector $\vec{c}$. The point of interest the camera is looking at is at position vector $\vec{p}$. Also, we fix the upward direction to $\hat{e}_z$. Then $\vec{a} = \vec{p} - \vec{c}$ is the displacement vector from $\vec{c}$ to $\vec{p}$. Together with vectors

$$\vec{u} = \vec{a} \times \hat{e}_z,$$

$$\vec{v} = \vec{u} \times \vec{a},$$

we can define the following right-handed frame of reference: the origin is at position $\vec{c}$, the right direction is $\hat{u}$, the up direction is $\hat{v}$, and the viewing direction is $-\hat{a}$. These frame vectors are always perpendicular to each other, which means that we have defined a local Cartesian coordinate system with respect to the camera just by a few simple operations.

B.2 Matrices

If vectors are treated as values, then matrices can be considered as functions that map the given vectors to other ones. For example, a vector can be rotated around the origin of the space with a certain kind of a matrix. Matrices can also be used to collect or augment vectors into one bundle so that they can then be operated on together at the same time. In both cases a *matrix* $M_{m,n}$ is an array of terms, numbers or symbols arranged in m rows and n columns denoted by

$$M_{m,n} = \begin{bmatrix} m_{1,1} & m_{1,2} & \cdots & m_{1,n} \\ m_{2,1} & m_{2,2} & \cdots & m_{2,n} \\ \vdots & \vdots & \ddots & \vdots \\ m_{m,1} & m_{m,2} & \cdots & m_{m,n} \end{bmatrix}$$

where $1 \leq m, n \in \mathbb{N}$. We can omit the size subscript when it is clear from the context. Since we allow both $m = 1$ and $n = 1$, we can consider row and column vectors as degenerate matrices of size $1 \times n$ and $m \times 1$, respectively. Also, it is possible to have a 1×1 matrix $M_{1,1}$ and, depending on the convention used, it can be considered as a scalar. However, we do not adopt this practice; to refer to $M_{1,1}$ as a scalar we use $m_{1,1}$ instead to keep the semantics clear.

To be able to consider a vector as a special kind of a matrix, all the vector operations must be maintained – not necessarily for all matrices but at least for the ones that are vector-like. It is worth seeking linkages of the concepts between vectors and matrices, because that induces a two-way effect: it enriches the world of matrices and, at the same time, the expressive power of matrices can be used as a tool with vectors.

As with vectors, to add two matrices together we simply add the elements in corresponding places. Naturally, this requires that the matrices are of the same size. When adding matrices A and B, the elements of the resulting matrix $C = A + B$ are defined as

$$c_{i,j} = a_{i,j} + b_{i,j}.$$

Conversely, in matrix subtraction $C = A - B$ the corresponding elements are subtracted:

$$c_{i,j} = a_{i,j} - b_{i,j}.$$

A vector $\vec{v}$ can be scaled by multiplying it by $r \in \mathbb{R} : r\vec{v}$. This generalizes directly to all matrices, and $C = rA$ is simply

$$c_{i,j} = r \cdot a_{i,j}.$$

How about multiplication? With vectors we have the dot product $\vec{v} \bullet \vec{w}$ and the cross product $\vec{v} \times \vec{w}$. The vector cross product can be represented with different concepts in the realm of the matrices, but the other direction lacks standard definitions. The dot product, however, can be generalized to a matrix operation which is called matrix multiplication. At first sight the definition of this operation seems quite baffling, but much of the power of matrices springs from it. Let us begin by presenting matrix multiplication from point of view of matrices, and then we will clarify its simplicity and briefly illuminate its connection to the vector dot product.

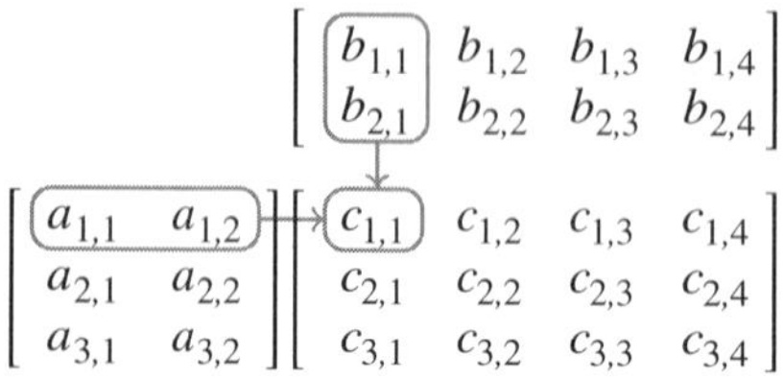

$$\begin{bmatrix} b_{1,1} & b_{1,2} & b_{1,3} & b_{1,4} \\ b_{2,1} & b_{2,2} & b_{2,3} & b_{2,4} \end{bmatrix}$$

$$\begin{bmatrix} a_{1,1} & a_{1,2} \\ a_{2,1} & a_{2,2} \\ a_{3,1} & a_{3,2} \end{bmatrix} \begin{bmatrix} c_{1,1} & c_{1,2} & c_{1,3} & c_{1,4} \\ c_{2,1} & c_{2,2} & c_{2,3} & c_{2,4} \\ c_{3,1} & c_{3,2} & c_{3,3} & c_{3,4} \end{bmatrix}$$

Figure B.7 An instance of the matrix multiplication defined by Equation (B.6): matrices of sizes 3×2 and 2×4 are multiplied together, resulting in a 3×4 matrix. The value $c_{1,1} = a_{1,1}b_{1,1} + a_{1,2}b_{2,1}$, and for example $c_{2,4} = a_{2,1}b_{1,4} + a_{2,2}b_{2,4}$.

Matrix multiplication imposes limitations on the matrices operated upon. Let us consider a matrix A of size $m \times n$ and a matrix B of size $n \times s$, where $1 \le m, n, s$. Observe that the number of columns in A equals the number of rows in B. Multiplying these matrices is defined to give as a result a matrix C of size $m \times s$ with elements

$$c_{i,j} = \sum_{k=1}^{n} a_{i,k}b_{k,j}, \tag{B.6}$$

where $1 \le i \le m$ and $1 \le j \le s$. The index k runs over the columns of A and the rows of B utilizing the aforementioned size requirement of the matrices being multiplied.

To give a mnemonic – and even a pen-and-paper method – for Equation (B.6), the multiplication can be depicted as shown in Figure B.7. For example, to multiply

$$A_{3,2} = \begin{bmatrix} a_{1,1} & a_{1,2} \\ a_{2,1} & a_{2,2} \\ a_{3,1} & a_{3,2} \end{bmatrix} \quad \text{and} \quad B_{2,4} = \begin{bmatrix} b_{1,1} & b_{1,2} & b_{1,3} & b_{1,4} \\ b_{2,1} & b_{2,2} & b_{2,3} & b_{2,4} \end{bmatrix}$$

we place A to the left of the result matrix $C_{3,4}$ and B above it. Each element in C is at the intersection of one particular row of A and column of B.

The schema of Figure B.7 holds for all matrix shapes that can be multiplied. For example, if a column matrix $B_{m,1}$ is multiplied by a row matrix $A_{1,n}$, the result is $B_{m,1}A_{1,n} = C_{m,n}$, a matrix of size $m \times n$. How about the other way around? The vectors must be of the same length and, if so, multiplication gives

$$A_{1,m}B_{m,1} = [a_{1,1} \quad a_{1,2} \quad \cdots \quad a_{1,m}] \begin{bmatrix} b_{1,1} \\ b_{2,1} \\ \vdots \\ b_{m,1} \end{bmatrix}$$

$$= a_{1,1}b_{1,1} + a_{1,2}b_{2,1} + \ldots + a_{1,m}b_{m,1}$$

$$\overset{\text{Eq(B.4)}}{=} \vec{a} \bullet \vec{b}$$

where both vectors $\vec{a}$ and $\vec{b}$ are the *column* vector interpretations of their corresponding matrices $A_{1,m}$ and $B_{m,1}$. This gives us a hint that the matrix multiplication and the vector dot product may have something in common.

At first sight, the definition of matrix multiplication may seem convoluted, but it has proved to be convenient. For example, assume that we have two sets of linear equations

$$x'' = a_3 x' + b_3 y' \qquad\qquad x' = a_1 x + b_1 y$$
$$\text{and}$$
$$y'' = a_4 x' + b_4 y' \qquad\qquad y' = a_2 x + b_2 y$$
(B.7)

and we want to represent x'' and y'' in terms of x and y. The substitution of x' and y' is simply

$$x'' = a_3(a_1 x + b_1 y) + b_3(a_2 x + b_2 y) = (a_3 a_1 + b_3 a_2)x + (a_3 b_1 + b_3 b_2)y$$
$$y'' = a_4(a_1 x + b_1 y) + b_4(a_2 x + b_2 y) = (a_4 a_1 + b_4 a_2)x + (a_4 b_1 + b_4 b_2)y$$
(B.8)

but because matrix multiplication, as defined, gives us

$$\begin{bmatrix} a_3 & b_3 \\ a_4 & b_4 \end{bmatrix} \begin{bmatrix} a_1 & b_1 \\ a_2 & b_2 \end{bmatrix} = \begin{bmatrix} a_3 a_1 + b_3 a_2 & a_3 b_1 + b_3 b_2 \\ a_4 a_1 + b_4 a_2 & a_4 b_1 + b_4 b_2 \end{bmatrix},$$

Equation (B.8) can also be represented compactly as

$$\begin{bmatrix} x'' \\ y'' \end{bmatrix} = \begin{bmatrix} a_3 & b_3 \\ a_4 & b_4 \end{bmatrix} \begin{bmatrix} a_1 & b_1 \\ a_2 & b_2 \end{bmatrix} \begin{bmatrix} x \\ y \end{bmatrix}.$$
(B.9)

In other words, the situation in Equation (B.7) can be captured with Equation (B.9) without the need for considering the details present in Equation (B.8).

To summarize, we can realize linear transformations just by using matrices. By doing this we have them in a format that is easy to combine (by matrix multiplication) and compute, which is why they are heavily used in, for example, computer graphics.

As we can see, for instance, in Equation (B.8) there are terms that resemble the calculations of the vector dot product. Let us look into this observation briefly. Consider the ith row of A as a row vector $\vec{a}_i$ and the jth column of B as a column vector $\vec{b}_j$. Clearly, $c_{i,j} = \vec{a}_i \bullet \vec{b}_j$:

$$A = \begin{bmatrix} a_{1,1} & a_{1,2} & \cdots & a_{1,n} \\ a_{2,1} & a_{2,2} & \cdots & a_{2,n} \\ \vdots & \vdots & \ddots & \vdots \\ a_{m,1} & a_{m,2} & \cdots & a_{m,n} \end{bmatrix} = \begin{bmatrix} \vec{a}_1 \\ \vec{a}_2 \\ \vdots \\ \vec{a}_m \end{bmatrix},$$

$$B = \begin{bmatrix} b_{1,1} & b_{1,2} & \cdots & b_{1,s} \\ b_{2,1} & b_{2,2} & \cdots & b_{2,s} \\ \vdots & \vdots & \ddots & \vdots \\ b_{n,1} & b_{n,2} & \cdots & b_{n,s} \end{bmatrix} = \begin{bmatrix} \vec{b}_1 & \vec{b}_2 & \cdots & \vec{b}_s \end{bmatrix},$$

$$C = \begin{bmatrix} \vec{a}_1 \\ \vec{a}_2 \\ \vdots \\ \vec{a}_m \end{bmatrix} \begin{bmatrix} \vec{b}_1 & \vec{b}_2 & \cdots & \vec{b}_s \end{bmatrix} = \begin{bmatrix} \vec{a}_1 \bullet \vec{b}_1 & \vec{a}_1 \bullet \vec{b}_2 & \cdots & \vec{a}_1 \bullet \vec{b}_s \\ \vec{a}_2 \bullet \vec{b}_1 & \vec{a}_2 \bullet \vec{b}_2 & \cdots & \vec{a}_2 \bullet \vec{b}_s \\ \vdots & \vdots & \ddots & \vdots \\ \vec{a}_m \bullet \vec{b}_1 & \vec{a}_m \bullet \vec{b}_2 & \cdots & \vec{a}_m \bullet \vec{b}_s \end{bmatrix}.$$

In other words, matrix multiplication can be viewed as the generalization of the vector dot product.

It is worth noting that matrix multiplication is not commutative – not only because of the size requirements – but even if the sizes of A and B matched, $AB \neq BA$. Otherwise, the following rules apply for matrices:

$$A + B = B + A,$$

$$A + (B + C) = (A + B) + C,$$

$$A(BC) = (AB)C,$$

$$A(B + C) = AB + AC,$$

$$(A + B)C = AC + BC.$$

If A is of size $n \times n$, we can define the power of the matrix A^k $(1 \leq k)$ as

$$A^k = \underbrace{AA \cdots A}_{k}.$$

We can also define $A^0 = I$, where I is the *identity matrix*

$$I = \begin{bmatrix} 1 & 0 & \cdots & 0 \\ 0 & 1 & \cdots & 0 \\ \vdots & \vdots & \ddots & \vdots \\ 0 & 0 & \cdots & 1 \end{bmatrix}.$$

Matrices have also an operation called *transpose*, which may, at first sight, appear to be an artificial construction, but it is as important as the other operations. Transpose is denoted by the superscript $^\top$ but does not relate to the power operation. If matrix A is of size $m \times n$, then its transpose matrix $T = A^\top$ is of size $n \times m$, where the elements have exchanged their rows and columns:

$$t_{i,j} = a_{j,i}.$$

Note that the elements on the main diagonal $a_{i,i}$ $(1 \leq i \leq \min\{m, n\})$ of the matrix are preserved. The transpose gives us yet another way to describe the dot product of two column vectors when they are interpreted as matrices: $\vec{v}^\top \vec{w}$.

To demonstrate how matrices hide the details and compact the method descriptions we present two examples. The first one shows how to rotate any number of position vectors with only one matrix multiplication. The second example discusses how to move (i.e. translate) vectors by matrix multiplication.

Example on bundling column vectors to a single matrix

Assume we have the following asymmetric concave quadrilateral, enclosed in a convenient unit square that is easy to scale to an appropriate size. Let us call it ACQ and utilize its two-dimensional form to test visually our vector- and matrix-related calculations.

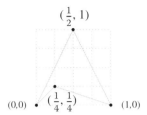

The vertices of ACQ can be defined by the position vectors

$$\vec{q}_0 = [0 \quad 0]^\mathsf{T}, \quad \vec{q}_1 = \left[\tfrac{1}{4} \quad \tfrac{1}{4}\right]^\mathsf{T}, \quad \vec{q}_2 = [1 \quad 0]^\mathsf{T}, \quad \vec{q}_3 = \left[\tfrac{1}{2} \quad 1\right]^\mathsf{T},$$

that form the endpoints of the counterclockwise sequence of line segments. To operate with ACQ as an one entity, the column vectors can be augmented side by side into one matrix,

$$A = \begin{bmatrix} 0 & \tfrac{1}{4} & 1 & \tfrac{1}{2} \\ 0 & \tfrac{1}{4} & 0 & 1 \end{bmatrix}.$$

Now, to rotate ACQ about the origin we multiply it by a rotation matrix $R_{2,2}$ that maps the vectors into their proper positions: $A'_{2,4} = R_{2,2}A_{2,4}$. Note that the rotation matrix must be of size 2×2 because we want the result to have the same size as A.

In general, a rotation matrix $R_{2,2}$ turns every vector $[x \ y]^\mathsf{T}$ about the origin counterclockwise by the given angle α measured in radians. Since α is the parameter of the rotation, the general definition for the matrix is as follows:

$$R_{2,2}(\alpha) = \begin{bmatrix} \cos\alpha & -\sin\alpha \\ \sin\alpha & \cos\alpha \end{bmatrix} \begin{bmatrix} x \\ y \end{bmatrix}$$

$$= \begin{bmatrix} \diagup & \diagup \\ \diagup & \diagup \end{bmatrix} \begin{bmatrix} x \\ y \end{bmatrix} = \begin{bmatrix} \diagup \cdot x + \diagup \cdot y \\ \diagup \cdot x + \diagup \cdot y \end{bmatrix} = \begin{bmatrix} x' \\ y' \end{bmatrix}$$

To give some intuition as to how the x and y values are changed, we have also depicted the trigonometric functions cos and sin in their domain $[0, 2\pi] \subset \mathbb{R}$.

If $\alpha = \pi/3$ (60°), the rotation matrix specializes to

$$R(\pi/3) = \begin{bmatrix} \tfrac{1}{2} & -\tfrac{\sqrt{3}}{2} \\ \tfrac{\sqrt{3}}{2} & \tfrac{1}{2} \end{bmatrix},$$

and then the actual application of the rotation gives

$$RA = \begin{bmatrix} \frac{1}{2} & -\frac{\sqrt{3}}{2} \\ \frac{\sqrt{3}}{2} & \frac{1}{2} \end{bmatrix} \begin{bmatrix} 0 & \frac{1}{4} & 1 & \frac{1}{2} \\ 0 & \frac{1}{4} & 0 & 1 \end{bmatrix}$$

$$= \begin{bmatrix} 0 & -\frac{\sqrt{3}}{8} + \frac{1}{8} & \frac{1}{2} & -\frac{\sqrt{3}}{2} + \frac{1}{4} \\ 0 & \frac{\sqrt{3}}{8} + \frac{1}{8} & \frac{\sqrt{3}}{2} & \frac{\sqrt{3}}{4} + \frac{1}{2} \end{bmatrix}$$

which can be visualized as

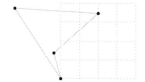

If there are tens, hundreds or even more vectors to be rotated, this method consumes both time and memory. Fortunately, some of the vectors can be left out of the bundle matrix A. For example, $\vec{q}_0$ is at the pivot of the rotation and, thus, its position does not change. Also, $\vec{q}_2$ is changed only by the leftmost column of the rotation matrix, and this is why the third column of RA is identical to the first column of R (i.e. both $\vec{q}_0$ and $\vec{q}_2$ can be left out of the calculation and their rotated positions can be determined by other and simpler means). The rationale is the same as with basis vectors: Linear combinations define new vectors. Therefore, all such linear combinations that are efficient to calculate are candidates for postponing their repositioning into a post-rotation phase.

Example on translating column vectors by matrix multiplication
If there are many phases in the matrix calculations, it saves time and memory to have all the constant matrices reduced and simplified as much as possible. For example, the matrix multiplications can be pre-calculated, because the order of calculations does not affect the outcome: $A(BC) = (AB)C = ABC$. This property has turned out to be crucial, for instance, in modelling physics and developing graphics pipelines.

But there is a fundamental operation that cannot be represented as a matrix multiplication: moving from one position to another. Moving a vector is also called *translation*. In other words, if all the matrices are constant but the sequence of operations required consists of an addition, the situation cannot be collapsed into one matrix only.

Fortunately, the restriction applies only within the dimension of concern. This means that if we are in two dimensions, there are no 2×2 matrices for translation. However, it is possible to have the same effect in three dimensions. Suppose we are moving the position $\vec{p} = [p_1 \ p_2]^\mathsf{T}$ by a displacement $\vec{r} = [r_1 \ r_2]^\mathsf{T}$. If we define a translation matrix

$T_{3,3}$ so that it is $I_{3,3}$ but its upper-right corner has the components of $\vec{r}$, and also an augmented vector $\vec{p}' = [p_1\ p_2\ 1]^\mathsf{T}$, then

$$T\vec{p}' = \begin{bmatrix} 1 & 0 & r_1 \\ 0 & 1 & r_2 \\ 0 & 0 & 1 \end{bmatrix} \begin{bmatrix} p_1 \\ p_2 \\ 1 \end{bmatrix} = \begin{bmatrix} p_1 + r_1 \\ p_2 + r_2 \\ 1 \end{bmatrix}.$$

Now, the effect of $\vec{p} + \vec{r}$ focuses on the first components of the result vector. This idea is an application of the so-called homogeneous coordinates. The other fundamental operations with matrices, including various projections, have similar interpretations in this system, which unifies them all with matrix multiplication.

The homogeneous coordinates are just one example of the attractions the continents of vectors and matrices have in store. Over their long history they have grown into a full range of concepts and tools that can be applied in diverse contexts. And, on top of all that, the explorer need not be a mathematician in order to benefit from them – and to have fun at the same time.

B.3 Conclusion

To complete this short introduction to vectors and matrices we have devised Algorithm B.1 that generates a fractal called Barnsley's wreath (Edgar 1991). The fractal consists entirely of hexagons that reproduce, translate (i.e. move) and rotate. The recursive routine BARNSLEY-WREATH is initiated with the invocation

1: $T \leftarrow \langle W_1, W_2, W_3, W_4, W_5, W_6 \rangle$
2: BARNSLEY-WREATH($img, T, D, d - 1$)

utilizing the following matrices:

$$W_1 = \begin{bmatrix} -\frac{1}{2} & 0 & \frac{1}{2} \\ 0 & \frac{1}{2} & 0 \\ 0 & 0 & 1 \end{bmatrix}, \quad W_2 = \begin{bmatrix} -\frac{1}{2} & 0 & -\frac{1}{4} \\ 0 & \frac{1}{2} & \frac{\sqrt{3}}{4} \\ 0 & 0 & 1 \end{bmatrix}, \quad W_3 = \begin{bmatrix} -\frac{1}{2} & 0 & -\frac{1}{4} \\ 0 & \frac{1}{2} & -\frac{\sqrt{3}}{4} \\ 0 & 0 & 1 \end{bmatrix},$$

$$W_4 = \begin{bmatrix} -\frac{1}{4} & 0 & -\frac{1}{4} \\ 0 & \frac{1}{4} & 0 \\ 0 & 0 & 1 \end{bmatrix}, \quad W_5 = \begin{bmatrix} -\frac{1}{4} & 0 & \frac{1}{8} \\ 0 & \frac{1}{4} & \frac{\sqrt{3}}{8} \\ 0 & 0 & 1 \end{bmatrix}, \quad W_6 = \begin{bmatrix} -\frac{1}{4} & 0 & \frac{1}{8} \\ 0 & \frac{1}{4} & -\frac{\sqrt{3}}{8} \\ 0 & 0 & 1 \end{bmatrix},$$

$$R = \begin{bmatrix} \frac{1}{2} & -\frac{\sqrt{3}}{2} \\ \frac{\sqrt{3}}{2} & \frac{1}{2} \end{bmatrix}, \quad D = \begin{bmatrix} 0 & 1 & 0 \\ 0 & 0 & 0 \\ 1 & 1 & 1 \end{bmatrix}.$$

The matrices W_i ($1 \le i \le 6$) describe the transformations that change the positions and orientations of the generated hexagons. The initial situation is defined by the matrix D that contains two-column vectors of size 2×1 in its upper left-hand corner. The vertices of the hexagons are produced by using the rotation matrix R.

The outcome of the algorithm is shown in Figure B.8 for the reader's pleasure.

Algorithm B.1 Barnsley's wreath fractal. Primitive routine *polygon* draws and fills the given polygon with the RGBA colour 0A0A0A0A$_{16}$.

BARNSLEY-WREATH(*img*, *T*, *D*, *d*)

  in: empty image *img*; sequence *T* of transformation matrices (constant); augmented matrix *D* of reference vectors; depth of recursion *d*

  out: filled greyscale image *img* in Figure B.8

  1: **if** $d = 0$ **then**   ▷ Terminate the recursion?

  2:   **return**

  3: **end if**

  4: $|D'| \leftarrow |T|$ ▷ Reserve space for $|T|$ matrices.

  5: **for** $i \leftarrow 0 \ldots (|T| - 1)$ **do**   ▷ Apply all the transformations in T.

  6:   $D'_i \leftarrow T_i D$ ▷ Transform the bundle of reference vectors.

  7:   *polygon*(*img*, HEXAGON-VERTICES(D'_i))   ▷ Draw the referred hexagons.

  8: **end for**

  9: **for** $i \leftarrow 0 \ldots (|D'| - 1)$ **do**   ▷ Descent in the recursion.

 10:   BARNSLEY-WREATH(*img*, *T*, D'_i, $d - 1$)

 11: **end for**

HEXAGON-VERTICES(*M*)

  in: matrix *M* of bundled column vectors

  out: sequence of position vectors of the vertices of a hexagon

  constant: rotation matrix R of $\pi/3$ rad (60°); centre position of a hexagon $\vec{p}_c$

  1: $\vec{p}_c \leftarrow [m_{0,0} \quad m_{1,0}]^\mathsf{T}$ ▷ Extract column vectors…

  2: $\vec{p}_t \leftarrow [m_{1,0} \quad m_{1,1}]^\mathsf{T}$ ▷ …of size 2×1 from M.

  3: $\vec{p} \leftarrow \vec{p}_t - \vec{p}_c$ ▷ Move to the origin.

  4: $V \leftarrow \langle \vec{p} \rangle$ ▷ The first and the last position is at $\vec{p}$.

  5: **for** $i \leftarrow 1 \ldots 6$ **do**   ▷ Create all the vertices of the hexagon.

  6:   $\vec{p} \leftarrow R\vec{p}$ ▷ Rotate $\vec{p}$.

  7:   $V \leftarrow V \parallel \langle \vec{p} \rangle$ ▷ A new vertex position for the hexagon.

  8: **end for**

  9: **for** $i \leftarrow 0 \ldots 6$ **do**   ▷ Move the positions in V by $\vec{p}_c$.

 10:   $V_i \leftarrow V_i + \vec{p}_c$

 11: **end for**

 12: **return** V

Figure B.8 Barnsley's wreath.

Bibliography

Abramson B 1987 The expected-outcome model of two-player games. Technical Report CUCS-315-87, Columbia University, New York.

Abramson B 1989 Control strategies for two-player games. *ACM Computing Surveys* **21**(2), 137–161.

Adams E 2014 *Fundamentals of Game Design* third edn. New Riders, Berkeley, CA.

Adams EW 2013 *Resolutions to Some Problems in Interactive Storytelling* PhD thesis University of Teesside Middlesbrough.

Aggarwal S, Banavar H, Khandelwal A, Mukherjee S and Rangarajan S 2004 Accuracy in dead-reckoning based distributed multi-player games *Proceedings of 3rd ACM SIGCOMM Workshop on Network and System Support for Games*, pp. 161–165.

Airey JM, Rohlf JH and Brooks, Jr. FP 1990 Towards image realism with interactive update rates in complex virtual building environments. *Computer Graphics* **24**(2), 41–50.

Albers S and Mitzenmacher M 1998 Average case analyses of list update algorithms, with applications to data compression. *Algorithmica* **21**(3), 312–329.

Aldous D and Diaconis P 1986 Shuffling cards and stopping times. *American Mathematical Monthly* **93**(5), 333–348.

Alexander T 2002 GoCap: Game observation capture In *AI Game Programming Wisdom* (ed. Rabin S) Charles River Media Hingham, MA pp. 579–589.

Alha K, Koskinen E, Paavilainen J, Hamari J and Kinnunen J 2014 Free-to-play games: Professionals' perspectives *Proceedings of the 2014 International DiGRA Nordic Conference*, Gotland, Sweden.

Ashlock D, Lee C and McGuinness C 2011 Search-based procedural generation of maze-like levels. *IEEE Transactions on Computational Intelligence and AI in Games* **3**(3), 260–273.

Auer P, Cesa-Bianchi N and Fischer P 2002 Finite-time analysis of the multiarmed bandit problem. *Machine Learning* **47**(2–3), 235–256.

Aylett R and Louchart S 2007 Being there: Participants and spectators in interactive narrative In *Virtual Storytelling. Using Virtual Reality Technologies for Storytelling. Proceedings of the Fourth International Conference, ICVS 2007* (ed. Cavazza M and Donikian S), vol. 4871 of *Lecture Notes in Computer Science*, pp. 117–128. Springer-Verlag, Berlin.

Bachrach R and El-Yaniv R 1997 Online list accessing algorithms and their applications: Recent empirical evidence *Proceedings of the 8th Annual ACM-SIAM Symposium on Discrete Algorithms (SODA'97)*, pp. 53–62. Society for Industrial and Applied Mathematics, Philadelphia.

Algorithms and Networking for Computer Games, Second Edition. Jouni Smed and Harri Hakonen.
© 2017 John Wiley & Sons Ltd. Published 2017 by John Wiley & Sons Ltd.

Bai J, Seah D, Yong J and Leong B 2009 Offloading AI for peer-to-peer games with dead reckoning *Proceedings of the 8th International Conference on Peer-to-peer Systems*, p. 3.

Balch T and Arkin RC 1998 Behavior-based formation control for multi-robot teams. *IEEE Transactions on Robotics and Automation* **14**(6), 926–939.

Balch T and Hybinette M 2000 Social potentials for scalable multi-robot formations *Proceedings of the 2000 IEEE International Conference on Robotics and Automation*, vol. 1, pp. 73–80.

Ballard BW 1983 The ∗-minimax search procedure for trees containing chance nodes. *Artificial Intelligence* **21**(3), 327–350.

Barr AH 1991 Teleological modeling In *Making Them Move* (ed. Badler NI, Barsky BA and Zeltzer D) Morgan Kaufmann San Francisco pp. 315–321.

Bartle R 1990 Interactive multi-user computer games. Technical report, British Telecom. ⟨http://www.mud.co.uk/richard/imucg.htm⟩.

Baughman NE and Levine BN 2001 Cheat-proof playout for centralized and distributed online games *Proceedings of the Twentieth IEEE Computer and Communication Society INFOCOM Conference*, Anchorage, AK.

Bayer D and Diaconis P 1992 Trailing the dovetail shuffle to its lair. *Annals of Applied Probability* **2**(2), 294–313.

Bellman RE and Zadeh LA 1970 Decision-making in a fuzzy environment. *Management Science* **17**(4), 141–164.

Benford S, Bowers J, Fahlén LE, Mariani J and Rodden T 1994 Supporting cooperative work in virtual environments. *Computer Journal* **37**(8), 653–668.

Benford S, Greenhalgh C, Reynard G, Brown C and Koleva B 1998 Understanding and constructing shared spaces with mixed-reality boundaries. *ACM Transactions on Computer-Human Interaction* **5**(3), 185–223.

Benford S, Greenhalgh C, Rodden T and Pycock J 2001 Collaborative virtual environments. *Communications of the ACM* **44**(7), 79–85.

Berglund EJ and Cheriton DR 1985 Amaze: A multiplayer computer game. *IEEE Software* **2**(3), 30–39.

Bernier YW 2001 Latency compensating methods in client/server in-game protocol design and optimization *Proceedings of the Game Developers Conference*.

Bettner P and Terrano M 2001 1500 archers on a 28.8: Network programming in Age of Empires and beyond. *Gamasutra*. ⟨http://www.gamasutra.com/features/20010322/terrano_01.htm⟩.

Bharambe A, Douceur JR, Lorch JR, Moscibroda T, Pang J, Seshan S and Zhuang X 2008 Donnybrook: Enabling large-scale, high-speed, peer-to-peer games *Proceedings of the Conference on Computer Communications (SIGCOMM)*, pp. 389–400.

Bjore S 2014 Techniques for formation movement using steering circles In *Game AI Pro: Collected Wisdom of Game AI Professionals* (ed. Rabin S) CRC Press Boca Raton, FL pp. 289–295.

Boulanger JS, Kienzle J and Verbrugge C 2006 Comparing interest management algorithms for massively multiplayer games *Proceedings of 5th ACM SIGCOMM Workshop on Network and System Support for Games*.

Box GEP and Muller ME 1958 A note on the generation of random normal deviates. *Annals of Mathematical Statistics* **29**(2), 610–611.

Bratley P, Fox BL and Schrage LE 1983 *A Guide to Simulation*. Springer-Verlag, New York.

Brown GW 1956 Monte Carlo methods In *Modern Mathematics for the Engineer: First Series* (ed. Beckenbach E) McGraw-Hill New York chapter 12, pp. 279–306.

Browne C, Powley E, Whitehouse D, Lucas S, Cowling PI, Rohlfshagen P, Tavener S, Perez D, Samothrakis S and Colton S 2012 A survey of Monte Carlo tree search methods. *IEEE Transactions on Computational Intelligence and AI in Games* **4**(1), 1–43.

Buck J 2015 *Mazes for Programmers: Code Your Own Twisty Little Passages.* Pragmatic Bookshelf, Dallas, TX.

Buschmann F, Meunier R, Rohnert H, Sommerland P and Stal M 1996 *Pattern-Oriented Software Architecture: A System of Patterns* vol. 1 of *Software Design Patterns.* John Wiley & Sons, Chichester.

Cai W, Lee FBS and Chen L 1999 An auto-adaptive dead reckoning algorithm for distributed interactive simulation *Proceedings of the Thirteenth Workshop on Parallel and Distributed Simulation*, pp. 82–89, Atlanta, GA.

Caillois R 2001 *Man, Play and Games.* University of Illinois Press, Urbana. Originally published in French 1958.

Canudo R 1988a The birth of a sixth art In *French Film Theory and Criticism: 1907–1939* (ed. Abel R) vol. I Princeton University Press Princeton, NJ pp. 58–66. Originally published in French 1911.

Canudo R 1988b Reflections on the seventh art In *French Film Theory and Criticism: 1907–1939* (ed. Abel R) vol. I Princeton University Press Princeton, NJ pp. 291–303. Originally published in French 1923.

Cavazza M, Charles F and Mead SJ 2001 Interactive storytelling: From computer games to interactive stories In *Proceedings of International Conference on Application and Development of Computer Games in the 21st Century* (ed. Sing LW, Man WH and Wai W), pp. 49–55, Hong Kong.

Chandler HM 2008 *The Game Production Handbook* second edn. Jones & Bartlett, Sudbury, MA.

Chang YC, Chen KT, Wu CC, Ho CJ and Lei CL 2010 Online game QoE evaluation using paired comparisons *IEEE International Workshop on Communications Quality and Reliability.*

Chang YI 1996 A simulation study on distributed mutual exclusion. *Journal of Parallel and Distributed Computing* **33**(2), 107–121.

Charles F, Mead SJ and Cavazza M 2002 Generating dynamic storylines through characters' interactions. *International Journal of Intelligent Games & Simulation* **1**(1), 5–11.

Chazelle B 1991 Triangulating a simple polygon in linear time. *Discrete & Computational Geometry* **6**(5), 485–524.

Chen BL, Chen L, Zou SR and Xu XL 2013 Quantitative measurement and method for detecting anti-community structures in complex networks. *International Journal of Wireless and Mobile Computing* **6**(5), 431.

Chen H, Chen L and Chen GC 2005 Effects of local-lag mechanism on task performance in a desktop CVE system. *Journal of Computer Science and Technology* **20**(3), 396–401.

Chen L, Yu Q and Chen B 2014 Anti-modularity and anti-community detecting in complex networks. *Information Sciences* **275**, 293–313.

Claypool M and Claypool K 2006 Latency and player actions in online games. *Communications of the ACM* **49**(11), 40–45.

Consalvo M 2007 *Cheating: Gaining Advantage in Videogames.* MIT Press, Cambridge, MA.

Cormen TH, Leiserson CE, Rivest RL and Stein C 2001 *Introduction to Algorithms* second edn. MIT Press, Cambridge, MA.

Costikyan G 2002 I have no words & I must design: Toward a critical vocabulary for games In *Computer Games and Digital Cultures Conference Proceedings* (ed. Mäyrä F), pp. 9–33, Tampere, Finland.

Coulom R 2007 Efficient selectivity and backup operators in Monte-Carlo tree search In *Proceedings of the 5th International Conference on Computers and Games (CG'06)* (ed. van den Herik HJ, Ciancarini P and Donkers HJ), vol. 4630 of *Lecture Notes in Computer Science*, pp. 72–83. Springer-Verlag, Berlin.

Crawford C 1984 *The Art of Computer Game Design*. Osborne/McGraw-Hill, Berkeley, CA.

Cronin E, Filstrup B and Jamin S 2003 Cheat-proofing dead reckoned multiplayer games In *Proceedings of the 2nd International Conference on Application and Development of Computer Games* (ed. Sing LW, Man WH and Wai W), pp. 23–29, Hong Kong.

Dahl OJ, Dijkstra EW and Hoare CAR 1972 *Structured Programming* number 8 in *A.P.I.C. Studies in Data Processing*. Academic Press, London.

Dawson C 2002 Formations In *AI Game Programming Wisdom* (ed. Rabin S) Charles River Media Hingham, MA pp. 272–281.

de Carpentier GJP and Bidarra R 2005 Behavioral assumption-based prediction for high-latency hiding in mobile games *Proceedings of 7th International Conference on Computer Games – CGAMES'05*, pp. 83–88, Angoulême, France.

de Sevin E, Chopinaud C and Mars C 2015 Smart zones to create the ambience of life In *Game AI Pro 2: Collected Wisdom of Game AI Professionals* (ed. Rabin S) CRC Press Boca Raton, FL pp. 89–100.

Defense Advanced Research Projects Agency 1981 Internet protocol Internet RFC 791. ⟨http://www.faqs.org/rfcs/rfc791.html⟩.

Derenick JC and Spletzer JR 2007 Convex optimization strategies for coordinating large-scale robot formations. *IEEE Transactions on Robotics* **23**(6), 1252–1259.

Dewdney AK 1984 Computer recreations: In the game called Core War hostile programs engage in a battle of bits. *Scientific American* **250**(5), 14–22.

Dijkstra EW 1968 Letters to the editor: Go to statement considered harmful. *Communications of the ACM* **11**(3), 147–148.

Diot C and Gautier L 1999 A distributed architecture for multiplayer interactive applications on the Internet. *IEEE Networks Magazine* **13**(4), 6–15.

Dubois D, Fargier H and Prade H 1996 Possibility theory in constraint satisfaction problems: Handling priority, preference and uncertainty. *Applied Intelligence* **6**, 287–309.

Duncan TP and Gračanin D 2003 Pre-reckoning algorithm for distributed virtual environments In *Proceedings of the 2003 Winter Simulation Conference* (ed. Chick S, Sánchez J, Ferrin D and Morrice DJ), pp. 1086–1093.

Ebert DS, Musgrave FK, Peachey D, Perlin K and Worley S 2002 *Texturing & Modeling: A Procedural Approach* Morgan Kaufmann Series in Computer Graphics third edn. Morgan Kaufmann, Burlington, MA.

Edgar GA 1991 A fractal puzzle. *Mathematical Intelligencer* **13**, 44–50.

Ekberg M 2016 *Monetization of free-to-play mobile games* Master's thesis University of Turku.

Entacher K 1999 Parallel streams of linear random numbers in the spectral test. *ACM Transactions on Modeling and Computer Simulation* **9**(1), 31–44.

Ercole A, Whittlestone KD, Melvin DG and Rashbass J 2002 Collusion detection in multiple choice examinations. *Medical Education* **36**(2), 166–172.

Erol K, Hendler J and Nau DS 1994a HTN planning: Complexity and expressivity *Proceedings of the Twelfth National Conference on Artificial Intelligence*, pp. 1123–1128, Seattle.

Erol K, Hendler J and Nau DS 1994b UMCP: A sound and complete procedure for hierarchical task-network planning *Proceedings of the Second International Conference on Artificial Intelligence Planning Systems*, pp. 249–254, Chicago.

Evans R 2002 Varieties of learning In *AI Game Programming Wisdom* (ed. Rabin S) Charles River Media Hingham, MA pp. 567–578.

Fédération Internationale de Football Association 2016 Laws of the game 2016/2017. ⟨http://www.fifa.com/development/education-and-technical/referees/laws-of-the-game.html⟩.

Feng WC, Kaiser E and Schluessler T 2008 Stealth measurements for cheat detection in on-line games *Proceedings of the 7th ACM SIGCOMM Workshop on Network and System Support for Games*, pp. 15–20, Worcester, MA.

Ferretti S 2008 Cheating detection through game time modeling: A better way to avoid time cheats in P2P MOGs?. *Multimedia Tools and Applications* **37**(3), 339–363.

Fields TV 2013 Game industry metrics terminology and analytics case study In *Game Analytics: Maximizing the Value of Player Data* (ed. Seif El-Nasr M, Drachen A and Canossa A) Springer-Verlag London pp. 53–71.

Fikes RE and Nilsson NJ 1971 STRIPS: A new approach to the application of theorem proving to problem solving. *Artificial Intelligence* **2**(3–4), 189–208.

Finkel RA and Fishburn JP 1982 Parallelism in alpha-beta search. *Artificial Intelligence* **19**(1), 89–106.

Fishburn JP 1983 Another optimization of alpha-beta search. *ACM SIGART Bulletin* **84**, 37–38.

Fournier A, Fussell D and Carpenter L 1982 Computer rendering of stochastic models. *Communications of the ACM* **26**(6), 371–384.

Frécon E and Stenius M 1998 DIVE: A scaleable network architecture for distributed virtual environments. *Distributed Systems Engineering* **5**(3), 91–100.

Fredslund J and Matarić MJ 2002 A general algorithm for robot formations using local sensing and minimal communication. *IEEE Transactions on Robotics and Automation* **18**(5), 837–846.

Freeman JA and Skapura DM 1991 *Neural Networks: Algorithms, Applications, and Programming Techniques*. Addison-Wesley, Redwood City, CA.

Fritsch T, Ritter H and Schiller J 2005 The effect of latency and network limitations on MMORPGs: A field study of Everquest2 *Proceedings of 4th ACM SIGCOMM Workshop on Network and System Support for Games*, pp. 1–9.

Fullér R and Carlsson C 1996 Fuzzy multiple criteria decision making: Recent developments. *Fuzzy Sets and Systems* **78**, 139–153.

Gamma E, Helm R, Johnson R and Vlissides J 1995 *Design Patterns: Elements of Reusable Object-Oriented Software* Addison-Wesley Professional Computing Series. Addison-Wesley, Reading, MA.

Gazzard A 2013 *Mazes in Videogames: Meaning, Metaphor and Design*. McFarland & Company, Jefferson, NC.

Gelly S and Silver D 2011 Monte-Carlo tree search and rapid action value estimation in computer Go. *Artificial Intelligence* **175**(11), 1856–1875.

Glover F 1989 Tabu search – part I. *ORSA Journal of Computing* **1**(3), 190–206.

Goldberg DE 1989 *Genetic Algorithms in Search, Optimization and Machine Learning.* Addison-Wesley, Reading, MA.

Google Brain Team 2016 TensorFlow. ⟨https://www.tensorflow.org/⟩.

Graetz JM 1981 The origin of Spacewar. *Creative Computing* pp. 56–67. ⟨http://www.wheels.org/spacewar/creative/SpacewarOrigin.html⟩.

Graham RL, Knuth DE and Patashnik O 1994 *Concrete Mathematics: A Foundation for Computer Science* second edn. Addison-Wesley, Reading, MA.

Greenhalgh C 1998 Awareness-based communication management in the MASSIVE systems. *Distributed Systems Engineering* **5**(3), 129–137.

Groh C, Moldovanu B, Sela A and Sunde U 2012 Optimal seedings in elimination tournaments. *Economic Theory* **49**(1), 59–80.

Guesgen HW 1994 A formal framework for weak constraint satisfaction based on fuzzy sets *Proceedings of ANZIIS-94*, pp. 199–203, Brisbane.

Gustafson JL 1988 Reevaluating Amdahl's law. *Communications of the ACM* **31**(5), 532–533.

Hakiri A, Berthou P and Gayraud T 2010 QoS-enabled ANFIS dead reckoning algorithm for distributed interactive simulation *Proceedings of the 14th IEEE/ACM Symposium on Distributed Simulation and Real-Time Applications*, pp. 33–42.

Hakonen H, Leppänen V and Salakoski T 2000 Object integrity while allowing aliasing In *Proceedings of Conference on Software: Theory and Practice* (ed. Feng Y, Notkin D and Gaudel MC), pp. 91–96 16th IFIP WCC2000, Beijing.

Han S, Lim M, Lee D and Hyun SJ 2008 A scalable interest management scheme for distributed virtual environments. *Computer Animation and Virtual Worlds* **19**(2), 129–149.

Hanawa D and Yonekura T 2006 A proposal of dead reckoning protocol in distributed virtual environment based on the Taylor expansion *Proceedings of the 2006 International Conference on Cyberworlds*, pp. 107–114.

Hanner N and Zarnekow R 2015 Purchasing behavior in free to play games: Concepts and empirical validation *Proceedings of the 48th Hawaii International Conference on System Sciences*, pp. 3326–3335.

Harabor D and Grastien A 2012 The JPS pathfinding system *Proceedings of the Fifth Annual Symposium on Combinatorial Search*, Niagara Falls, Ontario.

Harel D 1987 *Algorithmics: The Spirit of Computing.* Addison-Wesley, Wokingham.

Hartman C and Benes B 2006 Autonomous boids. *Computer Animation and Virtual Worlds* **17**(3–4), 199–206.

Hauk T, Buro M and Schaeffer J 2005 Rediscovering ∗-Minimax search In *Computers and Games, 4th International Conference, CG 2004, Ramat-Gan, Israel, July 5–7, 2004* (ed. van den Herik HJ, Björnsson Y and Netanyahu NS), vol. 3846 of *Lecture Notes in Computer Science*, pp. 35–50. Springer-Verlag, Berlin.

Hegel GWF 1975 *Aesthetics: Lectures on Fine Art* vol. II. Clarendon Press, Oxford. Originally published in German 1835.

Heger F 2013 *Scalable Propagation of Continuous Actions in Peer-to-Peer-based Massively Multiuser Virtual Environments: The Continuous Events Approach* PhD thesis Universität Mannheim.

Heijari V 2014 Current trends and best practices Aalto Game Monetization Design. ⟨https://youtu.be/JveS1WKUfeg⟩.

Hellekalek P 1998 Good random number generators are (not so) easy to find. *Mathematics and Computers in Simulation* **46**(5–6), 485–505.

Herrera F and Verdegay JL 1997 Fuzzy sets and operations research. Perspectives. *Fuzzy Sets and Systems* **90**, 207–218.

Hertel S and Mehlhorn K 1985 Fast triangulation of the plane with respect to simple polygons. *Information and Control* **64**(1–3), 52–76.

Higgins D 2002 Pathfinding design architecture In *AI Game Programming Wisdom* (ed. Rabin S) Charles River Media Hingham, MA pp. 122–132.

Hoglund G and McCraw G 2007 *Exploiting Online Games: Cheating Massively Distributed Systems*. Addison-Wesley, Reading, MA.

Hudak P 1989 Conception, evolution, and application of functional programming languages. *ACM Computing Surveys* **21**(3), 359–411.

Huizinga J 1955 *Homo Ludens: A Study of the Play-Element in Culture*. Beacon Press, Boston. Originally published in Dutch 1938.

Humphreys T 2015 Exploring HTN planners through example In *Game AI Pro 2: Collected Wisdom of Game AI Professionals* (ed. Rabin S) CRC Press Boca Raton, FL pp. 149–167.

Ida Y, Ishibashi Y, Fukushima N and Sugawara S 2010 QoE assessment of interactivity and fairness in first person shooting with group synchronization control *Proceedings of the 9th Annual Workshop on Network and Systems Support for Games*.

International Game Developers Association 2004 Foundations of interactive storytelling.

Islam MN, Haque SMR, Alam KM and Tarikuzzaman M 2009 An approach to improve collusion set detection using MCL algorithm *2009 12th International Conference on Computers and Information Technology*, pp. 237–242.

Jahn T and Loviscach J 2008 For bees and gamers: How to handle hexagonal tiles In *Game Programming Gems 7* (ed. Jacobs S) Cengage Learning Boston pp. 47–58.

Jensen K, Wirth N, Mickel AB and Miner JF 1985 *Pascal – User Manual and Report* third edn. Springer-Verlag, New York.

Johansson U, Sönströd C and König R 2003 Cheating by sharing information – the doom of online poker? In *Proceedings of the 2nd International Conference on Application and Development of Computer Games* (ed. Sing LW, Man WH and Wai W), pp. 16–22, Hong Kong.

Johnson G 2003 Avoiding dynamic obstacles and hazards In *AI Game Programming Wisdom 2* (ed. Rabin S) Charles River Media Hingham, MA pp. 161–170.

Kaukoranta T, Smed J and Hakonen H 2003 Understanding pattern recognition methods In *AI Game Programming Wisdom 2* (ed. Rabin S) Charles River Media Hingham, MA pp. 579–589.

Keil JM 1985 Decomposing a polygon into simpler components. *SIAM Journal on Computing* **14**(4), 799–817.

Kelley AD, Malin MC and Nielson GM 1988 Terrain simulation using a model of stream erosion. *Computer Graphics* **22**(4), 263–268.

Kelly G and McCabe H 2006 A survey of procedural techniques for city generation. *ITB Journal* **14**, 87–130.

Kelly G and McCabe H 2007 Citygen: An interactive system for procedural city generation *Proceedings of the 5th International Conference on Game Design and Technology*, pp. 8–16.

Kennedy J, Eberhart RC and Shi Y 2001 *Swarm Intelligence*. Morgan Kaufmann, San Francisco.

Ketola T 2014 Quantifying software development: Applying mobile monetization techniques to your software development process In *Proceedings of the 19th International Conference on Computer Games* (ed. Mehdi Q, Elmaghraby A, Marshall I, Lauf A, Jaromczyk JW, Ragade R, Begoña García Z, Chang DJ, Chariker J, El-Said M and Yampolskiy R), pp. 66–69.

Kimppa KK and Bissett A 2005 Is cheating in network computer games a question worth raising? In *Ethics of New Information Technology: Proceedings of the Sixth International Conference of Computer Ethics* (ed. Brey P, Grodzinsky F and Introna L), pp. 261–267, Enschede, The Netherlands.

Kimppa KK, Heimo OI and Harviainen JT 2015 First dose is always freemium. *Computers and Society* **45**(3), 132–137.

Kirkpatrick S, Gelatt CD and Vecchi MP 1983 Optimization by simulated annealing. *Science* **220**(4598), 671–680.

Kirmse A 2000 A network protocol for online games In *Game Programming Gems* (ed. DeLoura M) Charles River Media Hingham, MA pp. 104–108.

Kirmse A and Kirmse C 1997 Security in online games. *Game Developer* **4**(4), 20–28.

Knuth DE 1998a *Fundamental Algorithms* vol. 1 of *The Art of Computer Programming* third edn. Addison-Wesley, Reading, MA.

Knuth DE 1998b *Seminumerical Algorithms* vol. 2 of *The Art of Computer Programming* third edn. Addison-Wesley, Reading, MA.

Knuth DE 1998c *Sorting and Searching* vol. 3 of *The Art of Computer Programming* second edn. Addison-Wesley, Reading, MA.

Knuth DE 2011 *Combinatorial Algorithms, Part 1* vol. 4A of *The Art of Computer Programming*. Addison-Wesley, Upper Saddle River, NJ.

Knuth DE and Moore RW 1975 An analysis of alpha-beta pruning. *Artificial Intelligence* **6**(4), 293–326.

Kocsis L and Szepesvári C 2006 Bandit based Monte-Carlo planning *Proceedings of the 17th European Conference on Machine Learning (ECML'06)*, vol. 4212 of *Lecture Notes in Artificial Intelligence*, pp. 282–293. Springer-Verlag, Berlin.

Kohonen T 1995 *Self-Organizing Maps*. Springer-Verlag, Berlin.

Koskenvoima A and Mäntymäki M 2015 Why do small and medium-size freemium game developers use game analytics? In *Open and Big Data Management and Innovation* (ed. Janssen M, Mäntymäki M, Hidders J, Klievink B, Lamersdorf W, van Loenen B and Zuiderwijk A), vol. 9373 of *Lecture Notes in Computer Science*, pp. 326–337. Springer-Verlag, Cham, Switzerland.

Krasner GE and Pope ST 1988 A cookbook for using the model-view-controller user interface paradigm in Smalltalk-80. *Journal of Object-Oriented Programming* **1**(3), 26–49.

Kronmal RA and Peterson AV 1979 The alias and alias-rejection-mixture methods for generating random variables from probability distributions *Proceedings of the 11th Conference on Winter Simulation (WSC'79)*, vol. 1, pp. 269–280. IEEE Press, Piscataway, NJ.

Krumm-Heller A and Taylor S 2000 Using determinism to improve the accuracy of dead-reckoning algorithms *Proceedings of the Simulation Technology and Training Conference*.

Kruskal JB 1956 On the shortest spanning subtree of a graph and the traveling salesman problem. *Proceedings of the American Mathematical Society* **7**, 48–50.

Laasonen J and Smed J 2012 Co-ordinating formations: A comparison of methods In *Algorithmic and Architectural Gaming Design: Implementation and Development* (ed. Kumar A, Etheredge J and Boudreaux A) IGI Global Hershey, PA pp. 1–22.

Laasonen J and Smed J 2015 Soft play detection in shooter games using hit matrix analysis. *EAI Endorsed Transactions on Serious Games*. ⟨http://eudl.eu/doi/10.4108/icst.intetain.2015.259565⟩.

Laasonen J, Knuutila T and Smed J 2011 Eliciting collusion features In *Proceedings of 2nd ICST/CREATE-NET Workshop on DIstributed SImulation and Online gaming (DISIO 2011)* (ed. D'Angelo G and Ferretti S), Barcelona.

Lamport L and Lynch N 1990 Distributed computing: Models and methods In *Handbook of Theoretical Computer Science* (ed. van Leeuwen J) vol. B: *Formal Models and Semantics* Elsevier Amsterdam pp. 1157–1199.

Laurel B 1991 *Computers as Theatre*. Addison-Wesley, Reading, MA.

Laurens P, Paige RF, Brooke PJ and Chivers H 2007 A novel approach to the detection of cheating in multiplayer online games *12th IEEE International Conference on Engineering Complex Computer Systems*, pp. 97–106.

Lecky-Thompson GW 1999 Algorithms for an infinite universe. *Gamasutra*. ⟨http://ubm.io/2kADPPl⟩.

L'Ecuyer P 1988 Efficient and portable combined random number generators. *Communications of the ACM* **31**(6), 742–749,774.

L'Ecuyer P 1999 Tables of linear congruential generators of different sizes and good lattice structure. *Mathematics of Computation* **68**(225), 249–260.

L'Ecuyer P and Côté S 1991 Implementing a random number package with splitting facilities. *ACM Transactions on Mathematical Software* **17**(1), 98–111.

L'Ecuyer P, Blouin F and Couture R 1993 A search for good multiple recursive random number generators. *ACM Transactions on Modeling and Computer Simulation* **3**(2), 87–98.

Lee BS, Cai W, Turner SJ and Chen L 2000 Adaptive dead reckoning algorithms for distributed interactive simulation. *International Journal of Simulation Systems, Science & Technology* **1**(1–2), 21–34.

Lee H, Kozlowski E, Lenker S and Jamin S 2002 Multiplayer game cheating prevention with pipelined lockstep protocol In *Entertainment Computing: Technologies and Applications, IFIP First International Workshop on Entertainment Computing* (ed. Nakatsu R and Hoshino J), pp. 31–39, Makuhari, Japan.

Lescop D and Lescop E 2014 Exploring mobile gaming revenues: The price tag of impatience, stress and release. *Digiworld Economic Journal* **94**, 103–122.

Lewis JP 1987 Generalized stochastic subdivision. *ACM Transactions on Graphics* **6**(3), 167–190.

Lewis MA and Tan KH 1997 High precision formation control of mobile robots using virtual structures. *Autonomous Robots* **4**(4), 387–403.

Lewis PA, Goodman AS and Miller JM 1969 A pseudo-random number generator for the System/360. *IBM Systems Journal* **8**(2), 136–146.

Liew J 2008 29 business models for games. ⟨http://lsvp.com/2008/07/02/29-business-models-for-games/⟩.

LifeWiki 2014 Maze. ⟨http://www.conwaylife.com/wiki/Maze⟩.

Lindenmayer A 1968a Mathematical models for cellular interactions in development I. Filament with one-sided inputs. *Journal of Theoretical Biology* **18**(3), 280–299.

Lindenmayer A 1968b Mathematical models for cellular interactions in development: II. Simple and branching filaments with two-sided inputs. *Journal of Theoretical Biology* **18**(3), 300–315.

Liu ES and Theodoropoulos GK 2014 Interest management for distributed virtual environments: A survey. *ACM Computing Surveys* **46**(4), 51:1–51:42.

Lou JK, Chen KT and Lei CL 2009 A collusion-resistant automation scheme for social moderation systems *6th IEEE Consumer Communications and Networking Conference, 2009. CCNC 2009*, pp. 1–5.

Luton W 2013 *Free-to-Play: Making Money from Games You Give Away*. New Riders, Berkeley, CA.

Mackenzie D 2002 The mathematics of … shuffling: The Stanford flip. *Discover* **23**(10), 22–23.

Mark D 2015 Modular tactical influence maps In *Game AI Pro 2: Collected Wisdom of Game AI Professionals* (ed. Rabin S) CRC Press Boca Raton, FL pp. 343–364.

Mars C and Chanut J 2015 Hierarchical architecture for group navigation behaviors In *Game AI Pro 2: Collected Wisdom of Game AI Professionals* (ed. Rabin S) CRC Press Boca Raton, FL pp. 209–223.

Marsaglia G 1962 Improving the polar method for generating a pair of normal random variables. Technical Report D1-82-0203, Boeing Scientific Reserch Laboratories, Seattle.

Marsaglia G and Bray TA 1964 A convenient method for generating normal variables. *SIAM Review* **6**, 260–264.

Marsland TA and Campbell M 1982 Parallel search of strongly ordered game trees. *ACM Computing Surveys* **14**(4), 533–551.

Martel E 2014 Tips and tricks for a robust third-person camera system In *Game AI Pro: Collected Wisdom of Game AI Professionals* (ed. Rabin S) CRC Press Boca Raton, FL pp. 557–566.

Mateas M 2002 *Interactive Drama, Art and Artificial Intelligence* PhD thesis Carnegie Mellon University Pittsburgh.

Matias Y, Vitter JS and Ni WC 1993 Dynamic generation of discrete random variates *Proceedings of the 4th Annual ACM-SIAM Symposium on Discrete Algorithms (SODA'93)*, pp. 361–370. Society for Industrial and Applied Mathematics, Philadelphia.

Mazrooei P, Archibald C and Bowling M 2013 Automating collusion detection in sequential games *AAAI Conference on Artificial Intelligence.*

McLeod AI 1985 Remark AS R58: A remark on algorithm AS 183. An efficient and portable pseudo-random number generator. *Applied Statistics* **34**(2), 198–200.

Meyer B 1997 *Object-Oriented Software Construction* second edn. Prentice Hall, Upper Saddle River, NJ.

Michie D 1966 Game-playing and game-learning automata In *Advances in Programming and Non-Numerical Computation* (ed. Fox L) Pergamon Press Oxford pp. 183–200.

Miller GSP 1986 The definition and rendering of terrain maps. *Computer Graphics* **20**(4), 39–48.

Mogaki S, Kamada M, Yonekura T, Okamoto S, Ohtaki Y and Reaz MBI 2007 Time-stamp service makes real-time gaming cheat-free *Proceedings of the 6th ACM SIGCOMM Workshop on Network and System Support for Games*, pp. 135–138, Melbourne.

Monnerot-Dumaine A 2009 The Fibonacci word fractal.
⟨https://hal.archives-ouvertes.fr/hal-00367972⟩.

Morse KL, Bic L and Dillencourt M 2000 Interest management in large-scale virtual environments. *Presence* **9**(1), 52–68.

Morton G 1966 A computer oriented geodetic data base; and a new technique in file sequencing. Technical report, International Business Machines Co. Ltd., Ottawa.

Moussaïd M, Perozo N, Garnier S, Helbing D and Theraulaz G 2010 The walking behaviour of pedestrian social groups and its impact on crowd dynamics. *PLoS ONE* **5**(4), e10047.

Murdoch SJ and Zieliński P 2004 Covert channels for collusion in online computer games In *Information Hiding: 6th International Workshop* (ed. Fridrich J), vol. 3200 of *Lecture Notes in Computer Science*, pp. 355–369. Springer-Verlag, Berlin.

Naffin DJ and Sukhatme GS 2004 Negotiated formations In *Intelligent Autonomous Systems 8* (ed. Groen F, Amato N, Bonarini A, Yoshida E and Kröse B), pp. 181–190. IOS Press, Amsterdam.

Nealen A, Müller M, Keiser R, Boxerman E and Carlson M 2006 Physically based deformable models in computer graphics. *Computer Graphics Forum* **25**(4), 809–836.

Newzoo 2014 Top 100 countries represent 99.8% of $81.5bn global games market.
⟨https://newzoo.com/insights/articles/top-100-countries-represent-99-6-81-5bn-global-games-market/⟩.

Neyland DL 1997 *Virtual Combat: A Guide to Distributed Interactive Simulation*. Stackpole Books, Mechanicsburg, PA.

Novak J 2007 *Game Development Essentials: An Introduction* second edn. Delmar Cengage Learning, Clifton Park, NY.

Object Management Group 2005 *Unified Modeling Language: Superstructure, Version 2.0*. Formal/05-07-04.

Ögren P, Fiorelli E and Leonard NE 2002 Formations with a mission: Stable coordination of vehicle group maneuvers In *Electronic Proceedings of the 15th International Symposium on Mathematical Theory of Networks and Systems* (ed. Gilliam DS and Rosenthal J). ⟨http://www.nd.edu/~mtns/papers/4615_3.pdf⟩.

Orkin J 2003 Applying goal-oriented action planning to games In *AI Game Programming Wisdom 2* (ed. Rabin S) Charles River Media Hingham, MA pp. 217–227.

Palshikar GK and Apte MM 2008 Collusion set detection using graph clustering. *Data Mining and Knowledge Discovery* **16**(2), 135–164.

Parish YI and Müller P 2001 Procedural modeling of cities *Proceedings of the 28th Annual Conference on Computer graphics and Interactive Techniques (SIGGRAPH '01)*, pp. 301–308.

Park KS and Kenyon RV 1999 Effects of network characteristics on human performance in a collaborative virtual environment *Proceedings of IEEE International Conference on Virtual Reality*, Houston, TX.

Park SK and Miller KW 1988 Random number generators: Good ones are hard to find. *Communications of the ACM* **31**(10), 1192–1201.

Patel AJ 2003 Amit's thoughts on path-finding.
⟨http://theory.stanford.edu/~amitp/GameProgramming/⟩.

Pearl J 1986 Fusion, propagation, and structuring in belief networks. *Artificial Intelligence* **29**(3), 241–364.

Peinado F and Gervás P 2007 Automatic direction of interactive storytelling: Formalizing the game master paradigm In *Virtual Storytelling. Using Virtual Reality Technologies for*

Storytelling. Proceedings of the Fourth International Conference, ICVS 2007 (ed. Cavazza M and Donikian S), vol. 4871 of *Lecture Notes in Computer Science*, pp. 196–201. Springer-Verlag, Berlin.

Perlin K 1985 An image synthesizer *Proceedings of the 12th Annual Conference on Computer Graphics and Interactive Techniques (SIGGRAPH '85)*, vol. 19, pp. 287–296.

Perlin K 2001 Noise hardware *Real-Time Shading SIGGRAPH Course Notes* ACM New York chapter 2.

Perlin K 2002 Improving noise. *ACM Transactions on Graphics (TOG)* **21**, 681–682.

Perlin K and Hoffert EM 1989 Hypertexture *Proceedings of the 16th Annual Conference on Computer Graphics and Interactive Techniques (SIGGRAPH '89)*, vol. 23, pp. 253–262.

Peters C and Ennis C 2009 Modeling groups of plausible virtual pedestrians. *IEEE Computer Graphics and Applications* **29**(4), 54–63.

Pottinger D 1999a Coordinated unit movement. *Gamasutra*. ⟨http://www.gamasutra.com/features/19990122/movement_01.htm⟩.

Pottinger D 1999b Implementing coordinated movement. *Gamasutra*. ⟨http://www.gamasutra.com/features/19990129/implementing_01.htm⟩.

Pottinger DC 2000 Terrain analysis in realtime strategy games *2000 Game Developer Conference Proceedings*, San Jose, CA.

Prim RC 1957 Shortest connection networks and some generalizations. *Bell System Technical Journal* **6**, 1389–1401.

Pritchard M 2000 How to hurt hackers: The scoop on Internet cheating and how you can combat it. *Gamasutra*. ⟨http://www.gamasutra.com/features/20000724/pritchard_01.htm⟩.

Prusinkiewicz P and Lindenmayer A 1990 *The Algorithmic Beauty of Plants*. Springer-Verlag, New York.

Pulkkanen A and Seppänen M 2012 Freemium business models in technology product markets *ISPIM Conference Proceedings*, pp. 1–9.

Quax P 2007 *An Architecture for Large-scale Virtual Interactive Communities* PhD thesis Hasselt University.

Rabin S 2015 Agent reaction time: How fast should an AI react? In *Game AI Pro 2: Collected Wisdom of Game AI Professionals* (ed. Rabin S) CRC Press Boca Raton, FL pp. 31–34.

Rabiner LR and Juang BH 1986 An introduction to hidden Markov models. *IEEE Acoustics, Speech, and Signal Processing Magazine* **3**(1), 4–16.

Reynolds CW 1987 Flocks, herds, and schools: A distributed behavioral model. *Computer Graphics* **21**(4), 25–34.

Reynolds CW 1999 Steering behaviors for autonomous characters *Proceedings of the Game Developers Conference*, pp. 763–782. Miller Freeman Game Group, San Francisco.

Riedl MO 2004 *Narrative Generation: Balancing Plot and Character* PhD thesis North Carolina State University Raleigh.

Riemer T 2015 *Agent-based procedural quest generation for a role-playing game* Master's thesis IT University Copenhagen.

Rivest R 1992 The MD5 message digest algorithm Internet RFC 1321. ⟨http://theory.lcs.mit.edu/~rivest/Rivest-MD5.txt⟩.

Roden T and Parberry I 2004 From artistry to automation: A structured methodology for procedural content creation In *Proceedings of the Third International Conference on Entertainment Computing (ICEC 2004)* (ed. Rauterberg M), pp. 151–156. Springer-Verlag, Berlin.

Rollings A and Morris D 2000 *Game Architecture and Design*. Coriolis, Scottsdale, AZ.

Rouse, III R 2004 *Game Design: Theory and Practice* second edn. Jones & Bartlett, Sudbury, MA.

Ryan MD and Sharkey PM 1999 The causal surface and its effect on distribution transparency in a distributed virtual environment *Proceedings of IEEE International Conference on Systems, Man, and Cybernetics*, vol. 6, pp. 75–80, Tokyo.

Ryvkin D and Ortmann A 2008 The predictive power of three prominent tournament formats. *Management Science* **54**(3), 492–504.

Sacerdoti ED 1974 Planning in a hierarchy of abstraction spaces. *Artificial Intelligence* **5**(2), 115–135.

Salen K and Zimmerman E 2004 *Rules of Play: Game Design Fundamentals*. MIT Press, Cambridge, MA.

Samuel AL 1959 Some studies in machine learning using the game of checkers. *IBM Journal of Research and Development* **3**(3), 210–229.

Samuel AL 1967 Some studies in machine learning using the game of checkers. II – Recent progress. *IBM Journal of Research and Development* **11**(6), 601–617.

Sanderson D 1999 Online justice systems. *Game Developer* **6**(4), 42–49.

Savery C 2014 *Consistency Maintenance in Networked Games* PhD thesis Queen's University Kingston, Ontario.

Scarf PA and Shi X 2008 The imporance of a match in a tournament. *Computers & Operations Research* **35**(7), 2406–2418.

Schell J 2015 *The Art of Game Design: A Book of Lenses* second edn. CRC Press, Boca Raton, FL.

Schmidt D, Stal M, Rohnert H and Buschmann F 2000 *Pattern-Oriented Software Architecture: Patterns for Concurrent and Networked Objects* vol. 2 of *Software Design Patterns*. John Wiley & Sons, Chichester.

Sedgewick R 1977 Permutation generation methods. *Computing Surveys* **9**(2), 137–164.

Seidel R 1991 A simple and fast incremental randomized algorithms for computing trapezoidal decompositions and for triangulating polygons. *Computational Geometry* **1**(1), 51–64.

Seppänen A 2003 Regional case study: Finland *Game Developer Conference Mobile 2003 Proceedings*, San Jose, CA. ⟨http://www.gamasutra.com/features/gdcarchive/2003M/Seppanen_Antti.ppt⟩.

Seufert EB 2014 *Freemium Economics: Leveraging Analytics and User Segmentation to Drive Revenue*. Morgan Kaufmann, Burlington, MA.

Shafer G 1990 Perspectives on the theory and practice of belief functions. *International Journal of Approximate Reasoning* **4**(5–6), 323–362.

Sharkey PM, Ryan MD and Roberts DJ 1998 A local perception filter for distributed virtual environments *Proceedings of IEEE Virtual Reality Annual International Symposium*, pp. 242–249, Atlanta, GA.

Shi SW, Xia M and Huang Y 2015 From minnows to whales: An empirical study of purchase behavior in freemium social games. *International Journal of Electronic Commerce* **20**(2), 177–207.

Shim KH and Kim JS 2001 A dead reckoning algorithm with variable threshold scheme in networked virtual environment *IEEE International Conference on Systems, Man, and Cybernetics*, vol. 2, pp. 1113–1118.

Shirmohammadi S and Georganas ND 2001 An end-to-end communication architecture for collaborative virtual environments. *Computer Networks* **35**(2–3), 351–367.

Siira A 2004 *Automatic commentators* Master's thesis Department of Information Technology, University of Turku.

Singhal SK 1996 *Effective Remote Modeling in Large-Scale Distributed Simulation and Visualization Environments* PhD thesis Stanford University.

Singhal SK and Zyda MJ 1999 *Networked Virtual Environments: Design and Implementation*. Addison Wesley, Reading, MA.

Slany W 1994 *Fuzzy Scheduling* PhD thesis Technische Universität Wien Vienna. CD-Techical Report 94/66.

Slany W 1995 Comparing partial constraint satisfaction models *Workshop Notes of the CP'95 Workshop on Over-Constraint Systems*, pp. 151–159, Cassis, France.

Smed J 2014 Interactive storytelling: Approaches, applications and aspirations. *International Journal of Virtual Communities and Social Networking* **6**(1), 22–34.

Smed J and Hakonen H 2003 Towards a definition of a computer game. Technical Report 553, Turku Centre for Computer Science.

Smed J and Hakonen H 2005a Preventing look-ahead cheating with active objects In *Computers and Games, 4th International Conference, CG 2004, Ramat-Gan, Israel, July 5–7, 2004* (ed. van den Herik HJ, Björnsson Y and Netanyahu NS), vol. 3846 of *Lecture Notes in Computer Science*, pp. 301–315. Springer-Verlag, Berlin.

Smed J and Hakonen H 2005b Synthetic players: A quest for artificial intelligence in computer games. *Human IT* **7**(3), 57–77.

Smed J and Hakonen H 2006 Three concepts for light-weight communication in multiplayer games In *Proceedings of International Digital Games Conference (iDiG)* (ed. Dionísio J, Fernandes AR and Gomes P), pp. 199–202, Portalegre, Portugal.

Smed J, Kaukoranta T and Hakonen H 2002 Aspects of networking in multiplayer computer games. *The Electronic Library* **20**(2), 87–97.

Smed J, Kaukoranta T and Hakonen H 2003a AIsHockey—a platform for studying synthetic players In *Proceedings of the 2nd International Conference on Application and Development of Computer Games* (ed. Sing LW, Man WH and Wai W), pp. 183–188, Hong Kong.

Smed J, Kaukoranta T and Hakonen H 2003b Networking and multiplayer computer games – the story so far. *International Journal of Intelligent Games & Simulation* **2**(2), 101–110.

Smed J, Knuutila T and Hakonen H 2006 Can we prevent collusion in multiplayer online games? In *Proceedings of the Ninth Scandinavian Conference on Artificial Intelligence (SCAI 2006)* (ed. Honkela T, Raiko T, Kortela J and Valpola H), pp. 168–175, Espoo, Finland.

Smed J, Knuutila T and Hakonen H 2007 Towards swift and accurate collusion detection In *8th International Conference on Intelligent Games and Simulation (Game-On 2007)* (ed. Roccetti M), pp. 103–107, Bologna.

Smed J, Niinisalo H and Hakonen H 2005 Realizing the bullet time effect in multiplayer games with local perception filters. *Computer Networks* **49**(1), 27–37.

Smith G 2015 Procedural content generation: An overview In *Game AI Pro 2: Collected Wisdom of Game AI Professionals* (ed. Rabin S) CRC Press Boca Raton, FL pp. 501–518.

Smith JC, Fraticelli BMP and Rainwater C 2006 A bracket assignment problem for the National Collegiate Athletic Association men's basketball tournament. *International Transactions in Operational Research* **13**(3), 253–271.

Snook G 2000 Simplified 3D movement and pathfinding using navigation meshes In *Game Programming Gems* (ed. DeLoura M) Charles River Media Hingham, MA pp. 288–304.

Staab E and Engel T 2009 Collusion detection for grid computing *9th IEEE/ACM International Symposium on Cluster Computing and the Grid, 2009. CCGRID '09*, pp. 412–419.

Statista 2016 Statistics and facts about the film industry. ⟨http://www.statista.com/topics/964/film/⟩.

Steed A and Angus C 2005 Supporting scalable peer to peer virtual environments using frontier sets *Proceedings of the 2005 IEEE Conference 2005 on Virtual Reality*, pp. 27–34.

Steed A and Zhu B 2008 An implementation of a first-person game on a hybrid network *Proceedings of the First International Workshop on Massively Multiuser Virtual Environments (MMVE)*, pp. 24–28.

Street G, Petersen S and Kidd M 2001 How to balance a real time strategy game: Lessons from the Age of Empires series. ⟨http://www.gdconf.com/archives/2001/gstreetprintable3.ppt⟩.

Suits B 2014 *The Grasshopper: Games, Life, and Utopia* third edn. Broadview Press, Peterborough, Ontario. Originally published 1978.

Suovuo T, Lahti I and Smed J 2015 Game design frameworks and reality guides In *Handbook of Research on Gaming Trends in P-12 Education* (ed. Russell D and Leffey JM) IGI Global Hershey, PA pp. 85–104.

Swartjes I, Kruizinga E and Theune M 2008 Let's pretend I had a sword: Late commitment in emergent narrative In *Interactive Storytelling: First Joint International Conference on Interactive Digital Storytelling, ICIDS 2008* (ed. Spierling U and Szilas N), vol. 5334 of *Lecture Notes in Computer Science*, pp. 230–241. Springer-Verlag, Berlin.

Teller SJ and Séquin CH 1991 Visibility preprocessing for interactive walkthroughs. *Computer Graphics* **25**(4), 61–90.

Togelius J, Shaker N and Nelson MJ 2016 Introduction In *Procedural Content Generation in Games: A Textbook and an Overview of Current Research* (ed. Shaker N, Togelius J and Nelson MJ) Springer Cham, Switzerland.

Togelius J, Yannakakis GN, Stanley KO and Browne C 2011 Search-based procedural content generation: A taxonomy and survey. *IEEE Transactions on Computational Intelligence and AI in Games* **3**(3), 172–186.

Tozour P 2003 Search space representations In *AI Game Programming Wisdom 2* (ed. Rabin S) Charles River Media Hingham, MA pp. 85–102.

Uras T and Koenig S 2015 Subgoal graphs for fast optimal pathfinding In *Game AI Pro 2: Collected Wisdom of Game AI Professionals* (ed. Rabin S) CRC Press Boca Raton, FL pp. 145–159.

Vallvè-Guionnet C 2005 Finding colluders in card games In *Proceedings of the International Conference on Information Technology: Coding and Computing (ITCC'05)* (ed. Selvaraj H and Srimani PK), vol. II, pp. 774–775, Las Vegas.

van der Sterren W 2003 Path look-up tables – small is beautiful In *AI Game Programming Wisdom 2* (ed. Rabin S) Charles River Media Hingham, MA pp. 115–129.

van Verth J, Brueggemann V, Owen J and McMurry P 2000 Formation-based pathfinding with real-world vehicles *Proceedings of the Game Developers Conference*. CMP Game Media Group, San Francisco.

VanderKnyff CM, Bethea DJ, Reiter MMK and Whitton MC 2009 Statistical methods for user and team identification in multiplayer games. Technical report, University of North Carolina.

Verna D, Fabre Y and Pitel G 2000 Urbi et Orbi: Unusual design and implementation choices for distributed virtual environments In *VSMM 2000: Sixth International Conference on Virtual Systems and Multimedia* (ed. Thwaites H), pp. 714–724, Gifu, Japan.

Wallace N 2003 Hierarchical planning in dynamic worlds In *AI Game Programming Wisdom 2* (ed. Rabin S) Charles River Media Hingham, MA pp. 229–236.

Wang L and Hua W 2006 Survey and practice of 3D city modeling In *Technologies for E-Learning and Digital Entertainment* (ed. Pan Z, Aylett R, Diener H, Jin X, Göbel S and Li L), vol. 3942 of *Lecture Notes in Computer Science*, pp. 818–828. Springer-Verlag, Berlin.

Wang X and Devarajan V 2004 2D structured mass-spring system parameter optimization based on axisymmetric bending for rigid cloth simulation *Proceedings of the 2004 ACM SIGGRAPH International Conference on Virtual Reality Continuum and Its Applications in Industry*, pp. 317–323. ACM, New York.

Wang X and Yu H 2005 How to break MD5 and other hash functions In *Advances in Cryptology – EUROCRYPT 2005: 24th Annual International Conference on the Theory and Applications of Cryptographic Techniques* (ed. Cramer R), vol. 3494 of *Lecture Notes in Artificial Intelligence*, pp. 19–25. Springer-Verlag, Berlin.

Watson B, Müller P, Wonka P, Sexton C, Veryovka O and Fuller A 2008 Procedural urban modeling in practice. *IEEE Computer Graphics and Applications* **28**(3), 18–26.

Watt A 2000 *3D Computer Graphics* third edn. Addison-Wesley, Harlow.

Watte J 2008 Authentication for online games In *Game Programming Gems 7* (ed. Jacobs S) Cengage Learning Boston pp. 481–489.

Weallans A, Louchart S and Aylett R 2012 Distributed drama management: Beyond double appraisal in emergent narrative In *Interactive Storytelling: 5th International Conference on Interactive Digital Storytelling, ICIDS 2012* (ed. Oyarzun D, Peinado F, Young RM, Elizalde A and Méndez G), vol. 7648 of *Lecture Notes in Computer Science*, pp. 132–143. Springer-Verlag, Heidelberg.

Weidemann T 2014 Beginners intro to F2P Aalto Game Monetization Design. ⟨https://youtu.be/fdzk7x3W3kE⟩.

Wichmann BA and Hill ID 1982 Algorithm AS 183: An efficient and portable pseudo-random number generator. *Applied Statistics* **31**(2), 188–190. See also McLeod (1985); Wichmann and Hill (1984); Zeisel (1986).

Wichmann BA and Hill ID 1984 Correction: Algorithm AS 183: An efficient and portable pseudo-random number generator. Applied Statistics **33**(1), 123.

Witten IH, Moffat A and Bell TC 1999 *Managing Gigabytes: Compressing and Indexing Documents and Images* second edn. Morgan Kaufmann, San Francisco.

Wittgenstein L 2009 *Philosophical Investigations* fourth edn. Wiley-Blackwell, Malden, MA. Originally published in German 1953.

Woodcock S 2002 Recognizing strategic dispositions: Engaging the enemy In *AI Game Programming Wisdom* (ed. Rabin S) Charles River Media Hingham, MA pp. 221–232.

Worley S 1996 A cellular texture basis function *Proceedings of the 23rd Annual Conference on Computer Graphics and Interactive Techniques (SIGGRAPH '96)*, pp. 291–293.

Wu J and Sheng L 2001 An efficient sorting algorithm for a sequence of kings in a tournament. *Information Processing Letters* **79**(6), 297–299.

Yager RR 1981 A new methodology for ordinal multiobjective decisions based on fuzzy sets. *Decision Sciences* **12**, 589–600.

Yager RR 1988 On ordered weighted averaging aggregation operators in multicriteria decisionmaking. *IEEE Transactions on Systems, Man, and Cybernetics* **18**(1), 183–190.

Yager RR and Filev DP 1994 *Essentials of Fuzzy Modeling and Control*. John Wiley & Sons, New York.

Yampolskiy RV 2007 Online poker security: Problems and solutions In *GAME-ON-NA 2007: 3rd International North American Conference on Intelligent Games and Simulation* (ed. Fishwick P and Lok B), Gainesville, FL.

Yampolskiy RV 2008 Detecting and controlling cheating in online poker *Consumer Communications and Networking Conference, 2008. CCNC 2008. 5th IEEE*, pp. 848–853.

Yan J 2003 Security design in online games *Proceedings of the 19th Annual Computer Security Applications Conference (ACSAC'03)*, pp. 286–297, Las Vegas.

Yan J 2010 Collusion detection in online bridge *Proceedings of the Twenty-Fourth AAAI Conference on Artificial Intelligence (AAAI-10)*, pp. 1510–1515.

Yan JJ and Choi HJ 2002 Security issues in online games. *The Electronic Library* **20**(2), 125–133.

Yob G 1975 Hunt the Wumpus. *Creative Computing* **1**(5), 51–54.

Young BJ, Beard RW and Kelsey JM 2001 A control scheme for improving multi-vehicle formation maneuvers *Proceedings of the American Control Conference*, vol. 2, pp. 704–709.

Yu Q and Chen L 2013 A new method for detecting anti-community structures in complex networks. *Journal of Physics: Conference Series* **410**(1), 012103.

Yu SJ and Choy YC 2001 A dynamic message filtering technique for 3D cyberspaces. *Computer Communications* **24**(18), 1745–1758.

Zadeh LA 1965 Fuzzy sets. *Information and Control* **8**(3), 338–353.

Zander S, Armitage G and Branch P 2008 Covert channels in multiplayer first person shooter online games *33rd IEEE Conference on Local Computer Networks, 2008. LCN 2008*, pp. 215–222. IEEE, Los Alamitos, CA.

Zeisel H 1986 Remark ASR61: A remark on algorithm AS 183. An efficient and portable pseudo-random number generator. Applied Statistics **35**(1), 89.

Zetterström J 2005 *A legal analysis of cheating in online multiplayer games* Master's thesis School of Economics and Commercial Law Gothenburg, Sweden.

Zhang X, Gračanin D and Duncan TP 2004 Evaluation of a pre-reckoning algorithm for distributed virtual environments *Proceedings of the Tenth International Conference on Parallel and Distributed Systems*, pp. 445–452.

Zhao S, Li D, Gu H, Shao B and Gu N 2009 An approach to sharing legacy TV/arcade games for real-time collaboration *Proceedings of the 29th IEEE International Conference on Distributed Computing Systems*, pp. 165–172.

Zhou X and Zheng H 2010 Breaking bidder collusion in large-scale spectrum auctions *Proceedings of the Eleventh ACM International Symposium on Mobile Ad Hoc Networking and Computing - MobiHoc '10*, p. 121. ACM Press, New York.

Zobrist AL 1969 A model of visual organization for the game of Go *Proceedings of AFIPS Spring Joint Computer Conference*, pp. 103–112, Boston.

Ludography

Adams T, *Dwarf Fortress*. Bay 12 Games, 2006.

Atari, *Pong*. Atari, 1972.

Barlow S, *Her Story*. 2015.

Berglund EJ and Cheriton DR, *Amaze*. 1985.

Bioware, *Neverwinter Nights*. Infogrames, 2002.

Blizzard Entertainment, *World of Warcraft*. Blizzard Entertainment, 2004.

Blizzard North, *Diablo II*. Blizzard Entertainment, 2000.

Braben D and Bell I, *Elite*. Firebird, 1984.

Bungie Software, *Halo: Combat Evolved*. Microsoft Games, 2003.

CCP Games, *Eve Online*. CCP Games, 2003.

DevTeam, *NetHack 3.6.0*. ⟨http://www.nethack.org/⟩, 2015.

Dewdney AK, *Core War*. 1984.

DMA Design, *Grand Theft Auto III*. Rockstar Games, 2001.

Ensemble Studios, *Age of Empires II: The Age of Kings*. Microsoft Games, 1999.

Epyx, *Pitstop II*. U.S. Gold, 1984.

Frogmind, *Badland*. Frogmind, 2013.

Graetz JM, Russell SR and Witanen W, *Spacewar!*. 1962.

Grinding Gear Games, *Path of Exile*. Grinding Gear Games, 2013.

Gygax G and Arneson D, *Dungeons & Dragons*. TSR, 1974.

Hello Games, *No Man's Sky*. Hello Games, 2016.

id Software, *Doom*. id Software, 1993.

id Software, *Quake*. id Software, 1996.

Inkle, *80 Days*. Inkle, 2014.

King, *Candy Crush Saga*. King, 2012.

Konami, *Dance Dance Revolution*. Konami, 1998.

Lionhead Studios, *Black & White*. Electronic Arts, 2001.

LucasArts, *Indiana Jones and the Fate of Atlantis*. LucasArts, 1992.

Maxis, *The Sims*. Electronic Arts, 2000.

MicroProse Software, *Formula One Grand Prix*. MicroProse Software, 1991.

Mojang, *Minecraft*. Mojang, 2011.

Monolith Productions, *No One Lives Forever 2: A Spy in H.A.R.M.'s Way*. Fox Interactive, 2002.

Mossmouth, *Spelunky*. Mossmouth, 2008.

Namco, *Pac-Man*. Midway Games West, 1981.

Niantic, *Ingress*. Niantic, 2012.

Algorithms and Networking for Computer Games, Second Edition. Jouni Smed and Harri Hakonen.
© 2017 John Wiley & Sons Ltd. Published 2017 by John Wiley & Sons Ltd.

Nishikado T, *Space Invaders*. Taito, 1978.

Origin Systems, *Ultima Online*. Electronic Arts, 1997.

Origin Systems, *Wing Commander*. Origin Systems, 1990.

Pandemic Studios, *Star Wars: Battlefront*. LucasArts, 2004.

Procedural Arts, *Façade*. Procedural Arts, 2005.

Quantic Dream, *Heavy Rain*. Sony Computer Entertainment, 2010.

Raven Software, *Jedi Knight II: Jedi Outcast*. LucasArts, 2002.

Relic Entertainment, *Homeworld*. Sierra Studios, 1999.

Red Storm Entertainment, *Force 21*. Red Storm Entertainment, 1999.

Remedy Entertainment, *Max Payne*. Gathering of Developers, 2001.

Rockstar North, *Grand Theft Auto V*. Rockstar Games, 2013.

Rotobee, *Singles: Flirt Up Your Life*. Deep Silver, 2004.

Smed J, *AIsHockey*. 2003.

Sphere, *Falcon A.T.* Spectrum Holobyte, 1988.

Sullivan Bluth, *Dragon's Lair*. ReadySoft, 1989.

Supercell, *Clash of Clans*. Supercell, 2012.

Team Meat, *Super Meat Boy*. Team Meat, 2010.

Telltale Games, *The Walking Dead*. Telltale Games, 2012.

Valve Software, *Half-Life*. Sierra Studios, 1998.

Verant Interactive, *EverQuest*. 989 Studios, 1999.

Vicarious Visions, *Terminus*. Vicarious Visions, 2001.

Yob G, *Hunt the Wumpus*. 1975.

Zynga, *FarmVille*. Zynga, 2009.

Index

Algorithms and Networking for Computer Games, Second Edition. Jouni Smed and Harri Hakonen.
© 2017 John Wiley & Sons Ltd. Published 2017 by John Wiley & Sons Ltd.